· THE ·
LANGUAGE
· OF ·
LIFE

A Festival of Poets

· THE ·
LANGUAGE
· OF ·
LIFE

A Festival of Poets

BILL MOYERS

JAMES HABA, *Editor*

DAVID GRUBIN, *Contributing Editor*
ELIZABETH MERYMAN-BRUNNER, *Art Research*

BROADWAY BOOKS
New York

BROADWAY

First Broadway Books trade paperback edition published 2001.

Photographs by William Abranowicz, Lola Mae Aurty, Nancy Crampton, Gypsy P. Ray, Lynn Saville, Rona Talcott.

The Library of Congress Cataloging-in-Publication Data has cataloged the hardcover as:

Moyers, Bill D.
The language of life: a festival of poets / Bill Moyers; James
Haba, editor; David Grubin, consulting editor; Elizabeth Meryman-
Brunner, art research. – 1st ed.
p. cm.
Published to coincide with the premiere of the eight-part PBS
series of the same name.
Includes bibliographical references.
1. American poetry–20th century–History and criticism–Theory,
etc. 2. American poetry–Minority authors–History and criticism–
Theory, etc. 3. Minorities–United States–Intellectual life.
4. Poets, American–20th century–Interviews. 5. American
poetry–20th century. 6. Ethnic groups–Poetry. 7. Minorities–
Poetry. I. Haba, James. II. Grubin, David. III. Title.
PS325.M69 1995
811'.5409–dc20 95-10348
CIP

0-385-48410-0

12 11 10 9 8 7 6 5 4

Bill Moyers would like to thank the following people for their contributions to the television programs *The Power of the Word, Poet Laureate Rita Dove, A Life Together,* and *The Language of Life:*

Michael Allen, Kaye Armstrong, Michael Bacon, Glynda Bates, Frank Berman, David Besdesky, Rachel Bluestein, Tom Bobridge, Robbie Bolton, Paula Bolvin, Harry Bottorf, Ray Buccianti, Barbara Byrne, Joe Camp, Mark Chamberlin, Tricia Clark, Bryan Cole, Norm Craley, Pat Crooks, Jonathan Daitch, Hillary Dann, Marlene Dann, Nick Davis, Tom Donahue, Rob Featherstone, Frank Ferrigno, Tony Foresta, Tim Foster, Jacqueline Frank, Dana Fox, Michael Frattiani, Nancy Gerstman, Naomi Golf, Paul Goroff, Janet Graham, Eileen Griffin, David Grubin, Eve Grubin, Joan Grubin, Tom Guarcello, James Haba, Ned Hallick, Craig Harris, Scott Herde, Paul Hickey, Kate Hirson, Todd Holme, Ray Hoover, Marge Hubbard, John Hyater, Loretta Jones, Nancy Kennedy, Dan Klein, Alex Klymko, Chris Kogler, Michael Kreider, Marc Kroll, Ed Lee, Michael Lonsdale, Ann Mauze, Betsy McCarthy, William B. McCullough, Rick Malkames, Mark Mandler, Donna Marino, Alice Markowitz, Edward Marritz, Mike Mayes, Dena Mermelstein, Robert Miller, Judith Davidson Moyers, Suzanne Moyers, Roslyn Myers, Jonathan Nichols, Bill Nye, Eddie O'Connor, Claudia Odyniec, Elizabeth O'Mara, Judy Doctoroff O'Neill, Melissa Painter, Mitul Patel, Linda Patterson, Roger Phenix, Debra Phillips, Amanda Pollock, Stacey B. Pucillo, Rebecca Quick, Colleen Quinn, Scott Ramsey, Nick Renbeck, Chris Roberts, John Robinson, Richard P. Rogers, Deborah Rubenstein, Bernard Russo, Don Scarlotta, William B. Schamann, Amy Schatz, Adam Schenck, Joel Shapiro, Howard Sharp, Michael Shepley Public Relations, Gary Silver, Elissa Silverman, Art Sloane, Chuck Smith, Michael Smith, Jim Snarski, Peter Stader, Peter Steinberg, David Steward, John Sweyne, Eileen Taylor, Doris Lang Thomas, Buzz Turner, Pamela Mason Wagner, Cheryl Wang, Diana Warner, Sherie Lynn Weldon, Arthur White, Eric Wilson, The Paul Winter Consort, Midge Woolsey, Will Wynne.

For Jacqueline Kennedy Onassis
as you set out for Ithaka

CONTENTS

INTRODUCTION

When I was a schoolboy our teachers required us to memorize poems. By copying the lines over and over, I excelled at the sport. But it was only sport. The words I had committed to memory were divorced from meaning or emotions. I knew the poems but not the experience of them. Only later, when a series of English teachers gifted in Elizabethan theatrics began to read serious poetry aloud in class, did I hear the music and encounter the Word within the words. Now love truly became "a red, red rose;" "the road not taken" proved to be haunting; and I knew for certain that it is indeed wisdom "to follow the heart." Poetry that entered the ear traveled faster to the "upper warm garrets" of my mind than poetry perceived by the eye. I continue to value the architecture of a poem in print, but as Maya Angelou has said, "poetry is music written for the human voice." Hearing's the thing, and poetry readings are concerts of sheer joyous sound. In the words of Octavio Paz, "When you say life is marvelous, you are saying a banality. But to *make* life a marvel, that is the role of poetry." One only need attend a robust festival of poets to witness the marvel; better still, to experience it.

I used to think of the poet as living a lonely existence, waiting in solitude for the Muse to appear on beads of sweat coaxed from a secret chamber deep in the soul. That is true in a way, but it is not the whole truth. Poets love each other's company, and they love an audience. The first time the filmmaker David Grubin and I attended the Dodge Poetry Festival in New Jersey's historic village of Waterloo, we came upon thousands of poetry lovers, from a score of states, having the time of their lives. The festival is a biennial event, sponsored by the Geraldine R. Dodge Foundation as part of an effort to reconnect people to poetry through classroom workshops and public events. Nowhere will you find language more verdant and vibrant, an atmosphere more festive. Noted poets and newcomers read to large audiences under a big tent and conduct daily workshops with small groups of students and teachers. The music of the Paul Winter Consort rises from the stage intimately intertwined with the spoken words. Spontaneous audiences gather around young people reading their newly minted poems in the gazebo on the village green. There are moments rich in humor and wisdom, transcendent moments after which one sees the world differently, and moments when the play of language dazzles the ear as fireworks delight the eye on the Fourth of July.

The *New York Times* covered the most recent Dodge Festival as if it were the epitome of poetry's resurgence on the public stage. "Once the trademark of a Beat generation," the *Times* reported, "poetry readings have moved out of smoky cafes" to become a staple of the country's cultural scene. Poetry performances are held at over 150 places in the New York area alone. At the Nuyorican Poets Cafe in the East Village, audiences rate performances "like Olympic judges." But the renaissance of public poetry is nationwide. The Elliott Bay Book Company in Seattle schedules sixty readings a year. Among the many poetry readings in Southern California is one in Van Nuys, where people age sixty and older gather to share in verse "their war stories from the battlefield of life." In Bergen County, New Jersey, octogenarians and twelve-year-olds read each other's poems in a program called Joy. The *Bergen Record* says, "They learn from each other about experiences common to both—peer pressure, society's woes, death, the loss of a pet, nature, freedom, politics."

"Let Us Not Mince Words, Poetry's Big!" proclaims a headline in the *New York Daily News.* The story tells of MTV's "Fightin' Words," a campaign of political poetry videos; of rocker Patti Smith and the poet T. Coraghessan Boyle reading their poems to hundreds of fans in Central Park; of metaphors and images flying through the air in "poetry slams" at local clubs. Some people worry that the showmanship will erase "the elusive borders between literature and music, between entertainment and art," downgrading nobler forms of the art. Emily Dickinson on MTV? T. S. Eliot rapping?

Fear not; traditional poetry is secure, but every age calls forth new poets who create new forms, and our age is no exception. Like the Dodge Festival, contemporary poetry reading is a stage on which fresh voices take up the democratic conversation. No less a literary figure than Adrienne Rich has worried aloud about poetry's banishment to the margins, "hoarded inside the schools, inside the universities." She sees this exile as a form of censorship that "goes hand in hand with an attitude about politics, which is that the average citizen, the regular American, can't understand poetry and also can't understand politics, that both are somehow the realms of experts." Readings are returning poetry to the people. They recall those public gatherings in early America in which citizens assembled on the commons to read their broadsheets and discuss the news of the day.

Poetry is news—news of the mind, news of the heart—and in the reading and hearing of it, poet and audience are fused. Strangers converge but community emerges, the shared experience of being present when poetry reveals a particular life to be every life—my life, your life, you, me, us. It doesn't happen on the Internet in cyberspace; the mere transmission from afar of information or knowledge among parties with common interests is of course communication, but what occurs at poetry readings is communion.

The Nigerian novelist Chinua Achebe has often said that there are really three elements to any work of literature: the words themselves (the poem), the maker/arranger of the words (the poet), and the audience. Achebe goes on to say that in traditional African cultures where the poet and the storyteller still survive, there is a generally shared understanding that all three of these elements must be present for the poem to be realized; what begins as a crowd becomes a community; poem, poet, and public interact to produce a new and living organism. The poets I watched at the Dodge Festival—the poets in this book—seemed to be yearning for, and working toward, this sense of community. Connecting is crucial to being a poet.

As for the showmanship, Quincy Troupe reminds us that poetry began as song. It was performance. Troupe and other African-American poets still invoke the tradition of the griot, the roving troubadour who sang his poetry to villagers. "Language is a living thing," Troupe says. "It feeds on the living language of a community." When Troupe goes home to St. Louis to read his poetry at Duff's Restaurant, he knows from the response of people there if he has the rhythm and realities of life just right. His poem about Magic Johnson taking it "to the hoop" has them shouting and stomping and roaring with pleasure, as if they were watching the game itself. Poetry creates an experience that the audience lives. Troupe told me, "I used to write 'high academic poems,' you know, 'hither and thither and thou and thine.' But then I realized people want to hear the voice. They want to hear you sing. They want to hear something that connects to their life. You've got to write where you come from."

Because Americans come from so many places, the poets of our time are infusing powerful new energy and idioms into our language. Their poetry flows from different geographies and cultures, as immigration continues to transform this country and native-born Americans retrace the steps and recapture the voices of their ancestors. Moreover, the source of much new poetry is also spiritual, originating in some unmapped interior country waiting to be explored. Linda McCarriston held a packed house in silent thrall at the recent Dodge Festival as she read her poetry about the torments of a family ravaged by her violent father; until she started writing about these experiences, she said, she never felt that she possessed "as a woman" the authority to speak to the larger culture. As she read on, into poems about healing those wounds from her past, she ceased to be the victim and became instead sojourner and celebrant, whose praise of life wrapped her audience into the exaltation with her.

Listening that evening, I was struck by how much we owe our poets for reminding us that experience is the most credible authority of all. Democracy needs her poets, in all their diversity, precisely because our hope for survival is in recognizing the reality of one another's lives. "Is that a *real* poem," the student asks, "or did you just make it up?" It is real because it *is* made up—from life, so that even those of us who are not poets know when we hear it that the language is true. We nod yes and say, That is just how I felt when my father died, or when I spied the first crocus parting the snow, or when the maple withered outside our breakfast-room window, or when waking from surgery I looked into my wife's eyes, or when I took my new grandson's hand into mine.

Poetry is the most honest language I hear today. It can be unbearably honest. Such honesty is why even modest poems are useful—better a fumbling effort at truth than a slickly packaged lie—and good ones indispensable. Against the sybaritic images of advertising that daily wash over us, against the sententious rhetoric of politics, poetry stands as "the expression of faith in the integrity of the senses and of the imagination" (W. S. Merwin's description). The poets I have met would be incapacitated if they did not write from a place of truth. Revelation is their reason for being.

Revelation comes hard. As Stanley Kunitz once acknowledged, poetry is "the most difficult, most solitary, and most life-enhancing thing that one can do. It's a struggle because words get tired. We use them. We abuse them. A word is a utilitarian tool to begin with, and we have to re-create it, to make it magical. You have to kill off all the top of one's head, remove it, and try to plunge deep into self, deep into memories, deep into the unconscious life. And then begin again."

Now in his ninetieth year, Kunitz still plumbs the depths. He says that "poetry is a means of feeling that, solitary as you are, in the act of writing the poem you are in touch with the whole chain of being. You are always trying not only to get in touch with your most primal self, but with the whole history of the race."

If that were the only reason for poetry, it would be enough. In accepting the 1980 Nobel Prize for Literature, Czeslaw Milosz said: "Our planet gets smaller every year, and with its fantastic proliferation of mass media is witnessing a process that defies definition, characterized by a refusal to remember." *A refusal to remember.* Yet memory is critical if a people are not to be at the mercy of the powers-that-be, if they are to have something against which to measure what the partisans and propagandists tell them today. Memory is critical if, as democracy requires, we are to make midcourse corrections in the affairs of state and our personal behavior. Mark Twain wrote that a cat, once it had sat on a hot stove, would never do so again, but neither would it sit on a cold stove. We humans are different. We can reflect on our experiences and share the insights with others. Life becomes a conversation between generations—past, present, future. "New ages don't begin all at once," Bertolt Brecht said. "My grandfather lives in the new age. My grandson will still live in the old. New meat is eaten with old forks. From the new antennae come the old stupidities. Wisdom is passed from mouth to mouth."

It has often seemed to me that in the poems I most fancy, every word has hanging on it scores of remembrances, like pots and pans dangling from a prairie schooner trekking westward. The poet's yearning to haul to the surface those reverberations from the past is a yearning I share. My own puny, failed, and always furtive efforts to write poetry are in response to distant voices in my head. One belongs to my grandfather Joseph, who died when I was five. How long I have wished to unwrap from the enigma of that cold, waxen corpse the person I yearned as a child to know. I have tried, too, to call up my great grandmother, abandoned with three children in the 1880s by her husband who left Tennessee for California and never came back. There are family secrets only she can answer, and that I imagine the poet's muse coaxing from her.

I envy poets their ability to bring such voices to life. When I interviewed Mary TallMountain she talked of how as a child she had been torn from her Athabaskan village near the Arctic Circle and transported to a new home in the United States to be raised by stepparents. It was fifty years before she returned to that village. She endured her exile with the help of imagined conversations with her grandmother, Matmiya, whose name in English means "mountain":

> I see you sitting
> Implanted by roots
> Coiled deep from your thighs.
> Roots, flesh red, centuries pale.
> Hairsprings wound tight
> Through fertile earthscapes
> Where each layer feeds the next
> Into depths immutable.
>
> Though you must rise, must
> Move large and slow
> When it is time, O my
> Gnarled mother-vine, ancient
> As vanished ages,
> Your spirit remains
> Nourished,
> Nourishing me.

Garrett Kaoru Hongo, too, agrees that "poems are carriers of memories." His Japanese American grandfather was arrested in Honolulu the day after Pearl Harbor and held for questioning. He never forgot the pain and humiliation, and every night after dinner, bourbon in hand, he would repeat the story to the grandson whose poems are now a family's vessels of remembrance. Like Garrett Hongo,

> I want the dead beside me when I dance, to help me
> flesh the notes of my song, to tell me it's all right.

Sadly, a disconnection has occurred in society with respect to history, nature, and language that makes the deep longing for each more acute, as our frenetic lives hardly allow us to slow down for sunsets, memories, or poems. Of the many poetical insights in this book, one of my favorites comes from Naomi Shihab Nye:

> Walk around feeling like a leaf.
> Know you could tumble any second.
> *Then* decide what to do with your time.

I read these words soon after undergoing heart bypass surgery, and more than once during my recovery the image of that fragile leaf appeared in my head, persuading me of new priorities. Nye is right: "Poems allow us to savor a single image, a single phrase. Just think how many people have savored a haiku poem over hundreds of years. It slows you down to read a poem. You read it more than one time. You read it more slowly than you would speak to someone in a store. And we need that slow experience with words."

Here, then, for slow readers like myself, is the language of life. This book began with the 1989 PBS series *The Power of the Word,* in which David Grubin and I sought to suggest the variety of poetic voices we heard at the Dodge Poetry Festivals, including the incomparable Kunitz ("I dance/for the joy of surviving/at the edge of the road"). To those fifteen poets we have added others from our PBS productions *A Life Together: Donald Hall and Jane Kenyon, Rita Dove: Poet Laureate,* and *The Language of Life,* our series airing for the first time on public television in the summer of 1995. Our purpose with this latest series is to reveal just how the democratic discourse continues to be broadened and enriched by diverse voices, and to illuminate those wellsprings of poetry in each human being, however muted and suppressed, that can illuminate life's way.

My collaboration with David Grubin, who produced and directed both *The Power of the Word* and *The Language of Life,* and who is contributing editor of this book, began twenty years ago. I have lost count of the number of television programs we have done together, but our collaboration—the artist with the journalist—has been a deepening joy for me ever since it began. David's interests range across life and his body of work reflects them, whether he is recording the daily travails of a farming family in North Dakota, probing the world of N. C. Wyeth, recapturing the civic power of art in the Florence of the Renaissance, or returning to Normandy with the veterans of D day. His films on the life and times of FDR are widely considered to have been the best documentaries of 1993. David's love of language goes back to his youth—he majored in literature before turning to film—and is, I am convinced, a chief source of his artistry as a producer and director. His films are poetry in motion.

Both of us owe a large debt to the Geraldine R. Dodge Foundation for making possible classroom encounters between inspiring teachers and inspired poets, for poetry gatherings throughout the Garden State, and for the biennial festival. The trustees of the foundation have contributed $2 million over ten years to advance poetry's cause on many fronts, and Scott McVay, who heads the foundation, deserves the applause of poets and poetry lovers everywhere for his tireless advocacy.

I also want to salute the efforts of teachers across the country, across all the disciplines and down the years, who bring poetry to life for each new generation. Eleven of those teachers contributed their ideas and experience to the Teacher's Kit, which accompanies the PBS series and this book. I am grateful to them, and to the team led by Robert Miller of WNET in New York for the educational outreach that makes the series available to students across the country.

James Haba, the Dodge Festival coordinator and catalyst, advised the PBS programs and was the senior editor for this book. "When a man does not write his poetry," Emerson said, "it escapes by other vents through him." Jim is so busy teaching and creating forums for others that he has little time to write poetry himself, but serving the cause of poetry is his calling and poets throughout America have no better friend.

This book owes its survival through a forest of deadlines to the management skills of Debbie Rubenstein, who came to Public Affairs Television from New Orleans via the University of North Carolina. Smart, unflappable, and brimming with élan vital, from start to finish she has supervised the process without a bobble. She was ably assisted by Lisa Todorovich. Abby Kende and her staff at Tele-Cinema met the challenging task of obtaining clearances for the poems.

All of my endeavors are imprinted, in more ways than I can enumerate, with the intelligence and creativity of my wife and partner, Judith Davidson Moyers, the president of Public Affairs Television and coexecutive editor of every program we produce. It was she who encouraged me, one summer morning on the terrace, to act on the impulse to turn the approaching Dodge Festival—then just a few weeks away—into a television series and book. And it was she who became the main force in designing this book. She has yet to heed my counsel to release her own fine poetry into the world, but as Tennyson noted:

> To have the deep Poetic heart
> Is more than all poetic fame.

Our daughter, Suzanne Moyers—teacher, editor, writer—provided me with fresh research and insights into the poems and their authors. Because poetry is "the opening and closing of a door, leaving those who look through to guess about what is seen during a moment" (Carl Sandburg), I welcomed the response of a fresher intelligence and experience to the images and ideas of the poets and poetry at the festival.

I am grateful once again to Elizabeth Meryman-Brunner, the art researcher for my earlier book *Healing and the Mind,* who returned to elevate this endeavor too; to our company's vice president, the versatile Judy Doctoroff O'Neill, who keeps all our projects on the glide path; and to my indefatigable assistant, Eileen Taylor, the calm at the center.

Our efforts would have been for naught if my colleagues at PBS and at other public television stations around the country were not open to the poet's voice. Series like *The Language of Life* fulfill public television's unique mission, offering a forum to people who would never gain a hearing in the commercial media. Nor would the series have happened without the funding provided by Mutual of America Life Insurance Company, the Germeshausen Foundation, and the John D. and Catherine T. MacArthur Foundation. Thanks to them, millions of Americans will share the life-affirming passion of these poets.

All of the people who joined in this endeavor believe what Adrienne Rich put so well in her book *What Is Found There:*

> I knew—had long known—how poetry can break open locked chambers of possibility, restore numbed zones to feeling, recharge desire. And, in spite of conditions at large, it seemed to me that poetry in the United States had never been more various and rich in its promise and its realized offerings.

— BILL MOYERS

Carolyn Forché, David Grubin, Bill Moyers, Roger Phenix

EDITOR'S NOTE

A companion to Bill Moyers's 1995 public television series *The Language of Life,* this book completes a circle that began with the desire to bring poems out of what Stanley Kunitz has called "a very cold bed"—the page—and into the bodies of poets and audiences, thereby returning poetry to its physical roots, which nourished us long before print began to define, and in some ways to limit, our magical experience of words. So now these poems and conversations return enlivened to print, giving us still more of each poet and allowing us to revisit at will those moments of thought and feeling which speak most directly to us.

In the spirit of community at the heart of all poetry, this book also accompanies the other eight Bill Moyers public television programs featuring contemporary poets first broadcast between 1989 and 1994. These twenty-nine interviews generally include and expand their television counterparts as they assume the style and pace appropriate to the printed page. In addition to many of the poems heard on television, the reader will find here many others that never made it to the screen; and the recommended reading list that concludes this volume opens the way to still more poems.

Five poets—Octavio Paz, William Stafford, Sharon Olds, Galway Kinnell, and W. S. Merwin—also appeared in *The Power of the Word.* Each marks our progress through these interviews with poems, photographs, and a few words about their experience of poetry. So rich is the renewal of poetry in our time that it would be impossible even to list the many hundreds of poets who deserve to be in this series and in this book. This grouping merely represents one sampling of the remarkable talent and caring among the thousands of poets at work today.

Both catalyst and essential ground for the television programs and this book, the Dodge Poetry Festivals regularly offer the chance to experience directly the range of voices and the shared life of poetry so often acknowledged in these pages. But no images can adequately reveal and no words can fully describe what it is like to be there. I can only say, in the words of Coleman Barks's ocean frog as he tries to explain his world to the ditch frog: "I couldn't tell you. You have to go there. I'll take you there some day."

I am glad to join Bill Moyers in thanking the trustees of the Geraldine R. Dodge Foundation, whose early and renewed support has made the Dodge Poetry Festivals possible, and Scott McVay, the Foundation's executive director, who first envisioned them and then became their most loyal friend. My wife, Erica, brought belief and encouragement to every phase of the festivals' development. Robert Carnevale, Natalie Gerber, and Brett Anderson were among the many who helped mount the 1994 festival, and they stepped in again to assist with the preparation of these interviews. I owe Natalie Gerber particular thanks for her careful biographical and bibliographical research.

Joan Hunziker, Kathleen Murphy, and Karen and Norma Ritter faithfully processed the several stages of each interview. Lisa Todorovich lent skilled hands at just the right moments, as did Debbie Rubenstein, who gracefully coordinated this project after Judy Doctoroff O'Neill so ably launched it. Elizabeth Meryman-Brunner hunted down and chose the photographs, which remind us of the people from whom these words arise, and Doubleday editor Bruce Tracy consistently encouraged and wisely advised our progress throughout.

Special thanks to Galway Kinnell, W. S. Merwin, Sharon Olds, Octavio Paz, and William Stafford, who were not interviewed by Bill Moyers but who each kindly consented to being represented here by a photograph, a poem, and a few words about poetry spoken at the 1988 Dodge Poetry Festival.

Working with David Grubin, first on the television programs and then on this book, has been a complete pleasure—his keen and experienced eye improved both surface and substance. Judith Moyers passionately embraced this project from the outset and then steadily contributed to its success. We all owe Bill Moyers thanks for having over so many years been willing to devote precious broadcast time to bringing poets and poetry to new and ever-increasing audiences. The community within poetry finds expression in him and in his belief in our capacity to become fully human.

—JAMES HABA

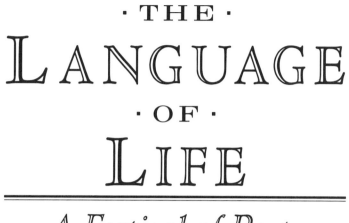

· THE ·
LANGUAGE
· OF ·
LIFE

A Festival of Poets

W. S. MERWIN

W. S. Merwin was recently described by the *New York Times* as "A Poet of Their Own" in recognition of his stature in the pantheon of contemporary American poets. He won the Pulitzer Prize in 1971 and the Academy of American Poets' first annual Tanning Prize in 1994. Merwin and his wife live in a remote section of Hawaii, where they are presently restoring an abandoned pineapple farm to its original state.

Any work of art makes one very simple demand on anyone who genuinely wants to get in touch with it. And that is to stop. You've got to stop what you're doing, what you're thinking, and what you're expecting and just be there for the poem for however long it takes.

Poetry, like all the arts, is an expression of faith in the integrity of the senses and of the imagination; these are what we have in common with the natural world. The animals have no doubt about the integrity of their senses—they're essential to them—and whatever the animal imagination may be, we can imagine it as being connected with their senses. Our remaining connections with what we call the natural world are our dreams, some of our erotic life, if we're lucky, and any sensual experience that we can still believe in.

We go into a supermarket and we have artificial light, canned music, everything's deodorized—we can't touch or taste or smell anything, and we hear only what they want us to hear. No wonder everybody wanders around like zombies! Because our senses have been taken away from us for a while. A supermarket brings the whole thing into focus. The things that are there don't belong there, they didn't grow there. They have a shelf life, which is being rented, so that we can buy them. It's only about selling things. This is a very strange kind of situation, but it's typical of our lives.

Poetry, like all the arts, not only reconnects us to the world, it emanates from the connection with the world of the senses and the imagination that remains. When that connection is no longer there, there will be no arts, and we won't even know what we missed—we really will be zombies walking around, if we can walk around at all, in a sort of eternal supermarket.

PLACE

On the last day of the world
I would want to plant a tree

what for
not for the fruit

the tree that bears the fruit
is not the one that was planted

I want the tree that stands
in the earth for the first time

with the sun already
going down

and the water
touching its roots

in the earth full of the dead
and the clouds passing

one by one
over its leaves

Poetry is like bread—everybody shares it.

CLARIBEL ALEGRÍA

Claribel Alegría, one of the major voices in Latin American letters, has published forty books, including fifteen collections of poetry. She began composing poems at age six but told no one for fear that "my girlfriends would mock me, and no boy ever invite me to a dance." Since 1980 she has lived in political exile from her homeland, El Salvador. But even her poems giving voice to the victims of dictatorship and death squads are love poems to the land and the people where she was nurtured. Her book *Sobrevivo ("I Survive")* received the Casa de las Americas poetry prize in 1978.

MOYERS: You begin "Desire" with a quote from Pizarnik, "And someone entered death / with his eyes open." How does such a thought become the inspiration for a whole poem?

ALEGRÍA: It happens to me a lot. I always keep what I call my "seed book." It's a simple notebook, and when I read something that really touches me, or when I hear something, or when I dream—I dream a lot—I put all these things into my seed book. This passage was one of them. Sometimes I go to my seed book and all of a sudden there's a click. That is what happened here.

DESEO

"Y alguien entra a la muerte
con los ojos abiertos".
    —A. PIZARNIK

Quiero entrar a la muerte
con los ojos abiertos
abiertos los oidos
sin mascaras
sin miedo
sabiendo
y no sabiendo
enfrontarme serena
a otros voces

DESIRE

"And someone entered death
  with his eyes open."
    —A. PIZARNIK

I want to enter death
with my eyes open
my ears open
with no masks
no fears
knowing
and not knowing
serenely facing
other voices

a otros aires	other airs
a otros cauces	other paths
olvidar mis recuerdos	forgetting my memories
desprenderme	detaching myself
nacer de nuevo	being reborn
intacta.	intact.

TRANSLATED BY D. J. FLAKOLL

MOYERS: You put the thought in there to germinate, so to speak.

ALEGRÍA: That's right. That seed germinated and the poem arose.

MOYERS: "The Mirror" is a very haunting poem. Mirrors show up again and again in your poems.

ALEGRÍA: I know. The mirror is an important symbol for me. In the long poem I am now writing mirrors appear throughout, and at the end I break them all.

MOYERS: Why?

ALEGRÍA: Because I get tired of seeing my face over and over, repeated endlessly, so tired that I break all the mirrors at the end of this long poem I am writing.

MOYERS: How did you become so intrigued by mirrors?

ALEGRÍA: When I was an adolescent and wanted to become an actress, I would go to my room and look at myself in the mirror. I wanted to become a tragic artist of the theater, so I started reciting and while I was reciting I always looked at myself in the mirror. Then I realized that I had a crooked face, that my left side was very different from my right side. With my left side I could be glamorous, but with my right side, no—there I was always very much down to earth. From then on mirrors haunted me. I would look at my face to see the side that wanted to be an actress and then to see if that side could pull the other side up, things like that. So mirrors haunted me all the time.

MOYERS: Do you find joy in writing poetry?

ALEGRÍA: Yes, sometimes, but other times I don't. It depends. Poems come to me in different ways. Sometimes I am very, very lucky and a line of poetry is given to me in a dream. I always keep a little notebook in my night table and I write my dreams in it. In *Luisa in Reality Land*—a sort of autobiographical book, vignettes and poems—I say that I have a gypsy in me that I dream of. The gypsy is a poet, it's me really, because she gives me the poems. So sometimes it's a great joy to write poems, they sort of come.

But other times I suffer when a poem dies in my hand; it's terrible when a poem dies a premature death. Then there are still other times when, even before I think of writing a poem, I hear the music.

MOYERS: The music?

ALEGRÍA: Yes, the music haunting me. Sometimes I hear music haunting me, and then I have to fill that music with words.

MOYERS: You do seem to be experiencing joy in "Ars Poetica." What is "the promised land" in that poem?

ALEGRÍA: Well, I was thinking of the promised land more than anything else in the world, but especially in relation to my country. I wrote that poem when there was war in El Salvador—it was terrible, destruction and death everywhere—but I always thought that there was something behind all that, and I thought that if I didn't keep in mind what was behind all that horror I would surely go crazy. Now I feel the same way for the whole world. I mean, it's so terrible when you think of Rwanda, for instance.

ARS POETICA

I,
poet by trade,
condemned so many times
to be a crow,
would never change places
with the Venus de Milo:
while she reigns in the Louvre
and dies of boredom
and collects dust
I discover the sun
each morning
and amid valleys
volcanos
and debris of war
I catch sight of the promised land.
TRANSLATED BY D. J. FLAKOLL

MOYERS: It's the oldest vision of all, is it not? The Vision of Eden.

ALEGRÍA: The Garden of Eden, exactly, and I think it *is* there. I am not so pessimistic as to stop believing in it. Sometimes I'm afraid of becoming cynical because of some hurtful influence that such feeling could bring into the world. I hope that will not happen.

MOYERS: I love the opening of "Ars Poetica," "I, / poet by trade." But what do you mean by the phrase "condemned so many times / to be a crow"?

ALEGRÍA: Sometimes I feel that I am a crow, that I have pitiless eyes, that I look at things in the way a crow probably would look, with pitiless eyes, and when I discover in myself something I don't like in others I also look at myself with pitiless eyes. When I look with those eyes I feel that I am a crow. Do you see?

MOYERS: Yes, but then what are you asking us to do in "Documentary" when you say to the reader, "Come, be my camera."

ALEGRÍA: Yes, there I *do* want you to see what I am seeing. I wrote that poem a long time ago, and some people said it was a political poem. I laughed. To me it was a love poem for my country, and I wanted everybody to come and see what I was seeing. I wanted them to see why it was such a desperate situation.

MOYERS: I saw your country with cameras during the war and I know what you mean. There was something else in those smoky mountains and green hillsides, something else in the serenity of the people living their lives in the midst of horror.

ALEGRÍA: Exactly. That's what I tried to say in that poem, that in spite of all this horror something else is going to come.

DOCUMENTARY

Come, be my camera.
Let's photograph the ant heap
the queen ant
extruding sacks of coffee,
my country.
It's the harvest.
Focus on the sleeping family
cluttering the ditch.
Now, among trees:
rapid,
dark-skinned fingers

stained with honey.
Shift to a long shot:
the file of ant men
trudging down the ravine
with sacks of coffee.
A contrast:
girls in colored skirts
laugh and chatter,
filling their baskets
with berries.
Focus down.
A close-up of the pregnant mother
dozing in the hammock.
Hard focus on the flies
spattering her face.
Cut.
The terrace of polished mosaics
protected from the sun.
Maids in white aprons
nourish the ladies
who play canasta,
celebrate invasions
and feel sorry for Cuba.
Izalco sleeps
beneath the volcano's eye.
A subterranean growl
makes the village tremble.
Trucks and ox-carts
laden with sacks
screech down the slopes.
Besides coffee
they plant angels
in my country.
A chorus of children
and women
with the small white coffin
move politely aside
as the harvest passes by.

The riverside women,
naked to the waist,
wash clothing.
The truck drivers
exchange jocular obscenities
for insults.
In Panchimalco,
waiting for the ox-cart to pass by,
a peasant
with hands bound behind him
by the thumbs
and his escort of soldiers
blinks at the airplane:
a huge bee
bulging with coffee growers
and tourists.
The truck stops in the market place.
A panorama of iguanas,
chickens,
strips of meat,
wicker baskets,
piles of *nances,*
nísperos,
oranges,
zunzas,
zapotes,
cheeses,
bananas,
dogs, *pupusas, jocotes,*
acrid odors,
taffy candies,
urine puddles, tamarinds.
The virginal coffee
dances in the millhouse.
They strip her,
rape her,
lay her out on the patio
to doze in the sun.

The dark storage sheds
glimmer.
The golden coffee
sparkles with malaria,
blood,
illiteracy,
tuberculosis,
misery.
A truck roars
out of the warehouse.
It bellows uphill
drowning out the lesson:
A for alcoholism,
B for battalions,
C for corruption,
D for dictatorship,
E for exploitation,
F for the feudal power
of fourteen families
and etcetera, etcetera, etcetera.
My etcetera country,
my wounded country,
my child,
my tears,
my obsession.

TRANSLATED BY D. J. FLAKOLL

MOYERS: Your very name means joy, doesn't it? You have such joy in your poetry, and yet you deal with painful stories of war and death and torture. How do you reconcile the art and the reality?

ALEGRÍA: It's very difficult sometimes to reconcile art and reality, but I have never thought that the poet had to be in an ivory tower just thinking beautiful thoughts. When there is so much horror around you, I think you have to look at it. You have to feel it and suffer with the others and make that suffering yours.

MOYERS: How do you capture that horror without surrendering to it?

ALEGRÍA: With hope, always with hope. And sometimes it is very hard to maintain hope because dreams come tumbling down. For twelve years I lived in exile and could not return to my country, then after the peace agreements were signed, I went back. I cried—it was fantastic to talk to my people—but so many of the poor, poor people that I talked to asked, "Why all these horrors? Why so many deaths?"

MOYERS: It *is* such a wounded country. You said at one of the workshops yesterday that in your country they plant coffee and angels. Why angels?

ALEGRÍA: Because so many children die. About every five minutes a child dies in El Salvador. So often, before a child is two years old he or she is an angel; so we bury the children and we plant angels.

MOYERS: At the end of "Documentary" you switch from the camera to the alphabet. Why is that?

ALEGRÍA: Yes, at the end of the poem I switch and begin to list what is so terrible—the wounds in my country, dictatorships, everything—then I switch and, in the end, I am alone.

MOYERS: At the end of the poem the documentary camera is gone and the impersonal eye of the camera is replaced by the weeping eye of the poet.

ALEGRÍA: Of the poet, yes. Exactly. First it's impersonal—I want you to be a camera, and I want you to see everything that I see as a camera—but then after that, it's just me as a human being.

MOYERS: The tragedy is that this powerful poetry didn't stop the war in El Salvador. So why write this kind of poetry if power is deaf to it?

ALEGRÍA: When I wrote this poem I had great hopes. I thought, "Something is going to happen." I thought, "Maybe my government, maybe the United States government, maybe the people of the Old Guard—some of these people may see a little bit of the light." One of my great hopes is that in my poems there might be a little grain of sun that I can communicate. That's my way of fighting for my country.

MOYERS: The irony is that your poetry is probably a more enduring record of the horror of El Salvador than our cameras.

ALEGRÍA: I don't know, the cameras are very powerful too, and sometimes the power of the cameras produces seeds from which a poem can arise.

MOYERS: Do you know if your poetry ever reached the *campesinos,* the peasants?

ALEGRÍA: You know, that is one thing I was very happy about. Somebody told me that during my twelve years of exile from El Salvador the guerrillas had read my poems on the radio. During that time a man came to me in Nicaragua and said, "You know what? Many of the *campesinos* now ask to read your poems," and he told me "Documentary" was one they especially liked.

MOYERS: Why were you exiled?

ALEGRÍA: Because on the same day in 1980 when I had been invited to the Sorbonne to give a reading, a friend called me in Paris to tell me that Archbishop Romero had been assassinated. I was horrified, of course, and my husband said, "Don't give a reading. Talk about that instead." So we stayed up all night composing a tribute to Monseñor Romero. With other poets from my country I realized that we had to do something just to feel a little bit of what Monseñor Romero had left us because he really was, as they always said, "the voice of the voiceless."

So I started my reading by talking about what the death squads were doing in El Salvador, and my cousin—who was the Minister of Defense in El Salvador at that time, imagine that!—sent word to me not to return to El Salvador because he could not be responsible for my safety. This was very hard because my mother died in 1982 while I was in Nicaragua. I adored my mother, and she wanted to see me, but my brothers telephoned and said, "Don't come because there will be two funerals instead of one."

MOYERS: Well, there is an old story that when a revolution occurred in some ancient European land the new ruler was asked, "What's the first thing to do?" and he said, "Kill the poets."

ALEGRÍA: That's right. Yes.

MOYERS: When did you start writing poetry?

ALEGRÍA: Very early in my life, but really seriously when I was about fourteen. I began because of a wonderful book that came into my hands, Rilke's *Letters to a Young Poet*. I stayed up all night reading Rilke. We had a beautiful, big house in Santa Ana, a typical Spanish house with a patio and corridors, and after reading Rilke I paced for hours up and down the corridors. Then I went to the patio and sat near the fountain. Finally I told myself, "This is what I want to be. This is it. I want to be a poet."

Then I started writing, and when I was eighteen I had the good fortune to come to the United States to learn English and to study at a university. In the United States I met Juan Ramón Jiménez, the Spanish poet and Nobel Prize winner. He got interested in my poetry and offered to be my mentor. When he learned that I was already trying to write free verse, he said, "You cannot do that. First you have to go through all the traditional forms. You can free yourself after that. Then you will know what you are doing."

He showed me that free verse is the most difficult poetry to write because the music is inside; you are not helped by rhyme and it is very easy to fail. He was wonderful to me, he taught me how to relate music and painting to poetry and he made me read a horrible lot from the troubadours. He was fantastic, but he was very harsh with me, too. I went to his house twice a week, and he never told me that he liked even one line in my poetry. He would say, "This is vulgar" or "This is easy," and I would come home almost crying, saying, "Maybe I don't have it." But I went on and after two and a half years of this, he called me to his house where he and his wife received me with very special smiles, so I said, "What's the matter?" Then he said, "You have a book!" From all the poems I had written he had chosen twenty-two and his wife had copied them. That was my first book of poetry. I was very lucky.

MOYERS: Young poets need mentors, don't they?

ALEGRÍA: Yes, I think so, but then they also need to get rid of their mentors. For instance, this long poem that I've been writing for about two and a half years is going to be called "Thresholds," and in it I am involved with poetry at each threshold. At one of these thresholds I meet my mentor whom I call Merlin, Merlin the Magician. Merlin teaches me lots of things and then he wants me to hide in a terrible tower where I won't see anybody, I will just write poetry. But I refuse because I already know what love is, so I fly from the tower and I leave Merlin, my mentor.

MOYERS: Were you encouraged to read and to write your own poems when you were a child?

ALEGRÍA: Yes. I was very fortunate. My house had lots and lots of books, and the writers and painters of the time would come to the house. My father loved to recite poetry, and my mother loved the Spanish poets. They recited all the time. I remember very well that my favorite poet was Juana de Ibarború. Once my father himself read a poem to me by that wonderful woman, "If I Were a Man," which said, "If I could be a man I would do such and such a thing." I loved that poem. I said, "That's wonderful." That's when I started to be a feminist.

MOYERS: At what age?

ALEGRÍA: I was about ten.

MOYERS: And you dictated poems to your mother, didn't you?

ALEGRÍA: That's right. I was very petulant. When I was about five or six I did not know how to read or write yet, but I would say to my mother, "Mother, here is a poem. Please write it down because it is wonderful." And she would, *she* was wonderful.

MOYERS: All of this reinforces the idea that the poet enjoys a much more prominent place in Central America than in our country. As a poet you're so much better known in your land than our poets are known here in the United States. Why is that?

ALEGRíA: Traditionally in Central America the role of the poet is very important. In Central America, but especially in Nicaragua, practically everybody is a poet. When one man says to another, "I have some poems I am going to read to you," the other says, "Great, but if you read to me, I read to you."

MOYERS: Tell me how you came to write "Summing Up."

ALEGRíA: I am seventy now and when I was nearly sixty-eight, I started thinking back on my life. "I have lived a long, long time," I said to myself, "so what have been the crucial moments in my life?" I wanted to be clear, and that's why I called it "Summing Up." Let's say that poem is an account of my life.

SUMMING UP

In the sixty-three years
I have lived
some instants are electric:
the happiness of my feet
jumping puddles
six hours in Machu Picchu
the buzzing of the telephone
while awaiting my mother's death
the ten minutes it took
to lose my virginity
the hoarse voice
announcing the assassination
of Archbishop Romero
fifteen minutes in Delft
the first wail of my daughter
I don't know how many years yearning
for the liberation of my people
certain immortal deaths
the eyes of that starving child

your eyes bathing me in love
one forget-me-not afternoon
and in this rainy hour
the desire to mold myself
into a verse
a cry
a fleck of foam.

TRANSLATED BY D. J. FLAKOLL

MOYERS: "the desire to mold myself / into a verse / a cry / a fleck of foam." Why at this age these images which conclude the poem?

ALEGRÍA: Because I really wanted to write the poem which would sum up *all* my life. I wanted to mold myself into doing that. I also wanted to cry out to everybody, a desperate cry telling them what has happened. Then sometimes I just want to disappear and float in the air.

MOYERS: Like a fleck of foam?

ALEGRÍA: That's right. Like a fleck of foam.

Claribel Alegría, Carolyn Forché, Daisy Zamora

James A. Autry

James A. Autry wrote his first book of poetry about his boyhood in the Delta region of Tennessee and northern Mississippi. It abounds in family reunions, church revivals, country funerals, and nights under a tin roof. Autry went on to become a successful Fortune 500 executive, Magazine Executive of the Year, and, until his retirement in 1991, president of the Meredith Corporation's magazine group. His later poems take up choices and issues confronted by business leaders, from the firing of a salesman to office romance. An Iowa resident, he cofounded the Des Moines National Poetry Festival.

MOYERS: Some people tell me they can't be poets because language doesn't *use* them.

AUTRY: I understand that. A lot changed for me when I quit trying to select words and use language in certain ways that I'd been taught and instead just kept simplifying, simplifying, simplifying. I found that if I expressed what I was feeling in the simplest possible language it was always better, and somehow that language would come to me. There are poems that I work very hard on, and then there are others that just seem to be delivered, as if I'm taking dictation. Those are always the best poems, and while I may come back and edit them technically, craft them, if it's not there in the beginning, I can't put it there.

MOYERS: Almost every one of these poems about your childhood in Mississippi includes some person you knew personally, some voice that you can still hear.

AUTRY: I do *hear* those voices. I hear those voices especially when I visit the cemetery where many family members are buried. I can walk into that church, which was my father's church, close my eyes, and I can hear him preaching. You could call it vivid imagination, but it's not deliberate action; it's not something that I'm working to call up.

MOYERS: How did you happen to write "Genealogy"?

GENEALOGY

You are
in these hills

Poetry gives you permission to feel.

who you were and who you will become
and not just who you are

> *She was a McKinstry*
> *and his mother was a Smith*

And the listeners nod
at what the combination will produce
those generations to come
of thievery or honesty
of heathens or Christians
of slovenly men or working

> *'Course her mother was a Sprayberry*

And the new name rises
to the shaking of heads
the tightening of lips
the widening of eyes

> *And his daddy's mother was a McIlhenney*

Oh god a McIlhenney
and silence prays for the unborn children
those little McKinstry Smith Sprayberry McIlhenneys

> *Her daddy was no count and her daddy's daddy was no count*

Old Brother Jim Goff said it
when Mary Allen was pregnant

> *Might's well send that chile*
> *to the penitentiary soons he's born*
> *gonna end up there anyway*

But that lineage could also forgive
with benign expectation
of transgressions to come

> *'Course, what do you expect*
> *his granddaddy was a Wilkins*

or

> *The Whitsells are a little crazy*
> *but they generally don't beat up nobody outside the family*

or

> *You can't expect much work out of a Latham*
> *but they won't steal from you*

In other times and other places
there are new families and new names

> *He's ex P&G*
> *out of Benton and Bowles*
> *and was brand management with Colgate*

And listeners sip Dewar's and soda or puff New True Lights
and know how people will do things
they are expected to do
New fathers spring up and new sons and grandsons
always in jeopardy of leaving the family

> *Watch young Dillard*
> *if he can work for Burton he's golden*
> *but he could be out tomorrow*

And new marriages are bartered for old-fashioned reasons

> *If you want a direct marketing guy*
> *get a headhunter after someone at Time Inc.*

Through it all
communities new and old watch and judge and make sure
the names are in order
and everyone understands

AUTRY: I was jogging by the house of people I knew down here and I thought, well they're the so-and-so's. Then I realized that with that name went a whole set of characteristics. In a sense, I *know* about them. I know whether they're likely to be honest, or whether they're generally hardworking people. I realized that genealogy is real and that people who have certain characteristics ascribed to them somehow seem to work out that way which, I now understand, is largely the result of expectation.

MOYERS: Particularly when you live in a closely knit neighborhood like this and everybody shares the *same* expectations. They expect you to be like your father or your uncle or your aunt.

AUTRY: All my life when someone was talked about—like Judith Moyers, for instance—people would say, "She was a Davidson." Every woman was always referred to by her married name *and* by her maiden name, and her maiden name carried some defining characteristics. If there's some characteristic that may come up when talking about a man, you'll hear, "Well, you know, of course his mother was a Wilkins," as if to say, "Well, what do you expect?" I've heard these conversations all my life. The impulse to write the poem came much later, and actually after a business conversation in which someone had said to me, "If you want a direct marketing guy, you ought to get one from Time, Inc." I thought, that's the *family* he comes from, and somehow it all came together then. And at that time I was working on what I call flashback or contrast poems in which I contrast my present life with this life down here.

MOYERS: How do you reconcile the world of rural Mississippi and the world of your company's boardroom?

AUTRY: I look for patterns that are the same—whether it's thinking about families and genealogy or watching a chief executive officer deciding something in the same way the head of the school board or the country supervisors would decide something. I always look for patterns because in the best of what business is there's a strong thread of common sense.

MOYERS: Your grandfather was a preacher. Your father was a preacher. Is poetry a form of proclaiming?

AUTRY: I believe it is. In fact, I was just talking to Brother Gant at the church and I said, "You know, tomorrow when I stand up in that pulpit, it's going to be the first time I've ever been up there. Maybe my poems are my way of preaching." I do think that's true—we all have different ministries.

MOYERS: What's the ministry in poetry?

AUTRY: I think the ministry in *Nights Under a Tin Roof* is trying to recapture for those who have experienced it, or capture for those who haven't, all those threads of community and ritual that are acted out in funerals and all-day singings and revival meetings that somehow weave the everyday fabric of our lives.

MOYERS: When you're writing, do you remember things you didn't know you'd forgotten?

AUTRY: All the time. When I get to moving thematically, the details just present themselves.

MOYERS: In one of the poems you read in church, you talked about love, fellowship, and community. As you read I felt love, fellowship, and community occurring in that little congregation.

AUTRY: I felt it too—it was palpable—and yet I was trying to explain to someone after the reading that I didn't get that feeling from their faces, because I didn't look at their faces that much, but I could just feel it happening, and when it happened it was almost like hearing a click. First they were stiff, and then it was as if they were one—I could feel that sense of community, that we were all here together sharing this history.

MOYERS: How do you explain that?

AUTRY: I don't know that I can explain it any better than by saying, it *is* the power of the word. What has meant most to me in writing poetry is that people consistently come up after a reading and tell me that they don't read poetry and they don't study poetry, but they understand *this*. I like to think of it as somehow re-creating for them an important part of the lives that we shared. I feel the same way whether it happens here in Mississippi or in the business world. I'm always trying to tap into the common experience, the things that make us community.

MOYERS: Do you experience in the business world any of the love and community so palpable in your experience in Mississippi?

AUTRY: Yes, I do.

MOYERS: But we don't think of the business world that way.

AUTRY: I know we don't, but to me an important part of the business world is trying to get through the macho veneer we've built around business and get to the feelings which are at the heart of business. I keep saying business is life, life is business, so where did we get this macho, tough guy stuff? In fact, you spend sixty percent of your waking hours on the job—you celebrate, you suffer, you worry, you feel anxiety and pain and fear and jealousy and joy right there in the workplace every day—and that is what I try to get into poetry. In a way, what I'm saying is if we deal with the humanity of business, then the business will take care of itself.

MOYERS: What is there about the business world that stifles emotional experience and builds barriers between people instead of connecting them as they were connected in your church?

AUTRY: Part of it is the masculine ethic of business. We keep expecting women coming into the workplace to help change that, but they haven't changed it much. In fact, they've adopted it more than they've changed it.

M O Y E R S : All those metaphors of competition that spill over from sports to business.

A U T R Y : Exactly. Sports and even battle metaphors are often used in business. I hardly use the word "team" in business; I use "community" much more frequently.

If I'm involved in anything that is of great moment in business, it is trying to help evolve or discover a new vocabulary for people in business to use with one another.

M O Y E R S : So you believe we take on the qualities of the language we use?

A U T R Y : Yes. If you think about winning, you've got to think about losing; so if you think of yourself as a winner, you must think of someone else as a loser, and that makes the whole thing a zero sum game. I want to be an instrument of changing that, and part of what must be done is to change the vocabulary. Sports metaphors and battle metaphors have played a destructive role in business. I know people who cannot enjoy improving their share of market without also looking at the competitor from whom they got that share and saying, "I kicked him." What that perspective ignores is that there are cycles in business and, in my belief, the best thing business people can do is make the good cycle absolutely as good as it can be and keep the bad cycle from going as deep as might be expected.

M O Y E R S : What was the response the first time you read poetry to business folk?

A U T R Y : I had written an essay which appeared in the *Des Moines Register*, and as a result I was asked to talk to a group of business people, so I just decided this is it, I'm going to talk and then read some poems. When I told them I was going to read poems, I could see their eyes widen and the shock in their faces, but after I read the first three, I could see tears in the eyes of some gray-haired men in the audience, and I thought, "I'm onto something here. They *want* this. They're *yearning* for someone to recognize and to honor the emotion of what they're involved in."

M O Y E R S : The language of poetry is such an honest language—intimate and honest. Does that language threaten business folk? And what does that mean to the business?

A U T R Y : I wouldn't claim writing and reading poetry has not closed some doors—I'm sure it *has*—but it has opened *more* doors than it has closed. It has allowed me to get close to people, to approach intimacies with people about their lives in business that they're not used to, and I don't think that would have happened if I hadn't begun to trust my own poems.

MOYERS: What happens when you read "On Firing a Salesman"?

ON FIRING A SALESMAN

It's like a little murder,
taking his life,
his reason for getting on the train,
his lunches at Christ Cella,
and his meetings in warm and sunny places
where they all gather,
these smiling men,
in sherbet slacks and blue blazers,
and talk about business
but never about prices,
never breaking that law
about the prices they charge.

But what about the prices they pay?
What about gray evenings in the bar car
and smoke-filled clothes and hair
and children already asleep
and wives who say
"You stink"
when they come to bed?
What about the promotions they don't get,
the good accounts they lose
to some kid MBA
because somebody thinks their energy is gone?

What about those times they see in a mirror
or the corner of their eye
some guy at the club shake his head
when they walk through the locker room
the way they shook their heads years ago
at an old duffer
whose handicap had grown along with his age?

And what about this morning,
the summons,
the closed door,
and somebody shaved and barbered and shined
fifteen years their junior
trying to put on a sad face
and saying he understands?

A murder with no funeral,
nothing but those quick steps outside the door,
those set jaws,
those confident smiles,
that young disregard for even the thought
of a salesman's mortality.

AUTRY: That was the first poem I read to a business group, and there was a lot of nodding. When I asked, "How many of you ever fired someone?" I got a good show of hands, so I asked, "How many of you ever felt that way?" and I got *another* show of hands. I realized that no one has ever said to them that firing somebody is a dirty, rotten, awful job—it's gut-wrenching; it breaks your heart; you're taking something from that person; in a way, you're taking their life—and no one has ever said it's all right to feel terrible about that. I found people coming up after these poetry readings and thanking me for, in effect, giving them permission to admit their feelings when they have to do something like that. The other side of it is that they also get permission to celebrate and to be happy about the pleasure that business can provide.

MOYERS: Many would argue that if you're going to go into the market you need the soul of *The Wall Street Journal* editorial page, not the soul of James Autry.

AUTRY: Well, I have no doubt the editors of *The Wall Street Journal* would agree with you, but you have to constantly be thinking about the difference between business and management. Management is a tool to do business, and business is a way to organize resources to do commerce; but we tend to think of business as just business. I'm involved in management which by classic definition is getting results through people, and it is not anything like what Ivan Boesky was involved with.

Like religion, business is revealed and made manifest through people. It doesn't exist without people, whether they are the customers or the vendors or the employers or the investors. It is an enterprise of humanity, and the manager's role deals precisely with that. As a manager, I worry about financial resources and buying paper for our magazines and how much that's going to cost and what the postal service is going to do and all the things that business people get involved with, but I can do all that perfectly and yet fail, because I do not manage the people well. On the other hand, if I can manage the people well—create the environment in which they can grow and feel fulfilled and be part of this new neighborhood, and friends as the new family, which is called the job—then they will themselves almost indemnify me against some of the mistakes I might make on the technical side.

MOYERS: How do you find the right word, the precise word, the word that expresses what you feel?

AUTRY: If you ran into me on any given day of the week and looked into my pocket, you would see lots of little scraps of paper—lines and phrases, themes of poems, things I want to try to think about—and every once in a while I take those out and look at them and I begin to respond to a developing theme. Words begin to come as I work and I may want to change them for others that more precisely represent what I want to say.

MOYERS: Do you read it aloud to yourself for the sound of it in your own ear?

AUTRY: Always. I must read it aloud to myself and hear it in my own voice. Reading it aloud sometimes leads to polishing and changing and I'm also always looking for the common ground—it's almost desperately important for me that people hear my poetry and experience it as part of their own story. There are poets who write principally for themselves—in some ways, you could say that's true of me, too—and yet, if that loop weren't closed, if I didn't have an experience such as I had this morning when I knew that I'd reached that common ground and I was somehow telling *our* story, the experience would be incomplete.

That is important to me with the business audiences, too. It makes them realize how important their story is, and it's critically important for business people to feel that what they're doing in business *is* life. There's *only* life, and business is part of *that*.

MOYERS: Why do you write poetry?

AUTRY: I write poetry because I have to, which is what all artists will say. I came to poetry very late. I thought I would write novels or short stories—and of course, I've written thousands of words of magazine articles and journalistic things—but in the late 1970s, I had spent a lot of my life trying *not* to be a white Southerner. When I could come back here to visit, I began to feel a sense of loss about all the changes in roads, landscape, culture and, at the same time, a sense of somehow needing to preserve it.

I had never written or studied poetry, but when I heard James Dickey read I was moved by the efficiency of the language, the ability somehow to capture so much in so few words, and I thought, "Well, I'll try that." There's a certain arrogance in that, but I *did* try it, and those early poems now make me laugh. Somehow, though, a narrative voice came into what I was doing, and I began to realize that I could put the actual voices that I was hearing from the past into that poetry. The next thing I knew, I was writing poetry and feeling good about it. From that time on I've really never considered writing anything besides poetry.

MOYERS: You felt some guilt over being a white Mississippian. Poetry seems to have helped you recover feelings about the South that had been stifled.

AUTRY: Yes. I had virtually condemned it all in my quest to *not* be the white Southerner, and I used to look back in anger quite a bit, but it *is* part of me and *I* am part of it. Then I understood that a lot of what was good here had to do with the way the people are together—the love and the ritual and the community and the support.

MOYERS: When you come back to your roots, what's the biggest change?

AUTRY: The most obvious change is all the cutting of the forests. I was noticing this time that lots of timber is being cut out, and it's changing the whole way the land looks and feels. The second most obvious change is how television spreads style and fashion, the way people dress and what they talk about, even the eyeglasses they wear.

MOYERS: And language too is changing under the assault of television?

AUTRY: Language is changing *enormously*. In fact, you just don't hear a lot of the language that used to be common down here. Years ago I drove up to Uncle Elond's house and asked him, "Where's Aunt Cassie?" He said, "She's yonder in bed with the sorriest of the Itis boys, Arthur." "Arthur Itis." This language is just disappearing; no one talks that way anymore. To me, the rhythm and the texture and the sound of the language is the everyday poetry. Some of the most vivid examples are comparisons like— can I say this on television?—"Busier than a one-legged man in an ass-kicking contest." I just did. And other comparisons like "It's just hotter than . . . or colder than . . . or busier than"—that kind of thing.

MOYERS: Are you in these Southern poems looking for that boy you once were? Was that a reason for writing?

AUTRY: Oh, it was, and coming back to face some of what made me what I am also led to rediscovering a less cynical self. I would come back here as an arrogant young man—late teens, early twenties—and think, these folks don't know about the real world. The real world is tough, the real world is mean. Since then, I've been asking, "Well, what *is* the real world?" If you use the word "real" as meaning authentic, then *this* is the authentic world, the real world. That search for authenticity both in myself and in the people in the world has, to a large degree, taken away my earlier cynicism, which involved believing that I knew how the real world was as opposed to how this sheltered world was.

MOYERS: Well, many of us look wistfully back to when we had permission to be adolescent.

AUTRY: Yes, the life of an adult entails accepting and in some way being responsible for pain. My poems are not without pain. I have a body of unpublished work that explores some of it. My mother and father—he was a Baptist minister—were divorced, and being divorced is in itself a painful experience for everyone involved. That poetry has been written more recently. I think I had to go through this rediscovery first.

MOYERS: Will the painful poems be published one day?

AUTRY: I'm sure they will. My wife, Sally, and I have a son, and that's been both a very painful experience as well as, in many ways, a joyful experience. I have two or three poems which explore that pain.

MOYERS: You said to me once that you saw the face of God in the face of your autistic son, Ronald.

AUTRY: Sometimes I look at him and he seems wise beyond anything that could be tested by scientific measurement. Sometimes we look at one another right in the eyes, and I think he understands. There have been revelations in my experiences with him which I think of as divine revelations. And I've also heard, as you have, that God reveals Himself in pain, and I do believe it.

MOYERS: There was so much pain in the South of our youth. I grew up in East Texas well-loved, well-churched, and well-taught—but too long unaware of the suffering caused by racism and segregation. Not many blacks show up in your early poems.

AUTRY: I believe—and let me quickly say, I don't believe this is a dodge— that we white Southerners have to deal with this history all the time. I believe that the communities were so much the same that what I have written about is an experience that really doesn't have color to it. There's one poem in the book based on the marriage of two black people, but I think the rest of the poems present pretty common community experiences.

MOYERS: The ugly side of it was that we *did* have so much in common but couldn't live as a community.

AUTRY: Yes, of course there is an ugly side of the relations between blacks and whites. Now, obviously, in my childhood, living among black people and white people, there was a lot of overt racism which I, too, experienced, but I didn't live through the open strife of the 1960s. I was a distant citizen, the man who looked back, who didn't stay down here and work in the midst of it. I was neither a journalist nor a resident at that time. It was a very painful period, but I didn't live it, so I don't write about it.

MOYERS: In the library right over there I found a 1930 Mississippi Law book. Regulation 11.61 says it's a misdemeanor punishable by a $500 fine or six months in prison for any person, corporation, or organization to teach, promulgate, promote, or in any other way disseminate the idea of social equality between the races. I mean, that was about the time we were born.

AUTRY: That was the law.

MOYERS: Not much to celebrate about that reality.

AUTRY: There *isn't* much to celebrate, but I didn't grow up with that as law; I grew up with that as *custom*. Nobody ever said, "You know what the law is, don't do this." You just didn't do it. I think I was probably in college before the whole social and political and economic inequality things hit me, and it hit me hard. I went to college in 1951, and the Brown vs. School Board decision didn't come down until May of 1954 when I was editor of the school paper at the University of Mississippi. I remember *The New York Times* called—one of the big thrills of my life—and said, "You're the editor of the school paper, what do you think?" I said, "The people down here will obey the law." That shows you how much I knew at the time.

MOYERS: Because you were writing about your church, family, community, and because Mississippi was segregated at the time, no blacks show up in your poetry. But do they ever acknowledge that your experiences were their experiences, too—in their own families, churches, and communities?

AUTRY: They do. I've had black people down here hear my poetry and come up to me and say that's just the way they lived. This book has been anthologized in a series from the University of Mississippi Press, from the Center for the Study of Southern Culture which focuses on writers whose childhood and youth were spent in Mississippi, and last June in Jackson, Mississippi, the third volume, which is the poetry volume, was introduced and poets were asked to come for an all-day reading. So we all read our poems all day in the old State Capitol—blacks and whites—and there were probably more black poets than white poets represented there.

In fact, several black poets told me they would have thought my poems were about black people had they not seen my picture on the jacket. It was a wonderful experience, and I wrote a poem about it.

MISSISSIPPI WRITERS DAY

The irony was lost on no one.
There we sat,
poets, writers, teachers, scholars,
in the chamber where some
of our grandfathers and great-grandfathers
deliberated on how to solve
the nigra problem,
then passed the poll tax
and set up separate but equal schools
and decided that everyone had to read
and understand the constitution
before he could vote.
We sat there,
in the chamber in the building
whose bricks were made by slaves.
We sat and listened
to black poets,
to angry black poets
who read their words
so that no one could ever feel safe
reading them in a white voice.

It was a lesson about words
and how their color changes.
It was a lesson about places
and how their power changes.
It was a lesson about people
and how their fear changes.

MOYERS: That's the poem about a changing Mississippi?

AUTRY: Yes, and I think underneath my lamenting the changes I have talked about is the realization that I can't give up the bad part without also giving up the good part. In order to bring about the change that we've seen in Mississippi—Mississippi has more elected black officials than any state in the Union—we have had to give up much of the rest of the past.

MOYERS: When you come back now, are you able to get *into* this culture again?

AUTRY: I never am fully away from the corporate world, but there are times when I can just plunge right back into the way it felt. It's not as easy. I can't come to this church and do it because this church is nicely appointed and air-conditioned, but what I want to see, which I know would create great discomfort for everybody else who's down here all the time, would be open windows, bats flying in, bugs buzzing around the lights, all the things I remember when I was a boy in these pews. On the other hand, I can go down into the deep woods or to the home place where my father and my uncle were born, and be right back again. Some things never change here. The land doesn't change. They cut the trees, but this red dirt, this red-orange sandy soil never changes, and either it's in me or I'm in it, but I can always come back to my emotions through it.

MOYERS: Most poets I know are fugitives, in a sense. Very few of them are where they used to be, and what they write about is where they are no longer. Why is that?

AUTRY: I don't know, but I remember when I saw the movie *E.T.* I thought, "He's *also* always looking for *his* people," and I related very much to that. It's as if somehow I left looking for my people, and I come back looking for my people, but in some way that I don't fully understand I may find my people through my poetry.

James A. Autry, Bill Moyers

When you work at a poem long enough—if you just do that one poem and don't worry about anything else—then the imagery of one verse line exudes a sparkling fountain of energy that fills your spirit.

——— Jimmy Santiago Baca ———

Jimmy Santiago Baca credits poetry with saving his life. An abandoned child, his life on the streets led to a maximum-security prison in Arizona, where he taught himself to read and write. His first poems were written there. His poems have been praised for their witness to spiritual rebirth, and *Martin and Meditations on the South Valley* received the American Book Award in 1988. Born in New Mexico of Chicano and Apache descent, he founded Black Mesa Enterprises in Albuquerque to offer young people alternatives to violence through a community centered around language.

MOYERS: What images have shaped your poetry?

BACA: Well, I used to watch these old cowboy movies when I was a kid—black-and-white movies—and I was fascinated by how they communicated with mirrors. You would see these Pancho Villa rebels flashing the little tins that they cooked on, and somehow the others who saw the flashes knew what was going on.

When I write poetry I see those flashes deep within the text even though, honest to God, I feel a futility in writing poetry because I don't believe I'll *ever* reach whoever those rebels are to ask them what they represent and what they're fighting. But I keep going up that mountain and I've fallen many times. To me it's no longer about achieving the poem, it's just about being in *pursuit* of the poem.

Then yesterday another image occurred to me—writing poetry is like going to see a relative who you don't know exists because you're pretty much an orphan as you come into the world. But we're *all* orphans. We know that our true parent is the earth or whatever God our religion may give us. So I keep crossing this desert that's filled with these minuscule shimmerings of light, and sometimes it seems that my own needs are my shortcomings because I also always see this mirage: "Ah, there's Aunt Louise." I run to her and she evaporates. Then I look at God and say, "Why do You put these expectations in me? Why can't I be the kind of person who can withstand the illusions and cross the desert like those fabulous prophets of old or these great heroes in films?"

When I ultimately reach my own rebirth, my own potential, it will not be an oasis or a mirage. It will be Aunt Louise waving in the dust storm, telling me I'm home, I'm home.

MOYERS: What would your life have been if you hadn't followed that urge to seek those mirages, to write poetry?

BACA: In fact, for me it was never really so much a process of following mirages as it was a question of not having a place to stand in, of having no door open, of taking on the mantle of the outcast. I was the kid in the village who was ostracized from a very early age. I've always been the enemy of secrets.

MOYERS: What do you mean?

BACA: Well, when I was a kid they didn't want me in the kitchen because I knew that my aunt was having an affair with Louie, who was not her husband. I would walk in and say, "But what about Louie?" "Out of here!"

My uncles were these massive, mythological giants, and the way they got things done was if you didn't have the bolt on the oil case unscrewed, they would kick you in the ribs and you would get it unscrewed right. But I was the kid who stood up and said, "Why are you kicking us? You can't do that. That's not right." And they would look at me and say, "Five thousand years of tradition and along comes this urchin who tells us we're not supposed to kick him?" I knew that if the green alfalfa had its freedom to grow all around us, then they had no right to kick me. So I always felt very much like the grasshopper in front of the threshing machine.

MOYERS: When did you first feel the urge to write?

BACA: It started when I was in the county jail. I had escaped several times, and there was an all points bulletin for me. I always wanted to be famous, but I didn't want my face on the post office, you know. I was seventeen and I called up this friend of mine who said, "You better turn yourself in because they'll shoot on sight."

So I turned myself in at the county jail and awaited extradition so long that I became a kind of trustee. One day I was trying to make points with the booking clerk when two detectives brought in an Indian and started to strip him, but he wouldn't let them take off his talisman. He allowed them to take everything off his body, but when they reached for the talisman around his neck, he screamed. Because I come from a Chicano background mixed with Native American—my grandfather is Apache and my grandmother Yaqui—I knew what that meant. You're not supposed to take that off because that makes—

MOYERS: The talisman is the . . . ?

BACA: The sacred bag around your neck that protects your soul. But they scoffed at him and ripped it off his neck. The woman I was flirting with had been telling me how expensive her college textbooks were, and she was laughing with them when she turned around to go to the filing desk to pull his record, so I reached my hand through the bars and took the top one and put it in my overalls and went to my cell. I figure I got her for seventy-five dollars, right? This was my only way of getting her back, and I regretted ever flirting with her.

When I got to my cell that night I had a pen flashlight and I began to read about somebody walking around water, and it enthralled me because when I was with my grandfather, who was a sheepherder and a boxer on the weekends, we always walked wherever we went. The fondest memories I have in life are those with my grandparents, so I desperately wanted to write about my grandfather walking along the *aceqias,* the ditches.

I read most of that night, then the following morning when I was handing out coffee to the inmates, one man threw the coffee at me when I filled his cup up. He scalded my body and my face, and for an insult like that you have to fight—you have to go for his jugular. When the guard opened the gate and left with the coffee and the other trustees, this guy was telling me, "Come on, come on." I wasn't afraid of him, but for the first time in my life fear entered into me in a very bone-searing way—the fear that I might not be able to finish reading this book about a man who reminded me of my grandfather who had been a sheepherder. I was afraid that I might not be able to write about my grandfather if I fought. When this guy looked at me and said, "You're a coward," I went through some horrible moments—

MOYERS: You wanted to go at him?

BACA: Yes, I wanted to go at him.

MOYERS: But if you went at him . . .

BACA: I might die, but I had never cared about that before then. It was like feeling this whale in me beginning to surface after being down for a long time. I went to the cubicles given to attorneys and their clients and locked the door and began to scream at myself that I was *not* a coward, that I *could* go fight this guy, and then all I could see was the book's page in front of me and I began to slam into the walls as hard as I could with my fists, thinking that by imposing enough pain I could take away this ludicrous idea of this stupid book, because books got you nowhere.

I mean, sissies read books. You couldn't do *anything* with a book. You couldn't fix a '57 Chevy with a book. You couldn't take money from some hustler with a book. You couldn't convince or persuade anybody with a book. Books were in the way. And not only that, they were the great enemies. Books were where you found the pain. Books were where you found the shame, and books were where you found the lies that my grandparents had been lazy Mexicans and that I was no good, that I couldn't be as good as the next person. *That's* what was in books. So why should I go open a book and give myself all this pain? I didn't *need* that. I would rather go numb with a good bottle of tequila.

MOYERS: And yet the power of the word . . .

BACA: Oh, it caught me up in the fiercest typhoon I have ever been in and from which I have never escaped. I have continually swirled like a leaf.

MOYERS: Read "It Started."

IT STARTED

TO RICHARD AND REX

A little state-funded barrack
in the desert, in a prison. A poetry workshop,
an epicenter of originality, companionship,
pain and openness,
                              For some,
the first time in their life writing,
for others the first time saying openly what they felt,
the first time finding something in themselves,
worthwhile, ugly and beautiful.

        I think of you and me. Last night I was
thinking of you. I am your friend. I don't want you
to think otherwise.

                I was thinking, when we first wrote to each other.
                I remember instances, of tremendous joy
                when receiving your letters,
                what cells I was in,
                what emotional state, under
                what circumstances.
                Your letters always fell like meteorites
                into my lap.
                You were my first friendship
                engendered in this state, perhaps,
                all my past life.

I showed you my first poem ever written,
        "They Only Came to See the Zoo"

                But you didn't treat me like a wild ape,
                or an elephant. You treated me like Jimmy.
                And who was Jimmy?

A mass of molten fury in this furnace of steel,
and yet, my thoughts became ladles, sifting carefully
through my life, the pain and endurance,
to the essence of my being.
        I gently, into the long night, unmolding
        my shielded heart, the fierce figures
        of war and loss, I remolding them,
        my despair and anger into a cry and song,
I took the path alone, nuded myself to my own caged animals,
and learned their tongues and their spirits,
and roamed the desert, went to my place of birth. . . .
        Now tonight, I am a burning bush,
        my bones a grill of fire,
        I burn these words in praise,
        of our meeting, our friendship.

BACA: This is a poem about the writing workshop I had wanted to attend but couldn't, so I wrote them a poem from my cell.

MOYERS: "But you didn't treat me like a wild ape, / or an elephant. You treated me like Jimmy. / And who was Jimmy?"

BACA: Jimmy was this very, very bad potato they had wrapped in paper that they make orphans eat with fish. Everybody spits out the potato. You know how we have that central cornerstone in jurisprudence of presumed innocence? I had always believed this when I was born, and then one day everything that was told to me about how bad I was came home to roost. I believed that even God hated me, and there was no way to express the rage and there was no way to perform the ritual of forgiveness because I had no language.

MOYERS: Read the poem about the day you're being taken to prison.

BACA: Okay. This poem is called "Cloudy Day."

CLOUDY DAY

It is windy today. A wall of wind crashes against,
windows clunk against, iron frames
as wind swings past broken glass
and seethes, like a frightened cat
in empty spaces of the cellblock.

In the exercise yard
we sat huddled in our prison jackets,
on our haunches against the fence,
and the wind carried our words
over the fence,
while the vigilant guard on the tower
held his cap at the sudden gust.

I could see the main tower from where I sat,
and the wind in my face
gave me the feeling I could grasp
the tower like a cornstalk,
and snap it from its roots of rock.

The wind plays it like a flute,
this hollow shoot of rock.
The brim girded with barbwire
with a guard sitting there also,
listening intently to the sounds
as clouds cover the sun.

I thought of the day I was coming to prison,
in the back seat of a police car,
hands and ankles chained, the policeman pointed,
    "See that big water tank? The big
      silver one out there, sticking up?
      That's the prison."

And here I am, I cannot believe it.
Sometimes it is such a dream, a dream,
where I stand up in the face of the wind,
like now, it blows at my jacket,
and my eyelids flick a little bit,
while I stare disbelieving. . . .

The third day of spring,
and four years later, I can tell you,
how a man can endure, how a man
can become so cruel, how he can die
or become so cold. I can tell you this,

I have seen it every day, every day,
and still I am strong enough to love you,
love myself and feel good;
even as the earth shakes and trembles,
and I have not a thing to my name,
I feel as if I have everything, everything.

MOYERS: Isn't that the story in all of these poems? You keep looking for how a man can be so cold and yet endure.

BACA: Yes! It *is* that story. It's the story of a human being stripped to the very core and witnessing the degrees to which we can vary in either direction to absolute cruelty or absolute ecstasy. And I witness that.

MOYERS: What about "I Applied for the Board"? Did you literally try to read them your poems?

BACA: I *did*. It was my only way of telling them *this* is who I'd become—*this* is who I am, and *this* is the record. But they said, "Our record indicates you haven't worked," to which I said, "*My* record is different—*this* is my record."

MOYERS: The poetry?

BACA: Yes, and they said, "We don't want to hear *your* record."

I APPLIED FOR THE BOARD

. . . a flight of fancy and breath of fresh air
Is worth all the declines in the world.
It was funny though when I strode into the Board
And presented myself before the Council
With my shaggy-haired satchel, awiry
With ends of shoestrings and guitar strings
Holding it together, brimming with poems.

I was ready for my first grand, eloquent,
Booming reading of a few of my poems—
When the soft, surprised eyes
Of the chairman looked at me and said no.

And his two colleagues sitting on each side of him,
Peered at me through bluemetal eyes like rifle scopes,
And I like a deer in the forest heard the fresh,

Crisp twig break under my cautious feet,
As they surrounded me with quiet questions,
Closing in with grim sour looks, until I heard
The final shot burst from their mouths
That I had not made it, and felt the warm blood
Gush forth in my breast, partly from the wound,
And partly from the joy that it was over.

MOYERS: That's a daunting problem for the poet—getting people to hear your poems.

BACA: They usually surface as history sooner or later. The historians find them.

MOYERS: Yes, but what good does it do *you*? You're gone.

BACA: You can't worry about that. You can't worry about when you're going to get paid for it either. If you worry about whether people are going to hear it, and if you worry about whether you're going to get paid, you are in the wrong biz.

MOYERS: How *do* you survive?

BACA: You really have to survive by an act of grace, as in that great title of Robert Bly's book *The Light Around the Body*. In the greatest way, you really have to have faith in the unknown, otherwise you won't write.

MOYERS: You write about a lot more than prison, but let me ask you this. You have seen so much violence in prison, the violence men do to each other. What causes that violence?

BACA: I think in my own case, it's the inability to forgive my own rage that I've internalized against myself, and from that comes the inability to forgive others. Forgiveness is a thing most prisoners have never been taught. Forgiveness necessitates shame—you go through the shame, you go through the fact that all of your friends thought you were a fool. They manipulated you and you were nothing.

You fight at a party—they brought you along to entertain them. Let the goons get drunk on Jim Beam. Let *them* fight. You have to realize all of that. Even that the women you loved so much out of your deepest heart didn't love you—you were just *there*.

You have to take *all* of that. You have to live through the teeth of this monstrous rat, as it gnaws you to bits. You have to live through the pain, and then live through the shame, the absolute hurt. It's almost like being without a mother. No one can imagine what it is not to have a mother—you can't imagine that because in fact you come from the womb—but you have to be born in that act of forgiveness for yourself. You have to forgive yourself for being such a terrible fool.

Being a human being without forgiveness is like being the guitarist without fingers or being the diva without a tongue. You have to forgive if you're going to be a human being. Violence is an act of wanting to be a human being and believing you *are* a human being and acting on that instinct violently.

MOYERS: Violence becomes an act of affirmation?

BACA: Absolutely. Absolutely. You don't understand what it means to have total unerring, unequivocal, and illuminable despair. You will do *anything* to get out of that. *Anything*. The sapling of violence first sprouts out of ultimate despair.

MOYERS: How did you learn to forgive yourself as well as all those people flashing mirrors at you?

BACA: I came out of my cell one day, and I said, "I'm not working anymore." Now, I was a gang leader—I had about twenty guys who were ready to kill anybody that I pointed to—but when I said, "I'm not going to go to work today," they said, "What are you talking about?" I said, "I'm not working anymore. I'm going to close down. I'm going to learn how to write. I want to know why ninety-five percent of the men in this prison are Chicanos, and why ninety-five percent can't read or write, and why ninety-five percent are killing each other for smokes and for coffee. I want to know the answer to that. I can't live without the answer." And they said to me, "You're a coward. You're nothing."

That same day they threw scalding water on me. They threw urine at me. They threw feces at me. And I was in ecstasy. I was joyous. Because it was the first time I had ever found my own thought, and the first time I had ever followed my own feeling. Here I was eighteen years old, having my first original thought. People were throwing stuff at me and booing me in the cell blocks. I didn't know how anything was going to turn out; I just knew that I was happy.

MOYERS: Read "Work We Hate and Dreams We Love."

BACA: Okay. This is a very short one.

WORK WE HATE AND DREAMS WE LOVE

Every morning
Meiyo revs his truck up
and lets it idle. Inside the small adobe house,

he sips coffee
while his Isleta girlfriend
Cristi
brownbags his lunch.
Life is filled with work
Meiyo hates,
and while he saws, 2 x 4's,
trims lengths of 2 x 10's on table saw,
inside his veins another world
in full color etches
a blue sky on his bones,
a man following a bison herd,
and suddenly his hammer becomes a spear
he tosses to the ground
uttering a sound we do not understand.

MOYERS: What's happening there?

BACA: Oh, that's that primal howl of the coyote in our bones. I have so many friends who work with their hands, and all of them fade as they're working. Their friendship with each other is likened back to these other men long ago who used to speak to trees and commune with the water and say prayers to the sun at dawn.

MOYERS: What does your poetry do for you?

BACA: It's kept me from becoming America's most wanted bandit! If I didn't write poetry I'd be out robbing banks or something exciting, you know? *Anything* but the nine to five.

MOYERS: Poetry can be as exciting as—

BACA: When you work at a poem long enough—if you just do that *one* poem and don't worry about anything else—then the imagery of one verse line exudes a sparkling fountain of energy that fills your spirit. So in the most difficult of circumstances, after working on the poem I walk out and I feel that, whatever wall there is in front of me, I will go right through it like the saxifrage flower that splits the rocks.

COLEMAN BARKS

Coleman Barks changed his life's direction in 1976 when Robert Bly showed him some scholarly translations of the ecstatic poems of the thirteenth-century Sufi mystic Jelaluddin Rumi. Bly told him, "These poems need to be released from their cages." Captivated by the humor, wisdom, and spiritual depth of a man as famous in the Islamic world as Shakespeare is in the West, Barks took up the challenge. In collaboration with Persian linguist John Moyne, he has become the primary conduit bringing Rumi's mystical consciousness into English, translating and publishing thirteen collections of Rumi's poems. A poet in his own right, he teaches at the University of Georgia in Athens.

MOYERS: Tell me about Rumi.

BARKS: Jelaluddin Rumi was a thirteenth-century mystical teacher who lived from 1207 to 1273. He was a teacher first and a poet only in relation to that activity. His poems—which sprang *spontaneously* from the work he was doing with the dervish learning community in Konya, Turkey—were *spoken* in Persian. Dervish means doorway, an open space through which something can happen, so a dervish is a surrendered person. You lose your personal identity and something can be done through you.

Rumi was an Islamic mystic, but of that particular kind called Sufi, which means an openhearted person. It doesn't have to do with doctrine. It has to do with the opening of the heart and exploring the mystery of what they call "union."

MOYERS: Scholar turned mystic. What moved him in this direction?

BARKS: Meeting *his* teacher, Shams of Tabriz, who wandered throughout the Near East trying to find someone on his own level of spiritual attainment. The story goes that Shams once prayed, "Can you give me some companion?" and a voice said, "Jelaluddin Rumi who lives in Konya is your companion." So Shams went to Konya, and there are many stories about their meeting.

In one of them Rumi was riding on a donkey and, grabbing the reins, Shams asked, "Who is greater, Muhammed or Bestami?" Rumi answered, "Muhammed." To which Shams responded, "But Bestami said, 'How great is my glory!' and Muhammed said, 'I cannot praise You as You should be praised.' " (Bestami was one of those drunken ecstat-

*Poetry is close
to madness.*

ics who shout and expand with any taste of the mystery while Muhammed was more quiet and expectant.)

Rumi realized the depth from which the question had come and fell off the donkey into a trance. When he was revived, he had an answer. Rumi said, "Bestami took one gulp and thought that was it—'How great is my glory!'—whereas Muhammed realized that you have to take small sips, that knowledge of the divine keeps unfolding." Then Rumi and Shams went into this friendship that has become one of the great icons of mysticism—it's called *sohbet,* which means "mystical conversation." They disappeared into a place of conversation, this sort of silent interview place, until the students of Rumi got jealous and drove Shams away.

Rumi sent for Shams and brought him back, but his students drove Shams away again, and eventually Shams seems to have been murdered by Rumi's jealous disciples. Rumi's poetry sprang out of that loneliness for this companion of his spirit.

MOYERS: He certainly was prolific. His poems literally number in the—

BARKS: Thousands. There are some odes that have numbers like No. 3748 on them. There are so many, and I've just done four hundred or so. A team of translators could spend their lives working on this.

MOYERS: Thousands of poems? What does that say about our idea of carefully constructing meaning from images and words? Here's a man pouring out thousands of poems.

BARKS: Well, look what Shakespeare did. Some people just have this abundance of creativity flowing through them and who knows how that happens? It came through Rumi, but he didn't think poetry was all that important. He said, "It's like tripe, but my friends want it." For him poetry was a way of being with his friends, it had something to do with community.

MOYERS: He said it was like "fixing tripe"?

BARKS: That's right. He thought that writing poetry was like cooking tripe, and he didn't like tripe but he said, "I'll put my hands down into it and fix it because my friends like it." So it was something he did almost against his better judgment, but he knew that writing or dictating whatever was coming was helpful to his friends and to the people in this community. He actually spoke these poems and his scribe took them down, and evidently then he would see a transcription and revise it a little, but mostly these are first drafts. He never looked back, he just kept going. I estimate that he must have spoken twelve or fourteen poems a day for the last twelve years of his life.

MOYERS: And they issued from a state of ecstasy he experienced?

BARKS: Yes, but I think the state was continuous. He could easily go from singing pure praise to settling some dispute among his people about chickens or land. So he went right from law and moral disputes to ecstatic poetry.

MOYERS: And the audience he was addressing?

BARKS: I think they were primarily addressed to the people in the community that he was a part of, and often they were to specific people so you get different pieces of advice that seem contradictory. To one person he says, "Be deliberate, be careful," to another he says, "Break open and do not think what you're saying. Just speak and sing everything." He is one of these great teachers who can see what each soul needs at any particular moment. The poems are precise as well as general. In another place, he says, "These poems are for the spiritual descendants who will come after."

MOYERS: Your books of translations—*We Are Three, Open Secret, Unseen Rain, Delicious Laughter,* just a few of the titles—suggest the enormous range of Rumi, and yet few of us had heard of him.

BARKS: Yes. I had one of the best literary educations you can get at the University of California at Berkeley and the University of North Carolina at Chapel Hill, and I had never heard of Rumi until 1976 when Robert Bly handed me a book and said, "These poems need to be released from their cages."

MOYERS: And you've been translating them ever since?

BARKS: For seventeen years now I've been working, pretty much every morning, trying to make what I am given—which is literal, scholarly transcriptions of poems—into what I hope are valid poems in American English.

MOYERS: Because so few people have ever heard of him, can he ever be appreciated on the American scene?

BARKS: I don't know. I don't have the big picture on this. I just get up every morning and work on it. I feel like an ant, you know, and I don't know what the anthill is doing.

MOYERS: Today here at the festival I heard you say that trying to imagine the Islamic world without Rumi is like trying to imagine the Western world without Shakespeare.

BARKS: Yes, he seems to function that way in their world. He is the model of imaginative freedom and power, much as Shakespeare is for us.

MOYERS: How does a Westerner, scientifically inclined and surrounded by technology, approach poetry like this?

BARKS: I think we all have a core that's ecstatic, that knows and that looks up in wonder. We all know that there are marvelous moments of eternity that just happen. We *know* them. We can't say they don't happen, can we? I can't.

MOYERS: You use the word "ecstatic." What *is* ecstasy?

BARKS: When I was a child in Chattanooga, seven or eight years old, I remember sometimes in April when that spring gold light would come at the end of the day and just be there for about ten minutes. You know what I'm talking about in the South?

MOYERS: Yes.

BARKS: That gold time, well, I could hardly stand it as a child. I would lie down and hug myself, and my mother and my father would be playing bridge with the Penningtons. Lying on the floor hugging myself, I'd look at her and I'd say, "Mama, I've got that full feeling again," and she'd say, "I know you do, honey." So I grew up in an ecstatic world in which it was okay to lie on the floor and hug yourself or maybe just sit out on the bluff and watch the river.

But this little story may help too. One day Rumi heard the hammers of the gold beaters in one of the streets of Konya, and this seemingly normal university professor started doing a turn, a whirling meditation, a slow reminder of the ecstasy of the galaxies. He heard music and started doing this turn and they say he did it for thirty-six hours, and then he fell down, but he said, "I didn't fall down. I just reached that part of myself that's invisible."

MOYERS: There's a physicality to that story that evokes the material world.

BARKS: Well, not all of his poems are reminders of an ecstatic state. Some of them are more practical. In one poem Rumi quotes Muhammed, "Deliberation is one of the qualities of God," and yet that same poem concludes with the ecstatic words "These leaves, our bodily personalities, seem identical, / but the globe of soul fruit / we make, / each is elaborately / unique." That we're not trying to make identical Buddhas in a row is an ecstatic idea, you know. Each one of us is so fantastically beautiful and unique in the making of our own soul fruit.

> A friend remarks to the Prophet, "Why is it
> I get screwed in business deals?
> It's like a spell. I become distracted
> by business talk and make wrong decisions."

Muhammed replies, "Stipulate with every transaction
that you need three days to make sure."

Deliberation is one of the qualities of God.
Throw a dog a bit of something.
He sniffs to see if he wants it.

Be that careful.
Sniff with your wisdom-nose.
Get clear. Then decide.

The universe came into being gradually
over six days. God could have just commanded,
Be!

Little by little a person reaches forty and fifty and sixty,
and feels more complete. God could have thrown
      full-blown prophets
flying through the cosmos in an instant.

Jesus said one word, and a dead man sat up,
but Creation usually unfolds,
like calm breakers.

Constant, slow movement teaches us to keep working
like a small creek that stays clear,
that doesn't stagnate, but finds a way
through numerous details, deliberately.

Deliberation is born of joy,
like a bird from an egg.

                     Birds don't resemble eggs!
Think how different the hatching out is.

A white-leathery snake egg, a sparrow's egg;
a quince seed, an apple seed: Very different things
look similar at one stage.

These leaves, our bodily personalities, seem identical,
but the globe of soul-fruit
we make,
each is elaborately
unique.

                             (*MATHNAWI*, III, 3494–3516)

M O Y E R S : So there's the Rumi of ecstasy, the Rumi of practicality and delib-
eration, and the Rumi of laughter. He had a great sense of humor.

B A R K S : He has a theology of laughter actually. He says that it may be that
God is the impulse to laugh and that we *are* the different kinds of laughter. Everybody
laughs differently, and maybe God, the invisible, has an impulse to laugh that takes the
form of different laughters.

I think for Rumi joy is primary. To some people, the world seems filled with grief,
but Rumi would say, "I think that the world is primarily graceful, a gift. Sure, we die,
but what have we ever lost by dying?" We keep dying to old selves and emerging into
new places through our griefs, so there is an uproarious, hilarious undercurrent in every-
thing he says.

M O Y E R S : Even when Rumi talks about searching for the joy at the center of
grief he doesn't deny the grief. The idea of "joy at the center of grief" seems incongruous
to our ears today, in this century marked by the Holocaust, war, and genocide. His time
was not without its horrors.

B A R K S : Yes. Millions of people were killed by Genghis Khan and the Cru-
sades in his lifetime, it was happening all around him, but he felt that God's mercy is
underneath God's wrath and in charge of it. It was just something he lived and knew.

M O Y E R S : When you were reading last night I couldn't be sure whether the
character who shows up again and again in the comical anecdotes was his creation or
yours.

B A R K S : Oh, Nasruddin? He's a Middle Eastern trickster figure about whom
there are still jokes being made up. He's very elusive and tricky, and he teaches in many
different ways. But, yes, there is that Nasruddin-ish character to some of Rumi's work
which also teaches through jokes and tricky little turns of phrase.

Here's an example of a Nasruddin story. Nasruddin is on a train and the conductor
comes to pick up the tickets, but Nasruddin can't find his ticket. He looks in his pants
pocket, he looks in his briefcase, he looks in his suitcase, he starts looking in other
peoples' suitcases, but he can't find his ticket. Finally the conductor says, "Nasruddin, I
know you've got your ticket. Most people keep theirs in their top left-hand coat pocket.
Why don't you look there?" And Nasruddin says, "Don't even mention that. If it's not
there, I have no hope."

M O Y E R S : Is that a Rumi story?

B A R K S : No, but it could easily be because for Rumi if it's not here in your
heart you're in big trouble.

MOYERS: One of the Rumi collections you have translated is called *This Longing*. What is the longing?

BARKS: I don't know whether you can say it. It's like asking what is love? What is the ache within an ache? What do we really want when we love a river or a grandchild? What is the something that doesn't ever get solved in being human? I feel that with my sons, you know, that I can never say how much I love them. There's some longing that just never gets satisfied or expressed and there's always this dissatisfaction with however we try.

MOYERS: I like the poem about longing which ends, "don't move the way fear makes you move." How *does* fear make us move?

Keep walking, though there's no place to get to.
Don't try to see through the distances.
That's not for human beings. Move within,
but don't move the way fear makes you move.

BARKS: Nervously, protectively, defensively. "Don't try to see through the distances"—that's hard, isn't it? The Sufis say, "Live in this moment."

MOYERS: And Jesus said, "Take no thought of the morrow."

BARKS: Yes, there's no difference, but I don't talk well about these things except through the poems. The minute that I start trying to talk about them, it's as if my mouth gets full of dust, as if the words were meaningless.

MOYERS: What's happened to you as you've worked with these poems? I mean, you clearly have embraced them and incorporated them into your own life.

BARKS: Yes, my life is unthinkable without this work. It has brought friends into my life that I wouldn't have had and it has given me a way of speaking to people that I wouldn't have had. It brought me this teacher and it has given me all this actual literary work to do, but that's not what you're asking, is it?

MOYERS: Do you know what I'm asking?

BARKS: You're asking, "What does it mean to have your heart opened? You have this sort of nice boy getting a Masters and a Doctorate and going on to teach in college and then this thing comes down and grabs him and sets him to working on it. So how does he feel about what happened to him?"

Well, it feels good, like an egg cracking open and then something else comes out of it. When this happened I had finished all my literary training and I had gotten a respectable job, and then in the mid 1970s I got divorced and found myself in a place where I felt very vulnerable and very lost.

MOYERS: You must have been vulnerable to longing.

BARKS: Yes, and to love stories. You remember when you loved love stories? I mean, they were so gorgeous, you'd go to the movies, for example, and that would start a search that took the form of a woman or a man or a friend or a teacher.

1246

The minute I heard my first love story
I started looking for you, not knowing
how blind that was.

Lovers don't finally meet somewhere.
They're in each other all along.

BARKS: The love story was just the way of showing you this longing. "What you long for," Rumi says, "is *in* the longing." Whereas we say, "How do I love thee? Let me count the ways. One, two, three, four, five." But for Rumi the longing is not for a human form.

MOYERS: That's difficult to get. He says the longing you express is what you're longing *for*?

BARKS: Yes, the longing is for itself. But you know I can understand these poems better when I read them to people who have also some experience of this so . . . that's the way I start to understand them.

MOYERS: It's like so much of poetry at this festival, there's a call and response. We may not know why the call or why the response, but there seems to be a kind of dance going on.

BARKS: That's exactly it. Rumi's poem which begins, "Do you think I know what I'm doing?" describes exactly the way I feel.

1359

Do you think I know what I'm doing?
That for one breath or half-breath I belong to myself?

As much as a pen knows what it's writing,
or the ball can guess where it's going next.

MOYERS: Do you find it hard to talk about mysticism?

BARKS: Yes, and I don't know whether I'm supposed to talk about it, really, particularly on television in an interview situation.

MOYERS: There's a danger of trivializing it?

BARKS: Well, I don't know how much to say.

MOYERS: But don't you think people understand spiritual reality when they encounter it?

BARKS: Yes, I guess I do believe that, and I do sometimes talk about experiences I have had that make the invisible world undeniable, but I don't try to teach Rumi's poetry.

MOYERS: What kind of experiences do you talk about with your students?

BARKS: You see, I don't know whether I'm supposed to talk about this on television either, but I'll tell you one experience that I've had in my life that is amazing to me. I don't know how to explain it other than to believe there's some kind of invisible reality that's joking around with me.

When I was six years old I was a kind of geography freak. I memorized all the capitals of all the countries in the 1943 Rand McNally World Atlas. I knew them all, I even wrote them all out and gave them to my father for a Christmas present. Why? They were already *in* the atlas! My father was the headmaster of a boys school, and we would eat all our meals over there in the dining hall with about four hundred people. Everybody there knew I was this weird child who could name the capital of every country, so they would yell countries at me across the quadrangle. You know, someone would yell "Uruguay!" and this little kid would yell back, "Montevideo!" or someone else would yell "Bulgaria!" and the little kid would yell, "Sofia!" or another person would yell "Bhutan!"

MOYERS: The capital of Bhutan—

BARKS: "Thimphu!" Anyway, one day this Latin teacher went to his classroom and got a country that didn't seem to have a capital and he thought, "This is what this child needs." So he said that when he yelled the name of the country out across the quadrangle and I tried to find the capital of it in my mental computer and couldn't, the look on my face *named* me. The word he yelled was "Cappadocia!"

From then on I was called Cappadocia, or Capp, until at age seventeen I left that round little hilltop. So you can understand why I almost fell down a few years ago when I realized that the capital of Cappadocia was Iconium or Konya, the city where Rumi lived and is buried. At the time I didn't have the least idea what that name was going to become for me. Do you understand what I'm saying? Is that just synchronicity or is there an intelligence working in here that's playful?

MOYERS: Questions like that took you to Konya where Rumi taught and where he's buried.

BARKS: I went there in 1984 and lovely things happened. I was there by myself during Ramadan, and I decided I would just follow the Islamic practice and fast between sunrise and sundown every day. I wandered in and out of Rumi's tomb and other sacred places during the day, then at night I would go to a restaurant and break the fast, and I always ordered bottled water with dinner, but somehow I always got a crowd when I ordered it. The people from the kitchen would come out to hear me order it, and then they'd want to hear me order it again and again. It turned out that what I was ordering with my meal was "the secret of the universe." I was saying *siri,* and I should have been saying *su* for bottled water.

MOYERS: Asking for water you were, in their ears, asking for "the secret of the universe"?

BARKS: Right, so there's this thing that's playing tricks on me and maybe the secret of the universe *is* bottled water for me!

MOYERS: Or maybe your longing is for the secret of the universe, and it seems that you *are* supposed to talk about these things.

BARKS: Well, I just haven't seen anything like this on television so I'm going to wait till I see it to decide, unless this is edited out, you know.

MOYERS: No, we won't edit this out. Why would we edit mysticism out? It's so rare, why would we lose it?

BARKS: Well, *this* is not it. I mean, this is talking about it, this is talking about experience, and poetry is not experience either, it's talking *about* experience. Everything is a kind of a longing.

MOYERS: That makes me think of "Strange Business."

STRANGE BUSINESS

3061

If you don't have a woman that lives with you,
why aren't you looking?
If you have one, why aren't you satisfied?
You have no resistance to your friend.
Why don't you become the Friend?
If the flute is too quiet to say,
teach it manners.
Someone's holding you back, break off.

You sit here for days saying, *This is strange business.*
You're the strange business.
You have the energy of the sun in you,
but you keep knotting it up at the base of your spine.
You're some weird kind of gold that wants to stay melted
in the furnace, so you won't have to be coins.
Say ONE in your lonesome house.
Loving two is hiding inside your self.

You've gotten drunk on so many kinds of wine.
Taste this. It won't make you wild.
It's fire. Give up,
if you don't understand by this time
that your living is firewood.

This wave of talking builds. Better
we should not speak it, but let it grow within.

BARKS: He's talking to people who want to stay in the ecstatic state and never get out, people who never want to go down on the street where you can take some form that is usefully exchanged, like money. He's saying, let your ecstatic energy of the furnace go into the melting and forming so you can become something useful. He's telling you to give yourself to some useful work.

There's a relationship between the two states, they're the same substance, but some people, like me, prefer to cultivate and stay in the ecstatic state. Such people want to stay in the place where the poem is just about to happen and the music doesn't quite know what it's going to do next, that place of permanent fluidity. I love that. That's my home, but I get nervous when I have to make a coin out of it.

MOYERS: And spend it?

BARKS: Yes. Spending it makes me a little uneasy but I get more troubled about the whole process of taking it, reducing it down, and putting a stamp on it. Even about saying I'm ready to publish this or I'm ready to say this. I'm more at home in that gold place where my mother is looking at me.

MOYERS: Perhaps this is what Jesus meant when he chided the miser for hoarding his treasure instead of spending it. Anyway, maybe you're *supposed* to talk about these things. What you've just been saying calls up poem number 549. By the way, I haven't seen poems numbered like this before. Don't they have titles?

549

We take long trips.
We puzzle over the meaning of a painting or a book,
when what we're wanting to see and understand
in this world, we *are* that.

BARKS: No, Persian poems don't have titles, they're just stacked together and numbered. Books of poems often have generic titles, but single poems don't have titles the way ours do. I've always thought about the truth of that poem in relation to teaching, you know? I believe it doesn't really matter what the teacher talks about. You remember all those classes you took in college? It doesn't matter what was said. What we remember are a few presences. What was being taught was the *presence* of a few people, and there was a connection between that presence and us. But we sat there and took notes and thought we were studying the French Revolution or duck embryos or something, when what we were really learning about was coming *through* the teacher.

MOYERS: Yes. I don't remember much of what Robert Cotter taught me about history at the University of Texas, but I remember Robert Cotter.

BARKS: Absolutely. Well, we puzzle over the meaning of a painting, we try to say what it means, when really we *are* what we're wanting to understand. It's like poem number 556. This is a really ecstatic poem. It's hard just to sit here and talk about this one. It just seems true.

556

Daylight, full of small dancing particles
and the one great turning, our souls
are dancing with you, without feet, they dance.
Can you see them when I whisper in your ear?

MOYERS: Maybe that's the most apt commentary on a poem, "It just seems true."

BARKS: And yet some of them, like number 568, don't seem so basically right to me. Some of them I don't identify with at a particular moment. Some I do. But that's the longing, "trying wildly to open."

568

The human shape is a ghost
made of distraction and pain.
Sometimes pure light, sometimes cruel,
trying wildly to open,
this image tightly held within itself.

MOYERS: Open to?

BARKS: The next, the next song, whatever the next is. This closed-in struggle, the desperation, is one image of what a human being is. Another one is when he tells you you are song, and then he changes it and says, "a wished-for song." So you're the poem that's coming.

2196

You're song,
a wished-for song.

Go through the ear to the center,
where sky is, where wind, where
silent knowing.

Put seeds and cover them.
Blades will sprout
where you do your work.

MOYERS: Don't you wonder how this happens? How there gathers in one person the resources to create more than twenty thousand poems?

BARKS: Well, they say there's an unbelievable abundance available to everyone if we would just open to it. Nature is like a mirror for that, it's so abundant.

MOYERS: You know, one reason it's hard to talk about may be because in our time "ecstasy" has come to mean a kind of drug, but that's not what Rumi's talking about at all.

BARKS: No. We've ruined the word, probably. I wonder what would be another word for it. "Joy" is still a pretty good word isn't it? But it's a detergent!

MOYERS: It is. So we really need that little poem which begins just with pronouns and brings us back to the central experience of ecstasy.

BARKS: Yes. That's so radical, isn't it?

I, you, he, she, we.
In the garden of mystic lovers,
these are not true distinctions.

MOYERS: What do you make of that?

BARKS: There's a certain state of awareness where individuality is not the truth. There *is* truth in the idea that we are a community, you know. Maybe around Jesus' table it was that way: take this bread, take this wine, and then you are me. You are not necessarily Peter or James or Andrew or Bartholomew anymore, you are all of these and you are something else. I think most mystics will say that while we are multiple, the fact that we are multiple is not so true as the fact that we are one. But again, just *saying* that is not experiencing it.

This poem carries Rumi's longing for that reality to enter into this reality a little more.

837

We can't help being thirsty,
moving toward the voice
of water.
            Milk-drinkers draw close
to the mother. Muslims, Christians, Jews,
Buddhists, Hindus, shamans,
everyone hears the intelligent sound
and moves, with thirst, to meet it.

Clean your ears. Don't listen
for something you've heard before.

Invisible camel bells,
        slight footfalls in sand.

Almost in sight! The first word they call out
will be the last word of our last poem.

MOYERS: The secrets of mysticism weren't meant to be published.

BARKS: Not originally. The word "mysticism" comes from the word *mystes* which named the members of the mystery cults in ancient Greece. It has to do with keeping the mouth closed and with silence. The *mystes* were the ones who did not speak their secrets.

MOYERS: But something has been called forth by longing. The mystics can't keep it to themselves.

BARKS: Song and conversation. I think Rumi opened up the whole possibility that we can talk about this now. The way that he and Shams began to do *sohbet,* this conversation on mystical subjects, revealed a kind of friendship that now can be out in the open. In their relationship we have the model of ecstatic discussion.

MOYERS: There is a danger in overanalyzing ecstasy. Best just to sit back and experience it.

BARKS: Well, the mind doesn't do it. The mind cannot understand Rumi's poetry and neither can desire, but there's some other way of knowing. Some deeper part of our being knows we are not in grief, knows that we are in fact in eternity, and that part sings out of that knowing. I think that's the mystery that cannot be said.

My teacher once told me a story when I asked him, "What is it like to be in your state?" He said, "Well, there was once a frog from the ocean who came to visit a frog who lived in a little ditch, three feet by four feet by two feet. After the little ditch frog jumped down into the ditch, swam across, and went up the other side, he said to the ocean frog, 'How do you like that? Isn't that something? What is it like where you live?' And the ocean frog said, 'I couldn't tell you. You have to go there. I'll take you there some day.'"

My teacher said, "That's what it's like trying to describe mystical reality to somebody who lives in the confines of the mind and the confines of desire. It's like the difference between that ditch and the ocean." So my hope is that maybe through mystical poetry we catch the fragrance of a salt breeze coming.

ROBERT BLY

Robert Bly has devoted much of his creativity as poet, translator, and critic to helping people connect poetry to their emotional lives. From the 1960s when he was an organizer of Poets Against the Vietnam War to the 1980s when he helped to define the men's movement, he has emphasized poetry as a moral force in public affairs and a healing influence in individual lives. A winner of the National Book Award, he lives in Moose Lake, Minnesota, and travels widely to teach and conduct workshops.

MOYERS: You began translating the poetry of other cultures years ago, and have introduced us to poets from many lands. What do you think when you look around this festival and see all these poets from so many backgrounds?

BLY: I think it's lovely. This year they had a little session at noon when anyone could come in and read poems of Pablo Neruda. Neruda's the greatest poet we've had on the South and North American continents since Whitman; so that's quite appropriate. But I'm delighted also to see unheard poetry from many groups—Chinese American, Native American, Japanese American, Latino American, African American—coming in now and being accepted as part of the poetry of this culture.

MOYERS: When so many poets are writing from their own particular experience of gender, race, and ethnicity, does poetry lose the capacity to speak to common human experience?

BLY: It is possible that poetry gets fragmented. There may be two sides to the healthy urge to support hearing poetry from many perspectives: One side leads to this new poetry's being welcomed, which is appropriate, the other side leads to the old tradition's being hated, and that's more ominous. Pablo Neruda, for example, wrote very wild poetry, but his connection to tradition was very strong. As long as the voice is genuine, as long as it comes from a genuine part of the culture, that's sufficient for poetry. But poetry requires many, many years of struggling to understand what is the natural voice, not the rhetorical voice but the naturally quiet spoken voice.

Bill Stafford did a lot of that struggling. When I first began to realize what Bill Stafford was doing I felt how different we were because I was trained on Neruda and I had written a lot of political poetry—especially a lot of antiwar poetry during the Vietnam period—and, in a way, that's poetry that shouts over the heads of those around us to get

*It's important that the words in your poems
be those you could speak to your friends.*

to the people *over there*. But what Bill always has done, and many others as well, is to speak a colloquial language that goes straight *into the heart*. So I must say that's what I have been trying to do more of late, too.

MOYERS: Where are you in your own poetry right now?

BLY: Well, I mentioned Bill Stafford, who died just over a year ago—he wrote a poem every day—so, two years ago I got tired of all this stuff with interviews and lectures and I said, "I'm just going to stay home and stay in bed and write a poem every day the way Bill Stafford used to do."

His feeling was that you take the first thing that's happened to you during the day—whether it is someone jogging past the house or something you think of—and that's the thread you start with, then you try to follow that thread. He had this wonderful quatrain from Blake:

> I give you the end of a golden string,
>   Only wind it into a ball,
> It will lead you in at Heaven's gate
>   Built in Jerusalem's wall.

Stafford believed that a thread well-followed, gently, will lead you to the center of the universe. In that place where there is no difference between night and day and no difference between men and women, no difference between good and evil—in *that* place. He called it following the thread. I love that process very much. You can simply begin with a story.

MOYERS: What about a poem like "A Third Body"? How did that come about?

A THIRD BODY

A man and a woman sit near each other, and they do not long
at this moment to be older, or younger, nor born
in any other nation, or time, or place.
They are content to be where they are, talking or not-talking.
Their breaths together feed someone whom we do not know.
The man sees the way his fingers move;
he sees her hands close around a book she hands to him.
They obey a third body that they share in common.
They have made a promise to love that body.

Age may come, parting may come, death will come.
A man and a woman sit near each other;
as they breathe they feed someone we do not know,
someone we know of, whom we have never seen.

BLY: Ruth and I were on a plane; and I think we were going to a meditation conference in Kansas. Our destination was somehow part of the poem.

MOYERS: What is that body they have in common?

BLY: I don't know what it is. Some invisible body.

MOYERS: A communion?

BLY: Yes. It's something that happens when two people are close. It's as if a third body has come out of the invisible world and walks with them. In *The Waste Land* Eliot mentions how when Shackleton and his friend were walking to the South Pole they had the feeling that a third man was walking next to them. It's that mysterious kind of thing. I remember sending this poem to Galway Kinnell when I did it—because we send poems to each other—and I had originally had "Age may come, parting may come, death may come." He said, "What do you mean 'death *may* come'?" I said, "Okay. Okay." I changed it to "death will come."

MOYERS: What about "A Dream of Retarded Children"?

A Dream of Retarded Children

That afternoon I had been fishing alone,
Strong wind, some water slopping in the back of the boat.
I was far from home.
Later I woke several times hearing geese.
I dreamt I saw retarded children playing, and one came near,
And her teacher, face open, hair light.
For the first time I forgot my distance;
I took her in my arms and held her.

Waking up, I felt how alone I was.
I walked on the dock,
Fishing alone in the far north.

BLY: I felt lonesome one day in fall, and so I drove north, toward Canada, where I knew I would feel even more lonely. I stopped overnight at some small resort cabins in northern Minnesota, and that night I had a dream.

When I thought about the poem later, I realized how many slow parts of us we were mean to, especially in high school, when we all wanted to be groovy. Perhaps these slow parts, almost retarded parts, get exiled. One of the good things about growing older is that you have a chance to welcome those slow or retarded people back in. The dream brings them in; I was surprised that there were retarded children inside me and that one of them was coming near, but I was amazed that *all* of those exiled parts or beings had a *teacher!* A woman teacher! That was so wonderful somehow.

MOYERS: What does it take to get to the truth of experience as you do? What does it take to be a poet?

BLY: I don't know. Some students asked me yesterday how I began to write poetry. I didn't know what to say. I said, "Well, I fell in love with a woman who wrote poetry so I tried to write some to impress her." I added, "It didn't do any good." But when I wrote down that first poem, I was surprised to find something on the page that I hadn't intended to put there. It's as if we have one person who does well, and that person's okay, you know—he passes exams—but also we have a second person who is much smarter and wiser and more subtle. That one will slip an image in when you're composing. I was surprised to see *that* person—whom I didn't really know—present on the page and setting down something I hadn't really intended to say.

I think writing poetry is a matter of agreeing that you have these two people inside: every day you set aside time to be with the subtle person, who has funny little ideas, who is probably in touch with retarded children, and who can say surprising things. Bill's writing a poem every day is meant to open the poem to that person.

Moreover, when you're writing a poem every day, you can't always write out of your best side—if you're writing one a week, you can—but if you write every day, you don't know what's going to happen.

MOYERS: If you're writing a poem every day, as Bill Stafford said to do, how do you make sure they're all good?

BLY: A man once asked Bill, "Is it true you write a poem every day?" Bill answered, "Yes." Then the man asked, "Well, what if you're not so good that day?" And Bill said, "I just lower my standards." That's the most helpful thing said about poetry in forty years!

MOYERS: Why?

BLY: The aim in writing—though not in publishing—is to evade the superego who will say, "*That image was terrible. Stop right there!*" Bill believes one needs to have an attitude of *inclusion.* When writing a poem it's important to be a good host—you allow to come in whatever appears. Of course, you may then write a lot of bad poems. So what? A bad poem is just a group of words. You can let that go. You don't need to publish it. Bill also said, "If everyone had standards as low as those I have, no one would ever have writer's block." He's being a trickster there because his standards are very high in the end.

MOYERS: Do you remember the first poem that spoke to you, that touched you?

BLY: Yes, certainly. As a freshman at St. Olaf College, I sat down in the library and came across the sixth section of Whitman's *Song of Myself*, which begins, "A child said *What is the grass?* fetching it to me with full hands."

Whitman admits he doesn't know what the grass is any more than the child; he starts speculating a little. It could be "the handkerchief of the Lord . . . designedly dropped." It could be "the produced babe of the vegetation." Then all at once he says:

> This grass is very dark to be from the white heads of old mothers,
> Darker than the colorless beards of old men,
> Dark to come from under the faint red roofs of mouths.

That's superb! Whitman says that the grass is very dark to have come from "the white heads of old mothers." Oh, then he goes to "the faint red roofs of mouths." One of the greatest leaps I've ever seen! I read these lines the other day to my oldest daughter, who was carrying her baby about, and we were both amazed that he went then to tongues, "O I perceive after all so many uttering tongues . . ." Just wonderful!

Bill Stafford believed that poetry amounted to "a certain attention to language." Whitman actually *heard* what he had just said about the roofs of mouths, and so then he went to tongues. You asked what led me to poetry? I *did* fall in love with a woman who wrote poetry, but I think all poems are love poems basically.

MOYERS: While there is sweetness in what Bill Stafford says about writing poetry, there's a hint of sadness and sometimes anger, even rage and bitterness in his poems. Why is that?

BLY: Well, perhaps if you love nature, you won't get too angry—for example, Wordsworth wasn't angry very much—but that changes if you love justice, and Stafford loved justice. Remember what he said at the end of "Thinking for Berky," a sort of outcast girl?

> We live in an occupied country, misunderstood;
> justice will take us millions of intricate moves.
> Sirens will hunt down Berky, you survivors in your beds
> listening through the night, so far and good.

Anger comes about when the community and its leaders don't support the values or people that you love. So I understand why Bill Stafford's poems could also be angry, even bitter. I've recently done a long poem which is called "Anger Against Children," and it's *all* anger.

FROM ANGER AGAINST CHILDREN

. . . .

Parents take their children into the deepest Oregon forests,
And leave them there. When the children
Open the lunchbox, there are stones inside, and a note saying, "Do your
    own thing."
And what would the children do if they found their way home in the
    moonlight?
The planes have already landed on Maui, the parents are on vacation.
Our children live with a fear at school and in the house.
The mother and father do not protect the younger child from the savagery
    of the others.
Parents don't want to face the children's rage,
Because the parents are also in rage.

. . . .

This is the rage that shouts at children.
This is the rage that cannot be satisfied,
Because each year more ancient Chinese art objects go on display.
So the rage goes inward at last,
It ends in doubt, in self-doubt, dyeing the hair, and love of celebrities.
The rage comes to rest at last in the talk show late at night,
When the celebrities without anger or grief tell us that only the famous are
    good, only they live well.

I sent that poem to the *Atlantic Monthly* and they wrote: "We haven't had a poem here in several years that has caused so much discussion in the office as yours, but we are not going to print it. Young editors ask, 'Why is this man so angry?'" I thought, "Well, would the editors say to someone from Bosnia, 'Why are you so angry?'" This analogy is not exact, but our culture is coming to a place where we don't want to look at the amount of mistreatment we do toward children. It's odd, this change, because a hundred years ago immigrants came to this country because they felt we were on the side of the young! Our greatest poet, Whitman, was on the side of the young. How could it be that we've reversed ourselves so deeply that now four dollars go to old people for every dollar that goes to children? And I notice, too, often people flying to Phoenix don't want any children on the airplane. They want to water their lawns in peace. I feel a great sadness over that.

MOYERS: What is the relation between that feeling and the feeling in your poem "For My Son Noah, Ten Years Old"? What can you tell me about that poem?

FOR MY SON NOAH, TEN YEARS OLD

Night and day arrive, and day after day goes by,
and what is old remains old, and what is young remains young and grows
    old.
The lumber pile does not grow younger, nor the two-by-fours lose their
    darkness;
but the old tree goes on, the barn stands without help so many years;
the advocate of darkness and night is not lost.

The horse steps up, swings on one leg, turns his body;
the chicken flapping claws up onto the roost, its wings whelping and
    walloping,
But what is primitive is not to be shot out into the night and the dark,
and slowly the kind man comes closer, loses his rage, sits down at table.

So I am proud only of those days that pass in undivided tenderness,
when you sit drawing, or making books, stapled, with messages to the world,
or coloring a man with fire coming out of his hair.
Or we sit at a table, with small tea carefully poured.
So we pass our time together, calm and delighted.

BLY: The poem begins with a lot of energy—a horse steps up, he swings on one leg, turns his body, the chicken claws onto the roof, and so on—but as we know our *real* life is *not* in those massive expenditures of energy. The poem says, "What is primitive is not to be shot out into the night and the dark." What *is* primitive? It is rage, or "GET OVER HERE AND DO THIS!"

The older I get, the more clearly I see that the moments of real life don't lie there, but in quiet moments, when there is tenderness. When men hold to that, then "the kind man comes closer, loses his rage, sits down at table." Maybe because some of the retarded children have been welcomed back in, he "loses his rage, sits down at table."

MARILYN CHIN

Marilyn Chin is a fiercely lyrical writer whose life straddles two cultures. A first-generation Chinese American born in Hong Kong and raised in Portland, Oregon, she opens the classic tales and poems of both East and West to reveal the ironies and beauties of each.

She writes often about the conditions of exile, assimilation, and loss, and her poetry has been hailed for powerfully addressing the subjugation of Asian women raised in patriarchal societies. She teaches at San Diego State University.

MOYERS: You were born in Hong Kong and raised in Portland, Oregon. You claimed San Francisco as your home and consider yourself once exiled to San Diego. Where do you most belong?

CHIN: I believe I belong with my passport. I see myself and my identity as nonstatic. I see myself as a frontier, and I see my limits as limitless. Somebody once accused me of being a leftist radical feminist, West Coast, Pacific Rim, socialist, neo-Classical, Chinese American poet. And I say, "Oh yes, I am all of those things." Why not? I don't believe in static identities. I believe that identities are forever changing.

MOYERS: I will suggest you are at home in poetry. Every poem you've written seems very strongly *there*.

CHIN: Because poetry is my passion. It is my art. It is my love, it is my *first* love, my love beyond all loves, beyond romantic love. It's as necessary for me as breathing is necessary for me. I can't live without it. I tell my students that you know you are a poet when you can't live without it, when you'd rather die than live without it. I believe I have a mission, and that I have many stories to tell on many levels—on a personal level, on the familial level, on the historical-social level. I feel that my poetry has a strong social and political context.

And I feel that I'm a conduit for many voices. Historical voices, ancient voices, contemporary feminist voices. Women's voices mostly.

MOYERS: There is something quite tender in so many of your poems. It's in the prelude to your book *The Phoenix Gone, the Terrace Empty*. What is the country that is lost?

Although the country is lost
rivers and mountains remain.
And we shall always live
in this poetry that you love.

© Lynn Saville

PRELUDE

To love your country
is to know its beginnings
not with the bald-face moon
or the complacent river—
but here within you.

Your heart is a house—
I/we are its inhabitants.
Although the country is lost
rivers and mountains remain.
And we shall always live
in this poetry that you love.

for my mother,
Wong Yuet Kuen

CHIN: This book is dedicated to my mother—who is very ill presently—and the country is, of course, China and all that has to do with our stock, a strong Southern Cantonese peasant stock. I'm the first generation educated here, and I don't have children yet but my children's generation may be the first generation not to speak Chinese. So much of my poetry is about assimilation—about fearing it and loathing it but also celebrating the wonderful magic of it.

MOYERS: Somewhere you write about Chinese Americans as "the Model Minority."

CHIN: Right, and of course I use that phrase, "the Model Minority," with an edge. The label "Model Minority" is a pernicious term. What is implicit in this term is that on the flip side of "Model Minority" is a minority group that is *not* "model." The politicians coined this phrase to pit Asian Americans against African Americans and Latino Americans. They stereotype Asian Americans as being hardworking, submissive, quiet, invisible; we're "not very creative," and "not adverse to rote-learning," which means that we won't rock the boat—as long as we keep our nose to the grindstone and contribute to the GNP of the dominant society, we're okay—but don't get too rich or too noisy or so smart as to take jobs from "our" children. The scenario goes on . . .

MOYERS: Is it just a myth that the Chinese American has been more easily assimilated?

CHIN: My identity as a Chinese American poet is not monolithic. I don't think in monolithic terms. Many of my Chinese American friends don't write about assimilation, but I'm thoroughly bi-cultural and bi-lingual, and I see myself as a Pacific Rim person. I have family in China, in Hong Kong, in Hawaii, and all over the West Coast. So assimilation is a particularly important issue for me.

I am afraid of losing my Chinese, losing my language, which would be like losing a part of myself, losing part of my soul. Poetry seems a way to recapture that, but of course the truth is we can't recapture the past. The vector only goes one direction and that is toward the future. So the grandeur of China—the grandeur of that past of my grandfather's, of my grandmother's, of my mother's and so forth—that will be all lost to me. I lose inches of it every day. Sometimes I think I lose a character a day.

MOYERS: A character from your life story?

CHIN: Perhaps a character in life, too, but I was thinking about the written word. I lose the language every day.

MOYERS: There's almost an elegiac quality to the last lines of "How I Got That Name."

> . . . Solid as wood, happily
> a little gnawed, tattered, mesmerized
> by all that was lavished upon her
> and all that was taken away!

Now what does that say about assimilation?

HOW I GOT THAT NAME

AN ESSAY ON ASSIMILATION

I am Marilyn Mei Ling Chin.
Oh, how I love the resoluteness
of that first person singular
followed by that stalwart indicative
of "be," without the uncertain i-n-g
of "becoming." Of course,
the name had been changed
somewhere between Angel Island and the sea,
when my father the paperson
in the late 1950s

obsessed with a bombshell blonde
transliterated "Mei Ling" to "Marilyn."
And nobody dared question
his initial impulse—for we all know
lust drove men to greatness,
not goodness, not decency.
And there I was, a wayward pink baby,
named after some tragic white woman
swollen with gin and Nembutal.
My mother couldn't pronounce the "r."
She dubbed me "Numba one female offshoot"
for brevity: henceforth, she will live and die
in sublime ignorance, flanked
by loving children and the "kitchen deity."
While my father dithers,
a tomcat in Hong Kong trash—
a gambler, a petty thug,
who bought a chain of chopsuey joints
in Piss River, Oregon,
with bootlegged Gucci cash.
Nobody dared question his integrity given
his nice, devout daughters
and his bright, industrious sons
as if filial piety were the standard
by which all earthly men were measured.

Oh, how trustworthy our daughters,
how thrifty our sons!
How we've managed to fool the experts
in education, statistics and demography—
We're not very creative but not adverse to rote-learning.
Indeed, they can *use* us.
But the "Model Minority" is a tease.
We know you are watching now,
so we refuse to give you any!
Oh, bamboo shoots, bamboo shoots!
The further west we go, we'll hit east;
the deeper down we dig, we'll find China.

History has turned its stomach
on a black polluted beach—
where life doesn't hinge
on that red, red wheelbarrow,
but whether or not our new lover
in the final episode of "Santa Barbara"
will lean over a scented candle
and call us a "bitch."
Oh God, where have we gone wrong?
We have no inner resources!

Then, one redolent spring morning
the Great Patriarch Chin
peered down from his kiosk in heaven
and saw that his descendants were ugly.
One had a squarish head and a nose without a bridge.
Another's profile—long and knobbed as a gourd.
A third, the sad, brutish one
may never, never marry.
And I, his least favorite—
"not quite boiled, not quite cooked,"
a plump pomfret simmering in my juices—
too listless to fight for my people's destiny.
"To kill without resistance is not slaughter"
says the proverb. So, I wait for imminent death.
The fact that this death is also metaphorical
is testament to my lethargy.

So here lies Marilyn Mei Ling Chin,
married once, twice to so-and-so, a Lee and a Wong,
granddaughter of Jack "the patriarch"
and the brooding Suilin Fong,
daughter of the virtuous Yuet Kuen Wong
and G. G. Chin the infamous,
sister of a dozen, cousin of a million,
survived by everybody and forgotten by all.
She was neither black nor white,
neither cherished nor vanquished,
just another squatter in her own bamboo grove

minding her poetry—
when one day heaven was unmerciful,
and a chasm opened where she stood.
Like the jowls of a mighty white whale,
or the jaws of a metaphysical Godzilla,
it swallowed her whole.
She did not flinch nor writhe,
nor fret about the afterlife,
but stayed! Solid as wood, happily
a little gnawed, tattered, mesmerized
by all that was lavished upon her
and all that was taken away!

CHIN: There's a doubleness to nearly all my work, to how I feel about things, and perhaps especially about assimilation. As I've said, my family's past is irretrievable, but assimilation *must* happen. There's *no way* I can force my children to speak Chinese. There's *no way* that the pure yellow seed, as my grandmother called it, will continue.

MOYERS: That's what your grandmother called the Chinese?

CHIN: Yes. The Chinese want to keep the blood pure—my grandmother used to sit on the porch with a broom and try to sweep away the white boys from dating us—but assimilation is inescapable. I live in California, which is a very multicultural world. We are beyond being yellow, white, black. We're a wonderful swirl of shades of a brown. Just as I think it's impossible to keep Chineseness pure, I think it's also impossible to keep whiteness pure. I think *everything* must merge, and I'm willing to have it merge within me, in my poetry.

MOYERS: Is that what you're getting at in these lines: "She was neither black nor white, / neither cherished nor vanquished, / just another squatter in her own bamboo grove / minding her poetry—"?

CHIN: Yes, that's self referential, and of course the self has many levels, so when I talk about myself the "I" is always personal and also always representative of other Chinese Americans like myself.

MOYERS: What do you mean "neither cherished nor vanquished"?

CHIN: I feel rather invisible at times—neither cherished nor vanquished. If I were black I would be vanquished; if I were white I would be cherished. So, I believe that much of my life has been lived in a kind of mysterious opaqueness—neither cherished nor vanquished, neither loved nor hated. When Americans talk about racial politics they talk about the poles of black and white, where one group may be demonized and one group may be sanctified. I think that we must meet in the gray space in between to find harmony.

MOYERS: Some of your poetry moves far beyond just the Chinese American experience. For example, in "The Floral Apron," which you read last night, I could see *my* mother's floral apron!

CHIN: Indeed.

THE FLORAL APRON

The woman wore a floral apron around her neck,
that woman from my mother's village
with a sharp cleaver in her hand.
She said, "What shall we cook tonight?
Perhaps these six tiny squid
lined up so perfectly on the block?"

She wiped her hand on the apron,
pierced the blade into the first.
There was no resistance,
no blood, only cartilage
soft as a child's nose. A last
iota of ink made us wince.

Suddenly, the aroma of ginger and scallion fogged our senses,
and we absolved her for that moment's barbarism.
Then, she, an elder of the tribe,
without formal headdress, without elegance,
deigned to teach the younger
about the Asian plight.

And although we have traveled far
we would never forget that primal lesson
—on patience, courage, forbearance,
on how to love squid despite squid,
how to honor the village, the tribe,
that floral apron.

MOYERS: That image goes to the childhood experiences of everyone who had older teachers who touched us, or someone else who was tender to us a long time ago. That poem pulls in a lot of experience.

CHIN: Yes, *everything* must begin with the self. I was raised by my mother and my grandmother—my father left us when I was very young—so I was raised by a matriarchy. "The Floral Apron" speaks to that circumstance in my own personal history and I hope that it has universal application as well.

MOYERS: It most certainly does. What about your father? Are you writing about him when you write "for all we know / lust drove men to greatness, / not goodness, not decency"?

CHIN: My uncle was very upset when he heard those lines. He was shocked that I would dare to expose such terrible things about my father, but I think the feeling there came out of my personal experience. One event in particular hurt me greatly, and it occurred when I was seven years old, shortly after we arrived in America.

My father had a white lover and he was on the phone with her in an adjoining room while my mother, who couldn't speak English, was in the living room sewing and not understanding anything about what was going on. That was a very damaging experience for me as a child and it's been painful ever since. I try to resolve that experience in my poetry. All my love poems work on the personal level, but they also work on this familial level, in which over and over again I try to speak to my father and to resolve what was unresolvable—to ask him why he left us and why he left us for a white woman. And once again in my poems the white woman works on the personal level in that, indeed, "she's" what fragmented our family. The white woman is also symbolic of the American dream and of what happens to the immigrant family—in this case, the Chinese family—upon reaching these shores.

This is the fragmentation that I write about over and over again, hoping to resolve this pain, hoping to speak through my mother's suffering, hoping to be a conduit for her voice and for the voices of other Asian women.

MOYERS: Have you resolved it?

CHIN: I don't think I've resolved it, and that's why I continue to write the same love poem over and over again. I meet the same failure trying to resolve this in my personal life. I try over and over to resolve this deep pain and guilt I feel for my mother.

TURTLE SOUP

You go home one evening tired from work,
and your mother boils you turtle soup.

Twelve hours hunched over the hearth
(who knows what else is in that cauldron).

You say, "Ma, you've poached the symbol of long life;
that turtle lived four thousand years, swam
the Wei, up the Yellow, over the Yangtze.
Witnessed the Bronze Age, the High Tang,
grazed on splendid sericulture."
(So, she boils the life out of him.)

"All our ancestors have been fools.
Remember Uncle Wu who rode ten thousand miles
to kill a famous Manchu and ended up
with his head on a pole? Eat, child,
its liver will make you strong."

"Sometimes you're the life, sometimes the sacrifice."
Her sobbing is inconsolable.
So, you spread that gentle napkin
over your lap in decorous Pasadena.

Baby, some high priestess has got it wrong.
The golden decal on the green underbelly
says "Made in Hong Kong."

Is there nothing left but the shell
and humanity's strange inscriptions,
the songs, the rites, the oracles?

FOR BEN HUANG

MOYERS: That may explain why I like so much your poem "Turtle Soup." You are apparently addressing the turtle: " 'Sometimes you're the life, sometimes the sacrifice.' " As a religious symbol the turtle has the capacity to sustain life, but it also sustains life as part of the food chain.

CHIN: Right.

MOYERS: But is that also a way of talking about your mother and other women who have been sacrificed?

CHIN: Yes. " 'Sometimes you're the life, sometimes the sacrifice.' " I see her as the bridge that brought us over, and there she's the sacrifice. She once commented that she saw herself as the peach tree that brought the peaches, and now that she's given fruit it's time for her to die. In fact, she's very ill right now. She's only sixty-two, but she bore this suffering for many, many years. This line refers to her personal and familial suffering and also to that of a whole generation of women like her. The turtle is such a revered Chinese mythological symbol—it's a symbol of longevity and patience and grandeur and antiquity—but the irony of this turtle is that it ends up in a swirl, in a soup, in Pasadena, California. I see these creatures in my poems as self-portraits.

MOYERS: This poem is written in the voice of the Americanized child reminding her mother of what is sacred from the old country.

CHIN: Yes. The daughter is the one who *wants* to preserve it. In my own case, my undergraduate degree was in Chinese literature, and I went back to Taiwan to try to learn classical Chinese. As a poet I believe I need to work in both Eastern and Western paradigms; I need to know *both* traditions. On the other hand, of course, my mother and my grandmother who are from solid peasant stock are practical, and they say I should *not* be a poet. They want me to fulfill a typical immigrant aspiration and become a lawyer.

So the speaker in the poem cannot comprehend the historical forces that made her mother—the revolutions, the famines, the vicissitudes of the times that peasant women suffered and which made her generation very practical. In this poem her mother poaches this turtle for food and is not interested in the turtle as a cultural symbol. Because food is an Asian American trope, I write a lot about it. In ethnic American literature you'll often find food as a major motif, and there are many reasons for this. We're trying to preserve our past through food, and food also asserts our difference. Food is celebratory, but its flip side is hunger and deprivation. Spiritual deprivation and hunger in the new country are important motifs of ethnic American literature.

Hunger in the "gold" country, in the land of the plenty is almost obscene, so there's always that doubleness in my work when I write about food.

MOYERS: I want to ask you about two images that run through your poetry. One of my favorite poems is the "Song of the Sad Guitar," and you mention the Sad Guitar throughout your poetry. What is it?

CHIN: There's a literary reference to a poem by the Tang Dynasty poet Po Chü-Yi, "The Song of the Sad Guitar." Also, because I like doubleness, there's the blue guitar in Picasso's paintings that helps to set the mood. For me the guitar is actually a lute, a Chinese instrument, and that's how I visualize it in my poems, but I translate it as a guitar. I see it as a female instrument—in her curvaceous shape, in her music, and in her sadness. It's a sad guitar. Once again, it's a symbol of my mother's sadness and my mother's suffering.

MOYERS: You truly seem to carry your mother's sadness.

CHIN: Well, perhaps it's my projection, but she is very sad and this is something I write out of guilt and out of love. I think children want their mothers to be happy, and the fact that my mother cannot be happy in this new country shall haunt me forever and shall haunt my poetry forever.

MOYERS: The other image that appears often is the golden mountain. A good example is "The Disorder." What were the *golden mountains*?

THE DISORDER

The only truth you know now is your hunger
growing wider as the season darkens.
And all the fasting and Hindu calisthenics
couldn't keep those inches off. The fat
adheres to you like cancer or a warm lichen
dependent on a tree trunk's insecurity
and unwilling to part.
                            Everywhere
you venture the mirrors whisper,
the pond's reflections resound your dolor.
The winter doldrums comfort the beasts
within all but yourself—
                            As you reach out
to gather more confections and sweet rewards,
as you attempt to fill an emptiness
not filled by the sun, as you wait
for your inevitable fall,
                            a small child
within you remembers: *so, these, these*
were the "golden mountains"!

CHIN: The promised land, but of course it's said with irony—the promise is never fulfilled. And this poem once again talks about hunger and not satiation or fulfillment. And henceforth golden mountain, the promised land, has fallen short of its promises. I worked in a psychiatric hospital as a bi-lingual counselor for a couple of years in California, and this poem was actually written for a patient, Diana Toy, who was an anorexic—she used to starve herself—which is unheard of in a Chinese family. Supposedly this doesn't happen, and especially not in the land of plenty, the "gold" country.

The issue here relates to what we were just saying about how food is an important motif and how the flip side of the food and satiation is starvation. In this case Diana Toy is spiritually starved, which is what happens to many of us who appear on the shores of the promised land.

MOYERS: Women are claiming new territory for poetry, and women like you who come from the world over are pushing those boundaries even further. Is there something happening right now in American life that invites this?

CHIN: America is no longer a monolithic, European-derived culture. It is no longer a mono-lingual or mono-cultural country, and the margins are moving toward the center. That's to say that those of us who have an urgent message or who have polyphonic voices or who have colorful backgrounds and interesting lives and pasts have a lot to say, and it's now *our* turn to *say* it. Indeed, there's more urgency in what we have to say, and the contemporary poetry world can't keep us out.

That's the thing. We're breaking new ground, and *this* is the voice of America. My voice is one of the *many* voices of America.

David Mura, Marilyn Chin, Victor Hernández Cruz

Poetry began when somebody walked off a savanna or out of a cave and looked up at the sky with wonder and said, "Ah-h-h!" That was the first poem.

LUCILLE CLIFTON

Lucille Clifton decided early not to accept other people's definitions and to question everything for herself. She even turned society's limited expectations for a young black child to advantage and dared become a poet. Self-taught, she uses plain and powerful language to explore life's complexities and to affirm the spirit's endurance. A prolific poet (twice nominated for the Pulitzer Prize), children's author, and screenplay writer, she acknowledges her six children as the inspiration for much of her work. A native of New York, she teaches at Columbia University and at St. Mary's College of Maryland. For three years she was poet laureate of Maryland.

MOYERS: The audience was really with you last night, riding every current of pleasure and surprise. I kept asking myself, should poetry *be* this much fun?

CLIFTON: I hope so. It *can* be fun, but that doesn't mean it's not serious. I'm very serious.

MOYERS: What happens to you when the audience comes back to you the way they did last night?

CLIFTON: Well, I sort of ride that energy. I often don't know what I'm going to read until I get in front of people, then I try to feel out where it seems to be going for them, and for me as well.

MOYERS: So, you're improvising—in a way.

CLIFTON: Well, I'm improvising what poems to read, yes. I often have a feeling for what *I* want to hear so I usually do include a couple of those poems, but I also try to feel out what this particular group of people needs or wants or what poem should follow this one. It's like riding a wave, or what I like to think riding a wave must be like.

MOYERS: Listening to you recite your poems I imagined you having had a very hard life.

CLIFTON: I don't know if I think I've had a hard life, but I *have* had a challenging life. Everybody's life is more difficult than people think, but I was blessed with a sense of humor, so there are a lot of things that I think are funny, which has saved me on occasion. I can also see what I have gained from being challenged in my life: *I know* I'm tough—I've seen it so I know it's true.

MOYERS: In "climbing" what's your connection to the woman above you on that rope?

climbing

a woman precedes me up the long rope,
her dangling braids the color of rain.
maybe i should have had braids.
maybe i should have kept the body i started,
slim and possible as a boy's bone.
maybe i should have wanted less.
maybe i should have ignored the bowl in me
burning to be filled.
maybe i should have wanted less.
the woman passes the notch in the rope
marked Sixty.   i rise toward it, struggling,
hand over hungry hand.

CLIFTON: Well, on the one hand, I don't want to be her; on the other hand I'm *going* to be her, and very soon! The woman above me is climbing towards sixty, and I'm going to be sixty in a couple of years. When I was younger and I thought about sixty, well, I thought life was over at that age, but now that I am almost sixty I don't remember changing or getting older. I'm not settled yet. I used to think people the age I am now were supposed to be settled and sing hymns and bake bread; but I don't do anything like that, and I probably won't.

MOYERS: I was struck by the refrain "maybe i, maybe i, maybe i . . ."

CLIFTON: I think we always try to figure out if this is where we expected to be. For example, I often wonder if this is where I would have ended up if I had made other choices or accepted other paths.

MOYERS: Why do you say "less" in the line "maybe i should have wanted less"? Why *that* question *now*?

CLIFTON: Maybe because this feeling that there is so much to do and even less time is a feeling that keeps you stirred up. I have *still* not accepted that this is what

I was going to grow up to be. When I look at other people, especially people over fifty-five, I believe that they are where they thought they'd be. Then I think that maybe if I had wanted to be a schoolteacher with a nice dress from Talbot's, maybe then there wouldn't be this hunger inside.

MOYERS: What *did* you want to be?

CLIFTON: I knew what I did *not* want to be. I didn't want to be ordinary. Isn't that odd? I don't put any value judgment around it; I just didn't want to be my parents. I'm a very curious person. I knew that there was something other in the world, and I wanted to see it and feel it. I always wanted not to be plain and I don't know what that means exactly, but when I was in school I didn't want to get a C—flunk me or give me an A.

MOYERS: Isn't there something liberating at the age of sixty when one is freed from dreams of future greatness and can accept some ordinariness?

CLIFTON: Well, of course, ordinariness also has a greatness about it, and I don't know if I wanted to be great. I *did* want to be sure that I was all that I could be and that I saw the truth clearly.

MOYERS: The poem suggests that you're still climbing.

CLIFTON: Absolutely! I hope I'm still climbing because I'm human. I'm alive.

MOYERS: Has poetry helped you climb?

CLIFTON: Oh, poetry's probably saved my life. It has been *the* stable thing, something to love. Even in the middle of the most amazing and interesting things, there's a line that I could come to or that would come to me and help me through it. I think poetry has been the one faithful, good thing.

MOYERS: By doing *what* for you? Exactly what does it mean to sit and wrestle with those words until they line up on the page just the way you want them?

CLIFTON: I'm not sure that's how it happens exactly. I have a feeling that sometimes rather than wrestle and look for words, you have to be still and let them come. I was not trained as a poet, and I've never taken poetry lessons or had workshops. Nobody taught me anything much, really. So, I learned how to learn, and what I learned is that I could be still and allow the world and the impressions and the feelings—I'm very good with feelings—to come to me, and I could use our language to write them down.

MOYERS: You're good with feelings?

CLIFTON: I never learned to cut feelings off. I never learned that you were supposed to contain your feelings if you were an educated person, a sophisticated person. I did learn that I had to see things wholly and I learned to feel wholly as well, especially the complexities of what it means to be human and the complexities of what it means to be me.

MOYERS: It's been interesting to me to hear the male poets at this festival express so much emotion.

CLIFTON: Well, poets always have been given that license, and that's why male poets have traditionally had a hard time. They've been considered a little outside because *as poets* they have had permission to experience feelings, even ecstasy. But in this culture females have not even had permission to be poets until fairly recently. As an African American person I'm fortunate in being outside those boundaries of definition, so I could be whatever. I mean, no one thought I was going to be a poet anyway. As a rule in this culture those boundaries about what one is supposed to be as a visible human being didn't include people of African descent, so I ignored them.

I've said many times that one of the blessings of being born an African American woman on this continent is that I learned early not to buy other people's definitions, and primarily about who I was. That refusal led me to wonder about *every* definition, so I was then able to try to define the world for myself. Male poets are fortunate in that, as poets they have been given permission to express experience and feeling publicly, but I think female poets are only beginning to express feeling publicly.

People are beginning to understand that especially in poetry feeling transcends boundaries of race, culture, class, economics. They are also beginning to understand that intellect does *not* do that. On the other hand, the way we feel, the way we fear, the way we love, the way we hope—these are the same kinds of things for all of us. So poetry that is both intellectual and intuitive seems to me to be poetry that will get past any of the artificial boundaries which separate us.

MOYERS: That's why I can listen, for instance, to David Mura—whose Japanese American experience is totally foreign to me—and sense what he's feeling for his mother or father and why I can read one of your poems and experience what you seem to be feeling for those long-dead folks back on the plantation.

CLIFTON: Yes, and I think another reason is that something inside can say to you, "This is what it feels like to be a human being *of this sort,* but a human being." I tell audiences all the time that there are people who would say they can't relate to my poetry because I'm an African American woman and they are not; but I only write about being human, and I believe other humans can always recognize that. If I do it truly, if I do it honestly and authentically, which I try to do, then other humans can feel something from what I write.

MOYERS: Much of poetry is fiction, fact, and history all boiling in the cauldron. It must be *feeling* that gives it authenticity.

CLIFTON: Probably. Now, history and truth may sometimes be different things. Poetry doesn't have to be fact, it only has to be true. Sometimes it *is* fact, that's cool, but it doesn't have to be.

MOYERS: And by "true" you mean?

CLIFTON: I don't know if you can put what is true into linear, rational terms. Faulkner gets at it this way—if the truth is one thing to you and another to me, how do we know which is true and not true? The answer is that the heart already knows.

There is something in us that recognizes what is so; and even if it is not so for us, there is something in us that recognizes rightness. It may be that in our culture we've become accustomed not to listen to that voice, but just because we don't consciously listen to it with our ears doesn't mean we don't hear it.

MOYERS: Poetry nurtures that silent voice. I can't think of a better example than this poem.

at the cemetery,
walnut grove plantation, south carolina,
1989

among the rocks
at walnut grove
your silence drumming
in my bones,
tell me your names.

nobody mentioned slaves
and yet the curious tools
shine with your fingerprints.
nobody mentioned slaves
but somebody did this work
who had no guide, no stone,
who moulders under rock.

tell me your names,
tell me your bashful names
and i will testify.

the inventory lists ten slaves
but only men were recognized.

among the rocks
at walnut grove
some of these honored dead
were dark
some of these dark
were slaves
some of these slaves
were women
some of them did this
honored work.
tell me your names
foremothers, brothers,
tell me your dishonored names.
here lies
here lies
here lies
here lies
hear

CLIFTON: Well, let me tell you what happened with that poem. I went to Walnut Grove Plantation in South Carolina in 1989 and I was the only person of color on the tour. It's a wonderful two thousand acres, but on the tour there was no mention of slaves. The plantation had the original furniture, and the guide talked about the difficulty of the work for a small family, but there was no mention of slavery. Now I'm very nosy—I want to know everything when I travel to give readings, all the gossip, everything. I like to know what happened here, so I always ask about the people who were here before *these* people? And then the uncomfortable question always is "Where are they *now*?"

Well, Walnut Grove Plantation has the family burying ground, and on the sides of the roped-off path leading to that burying ground there are crosses and rocks and other things sitting on edge that to me clearly mark the graves of slaves. So I asked, "Why don't you mention slaves?" The first answer was "Maybe the guide didn't want to embarrass you." "Well," I said, "*I'm* not a slave. I don't know why he would think I'd be embarrassed." Then I asked again, and the answer was, "Maybe they didn't have any." Well, they had two thousand acres in South Carolina in the early part of the nineteenth century. Be serious!

When I suggested that the guide check the inventory—because slaves were considered property and were often inventoried—they discovered that the plantation had an inventory of ten slaves, but they might have had more because women weren't counted. Now, well, I had to find out about that! I mean, some things say, hey, like "No!" Then when I learned that the women were not considered valuable enough to inventory, I definitely wanted to write about that.

MOYERS: What do you want the readers to do at the end of the poem when you change the word "here" to "hear"?

CLIFTON: I want them to recognize that only half the truth was being told. At that time schoolchildren were taken there on field trips to Walnut Grove, and half the children in the town were denied the knowledge that their ancestors had helped to build that plantation. That is unjust, and I'm into justice big-time.

I read that poem in South Carolina a lot, and someone in the audience—I think she was the director of the group which has restored the plantation—wrote me a letter saying that she just didn't realize. Two years ago they began building a model slave cabin, and now they are going to include all the people who lived there in the tour. So that's one poem doing something, making a difference. Then once when I did a reading at the nearby town a woman came up and told me that her family had owned Walnut Grove, but she had never gone back—she was ashamed—so I said the next time I come here, we must go together. You see, we cannot ignore history. History doesn't go away. The past isn't back there, the past is *here* too.

MOYERS: Is it part of poetry's job to recover history, to proclaim it, and to correct it when necessary?

CLIFTON: Yes. All that may be needed is that the injustice in the world be mentioned so that nobody can ever say, "Nobody told me."

MOYERS: You have another poem about a slave cabin, on Sotterly Plantation, also in Maryland and also dated 1989.

slave cabin,
sotterly plantation, maryland, 1989

in this little room
note carefully

    aunt nanny's bench

    three words that label
    things
    aunt
    is my parent's sister
    nanny
    my grandmother
    bench
    the board at which
    i stare
    the soft curved polished
    wood
    that held her bottom
    after the long days
    without end
    without beginning
    when she   aunt nanny   sat
    feet dead against the dirty floor
    humming for herself   humming
    her own sweet human name

CLIFTON: Yes, I did a lot of plantations that year. Sotterly is near where I teach, at St. Mary's College in southern Maryland. They have a slave cabin still standing—I think it was inhabited until 1910, something like that—and it was interesting to me that they should be glad about having that cabin. For a number of reasons I'm proud of Maryland for that. You can't go into it, but on the door there is a little sign which I refer to in the poem.

My problem here was that "aunt nanny" isn't anybody's name; so to have "aunt nanny's bench" is not to tell you about her, or about anybody. It only tells you about their perception of her. So I just wondered, "What *was* her name?"

MOYERS: You need the name before you can testify?

CLIFTON: It is important for us to know what people call themselves and not to mistake what *we* call them for what they call themselves. We have the right as living creatures to name ourselves. Then when people call us something else, we can allow it or not. But "aunt nanny's bench"? Even at their most wonderful, the people who gave her that name perhaps didn't know who she was.

MOYERS: That's why so many poets "still believe in the magic of naming names."

CLIFTON: Yes, me too. I believe that's why the change of name movement among black people in the 1960s was so important, and it's interesting how resistant the larger culture was to it—if you have the right to name me, you have power over me, or you think you do; but as a living creature I have the right to be who I say I am.

MOYERS: Why did you dedicate "fury" to your mother?

fury

FOR MAMA

remember this.
she is standing by
the furnace.
the coals
glisten like rubies.
her hand is crying.
her hand is clutching
a sheaf of papers.
poems.
she gives them up.
they burn
jewels into jewels.
her eyes are animals.
each hank of her hair
is a serpent's obedient
wife.
she will never recover.
remember. there is nothing
you will not bear
for this woman's sake.

CLIFTON: Because it's my mother's story in a lot of ways. My mother used to write poetry. Neither of my parents graduated from elementary school, but my mother wrote very traditional, iambic pentameter poetry. She used to see me writing—I didn't write the way she did—and she'd say, "Aw, baby, that ain't no poem. Let me show you how to write a poem," so she would. I cannot imagine how this happened, but she once got a letter inviting her to put some poems in a book. She was very shy, a homebody kind of woman, and my father wouldn't let her do it. I am very quick to say at readings that it wasn't because he was an evil man. It was because it was the 1940s when husbands liked to think they could tell wives what to do—a very strange idea—but when my father did that, my mother burned her poems. She took them down in the basement to the coal stove and put them in the fire, and I was standing on the basement steps when she did it.

My mother's been dead thirty-five years, and as I was driving in the car many years after her death I suddenly thought, "Oh, that's what rage looks like. That's what fury looks like." Fury was my mother's hand as she was putting those poems into the furnace. I understood something then.

MOYERS: I have a hard time figuring out what this society expects of poets.

CLIFTON: I think our society often expects them to be odd, over there in their little corner. It's a shame.

MOYERS: Yes, but that's changing. You give a lot of readings, do you have any sense of a change?

CLIFTON: I *hope* it's changing. For too long poetry has been seen as an elite activity that only happens in the academy, but poetry is a very human urge and there have always been people attempting to express themselves in poems. I think there's a great renaissance of poetry in this country, and I think that we are beginning to remember that the first poets didn't come out of a classroom.

Poetry began when somebody walked off a savanna or out of a cave and looked up at the sky with wonder and said, "Ah-h-h!" *That* was the first poem. The urge towards "Ah-h-h!" is very human, it's in everybody. People express it in different ways, and I think the world is beginning to recognize that that urge in themselves is also poetry. Unfortunately, we've been taught that only certain things are poetry.

MOYERS: You said earlier that you don't *write* poems and that often they simply come to you: you just remain still, at the center, waiting for them.

CLIFTON: Well, why write them all the time? I *am* a poet all the time; but, yes, I learned how to wait for them.

MOYERS: What if you do not want to hear it? What if it frightens you? What if it is a terrible truth about the past or your family?

CLIFTON: Oh, all that certainly has happened, and lots of times. But too bad for me; I just have to accept it anyway. You cannot play for safety and make art. You have to get past your own fear. It's all right to be afraid. It's human to be afraid—there *are* fearful things in the world—so I think you almost *have* to be afraid, but if you draw back from what frightens you, then you may as well stop writing because, in a way, everything is frightening. Every morning you wake up to the unexpected, to what might kill you, but you have to do it anyway. Once you decide, "I will see clearly, I will speak clearly, I will say what I see," then you have to do it all.

MOYERS: When that dark figure enters, do you try to shift its shape?

CLIFTON: No, I don't think so. I try to say what it *is,* to name it because I know it doesn't just come to me and I believe my naming it can name it for others as well. I've sometimes said that if I have a strength as a poet and as a human being, it is not because I understand that I'm just like everybody else—it's much more difficult than that—it is because I understand that everybody else is just like me. So with that understanding, I believe that my naming can help those who are unable yet to name. I don't know if I do it clearly or not, all I know is that I make the attempt so that others who walk away may be a little safer.

MOYERS: Who is the shapeshifter in your shapeshifter poems? I've never before heard that term.

CLIFTON: This is a series of poems about the sexual abuse of children. In these poems there is a child, a girl child, who is being interfered with by her father, someone she trusts and loves, someone she thinks of as an authority figure. I read these poems quite a lot—this is a pervasive problem in our society—and I have found that they speak to so many people in all kinds of audiences. I've gotten very accustomed to having people come up to me—somebody did it again just the other day—and say, "Thank you for the shapeshifter poems." These are people from all kinds of places, and I understand this is their way of telling me that they know this problem.

I was startled the first time someone came up to me and said, "Thank you for those poems. *I* was a shapeshifter." I should also say that this person was female, and when she said, "Thank you," all I could do was hug her—but I'm not about judging any of them, you know.

MOYERS: Poetry can heal.

CLIFTON: I think so. It *can* be healing—certainly for me as poet—and I think for the listener too.

shapeshifter poems

1

the legend is whispered
in the women's tent
how the moon when she rises
full
follows some men into themselves
and changes them there
the season is short
but dreadful   shapeshifters
they wear strange hands
they walk through the houses
at night   their daughters
do not know them

2

who is there to protect her
from the hands of the father
not the windows which see and
say nothing   not the moon
that awful eye   not the woman
she will become with her
scarred tongue   who   who   who   the owl
laments into the evening   who
will protect her   this   prettylittlegirl

3

if the little girl lies
still enough
shut enough
hard enough
shapeshifter may not
walk tonight
the full moon may not
find him here
the hair on him
bristling
rising
up

4

the poem at the end of the world
is the poem the little girl breathes
into her pillow   the one
she cannot tell   the one
there is no one to hear   this poem
is a political poem   is a war poem   is a
universal poem but is not about
these things   this poem
is about one human heart   this poem
is the poem at the end of the world

CLIFTON: While many people have said to me that they suspect the shape-shifter poems might be about the sexual abuse of children, I also think people tend *not* to want to think that's what these stories are about. I have another poem, "the lost baby poem," which is about an abortion, but people like to think it might be about a miscarriage because it makes them feel better for me. You know, often one's mind doesn't want to go beyond certain barriers.

MOYERS: Do you know the little girl in those poems?

CLIFTON: I surely do know her. She was me.

MOYERS: You were the child being abused?

CLIFTON: Yes. That seems stark because I want to assure you that I've written many other poems about this subject. This is *not* my identity. I've had lots of things in my life that are not my identity, nor was this my father's identity either. When I talked about seeing things wholly, surely *I* am one of the people I want to see wholly, and my father is another person I want to see wholly since I inherited from him so many strong and good qualities, including stubbornness, strength, intelligence, and curiosity. He was a remarkable man.

But my father was abused by the United States of America, and quite often. I have a line in a poem about him, "if he could have done better he would have." I have another poem called "forgiving my father." When I wrote it, I showed it to my husband, and I said, "There, have I done it?" He read the poem, looked at me, and said, "No." I thought, "Well, gee."

I'm not a person who forgets things, and I'm not sure that I forgive things, but I don't want to make the whole judgment because, ultimately, if you fill yourself with venom you will be poisoned, and I don't want to be. I'm a survivor from my heart. I figured that out a long time ago.

MOYERS: Do you read your poems to your own children?

CLIFTON: I have six children and my baby's twenty-eight. My kids think my being a poet is the strangest thing, but now they're used to it. And, yes, I do read to them; they say things like, "Oh, that's nice, Mommy," or "I think that one's good." When they're asked how it feels that I'm their mother, they say, "Everybody's mother does something. She just does that." I also write children's books, and when they were young I was invited to every class in school but theirs. Kids are always embarrassed by their parents anyway. They would say, "Don't come to our class." Then when I finally did go to their classes, they gave me a lesson the night before: "You know how you walk? Don't walk that stupid walk. You know how you talk? Don't talk like that. Don't laugh your laugh. Don't wear your clothes." I was so embarrassed and so nervous by the time I went into their classes, it was amazing.

MOYERS: You—nervous?

CLIFTON: I don't get nervous that often, to tell the truth.

MOYERS: Tell me about "she lived."

she lived

after he died
what really happened is
she watched the days
bundle into thousands,
watched every act become
the history of others,
every bed more
narrow,
but even as the eyes of lovers
strained toward the milky young
she walked away
from the hole in the ground
deciding to live.   and she lived.

CLIFTON: Well, I've been widowed for over ten years. My husband's death was unexpected. He was quite a strong person, and we had been together about thirty years. I think people sometimes feel if they've been with somebody a long time and it's been a challenging but good marriage—I can't imagine anybody else as his wife, he was so quirky, which I rather like—that part of their life has died and they're going to spend the rest of their lives as "the widow of." But I never wanted to be a person like that.

So there was a time when I had to ask myself, "All right, am I going to sit here and be Fred's wife even if Fred's not alive?" When you're widowed you start filling in the blanks on forms—you know, "married or single"—and for a while I thought, "I'm married, he's just dead." But I figured out that to honor what we had together in his life, I must continue to live. I've had so many losses—parents, siblings, my husband—but you continue to live, and in continuing you honor those who didn't continue.

M O Y E R S : So, "she walked away / from the hole in the ground."

C L I F T O N : "deciding to live.   and she lived." I think that's what happened, though that's not exactly fact, because he was cremated.

M O Y E R S : So, this is not a literal event.

C L I F T O N : Well, it is, really. The hole in the ground sounds buried and he wasn't buried—he was cremated—but the truth of it is that I walked away from that end into a new beginning, a difficult beginning. You suddenly find yourself not in the mainstream of people who are part of ongoing life—"every act become[s] / the history of others." As a widow in my fifties I noticed that gentlemen in their fifties were looking at my daughters who were in their thirties. I wasn't fond of that, and I'm still not fond of that: "the eyes of lovers / strained toward the milky young." But you don't think about all that stuff—"she walked away / from the hole in the ground / deciding to live.   and she lived."

M O Y E R S : Not easy. Not easy at all. Your poem which begins "each morning I pull myself" seems to come from this daily struggle.

C L I F T O N : Some poets think, "Well, that's not a Lucille poem," as if I can't be complex. I mean, *please!* Humans *are* complex. Sometimes black folks buy into the idea that we're not complicated, but everybody's complicated, everything's complicated. I just don't know how we manage.

As I've said, my baby's twenty-eight years old, I'm widowed, and every day I'm attempting to be present, to continue. And still every day there are things that would make one hate. So you have to mention them and as much as possible try not to hate. Every day there is something that would make you afraid, and you have to try not to let it stop you.

That's where the honor is. Honor is *not* in not acting because you are afraid. Nor is there honor in acting when you are not afraid. But acting when you *are* afraid, *that's* where the honor is.

WILLIAM STAFFORD

William Stafford put no stock as a young man in received opinion. His tenacious personal code caused him to be interned as a conscientious objector from 1940 to 1944. His quiet, plain poems encourage others to venture beyond their known boundaries of knowledge and sympathy. He served as poetry consultant to the Library of Congress (now called poet laureate) in 1970–71 and poet laureate of Oregon from 1975 until his death on August 28, 1993. These remarks were made in October 1988.

A poem is anything said in such a way, or put on the page in such a way, as to invite from the hearer or the reader a certain kind of attention.

Writing is peculiarly susceptible to this wonderful resource, language. I didn't invent it, I don't control it. It just rolls on. It comes from everybody. It's not something I learned from other writers, by any means. It's not something I learned from critics, by any means. It is a great river of possibilities swirling around us all the time. People talk to each other and come upon—I guess I do it like a gull—these great swoops of realization and vistas that veer off toward other formulations in language. And even the *syllables* have meaning!

In writing I don't know *what* my intention is. This may sound strange, but I want to be on guard against trying to write good poems. Most writers say, "Oh, excellence! There's no use doing it if you don't do excellent things." But I don't feel that way at all. I feel that writing is an activity that brings all sorts of rewards, not just good poems. I'd give up everything I've written for a *new* one, for a *new* writing experience. It feels so good to go that trancelike way through a succession of realizations in language toward—

what? It's an adventure. It's exploration, rather than crafting a predetermined object. At least, that's the way I feel.

ASK ME

Some time when the river is ice ask me
mistakes I have made. Ask me whether
what I have done is my life. Others
have come in their slow way into
my thought, and some have tried to help
or to hurt: ask me what difference
their strongest love or hate has made.

I will listen to what you say.
You and I can turn and look
at the silent river and wait. We know
the current is there, hidden; and there
are comings and goings from miles away
that hold the stillness exactly before us.
What the river says, that is what I say.

Poetry gives us revelations, flashes,
which illuminate those things
which were mysterious to us.

— Victor Hernández Cruz —

Victor Hernández Cruz infuses his poetry with the rhythms, colors, and textures of Puerto Rico, his homeland, and the Lower East Side of New York City, where he grew up. He has reached out to the several communities that have shaped his work and involved their residents in artistic projects. He is a founding member of the Before Columbus Foundation, which seeks to make Americans aware of literature often overlooked by the establishment. Cruz has taught most recently at the University of California in San Diego.

MOYERS: No one has been able to pigeonhole you. Your poetry contains the sounds of the street, Caribbean fiction, jazz, popular music, black English, Puerto Rico, New York, Africa, Asia—where do all these sounds come from?

CRUZ: In one sense, it's the history of my body—the history of the migrations I have participated in. As a young child, my family left the small tropical town in the middle of Puerto Rico which had been home and migrated to New York City, one of the largest cities on the planet Earth. It was just like moving from one age into another.

The Caribbean is made up of many different peoples whose cultures overlay the cultures of the indigenous peoples who were originally there. So in my childhood world a lot of languages and cultural information came together all around me. Then the neighborhood where I grew up, near the Avenue D housing project on Manhattan's Lower East Side, was mostly African American and Puerto Rican, and there was a constant blend of these cultures on the street. So I naturally combine *all* these influences, and when I travel from New York to California I pick up still more forms of English and still more and different cultural information.

MOYERS: Were you exposed to poetry when you were a child?

CRUZ: Yes, to the oral tradition of Puerto Rican society. My grandfather Julio was a tobacconist in a small shop in Puerto Rico—he rolled the cigars. The tradition of a tobacconist was to tell stories, and tobacconists would sometimes have a reader come in to read aloud as they worked. They might hear a whole novel, a chapter a day.

When my parents moved to New York I drew from my memory of Puerto Rico and tried to write in traditional Spanish rhyming forms, but that was very frustrating because it's much more difficult to write rhymes in English. So I abandoned those forms early on and began to develop a voice that grew out of my neighborhood in New York City.

today is a day of great joy

when they stop poems
in the mail & clap
their hands & dance to
them

when women become pregnant
by the side of poems
the strongest sounds making
the river go along

it is a great day

as poems fall down to
movie crowds in restaurants
in bars

when poems start to
knock down walls to
choke politicians
when poems scream &
begin to break the air

that is the time of
true poets that is
the time of greatness

a true poet aiming
poems & watching things
fall to the ground

it is a great day

MOYERS: Yes, I hear the sounds and rhythms of New York in "today is a day of great joy." You were expecting poems to do a lot there.

CRUZ: When I was younger I felt that I had to get the city, *the actual pavement,* out of the way because I felt the physical setting of the city was hiding the mountains that I knew as a child, hiding the palm trees and the pineapple fields. I was reacting with deep hostility to the urban environment around me.

MOYERS: You had just come from the mountains of Puerto Rico to the concrete canyons of New York City.

CRUZ: Yes, and in the middle of *winter!*

MOYERS: Did you really expect poems to knock down walls and to choke politicians?

CRUZ: I think you have those illusions when you're younger, but because language is the natural force that it is, in fact it *does* have quite a lot of power. The first thing people do when they go crazy is to start talking to themselves. So the important task of poetry is to use the power to control language to grasp who we are inside—by which we can get hold of our lives.

MOYERS: You wrote, "going uptown to visit miriam" some twenty-five years ago. Read that one.

going uptown to visit miriam

on the train
old ladies playing football
going for empty seats

very funny persons

the train riders
                    are silly people
                    i am a train rider

but no one knows where i am
going to take this train

to take this train
to take this train

the ladies   read popular
paperback   because they
are popular   they get off
at 42 to change for the
westside line   or off
59 for the department store

the train pulls in & out
the white walls   dark-
ness   white walls   dark-
ness

ladies looking up   i
wonder where they going
the dentist   pick up
husband pick up wife
pick up kids
pick up? grass?
to library   to museum
to laundromat   to school

but no one knows where i am
going to take this train

MOYERS: Why do you repeat several lines from time to time?

CRUZ: Repetition is very important. I get that from the forms of bolero, the romantic love song of the Americas, in which there's always a chorus and there's always a line that gets repeated. That happens in salsa music, too—there's a question and then an answer. There's a call and response in Caribbean rhythms that comes from Africa. Because I grew up with all those calls and responses, all that repetition, I naturally used it in English forms.

MOYERS: Salsa is . . .

CRUZ: Salsa is how we've labeled the music of Puerto Rico, Cuba, and Santo Domingo. We used to call it the rumba, the mambo, all forms that now meet in the Latin communities of New York and mix with jazz and rhythm and blues and come out as salsa. The root is in African Caribbean music.

MOYERS: In one of your poems you talk about the "singing magic words of our ancestors."

CRUZ: "Magic words of our ancestors." Yes. There was a form of epic poetry which was sung and danced in a round circle with musical instruments. This was literature in song form, poetry passed on from generation to generation.

MOYERS: One of your poems is entitled "Puerta Rica." You end the name of your native island with the feminine *a* instead of the masculine *o*. Why?

CRUZ: Because *puerta* means door. It means rich door. *Puerta* is door and *puerto* is port. I was trying to throw light on the words *puerto* and *rico* which make up the European or Spanish invented name of our island. The original name was *Borinquen*. In this poem I wanted to dismantle the *new* name and investigate what it really means.

PUERTA RICA

Free Puerto Rico
Puerto Rico free
Puerto Rico for $12.50
Puerto Rico on credit
Get some rich port
free
free sand and free soil
Free Puerto Rico now
Give away Puerto Rico
for nothing
Port Rich
Rich Port
Rich free
Port free
Puerto Rico for a
thousand dollars
Free Puerto Rico now
Free Puerto Rico then
Free Puerto Rico always
Puerto Rico on layaway
Puerto Rico as thing
Puerto Rico as word
Puerta Rica
Puerto Rico as blood
as water as gold
Puerto Rico as idea
inside of briefcases
Going to colleges
Puerto Rico patches
Puerto Rico buttons

Puerto Rico as flag
waving
Puerto Rico as in the heart
as in the ocean
The sand as hot as
frying pan
Puerto Rico as lament
Puerto Rico as cement
Puerto Rico as my uncles
house
As Julia María
As Borinquen
Going from house to house
In the mountains
for more and more soft
Brown legs
Puerto Rico as the corner
where I stood
And when the sugar cane
trucks went thru town
All that fell down
all you could grab
Was free.

Puerto Rico as
abusement
As absent from your
center of discussion
Puerto Rico as amusement
Puerto Rico free
Puerto Rico as jail
Escape Puerta Rica
like the Maya
Invisible urbanites
take electric
Mayaris
Estudy new ways
not freeways
out of town

MOYERS: To the Europeans it was a rich port, but to you it was a rich door?

CRUZ: It *was* a rich door to me because out of that culture of conquest and slavery we have created a culture that has survived. We have survived the plantations, the hacienda, the forced labor, and *all* of that survival is in the music and the poetry of the Caribbean.

MOYERS: "Estudy new ways / not freeways / out of town." That's a powerful image.

CRUZ: Yes. I think one of the centers of my poetry is agricultural or rural, and in my work there's always a tension between the rural and the urban or the preindustrial and the industrial. There's always a battle against the industrial contamination not only of our island but, by extension, the planet Earth.

I also keep asking whether there's a shared sensibility among all agricultural peoples, all the peasant societies of the planet. If you study the costumes and tools of Czechoslovakian peasants, of Eastern European and Russian peasants, of Guatemalan campesinos and Indonesian farm laborers, there seem to be connections among these world rural communities. I think these connections have always been there, but on top of them there is now a layer of industrialization and urbanhood that stifles the real organic spirit of the Earth. I'm in constant search for that spirit of the Earth in all of my poetry.

MOYERS: Trying to preserve it?

CRUZ: Trying to find it, trying to preserve it, and trying to use it in a literary way.

MOYERS: What about the poems you've done about hurricanes? You sometimes spell the word *H-U-R-A-K-A-N*.

CRUZ: *Hurakan* is the god of the wind, and *hurakan* is, of course, what the English word *hurricane* comes from. A lot of native words have gone into the English language—for example, *barbecue* came from cooking practices in native societies—they're always cooking out in the open, *balbacoa*, which we now know as *barbecue*.

MOYERS: In "Problems with Hurricanes" you connect mangoes and bananas, all such sweet things, with the terror and violence of a hurricane.

PROBLEMS WITH HURRICANES

A campesino looked at the air
And told me:

With hurricanes it's not the wind
or the noise or the water.
I'll tell you he said:
it's the mangoes, avocados
Green plantains and bananas
flying into town like projectiles.

How would your family
feel if they had to tell
The generations that you
got killed by a flying
Banana.

Death by drowning has honor
If the wind picked you up
and slammed you
Against a mountain boulder
This would not carry shame
But
to suffer a mango smashing
Your skull
or a plantain hitting your
Temple at 70 miles per hour
is the ultimate disgrace.

The campesino takes off his hat—
As a sign of respect
towards the fury of the wind
And says:
Don't worry about the noise
Don't worry about the water
Don't worry about the wind—

If you are going out
beware of mangoes
And all such beautiful
sweet things.

CRUZ: Yes, I think of life that way. And sure enough, when Hugo came, my town had a green carpet. The leaves were scattered and breadfruits were rolling everywhere, plantains were everywhere—everybody got free fruit that day. But you can't take for granted the things that are sweet, and you can't keep them separate from what is painful and destructive.

MOYERS: What is it about the Caribbean that has most influenced your poetry?

CRUZ: The climate. The mountains. The contrasts. The tastes of many types of fruits. The coalitions of history that have created an international community. The racial blendings. The many ways people look. All the gestures of the human race, coming together. All the combinations—the different eyes, noses, mouths, lips, hair. The musics that have merged—a guitar next to a drum, Spanish medleys with African rhythms, the feel for *all* those rhythms simultaneously. This is Caribbean society. It's not so much multicultural as it is multiracial. It's three races, one culture. *That* is the Caribbean.

MOYERS: And what does poetry from the Caribbean bring to the mainland?

CRUZ: It brings a language which is still connected to agriculture and to nature in ways that North American poetry is not. Nature still survives in our part of the Americas, and the past is still around, too—Neolithic man with twentieth-century man.

The past shows up in our painting, in our music, and in our literature: the past which doesn't go away, the past which is going to be in the future. In Mexico, think of pyramids standing next to modern buildings. In Utuado, Puerto Rico, think of pictographs in the rocks. Think of the first books, the first letters, the first signs, the first pictures. Think of poetry in rocks. To see the true Puerto Rican literature you'd have to go out there and bring those rocks into the classroom: "Here, look at this sign, this symbol which was done thousands of years ago and which is still present."

MOYERS: Aren't the people coming to the United States from the Caribbean leaving behind that past?

CRUZ: The Caribbean is *always* in transit. I try in my poetry to capture the past and hold it. I don't write so much about my own personal biography. I write about myself as a Caribbean man, a man within a larger tapestry; and I try to see the connections between everything—between myself and history. By explaining myself to myself, maybe other people can also see themselves.

MOYERS: I like that. "Explaining myself to myself." That's what the poet does.

CRUZ: Very often. That's the purpose of the poet—to throw light on his or her individual situation within a human society.

MOYERS: You said the other day that "poetry is God's music."

CRUZ: Yes, I think poetry is like a sixth sense because not all of it comes from the outside. We hear it deep inside, where we combine everything that we get from our five senses. The poem goes back outside and exposes portions of the world, connections between things. Poetry gives us revelations, flashes, which illuminate those things which were mysterious to us.

Through language we reveal the embroidery of our lives and our culture. It's like capturing what has been occulted. In its cadences language exposes us to its mysteries. It helps us understand where we are standing, our local place and how we got there.

Jimmy Santiago Baca, Victor Hernández Cruz

RITA DOVE

Rita Dove is the first African American to be designated poet laureate of the United States—and, at forty-one, the youngest person ever to hold that position. In the role (October 1993–September 1995) she has brought new voices and audiences for poetry to the nation's capital and vigorously promoted poetry across the country. Her poems in *Thomas and Beulah,* about imagined moments in the lives of her maternal grandparents, won the Pulitzer Prize in 1987. She teaches at the University of Virginia.

MOYERS: How is life as our poet laureate?

DOVE: Very hectic but extremely gratifying. Even more people than I had hoped are interested in poetry—I've got letters backed up to the ceiling from all kinds of people and from students of all ages. People often simply want to know where they can find poetry.

MOYERS: I can imagine Thomas Jefferson doing a double take upon finding you the poet laureate sitting here in the Jefferson Building at the Library of Congress, which houses his original library. You must know that he felt blacks were innately incapable of writing poetry. He even said of Phillis Wheatley, the black female poet, that her poems were below the dignity of criticism.

DOVE: Yes. It's troublesome to read those words and then to read other words of Jefferson's which really make a wonderful case for the quality of all men. It's a paradox I've been wrestling with, but he was a man of his time—in the world in which he lived blacks were commonly thought to be inferior. It may be a blind spot, one that enabled him to lead the life he wanted to lead.

MOYERS: Slaves were his economic base.

DOVE: He could not have run Monticello and he could not have built the University of Virginia.

MOYERS: If Jefferson were here today, which poem would you read to him?

DOVE: I would read him "Lady Freedom Among Us," which is about his city, Washington, D.C., and which also has something to do with the body politic and with the political person. That poem would be closer than most to what he was comfortable with and knew in his life.

By making us stop for a moment, poetry gives us an opportunity to think about ourselves as human beings on this planet and what we mean to each other.

LADY FREEDOM AMONG US

don't lower your eyes
or stare straight ahead to where
you think you ought to be going

don't mutter *oh no*
not another one
get a job   fly a kite
go bury a bone

with her oldfashioned sandals
with her leaden skirts
with her stained cheeks and whiskers and heaped up trinkets
she has risen among us in blunt reproach

she has fitted her hair under a hand-me-down cap
and spruced it up with feathers and stars
slung over one shoulder she bears
the rainbowed layers of charity and murmurs
all of you   even the least of you

    don't cross to the other side of the square
don't think *another item to fit on a tourist's agenda*

consider her drenched gaze   her shining brow
she who has brought mercy back into the streets
and will not retire politely to the potter's field

having assumed the thick skin of this town
its gritted exhaust its sunscorch and blear
she rests in her weathered plumage
bigboned   resolute

don't think you can ever forget her
don't even try
she's not going to budge

no choice but to grant her space
crown her with sky
for she is one of the many
and she is each of us

MOYERS: You wrote that one after the statue of Lady Freedom was removed for cleaning and then brought back by helicopter to her place atop the Capitol Building right across from where we're sitting. That was in—

DOVE: In September 1993—about a month before the statue was brought back. Lady Freedom had been haunting me—sitting in the parking lot looking forlorn—so when the historian of Congress asked me if I would like to say a few words at the ceremony for her reinstallation I thought, "I have more than a few words to say."

MOYERS: What do you hope we'll take away from that poem?

DOVE: I would like us to think more deeply about freedom and how it affects the way human being relates to human being. That's why I wanted us to experience Lady Freedom as a human being—if we saw someone like her on the street, would we shy away from her obvious idealism and sense of herself? Hence the poem's comparisons to homeless people, who remind us that we are in this together. We really can't just imagine these people and think, "I've got my life and I'm going to keep going." They remind us that we're all connected.

MOYERS: So is Washington any place for a poet to be?

DOVE: Every place is a place for a poet to be, and every town needs its poets. Washington is a marvelous mix of contradictions in people. It's a town with beautiful white buildings and incredible slums. I find it exciting, but I also often find it indifferent to everyday life—reflected, for example, in the immense violence in this city and also in this thick skin that doesn't want to admit it or do anything about it.

MOYERS: When President Johnson sponsored a cultural festival at the White House the poet Robert Lowell denounced the Vietnam War and rebuked the president. LBJ threw up his hands and said, "I don't want anything to do with any poets. Don't bring me any poets." What does poetry have to say to power?

DOVE: By making us stop for a moment, poetry gives us an opportunity to think about ourselves as human beings on this planet and what we mean to each other. In that way, poetry becomes a voice to power that says, "Power is not the end-all or the be-all." Equally important is the connection poetry emphasizes of human being to human being: what *are* we doing to make the lives of everyone better, and not just materially but spiritually as well? I think that's why poetry has often been considered dangerous.

MOYERS: It seems to me that almost alone in our society poets exist to tell the truth, the one commodity in this town that politicians prefer in short supply.

DOVE: Truth can be difficult and slow. I think the American people want the truth, and they know that very often they aren't getting it, not only in politics but in the kind of entertainment they're being fed. There's this incredible longing to find something that really matters and that really helps us in our lives.

MOYERS: You told some teachers at the Dodge Poetry Festival that you wrap yourself in prose, but in poetry you get pulled into a well. I think many of us yearn to write poetry, but I for one can never find the well.

DOVE: It takes patience and when you find the well, or when the well finds you—and sometimes that's the case—it can be very frightening because the well pulls you down into yourself in a way that threatens your ability to communicate.

MOYERS: "The well" is the unconscious?

DOVE: Partly, but it's all the extraneous thoughts and all the connections that make up our interior life while on the surface we go about our daily outward lives. It's all the questions we don't ask ourselves because asking them means possible paralysis, questions like, "Who am I and who are human beings? What is our purpose? How do we fit into the universe?"

The well is a way of talking about time, too. We tend to think about time as something that we've got to get through—we chart it, slot it out, then we go through the day. But there's another kind of time that exists in us: the time of our entire lives, the things that we see every day that remind us of something in our childhood, the connections that we can see between our lives and history—that other people had dreams and ambitions and also lived and walked these same streets. Seeing one's own image reflecting up out of that well pulls us into a quieter space.

MOYERS: How did the associations in "Canary" come about?

CANARY

FOR MICHAEL S. HARPER

Billie Holiday's burned voice
had as many shadows as lights,
a mournful candelabra against a sleek piano,
the gardenia her signature under that ruined face.

(Now you're cooking, drummer to bass,
magic spoon, magic needle.
Take all day if you have to
with your mirror and your bracelet of song.)

Fact is, the invention of women under siege
has been to sharpen love in the service of myth.

If you can't be free, be a mystery.

DOVE: Jazz musicians often referred to the female vocalist as the canary, and
I've always been a big fan of Billie Holiday. For me, she embodies the notion of the
singing bird in a cage because she was this exquisite, consummate musician and stylist
and also a woman of incredible grace and pride who through her life was forced to
endure many indignities. Because she was black there was no bathroom for her in the
clubs when she toured, and because no hotels accepted blacks she had to stay in private
homes. Yet through it all she maintained an amazing dignity as if to say, "I know that I
am worth something."

MOYERS: There's a powerful line in that poem, "the invention of women
under siege/ has been to sharpen love in the service of myth."

DOVE: It's the idea that women who were denied power and who had no
access to power for so many years used what they had—their wiles, whatever—to gain
some measure of dignity and control. In fact, they played up to the myth of what women
were supposed to be—delicate, something to be worshiped—in order to gain respect.
But Holiday took it another turn: by her very *presence* she demanded respect; she de-
manded her pedestal while showing that she was tough, too.

MOYERS: The women in "The Island Women of Paris" who were from the
colonies of France in a sense turned the empire upside down just by being quintessen-
tially feminine.

THE ISLAND WOMEN OF PARIS

skim from curb to curb like regatta,
from Pont Neuf to the Quai de la Rappe
in cool negotiation with traffic,
each a country to herself
transposed to this city
by a fluke called "imperial courtesy."

The island women glide past held aloft
by a wire running straight to heaven.
Who can ignore their ornamental bearing,

turbans haughty as parrots,
or deft braids carved into airy cages
transfixed on their manifest brows?

The island women move through Paris
as if they had just finished inventing
their destinations. It's better
not to get in their way. And better
not look an island woman in the eye—
unless you like feeling unnecessary.

DOVE: Exactly. Oh, those island women! When I first saw them in the streets of Paris I thought, "Yes, that's the way *all* of us should walk. We should all be so proud to exist in our skins, as if to say; 'Isn't it amazing that human beings are walking on the face of this earth!'" Their natural sense of themselves and their worth as human beings reminded me of how often many of us actually seem apologetic for existing.

MOYERS: What is their sense of "destination," as you call it?

DOVE: It's a destination that *they* determine. They never seem to be going somewhere because someone sent them there. They invent their destinations themselves.

MOYERS: You went to Europe in—

DOVE: In 1974, when I was just out of college.

MOYERS: And the experience changed you?

DOVE: It had an incredible impact on me. I had never been west of the Mississippi, so making this big trip alone—I was there for a year on a Fulbright scholarship—meant that I had to get some sense of myself to keep from being lost. When for the first time I could look back and see the United States through different eyes, I began to stop taking for granted that what I heard about our foreign policies was necessarily the truth. Being in Germany for a year and intimately in contact with another language sharpened my appreciation for my own language—what it could do, and what I hadn't asked it to do for me.

MOYERS: Your poems suggest you visited some of the old battlefields of the two world wars.

DOVE: The first time I was in Europe I visited concentration camps and World War II battlefields. Since then I've visited a lot of battlefields where black soldiers fought during World War I. I was intrigued by the great irony that these men who wanted to fight in the war to make the world safe for democracy—as World War I was touted—could not find a place for themselves in the United States Army, so they fought under French command. It is incredibly ironic that Americans who distinguished themselves brilliantly in World War I could not fight under their own flag in this war for democracy.

ALFONZO PREPARES TO GO OVER THE TOP

(BELLEAU WOODS, 1917)

"A soldier waits until he's called—then
moves ass and balls up, over
tearing twigs and crushed faces,
swinging his bayonet like a pitchfork
and thinking *anything's better*
than a trench, ratshit
and the tender hairs of chickweed.
A soldier is smoke
waiting for wind; he's a long corridor
clanging to the back of a house
where a child sings
in its ruined nursery . . .
                    and Beauty is the
gleam of my eye on this gunstock and my spit
drying on the blade of this knife
before it warms itself in the gut of a Kraut.
Mother, forgive me. Hear the leaves? I am
already memory."

MOYERS: Was Alfonzo a real person?

DOVE: Yes, there was a real Alfonzo who fought in the battle of Belleau Woods. I tried very carefully to have authentic names to set these men in place and then to imagine what they could have been thinking at that moment. I'm still working on some of those poems.

MOYERS: You write that "A soldier is smoke / waiting for wind"—here one moment and gone the next. The anguish is palpable.

DOVE: Yes, it's true. Those poems were terribly difficult to write, and they sadden me immensely. Every time I work on them I get sad again. I had to go back to the battlefields because I was worried about not ever having had that experience, and yet I fervently believe that we can relate to experiences that we never could have had. In going back to the fields themselves, I thought of what Toni Morrison says in *Beloved,* "The 'thought picture' of what happened in a place is still out there. It's as if the action is still going on: if you stand very quietly you know they're still there; you just can't see them." That's how I felt walking through some of those battlefields.

MOYERS: The realities of trench warfare—the balls and ass and ratshit— may not be what people expect at a poetry festival. You make it clear, though, that the real obscenity is not in the words but in the trench warfare and in the black Americans having to fight under a foreign flag in order to serve their own flag.

DOVE: Yes, that's true. I also wanted to show that poetry doesn't have limits. Poetry is about life, and that means *all* of life—not only the roses but the trenches also.

MOYERS: One of the poems you read at the Dodge Festival was so physical that it caused a stir in the audience, "After Reading *Mickey in the Night Kitchen* for the Third Time Before Bed." That poem is not easy for some to hear.

AFTER READING *MICKEY IN THE NIGHT KITCHEN* FOR THE THIRD TIME BEFORE BED

I'M IN THE MILK AND THE MILK'S IN ME . . . I'M MICKEY!

My daughter spreads her legs
to find her vagina:
hairless, this mistaken
bit of nomenclature
is what a stranger cannot touch
without her yelling. She demands
to see mine and momentarily
we're a lopsided star
among the spilled toys,
my prodigious scallops
exposed to her neat cameo.

And yet the same glazed
tunnel, layered sequences.

She is three; that makes this
innocent. *We're pink!*
she shrieks, and bounds off.

Every month she wants
to know where it hurts
and what the wrinkled string means
between my legs. *This is good blood*
I say, but that's wrong, too.
How to tell her that it's what makes us—
black mother, cream child.
That we're in the pink
and the pink's in us.

DOVE: No, and it's not easy for me to read either, and yet I think it's absolutely necessary to talk about these things, particularly in the United States. I think we try to ignore our bodies—in some ways we seem to feel ashamed that we even have bodies—and yet what a marvelous thing a body is. Think of how it works, it's amazing!

MOYERS: Everything private is so public now—soft porn on television, Oprah and Donahue and Geraldo touting the latest techniques of sex. I'm old-fashioned enough to want some experiences kept private. On the other hand, the audience responded warmly—and when my wife, Judith, heard that poem she was reminded that such bonding intimacy between a mother and a child was not possible between her mother and her.

DOVE: Or between *my* mother and me. A lot of the talk today about sex is very exhibitionist and not really rooted in honesty. It's done for attention or manipulation or titillation, but the real point of that poem is not the naming of sexual organs; it is, as your wife understood, the moment of intimacy between a mother and a daughter, something about the body we share which one generation can teach the next. It's also about being able to answer without embarrassment the questions that a child, who doesn't have the sense to be embarrassed, asks about his or her body. To be able to answer those questions without making the child feel ashamed is something I had to learn.

MOYERS: Were you a voracious reader as a child?

DOVE: Oh, I read everything I could get my hands on—the backs of cereal boxes, anything; I had to have something to read all the time. Sometimes it was agony to be at the dinner table. My parents would say "Don't bring a book to the table," because all of us children would drag books along. Our parents allowed me and my siblings to read whatever we wanted to read. Some of my most wonderful memories are of wandering along the bookshelves in our house thinking, "What book am I going to read this time," and not knowing what book it was going to be.

MOYERS: I like your poem "The First Book." What's behind it?

THE FIRST BOOK

Open it.

Go ahead, it won't bite.
Well . . . maybe a little.

More a nip, like. A tingle.
It's pleasurable, really.

You see, it keeps on opening.
You may fall in.

Sure, it's hard to get started;
remember learning to use

knife and fork? Dig in:
you'll never reach bottom.

It's not like it's the end of the world—
just the world as you think

you know it.

DOVE: I was shocked when I visited some classes at my daughter's school and realized that many kids were afraid of reading, that reading wasn't a joy for them and that somehow they were afraid they were going to fail at it—they're much more adept with computers and other electronic media—so "The First Book" is about encouraging someone to discover the joy of reading.

MOYERS: You say reading is like eating.

DOVE: As a child reading was very physical for me—I really felt I was chewing my way through the book, and I also associated reading with eating because I would take snacks and match them to books. The summer when I was twelve I decided to read all of Shakespeare—I didn't make it—but when I began to read the plays, I found I couldn't read them in one sitting, so I would have to get snacks. I remember going through *Macbeth* and thinking that it was so dark and bleak that I should only eat toast or dried bread, nothing extravagant: I got pulled so deeply into that world that I wanted to feel a little like it, too. I was trying to engage all my senses. So it became a kind of game: what snack am I going to eat when I read *Romeo and Juliet*?

MOYERS: You talk as if reading Shakespeare provided pleasure in the same way that delicious food does.

DOVE: Yes, I had this wonderful advantage—no one told me that Shakespeare was supposed to be difficult. No one asked me, "Are you sure you understand that?" I just picked it up and began reading. I didn't understand every word, but I could understand five or six lines here and there, and the language was just so beautiful, it was like going on a ride.

MOYERS: Did your parents insist, "Rita, to succeed you're going to have to give your summers to Shakespeare"?

DOVE: No, but they did push us by saying, "Education is the key to doing whatever you want to do." They always insisted that we did our homework and that we tried to do the very best we could. If we brought home a grade that was less than perfect, the question always was "Did you do the best you could?" So the standard became ourselves.

MOYERS: They were middle-class people in Akron, Ohio.

DOVE: Yes. They were also the first generation in the family to enter the middle class. My father was the only one of ten children to make it through high school and into college. Education provided his way into a middle-class existence. My father had a dictionary next to his chair, and if he didn't know a word whenever he read anything, he'd look it up. So we couldn't go to him and ask, "What does this word mean?" We knew exactly what he would say: "There's the dictionary. Look it up." To keep reading we learned how to use the dictionary.

MOYERS: Did you ever make a bad grade?

DOVE: Oh, yes. I remember flunking a biology quiz. That was a shock.

MOYERS: What happened.

DOVE: Well, I came home and said, "I flunked a pop quiz," and my father said, "You should always be prepared for pop quizzes; they're going to come up all your life." The punishment was my own feeling of having failed myself.

MOYERS: So that explains "Flash Cards." It's about your childhood.

FLASH CARDS

In math I was the whiz kid, keeper
of oranges and apples. *What you don't understand,
master,* my father said; the faster
I answered, the faster they came.

I could see one bud on the teacher's geranium,
one clear bee sputtering at the wet pane.
The tulip trees always dragged after heavy rain
so I tucked my head as my boots slapped home.

My father put up his feet after work
and relaxed with a highball and *The Life of Lincoln.*
After supper we drilled and I climbed the dark

before sleep, before a thin voice hissed
numbers as I spun on a wheel. I had to guess.
Ten, I kept saying, *I'm only ten.*

DOVE: That's my daughter's favorite poem because I made her do flash cards, too, and I had sworn I would never do that to a child. There was stress there for me mainly because flash cards never end, but I didn't realize that they were really preparing me for life, where things don't end either.

MOYERS: When you graduated from high school in 1970 you were a presidential scholar, one of one hundred top high school students in the country. Did you feel that you were destined for something?

DOVE: Not at all. I knew I got good grades, but I just felt that I was doing what everyone wanted me to do. So when I got the telegram that I had been chosen to be a Presidential Scholar, it made no sense to me whatsoever, and I don't think I ever really believed it, even when it was going on.

MOYERS: Was there any pain in your childhood?

DOVE: Oh, sure. I was a very shy child, and I still fight shyness. I was a good student, so there was some pain in school, being teased.

MOYERS: For being good?

DOVE: Yes, and I was also called "brainiac," things like that. I wanted to be popular, to fit in, but I never really fit in because I got those good grades.

MOYERS: Was race ever the source of pain?

DOVE: Yes. There were some incidents involving race. One that I've described in my novel is related to grades as well. It's a moment with a person I thought was a very good friend, a white girl. We usually went home from school together and we played together. I had shown her my report card—I assumed everybody had good report cards, I was not quite with it—but she got angry and called me "nigger." It was a moment when it all crashed in on me. Sometimes you can seem to have a wonderful relationship with someone, but when it comes down to this bottom line, you're in for quite a revelation.

MOYERS: Did you tell your parents?

DOVE: Yes, I told them both. My mother tried to make me feel better by saying, "Well, she's just ignorant anyway," while my father muttered about the stupidity of some people and told me not to talk to her anymore, which kind of bothered me, too. I remember feeling very torn, so I just avoided her from then on.

MOYERS: Had your father's life been hard?

DOVE: Yes, and I didn't realize it at that point. My father kept his trials and tribulations secret from us for many, many years. He had been one of the top students in his graduating class—he had a master's degree in chemistry—and all of his classmates got jobs as chemists with the tire and rubber industry in Akron, but he was hired as an elevator operator. So for years while he was raising his budding family he was ferrying his former classmates up and down on this elevator. One of his professors from the university kept bugging the administration at Goodyear: "This is absurd. You have this incredible student employed as an elevator operator!" Finally my father became the first black chemist in the entire rubber industry.

But I knew nothing of all that until I was in college. When I thought that my father was insisting too much that we do it on our own, my mother would sometimes say, "Your father really means the best for you. He knows what it's like. Just trust me on this."

ELEVATOR MAN, 1949

Not a cage but an organ:
if he thought about it, he'd go insane.

Yes, if he thought about it
philosophically,
he was a bubble of bad air
in a closed system.

He sleeps on his feet
until the bosses enter from the paths
of Research and Administration—
the same white classmates
he had helped through Organic Chemistry.
A year ago they got him a transfer
from assembly line to Corporate Headquarters,
a "kindness" he repaid

by letting out all the stops,
jostling them up and down
the scale of his bitterness
until they emerge queasy, rubbing
the backs of their necks,
feeling absolved and somehow
in need of a drink. *The secret*

he thinks to himself, *is not
in the pipe but
the slender breath of the piper.*

MOYERS: This is the same man who went home in the evening to read *The Life of Lincoln.*

DOVE: Yes, that poem *is* about my father. That he could return home to his children and be a kind man was a lesson for all of us. While we were growing up and very fragile, he gave us a sense of believing that if we studied hard we would get our due. We were aware of discrimination, but we still believed that things were changing, so we had confidence.

MOYERS: That sign above your desk says "One lives by memory, not by truth." What does that mean to you?

DOVE: Memory is untruthful and inaccurate. The memories that inform and haunt us are actually probably very skewed—they aren't exactly what happened so much as how we felt about what happened. So our sense of ourselves is often rooted in how we felt in certain situations, but that's only a kind of truth.

MOYERS: And what we make of our experience, how we interpret it, is an ongoing process?

DOVE: Yes. I think even when we begin to understand how wrong we might have been about a certain situation, we still carry the memory of how we *felt* about it when we thought it happened in a certain way. So what's really strong in us is not truth but memory.

MOYERS: I think it was James Merrill who wrote that one only knows eternity in a grain of sand and one only knows history in the family around the table. Is that why you write so often about your family?

DOVE: Yes, I think we understand history through the family around the table and those who aren't there anymore but who are called in from the past. For example, in *Thomas and Beulah* I call my grandparents in to show how grand historical events can be happening around us but we remember them only in relation to what was happening to us as individuals at that particular moment.

MOYERS: How do you get into their world and into their emotions?

DOVE: Their experiences had to be imagined at some level, and my imagining began with an actual occurrence described in "The Event." My grandmother had told me about my grandfather's coming North as part of a song-and-dance team working on a paddleboat, and about his best friend's drowning in the Mississippi because an island sank. The question for me was, "How did this man, who must have been racked with guilt over the death of his friend, come to terms with his guilt?" So as I was writing these poems I was working toward this sweet, wonderful, quiet man that I knew as my grandfather.

MOYERS: What does writing a poem about kinfolk do for you?

DOVE: I can't imagine living without writing. Writing a poem for me means putting a name to a face, to memories. It means calling up emotions that I don't quite have a handle on, and beginning to understand them a little better by writing about them. But it also means reaching out and connecting with someone else. I think without that it wouldn't be worth it for me, it wouldn't have the same pull—because the final reward is when someone comes up to me and says, "I know exactly what you mean," or "That happened to me, too," or "You know, that could have been my grandmother." To feel that we human beings are more alike than we are different, and that we all have emotions that we can connect with, is the final thrill of writing.

MOYERS: And yet to so many poetry seems an alien experience.

DOVE: I always feel like telling people, "You don't know what you're missing!" Part of my self-appointed mandate as poet laureate is to help people see that poetry is not something above them or somehow distant; it's part of their very lives and it *is* enjoyable.

MOYERS: As a poet, how would you like to change us?

DOVE: I would like to remind people that we *have* an interior life—even if we often don't talk about it because it's not expedient, because it's not cool, because it's potentially embarrassing—and without that interior life, we are shells, we are nothing.

MOYERS: At the White House you read "Parsley" to an audience that included the president and the first lady, the vice president and Mrs. Gore, and many other Washington notables. What is the story of that poem and why did you read it there?

PARSLEY

1. *THE CANE FIELDS*

There is a parrot imitating spring
in the palace, its feathers parsley green.
Out of the swamp the cane appears

to haunt us, and we cut it down. El General
searches for a word; he is all the world
there is. Like a parrot imitating spring,

we lie down screaming as rain punches through
and we come up green. We cannot speak an R—
out of the swamp, the cane appears

and then the mountain we call in whispers *Katalina*
The children gnaw their teeth to arrowheads.
There is a parrot imitating spring.

El General has found his word: *perejil*
Who says it, lives. He laughs, teeth shining
out of the swamp. The cane appears

in our dreams, lashed by wind and streaming.
And we lie down. For every drop of blood
there is a parrot imitating spring.
Out of the swamp the cane appears.

2. THE PALACE

The word the general's chosen is parsley.
It is fall, when thoughts turn
to love and death; the general thinks
of his mother, how she died in the fall
and he planted her walking cane at the grave
and it flowered, each spring stolidly forming
four-star blossoms. The general

pulls on his boots, he stomps to
her room in the palace, the one without
curtains, the one with a parrot
in a brass ring. As he paces he wonders
the little knot of screams
is still. The parrot, who has traveled

all the way from Australia in an ivory
cage, is, coy as a widow, practicing
spring. Ever since the morning
his mother collapsed in the kitchen
while baking skull-shaped candies
for the Day of the Dead, the general
has hated sweets. He orders pastries
brought up for the bird; they arrive

dusted with sugar on a bed of lace.
The knot in this throat starts to twitch;
he sees his boots the first day in battle
splashed with mud and urine
as a soldier falls at his feet amazed—
how stupid he looked!—at the sound
of artillery. *I never thought it would sing*
the soldier said, and died. Now

the general sees the fields of sugar
cane, lashed by rain and streaming.
He sees his mother's smile, the teeth
gnawed to arrowheads. He hears
the Haitians sing without R's
as they swing the great machetes:
Katalina, they sing, *Katalina,*

mi madle, mi amol en muelte. God knows
his mother was no stupid woman; she
could roll an R like a queen. Even
a parrot can roll an R! In the bare room
the bright feathers arch in a parody
of greenery, as the last pale crumbs
disappear under the blackened tongue. Someone

calls out his name in a voice
so like his mother's, a startled tear
splashes the tip of his right boot.
My mother, my love in death.
The general remembers the tiny green sprigs
men of his village wore in their capes
to honor the birth of a son. He will
order many, this time, to be killed,

for a single, beautiful word.

D O V E : "Parsley" is based on an historical event that occurred in the Dominican Republic in 1937. Rafael Trujillo, the dictator at the time, selected for execution twenty thousand Haitian blacks who worked side by side in the cane fields with Dominicans. He did this in a very bizarre and ultimately creative manner. The Haitians spoke French Creole, in which—unlike Spanish—you don't roll the r, so the r sounds like an l. Trujillo had all the cane workers pronounce *perejil*, Spanish for parsley. Those who could not pronounce it correctly—whoever said *"pelejil"* instead of *"perejil"*—were Haitian and were executed. That he had them pronounce their own death sentence, this ultimate little twist in cruelty, was what haunted me. The poem deals with that and with how he arrives at that moment.

Here I was, at the White House at the highest administrative level of power, and I wanted to talk about the uses to which power has been put. I also wanted to talk about how necessary it is in all avenues of life to be able to imagine the other person. In that poem, I've tried to help us to understand how Trujillo arrived at this word—not just to say that he was a horrible dictator, but to make us realize that evil can be creative.

MOYERS: What was the reaction when you read this at the White House?

DOVE: It was an after-dinner event, and when I introduced the poem there was a moment of tension in the room—I think people were worried that this was not going to be politically appropriate, but that changed fairly rapidly. Having been invited to the White House, I felt that I should really show what poetry could do and that, in fact, it covers many different aspects of human joy and triumph and tragedy. That was one reason for reading this poem, and in the end I think it was very well received.

MOYERS: So poetry does have something to say to power?

DOVE: Oh, yes, I think it does.

© William Abranowicz

CAROLYN FORCHÉ

Carolyn Forché is at home with poetry and politics. Her experience as a human rights advocate and journalist for Amnesty International in El Salvador forged her poetry of witness and produced the poems in *The Country Between Us*, which won the Lamont Poetry Prize in 1981. She has recently collected works by political poets around the world as a poetic testament to the power of remembrance in a century of atrocities. She presently teaches at George Mason University and is director of the Associated Writing Programs.

MOYERS: Let's talk about "The Morning Baking." The joy of poetry shines through it.

FORCHÉ: That poem is about my grandmother from Czechoslovakia, born in the nineteenth century. She wore babushkas and little wire-rimmed glasses, and I remember her as very old and very big. I remember thinking her legs were like elephant legs, they went right down into her shoes. She made up English words all the time because she didn't know English very well. "The Morning Baking" is a poem of love and longing for her.

MOYERS: Was she still living when you wrote this poem?

FORCHÉ: She had died four years earlier. I think the first poems that came out of the depths of my feeling were the poems I wrote for her. My feelings about her were very ambivalent, richly ambivalent because I loved her dearly and because she was ragingly powerful and frightening at the same time. And foreign, from the old country. I think she shaped my soul in a lot of ways when I was younger, and when I first understood what poetry was and what it could be I went back in my heart to her for my first poems.

THE MORNING BAKING

Grandma, come back, I forgot
How much lard for these rolls

Think you can put yourself in the ground
Like plain potatoes and grow in Ohio?
I am damn sick of getting fat like you

Poetry allows the human soul to speak.

Think you can lie through your Slovak?
Tell filthy stories about the blood sausage?
Pish-pish nights at the virgin in Detroit?

I blame your raising me up for my Slav tongue
You beat me up out back, taught me to dance

I'll tell you I don't remember any kind of bread
Your wavy loaves of flesh
Stink through my sleep
The stars on your silk robes

But I'm glad I'll look when I'm old
Like a gypsy dusha hauling milk

MOYERS: "What poetry was and could be?" What *is* poetry?

FORCHÉ: Rilke said "poetry is the natural prayer of the human soul," and that's what I think poetry is because reading and writing poetry enables us to sustain and to extend our capacity for contemplation. I think we're living in an age when the velocity of human experience has so accelerated that perhaps our capacity to sustain contemplation is being eroded. Sometimes I think that certain kinds of human consciousness can become extinct and that we can preserve ourselves by paying serious attention to our language, to reading and writing.

MOYERS: What's the consciousness poetry liberates?

FORCHÉ: I think that poetry is the voice of the soul, whispering, celebrating, singing even. When I was reading and gathering poems written by poets of the twentieth century who had survived conditions of extremity—wars and imprisonment—I prefaced the gathering of these poems with some lines from Bertolt Brecht: "In the dark times, will there also be singing? Yes, there will be singing. About the dark times."

So poetry is the consciousness which gives rise to voice. Poetry allows the human soul to speak. I tell my students that in order to make a poem you must place yourself in contemplative expectation before a blank piece of paper. Put your hand on the paper and your hand will write your way to the poem. I tell them, "You can't think your way to good poems and then write the good poem. Think the bad poem, write the good poem. You have to just keep writing and keep writing until the poem emerges from your soul."

MOYERS: What happens when, as in my case, the hand doesn't get the message?

FORCHÉ: I think there are people who were born able to listen to poetry. And there are other people, like my husband who is a photographer, born able to see the world visually and to see arrangements of colors and light. He's always stopping me and saying, "Look at that light falling on this. And that shadow. And this formal angle." But I miss all of that, for me it's language. Walking down the street, I hear poetry in people's speech. I hear it floating past me, from something someone's saying. It's just something that I notice in life.

MOYERS: You apparently hear the language before it appears. Do you mean it appears to you silently in your consciousness before someone speaks it?

FORCHÉ: I think there are poets who actually hear rhythms before they have words for them, and then the words kind of fall into the poem. But I have more of a visual imagination, I see the poem and somehow I translate it. Maybe that process is a secondary order of poetry, but I took advice from Flannery O'Connor who said you must take it seriously and sit down every day before your writing table and wait for the Muse to come. If you don't keep your appointment, the Muse goes over to the next poet's house and gives that poet the poems. So you wait. You wait for an hour and if you get nothing, that's it, you get up and walk away. But if you sit down, and if you are regular and faithful, you will get your poems. So maybe you need to sit down more.

MOYERS: That's true. But when I do sit down, I'm more likely to have a book in my hand like this one of yours, *The Country Between Us*. What *is* the country between us?

FORCHÉ: It's complicated because that book emerged while I was working as a human rights activist in Central America and in the United States and those poems turned out to be very different from the poems I had previously written. They were still first-person lyric narrative free-verse poems, but I didn't realize how much I'd been changed by my experiences in El Salvador until those poems reflected that change.

The country between us is perhaps the distance between one human being and another, how long it takes one human voice to reach another human voice. It's probably also a reference to El Salvador, which was the country that came into my heart when I was just becoming an adult, and the country which probably shaped my moral imagination. But perhaps it is the United States too, because for me the United States is very complex. It was the people of the United States who all through that war were very concerned and who cared about human rights and responded very favorably to all appeals while at the same time the United States was a government that didn't seem to know how to listen to any of that. So I have two countries in my mind: the country of my people and the country of the government that I knew as I was growing into adulthood.

MOYERS: Your mention of El Salvador brings to mind "The Colonel." It's the poem of yours most quoted in anthologies and most used in classes. How did it come about?

FORCHÉ: I was in El Salvador. It was 1978. Very few Americans who didn't work for the embassy were there. There were a few Peace Corps people, but it was an unusual occurrence for an American to come into the country. I was being taken around and educated about conditions in Salvador by members of Claribel Alegría's family. My presence in the country came to the attention of the military, they were intrigued and wondered if I wasn't also working for the U.S. government because, in a way, everyone thinks that all North Americans there are doing that.

So officers began to want to talk to me. I realize today that they were hoping that the United States would desire their services and pay them for information and intelligence and so on, but I didn't know that then. It became clear to me, however, as I was having these meetings with military officers, that they were very upset about the human rights policy of President Carter. They believed that the United States was being hypocritical in its relation to them: they were still getting support, but they were embarrassed because they were being insulted internationally about their human rights behavior.

On this occasion I was taken to dinner at a very high-ranking officer's house and I don't think he realized that what I said about myself was true—I really *was* just a twenty-seven-year-old American poet. He got a little intoxicated and angry, and he wanted to send a message to the Carter administration. He wanted *me* to go back to Washington and tell President Carter, "We've had enough of this human rights policy," and his actions were his way of demonstrating his contempt.

THE COLONEL

What you have heard is true. I was in his house. His wife carried a tray of coffee and sugar. His daughter filed her nails, his son went out for the night. There were daily papers, pet dogs, a pistol on the cushion beside him. The moon swung bare on its black cord over the house. On the television was a cop show. It was in English. Broken bottles were embedded in the walls around the house to scoop the kneecaps from a man's legs or cut his hands to lace. On the windows there were gratings like those in liquor stores. We had dinner, rack of lamb, good wine, a gold bell was on the table for calling the maid. The maid brought green mangoes, salt, a type of bread. I was asked how I enjoyed the country. There was a brief commercial in Spanish. His wife took everything away. There was some talk then of how difficult it had become to govern. The parrot said hello on the terrace. The colonel told it to shut up, and pushed himself from the table. My friend said to me with his eyes: say nothing. The colonel returned with a sack used to bring groceries home. He spilled many human ears on the table. They were like dried peach halves. There is no other way to say this. He took one of them in his hands, shook it in our faces, dropped it into a water glass. It came alive there. I am tired of fooling around he said. As for the rights of anyone, tell your people they can go fuck themselves. He swept the ears to the floor with his arm and held the last of his wine in the air. Something for your poetry, no? he said. Some of the ears on the floor caught this scrap of his voice. Some of the ears on the floor were pressed to the ground.

MAY 1978

MOYERS: He *literally* poured ears on the floor?

FORCHÉ: He poured them on the table. I learned later there were a number of officers who had a practice of keeping bounty of various kinds. Some Vietnam veterans also told me that had happened in Vietnam, so what I saw was not as uncommon as I thought when I first saw it. I remember feeling sick and dizzy, but nothing happened to me. Everything was fine. His wife brought us out into the living room for coffee and tried to make everything better because she felt the dinner party was ruined. But he was not the worst man I met, not even the worst officer. In fact, this officer tried to warn priests when they were in danger.

MOYERS: "Some of the ears on the floor were pressed to the ground." Are they listening to something?

FORCHÉ: I'm happy you know that about the image, because sometimes people are puzzled, they don't understand why I describe in this way. But there's an expression, "ear to the ground," you know the way you can hear a train coming if you put your ear to the ground? I think that when we're writing a poem, sometimes our

associational memory magically makes these connections. There were many such mo-
ments writing "The Colonel."

I thought the moon in the poem was just the moon until someone pointed out that
it seems to be a white lamp shining in a box in an interrogation room. People have
interpreted many features of this poem, but when I wrote it, I was just trying to capture
details so that I would remember. I didn't even think it was a poem. I thought it was a
piece of a memoir that got mixed up with my poetry book. So when a scholar read the
manuscript and said, "This is the best one. This is the best poem," I said, "Oh, no. That's
a mistake. That's not a poem." It took me years to accept it as a poem and not just a
block of memory.

MOYERS: The Colonel, what happened to him?

FORCHÉ: He's dead.

MOYERS: The victims?

FORCHÉ: Dead.

MOYERS: But the poem survived, so for whatever consolation it is, memory
has a chance.

FORCHÉ: Yes. That's the hope.

MOYERS: Had I reported that incident as a journalist, I would have been
quite literal: who, what, when, where, and why. What's the relationship between these
facts as a journalist would report them and the truth that you're trying to reveal?

FORCHÉ: Some writers whom I admire very much say that facts often have
little to do with the truth. What I was trying to do with this piece, as I finally allowed it
to be in *The Country Between Us,* was to acknowledge that something important had
actually occurred. But the poem also contains a truth about the brutality of that situation
which seems to reach deeply into people. When I came back to the United States and
began reading the poem, I noticed that some people were very moved by it and others
were very angered by it. And some people simply didn't believe it, they said it could not
have happened.

There was a fierce denial and yet several years later a reporter for *The Washington
Post* interviewed soldiers in El Salvador and they apparently talked about the practice of
taking ears and all of that. In fact, one of these soldiers read the news story about his
practice of taking ears and was so proud of the story that he actually clipped it out and
laminated it and carried it in his wallet. Because now he was famous, you know, for this.

MOYERS: That's what can happen to a journalist's account. But the poem is a condemnation.

FORCHÉ: It *is* a condemnation. As a journalist, maybe you wouldn't have been able to use the obscenity, and perhaps you wouldn't have been able to quote him directly. But more than that, I don't think it would've happened to you because I don't think the message was intended for the press. It was intended for a quiet communication back to Washington, and unfortunately they told the wrong person. They told a poet.

MOYERS: Lesson for politicians and military leaders: Never talk to poets.

FORCHÉ: Never.

MOYERS: And wasn't it a poet who brought you to El Salvador in the first place?

FORCHÉ: Yes, Claribel Alegría. When I was working as a teacher in San Diego, her daughter Maya was my friend. Maya would always say to me, "My mother's a poet, my mother's a poet. You should meet my mother and read her poems." Well, I thought, everybody's mother is a poet, so I ignored her. Finally one day she brought out all of Claribel's books and she asked, "What languages do you read?" Then I said, "But your mother's a poet!" and she said, "That's what I've been telling you."

There was no English on the table amongst those books. Claribel Alegría's poems had never been translated into English. So I decided that I would bring her into English and I thought, well, I'll just buy the thickest Spanish-English dictionary I can find and simply look up all the words I don't know.

But even though my Spanish was terrible, Spanish was not the problem. The problem was that of course Claribel had grown up in a very different reality. Claribel had grown up under a military dictatorship, and she had witnessed a massacre when she was a child in 1932 in El Salvador. All of this came through in the poems, and I didn't know what was metaphorical and what was literal. I didn't understand that the guitar player's mangled hands were not symbolic, that they were actually mangled.

MOYERS: What about "The Memory of Elena."

THE MEMORY OF ELENA

We spend our morning
in the flower stalls counting
the dark tongues of bells
that hang from ropes waiting

for the silence of an hour.
We find a table, ask for *paella*,
cold soup and wine, where a calm
light trembles years behind us.

In Buenos Aires only three
years ago, it was the last time his hand
slipped into her dress, with pearls
cooling her throat and bells like
these, chipping at the night—

As she talks, the hollow
clopping of a horse, the sound
of bones touched together.
The *paella* comes, a bed of rice
and *camarones*, fingers and shells,
the lips of those whose lips
have been removed, mussels
the soft blue of a leg socket.

This is not *paella*, this is what
has become of those who remained
in Buenos Aires. This is the ring
of a rifle report on the stones,
her hand over her mouth,
her husband falling against her.

These are the flowers we bought
this morning, the dahlias tossed
on his grave and bells
waiting with their tongues cut out
for this particular silence,

1977

FORCHÉ: That is a poem is about a woman whose husband was a very prominent journalist in Argentina. The night of their wedding anniversary they went out to dinner, and after dinner they took a walk along the Río de la Plata and then hailed a taxicab to take them home. When they climbed into the taxicab, they gave the address but apparently somehow the police were in communication with that cab because when they pulled in front of the house her husband was machine-gunned to death and she was wounded in the mouth. She was taken to police detention for twenty-four hours and then so many people in Buenos Aires followed her husband's coffin during his funeral that she was saved, she was allowed to leave the country and go into exile. Elena is a very close friend of Claribel's.

MOYERS: Why a poem about a subject so grim?

FORCHÉ: Because I was a human rights person taking the histories and testimonies of people from all over Latin America who have suffered under dictatorships and political oppression, and sometimes I would be taking these histories in a setting so very different from the story that was being told to me. In this case, a café in a calm European country where I made the mistake of ordering food before hearing a very brutal, very difficult story. So I began not to write about her story but about how her story affected the listener.

One of the things that I believe happens when poets bear witness to historical events is that everyone they tell becomes a witness too, everyone they tell also becomes responsible for what they have heard and what they now know. So the poem began in my puzzlement over the enigma of having a calm, civilized lunch and talking about something as horrible as the twenty-four hours she spent in detention after her husband's murder.

MOYERS: Witnessing is almost an obsession with you, isn't it?

FORCHÉ: I suppose. Yes.

MOYERS: *The Angel of History* begins with an image of a child. "There are times when the child seems delicate," you write. And the witness of that child remains constant throughout these poems, almost like an angel in a frieze overlooking the cathedral where the cardinal is being murdered.

FORCHÉ: Yes.

MOYERS: The child as witness—that's the image.

FORCHÉ: Yes. It's the childhood of humanity, the innocence born within each of us. And then, it is also what we are given to see and to know on the earth and how we are able to respond to this, what we are able to pass on to others, so it has to do with the preservation of memory.

MOYERS: Is the "Angel of History" a child?

FORCHÉ: No, the angel of history actually comes from Walter Benjamin, a German Jewish philosopher, who wrote something called "Theses on the Philosophy of

History." I think he was trying to come to terms with the progression of history and with the piling up of ruins, fragments, broken worlds, broken civilizations, wounded imaginations, shattered minds and hearts, the accumulation of this wreckage and what it meant. He begins with something called "The Angel of History":

> This is how one pictures the angel of history. His face is turned toward the past. Where we perceive a chain of events, he sees one single catastrophe, which keeps piling wreckage and hurls it in front of his feet. The angel would like to stay, awaken the dead, and make whole what has been smashed. But a storm is blowing in from paradise; it has got caught in his wings with such a violence that the angel can no longer close them. The storm irresistibly propels him into the future to which his back is turned, while the pile of debris before him grows skyward.

And Benjamin's final sentence in this passage is "this storm is what we call progress."

So the idea for my angel of history was a tribute to him. Also because I had been doing human rights work in different parts of the world—in El Salvador, in Lebanon, and in South Africa with my husband, a journalist—I began to feel something strange happening to my poetry and to my language and my imagination. There was a kind of shattering or fragmenting, one event slid into the next and interrupted the next, one voice came in after another. I had this idea that while the earth, our planet, might be rocked in its weathers and its winds, maybe every human utterance that's ever been spoken lifts away from the earth and clings to it, too, like a weather of risen words. Then I thought that, as a poet, if I was calm enough and quiet enough and steady enough, I could hear these words and I could write them. That is sometimes how I felt writing this book, just allowing the voices to interrupt each other and letting this symphony of voices be one voice.

MOYERS: There is, in all of these poems, the act or attitude of remembering. Everything, even the future, is haunted by the past, and that's driven home for me in "Elegy" with this beautiful line, "And so we revolt against silence with a bit of speaking." Is this a function of poetry, to give memory a chance?

FORCHÉ: Yes. Yes.

ELEGY

The page opens to snow on a field: boot-holed month, black hour
the bottle in your coat half vodka half winter light.
To what and to whom does one say *yes*?
If God were the uncertain, would you cling to him?

Beneath a tattoo of stars the gate opens, so silent so like a tomb.
This is the city you most loved, an empty stairwell
where the next rain lifts invisibly from the Seine.

With solitude, your coat open, you walk
steadily as if the railings were there and your hands weren't passing
    through them.

"When things were ready, they poured on fuel and touched off the
    fire.
They waited for a high wind. It was very fine, that powdered bone.
It was put into sacks, and when there were enough we went to a
    bridge on the Narew River."

And even less explicit phrases survived:
"To make charcoal.
For laundry irons."
And so we revolt against silence with a bit of speaking.
The page is a charred field where the dead would have written
We went on. And it was like living through something again one
    could not live through again.

The soul behind you no longer inhabits your life: the unlit house
with its breathless windows and a chimney of ruined wings
where wind becomes an aria, your name, voices from a field,
And you, smoke, dissonance, a psalm, a stairwell.

M O Y E R S : Why these images—smoke, dissonance, a psalm, a stairwell?

F O R C H É : The poem was written for Terrence DePres who died several years ago. It's his elegy. He wrote a book called *The Survivor: An Anatomy of Life in the Death Camps,* and he awakened in me an understanding that for us some words would forever resist metaphor. Crematoria would always be crematoria and would never be symbolic of anything else. Ashes, the same. Smoke. Smoke linked to chimney linked to wire linked to crematoria would always be an actual event, particular in history. Tangible and real. These words would resist metaphor in a very definite way.

I was in mourning after his death because he was many things—a friend, a mentor, and a professor—and I wanted to give tribute to him. I imagined two things: I imagined that when he died, he had twelve million souls to welcome him to heaven and that comforted me somewhat. I also imagined that he had gone back to a memorial that he had told me to visit when I was young and in Paris. He had said, "Okay, you're going to Paris. Go to Notre Dame Cathedral, everybody goes there. But don't just go there. Go behind the cathedral, walk across the *quai* where you'll see a black iron gate and a white stairwell. Go down there. I'm not going to tell you what you will find."

So the first thing I did when I got off the bus was to take a cab immediately to Notre Dame Cathedral with my bags, my heavy bags. I went there and found that it was the memorial to the two hundred thousand people deported from France to the camps. The stairwell is that stairwell, leading down below the river.

I pictured him in my heart going there, only he's a ghost now, so his hands—he tries to hold on to the railing and nothing happens, there's no railing for him, he goes right through it. So, in a way, I was trying to tell him "It's okay to be dead. Don't be scared. We love you. We remember you."

MOYERS: Did you start out thinking that *The Angel of History* would be a book, a series of progressive, related poems?

FORCHÉ: One should never be ambitious, but I had this ambition to write a long poem which, when I finally did it, needed to be broken up into parts. This book took me about ten years to write, and it was originally much longer. But it kept compressing, and then expanding again. I didn't really understand this book until maybe the last two years of its coming, and then it shaped itself. One day when it was almost finished, I was walking in my study trying to put away boxes of old notes from this book when a piece of yellow legal paper flew to the floor. I picked it up, and I saw the word "angel" written in my own hand.

I thought, "Oh." I looked at it, and it was a quote I had copied from Paul Valéry years ago. It just fell to my feet and it closed the book. It's how I really see this book because the book does float around. It is a very strange book. But this quote came right to my feet and I picked it up:

> The angel handed me a book, saying, "It contains everything that you could possibly wish to know." And he disappeared.
> So I opened the book, which was not particularly fat.
> It was written in an unknown character.
> Scholars translated it, but they produced altogether different versions.
> They differed even about the very senses of their own readings, agreeing upon neither the tops of them nor the bottoms of them, nor upon the beginnings of them nor the ends.
> Toward the close of this vision it seemed to me that the book melted, until it could no longer be distinguished from this world that is about us.
> —PAUL VALÉRY

Paraphrasing it is not the act of reading a poem. The act of reading a poem is to take it in and to be changed or altered by it.

DONALD HALL

Donald Hall has become one of America's most venerated poets. A graduate of Harvard and Oxford, he began writing poetry as an adolescent. It was when he returned to his family's ancestral New Hampshire farm that he centered his powers as poet and storyteller, producing a procession of poems, plays, essays, short stories, and children's books. He remains active in the small community and serves as deacon in the local church. Poet laureate of New Hampshire from 1984 to 1989 and a member of the American Academy of Arts and Letters, he is married to the poet and translator Jane Kenyon.

MOYERS: Do you know where a poem really comes from?

HALL: I don't know where a poem comes from until after I've lived with it a long time. I've a notion that a poem comes from absolutely everything that ever happened to you. It's almost the secret of being a poet to let everything that ever happened to you be available to the page and the language. For me that usually takes a long time. I've had lines and stanzas come to me as if dictated by the mother ship, but never a whole poem.

You do get inspired. Things come to you that you don't understand, but then the intelligence comes in. I speak of the way I work, at any rate. I need to go over and over a poem, and by the time I've finished it, I know a great deal about it and to a considerable degree where it came from. Some of it, of course, comes from reading, and a lot comes from experience. Part may come from when you were five years old and part from when you were fifty-five years old, and eventually, you may be able to see all these layers of time.

MOYERS: The mystery to me in what you're describing is that the unconscious seems to contain everything that ever happened to us and everything that might ever happen to us.

HALL: Absolutely, and the poem is a way of tapping that source of power and strength and putting things simultaneously together which are apparently quite different. To me this is what distinguishes poetry from most prose, which is linear and sequential. In poetry many things are going on at the same time and these layers of time and density of language make the poem uniquely poetic.

MOYERS: What did you mean when you said that you take this chaos from the unconscious and apply the intelligence to it?

HALL: I say that everything in my poetry is intended because I didn't cross it out. It's typical for me to spend three to five years on a poem, but not working on it every day but maybe every day for six months, then nothing for six months, then starting in again. At the beginning, every draft changes a lot, but toward the end I may spend a lot of time changing a word from the end of one line to the beginning of the next, or changing commas to semicolons, or taking one word out then putting it back in again. I'm searching for something that will be fixed and final and that expresses, as much as it possibly can, this doubleness, this density of the language. I need to work on that poem and sleep on it and sleep on it. I need to sleep on it five hundred times.

MOYERS: What's the longest it's taken you to write a poem?

HALL: Well, there are different ways to answer that. There are poems that I've thought were finished and I've put them away and haven't touched them for five years and then brought them back and worked on them. There are several poems that I've worked on over twenty years. "The One Day" took about seventeen years, but I didn't work on it every day. There were many years when I didn't work on it at all. I knew it was there waiting for me, but I was scared to get to it. It was hard and it had difficult subject matter.

MOYERS: Is it true that you often don't know when you start what you've got or where you're going with it?

HALL: Oh, absolutely. Occasionally you do, but there's no rule. The most exciting thing is when you don't know. The beginning words or lines come to you heavy and freighted with feeling, covered with signs saying, "Pay attention to this. This is important." But you don't know why.

MOYERS: You've said at times you have long and frequent "assaults of language."

HALL: Yes. And then comes the process of working it over which I do every day, on schedule. The process of working it over is the process of understanding the poem.

MOYERS: Talk a little bit about what you think Socrates meant when he said, "There is no invention in the poet until he has been inspired out of his senses and has no mind."

HALL: I think Socrates, or Plato, was busy being superior to poets. This is the same philosopher who kicked them out of his republic because they were not reasonable. What Socrates said *does* describe the onset of a poem, but it doesn't describe the whole act of writing. It condescendingly looks upon the poet as beautiful but dumb. This is another salvo in the old war between the philosophers and the poets.

MOYERS: The war?

HALL: The war is the philosophers saying, "You're not really serious," and the poets saying, "Our way of expression—which is to use the unconscious and inspiration to create this density of language, which communicates from one internal soul to another—is the way of understanding, not your external rational way."

MOYERS: But I don't think of good poets as using dense language. If they did, laymen like me would have no access to it.

HALL: I think you can frequently understand a poem on a visceral level, and have the sense of communication with another human being, without being able to write an essay about it. With time enough and skill enough you can write an essay about it, but that's not the primary act of reading a poem. Paraphrasing it is *not* the act of reading a poem. The act of reading a poem is to take it in and to be changed or altered by it.

MOYERS: When I hear a good poem, I think to myself, "I could have written that," but if I read a tract of philosophy I rarely think I could have thought that.

HALL: I'll grant that difference. That's one thing in favor of poetry for me, too.

MOYERS: You keep notebooks, you write words down, then you leave them for a while to bubble and twist and turn, right?

HALL: I do *everything* to words. I'd be happy to send them to Florida or buy them hot dogs, anything, if they'll just come through. The work is prosaic, sitting at the desk every day and saying, "How can I make this better?" Such work is not, in itself, inspired, but by looking regularly at the poem I get so familiar with it that I'm working on it when I'm asleep. I wake up in the morning, look at the poem I worked on the day before, and see something I had not seen. Something has happened in between, probably sleep work. For that matter, something inside you is always working even when you're awake.

MOYERS: "A successful poem is impulse validated by attention"—your line. Is the attention at the desk there? Is that where you're sweating over it?

HALL: Sure. It's twenty seconds of impulse and two years of attention, but the impulse may be more important than the attention.

MOYERS: Someone has said that your poems are marked by either the pleasure of sound or the spirit of place, and sometimes by both.

HALL: Sound was my doorway into poems, and one of my faults is that I may deceive myself into writing a phrase down that sounds beautiful but doesn't mean a damned thing. When I was twelve, it was Edgar Allan Poe who started me writing poetry, his spookiness, but also his sound. Now Poe's sound is gross to me—it's too obvious, not delicate at all.

I say you read poems with your mouth, not with your ears, and they taste good. When I read a book silently, sitting in my chair, my throat gets tired. My mouth is really working, chewing on these sounds.

MOYERS: Your poem that for me best combines both the pleasure of sound and the spirit of place is "Mount Kearsarge." Is that one of your favorites?

MOUNT KEARSARGE

Great blue mountain! Ghost.
I look at you
from the porch of the farmhouse
where I watched you all summer
as a boy. Steep sides, narrow flat
patch on top—
you are clear to me
like the memory of one day.
Blue! Blue
The top of the mountain floats
in haze.
I will not rock on this porch
when I am old. I turn my back on you,
Kearsarge, I close
my eyes, and you rise inside me,
blue ghost.

HALL: Yes. It's a poem written about where I live now, but it was written when I didn't live here and thought I couldn't live here. So it's a poem saying, "I can never live there, damn it." Reading it now, I realize I was wrong and how wonderful to have been wrong about that.

MOYERS: You wrote, "I will not rock on this porch / when I am old." Why did you think you couldn't live here? Isn't this your ancestral home?

HALL: Right. My grandmother was born here, my mother was born here, and I wanted to live here as a kid, but along about the time I was nineteen or twenty I got practical and realized I couldn't farm here. An attack of realism convinced me that I could not make even the base living my grandparents had, at what used to be called subsistence farming. I wanted to write poems rather than have an apple orchard or strawberry farm, so I gave up the notion of coming here. And then, amazingly, I was able to come back and make a living as a freelance writer when I was forty-six years old.

MOYERS: But by moving back to New Hampshire, weren't you fearful that you might be narrowing your life enormously?

HALL: I had been writing about New Hampshire all along, in Michigan and in England, so when I came back here I thought, "Now I won't be writing out of missing it, so I won't write about New Hampshire anymore." But when I came back, the memories came back, and living in this house full-time was just extraordinary—I'm so close to my dead grandparents—so I certainly found my subject again.

MOYERS: Why did you choose poetry as a way of life?

HALL: I loved it so much. What other reason would you have for choosing poetry? I loved other people's poems and I wanted to make something like what I loved. That's how it started when I was twelve, but I really got serious when I was fourteen and decided I'd be a poet for the rest of my life.

MOYERS: Do you remember one of the poems you wrote at fourteen?

HALL: No, but I remember the first one I wrote as a morbid twelve-year-old reading Poe. It doesn't sound like Poe, but it has morbidity.

Have you ever thought
of the nearness of death to you?
It reeks through the day.
It shrieks through the night.
It follows you through the city
until it calls your name
in monotones loud.
Then, then comes the end of all.

MOYERS: You truly were a morbid kid?

HALL: I think I was. When I was nine years old, maybe three of the Connecti-cut great-aunts and uncles died within a year of cancer, and I remember lying in bed saying a sentence over and over again to myself, "And now death has become a reality." I was a rather literary nine-year-old, I suppose, and vain, writing my own biography: "And for Hall, at the age of nine, death became a reality." But the feelings were real all the same.

I write a lot of elegiac poetry. Poetry is trying to preserve place, and certainly elegiac poetry tries to keep the dead around. Poetry enacts our own losses so that we can share the notion that we all lose—and hold each other's hands, as it were, in losing. When somebody close to me dies, there are poems from the seventeenth century that I go back to, for example Bishop Henry King's "The Exequy." It's his only poem, more or less, and it's for his wife who died young. That poem talks to me across three hundred-odd years. When I make poems I'm consoling myself by making the poem out of loss, but I also have some notion that I'm talking to somebody else at any time now or in the future. The definition of a poem includes readers. I don't write a poem for myself.

MOYERS: It's a very public experience.

HALL: Young people feel as if they were writing for themselves, but that's only the beginning of the poem. When it's completed, the poem is a bridge from one to another.

MOYERS: Your father died in middle age. In *The One Day* you write, "my father drove home / from his work at the lumber yard weeping, / and shook his fist over my cradle: He'll do / what he wants to do." Did that really happen?

HALL: Yes, though his working in the lumber yard is fiction. This was one of the family stories that you grow up with, that create you. I remember being told from an early age how he had come home when I was a baby in the crib and said, "He'll do what he wants to do."

The implied matter is that my father was not doing what *he* wanted to do. He had wanted to be a teacher. The first child of self-made parents—immigrant mother, father who'd gone through fifth grade and had worked like crazy to build a business—my father could never do anything quite right. He had a job teaching for a couple of years—a thousand dollars a year—in a prep school, but he wanted to get married. My mother also taught, but married women couldn't teach. There were no two jobs. To get married he had to quit his teaching job and go to work for his father, the tough self-made man for whom he could never do anything quite right. My father was miserable in the business and he died there. Maybe three years after he went back to business he apparently shook his fist over my cradle and said those words.

When it turned out that what I wanted to do was poetry, he sort of gulped but then stuck with it. After he realized that I would probably be a teacher in order to support my poetry habit, he was pleased because he thought of teaching as the ideal life.

MOYERS: There's a haunting reference to your father in "White Apples."

WHITE APPLES

when my father had been dead a week
I woke
with his voice in my ear
                              I sat up in bed
and held my breath
and stared at the pale closed door

white apples and the taste of stone

if he called again
I would put on my coat and galoshes.

HALL: Yes. I've written about him a great deal. I began that poem shortly after the experience of hearing him, a few weeks dead, call for me. I didn't get out of bed to go see him. It was snowing and he was clearly calling outside by the front door. I was scared to go, and he didn't call again. So I wrote it down and I wrote it and I wrote it.

At first I had trouble with pronouns—the son was a "he" and the father was a "he"—so I changed the child to a daughter. But by making myself a woman I had distanced myself so much from the experience that it had become a phony poem. I published it in *The Times Literary Supplement,* but when I read it I knew it was no good. I had kidded myself and the editors who printed it, so I put it away. Then, years later, I found it again and restored the males, making the pronouns "I" and "he," and wrote it some more.

This is a poem that elapsed over seventeen years, and I still didn't get it right. I had put it away again for about a year, knowing it wasn't right, when one day as I was crossing the yard of my house in Ann Arbor a line came into my head—"white apples and the taste of stone"—with a little tag on it that said it belonged with this poem. I ran up to the attic, reached into a drawer, pulled out this poem, and wrote in "white apples and the taste of stone," which is syntactically disconnected from the rest of the poem and spatially disconnected too. It just stands there in the middle. But I think it gives a visual or imagistic location for a kind of fear. What *is* a white apple? Perhaps an apple made of stone that you break your teeth on, maybe a snowball, but it is certainly *not* nutritious. A white apple is an oxymoron, really. The "taste of stone" reinforces the scary oxymoron of "white apple." But for me, it was a line that came in to fix—to make permanent—the kind of fear I had, and what I was frightened of.

MOYERS: Well, I couldn't figure out "white apples and the taste of stone." Then I thought of a cemetery and the white apples that are sometimes on the frieze of a big mausoleum, and I thought a little boy writing this poem would be thinking about his father lying there.

HALL: You know, this is one of those moments where you find out something more about a poem years after you finished it! That house where I was living backed up to a cemetery. When that line came into my head, I could look out and see the monuments there! I had forgotten all about that. Thank you. That's where it came from, I'm sure.

MOYERS: What did you learn and what are you trying to preserve in "My Son, My Executioner"?

MY SON, MY EXECUTIONER

My son, my executioner,
  I take you in my arms,
Quiet and small and just astir
  And whom my body warms.

Sweet death, small son, our instrument
  Of immortality,
Your cries and hungers document
  Our bodily decay.

We twenty-five and twenty-two,
  Who seemed to live forever,
Observe enduring life in you
  And start to die together.

HALL: That was a poem written when my first child was born, my son Andrew. I may have felt my decay more at twenty-five than I do approaching sixty-five! But when he was born I was shocked by this feeling, which came over me very strongly, that my replacement had arrived.

I worried about what my son would think of this particular poem when he grew up. When he was about fourteen he said to me, "That wasn't really about you and me. That was about you and your father." I think it was. My father was still healthy—he had not contracted cancer—but he died just a year and a half later. He was not a vigorous man, he was an old fifty when my son was born, and perhaps I was worried about replacing him myself. A poem is so often, obviously and correctly, pointing south while at the same time something under it is going north.

MOYERS: Your neighbors tell me you are a regular at church.

HALL: Oh, sure. I don't miss going unless I'm traveling and away. We had a minister when we first came here named Jack Jensen who died three years ago at the age of fifty-seven. In his faith he alternated between a kind of philosophical dryness and a wonderful spiritual dampness. He gave me permission to feel Christian, and to enjoy and identify with what I could, even at moments when I could not give ultimate assent to the organization of the world by Christianity.

MOYERS: "Oh, Lord, I believe. Help Thou my unbelief."

HALL: Oh, yes. Absolutely.

MOYERS: Does writing poetry help you overcome skepticism?

HALL: No, I don't think writing poetry does. I wrote for a long time when I was not a Christian. I think writing poetry is separate from my Christian belief. I was raised a Christian, and I now recognize that I had a yearning for it, in years when I thought I was perfectly immune to it. I used to go to a church in England every Sunday. I lived in a village with a beautiful church and a preacher whom I loved, and I went there thinking that I was immune to the doctrine but enjoyed the experience esthetically. In retrospect, I think I was doing what I've accused a lot of other people of doing— licking the sugar off the pill, being worried about taking the pill: What do you have to do, if you say, "I'm a Christian"? Then when I came back here to this house, we started going to the church I had gone to as a child, and we found in the community of people there—not all the people but enough of them—a kind of hive of goodness.

Doctrine came first from our friend and minister, who, as I said, was sometimes filled with the spirit. When he wasn't, he would talk about what St. Paul said or about his own thinking. So we come from different sides, from an intellectual side—a philosophical and doctrinal side—and also from the side of feeling and identification.

MOYERS: In a little poem that I like called "A Grace" you grieve for the unripe dead. Who are they?

A GRACE

God, I know nothing, my sense is all nonsense,
And fear of You begins intelligence:
Does it end there? For sexual love, for food,
For books and birch trees I claim gratitude,
But when I grieve over the unripe dead
My grief festers, corrupted into dread,
And I know nothing. Give us our daily bread.

HALL: They are the dead whose deaths I particularly regret, who seem to have died before their time. We've talked about my father earlier, and surely he would be one, but there are more recent examples. People rarely seem to me to have lived out their lives and to be finished when they die. When someone I love dies before that time, I regret it—and this is something I reproach myself for. If I accept God's control of the universe I should accept these deaths, and yet I don't. I don't believe that God oversees the fall of the tiniest sparrow in the sky. My sense of the control of a god over human life is minimal, tenuous.

Meister Eckhart says that when we pray for something, we pray to nothing. When we pray for nothing, we pray to something. When we ask for things from God, we are doing less than nothing. I read Meister Eckhart a great deal. He's my favorite mystic or theologian.

MOYERS: Do you read your poems at church?

HALL: I did years ago, but I don't regularly. In the church we sometimes have Old Home Day—a New Hampshire holiday that reflects the diaspora of the old farmers, it's been going for almost a hundred years now—and somebody will play the piano or speak a poem. I might read a poem then. I've read on the Fourth of July and at local churches, not during church but to a kind of assemblage of church people afterwards. I've read at libraries.

MOYERS: What do your neighbors think of having a poet around?

HALL: It's marvelous compared to the colleges and universities. In the university somebody will have a couple of martinis and say, "And how is our great poet today?" It drives you nuts. There's deference, but it's ironic and full of anger, because the way of getting ahead in the university is to write books. If you write books because that's your nature, not to get promoted but because you're a writer, you get deference—and irony and envy with the deference. Around here, I meet somebody and he says, "Nice piece about ye in the papuh." That's the end of it.

MOYERS: Do they ever get the idea that you might be hovering, looking for material?

HALL: Sure. I get teased about it. Teasing is a big thing in the country here. I wrote a prose book in which I invented an abandoned railroad on Ragged Mountain up here, and I get teased about that every day. I remember talking to Gifford Wiggin, who reminisced for me and then as I was leaving said, "You gonna put this in a book?" I said, "Well, maybe, Gifford." He said, "Told ye a lotta lies."

MOYERS: The language in your poems evokes people I knew in Marshall, Texas.

HALL: Good. It *is* about where I live. I love the characteristic turns of humor that belong to different places. I don't know about Marshall, Texas, but in New Hampshire that humor depends upon use of language. I remember a story about my own son-in-law's father, who worked in a lumberyard pulling a piece of chain. Somebody said, "Why's Dean pullin' that chain?" And the boss said, "Did you ever see anybody *push* one?"

Or, "Do you think it's gonna rain?" "Well, it always *has*."

MOYERS: Do you think about death—your own death?

HALL: I always have, but I've been quite ill with cancer in the last few years and now have more reason to think of it. A little over three years ago I had colon cancer and then last year the colon cancer metastasized to the liver and I lost two thirds of my liver. I'm already sixty-four, but my chances for living to seventy are not terribly good. At the moment I have no discernible cancer in me. It's just that, statistically, people with my history mostly don't live very long. I'm likely to get a return of cancer. I have thrown all these organs out of the back of the sled with the wolves following the sled, so I'm going to run out of organs to throw to the wolves before long.

MOYERS: When did you write "Tubes"?

FROM TUBES

I

"Up, down, good, bad," said
the man with the tubes

up his nose, "there's lots
of variety . . .
However, notions
of balance between
extremes of fortune
are *stupid*—or at
best unobservant."
He watched as the nurse
fed pellets into
the green nozzle that
stuck from his side. "Mm,"
said the man. "Good. Yum.
(Next time more basil . . .)
When a long-desired
baby is born, what
joy! More happiness
than we find in sex,
more than we take in
success, revenge, or
wealth. But should the same
infant die, would you
measure the horror
on the same rule? Grief
weighs down the seesaw;
joy cannot budge it."

. . . .

5

"Of all illusions,"
said the man with the
tubes up his nostrils,
IVs, catheter,
and feeding nozzle,
"the silliest one
was hardest to lose.
For years I supposed
that after climbing

exhaustedly up
with pitons and ropes,
I would arrive at last on the plateau
of *Walking-level-*
forever-among-
moss-with-red-blossoms,
or the other one
of *Lolling-in-sun-*
looking-down-at-old-
valleys-I-started-
from. Of course, of course:
A continual
climbing is the one
form of arrival
we ever come to—
unless we suppose
that the wished-for height
and house of desire
is tubes up the nose."

HALL: I wrote that in between the two surgeries. The man with all these tubes in him is not really going to be making these speeches, but he does have a sense of humor. There are five little speeches here, and they're all sort of deathbed speeches. The first one actually is my favorite and the last one's my second favorite.

MOYERS: How have these serious illnesses affected your poetry?

HALL: I'm working more. I always have worked on poetry, maybe three hundred and twenty days of the year, but typically I probably have worked an hour, or an hour and a half. Since the colon cancer I have taken to working two or three hours a day. I'm working on more poems at the same time. I'm probably doing as many drafts as ever, but I'm putting in more hours and I'm finishing more poems now.

MOYERS: What inspired "Ox Cart Man?"

HALL: When we first came back to this house in the fall of 1975 my cousin Paul Fenton told me that story. Paul was a great storyteller. His face would crinkle a little bit and the corners of his mouth would turn up. You'd know he was thinking of a story. So Paul said, "Did you ever hear the story about the fella used to live around here? Every autumn he loaded up his cart," and then told me pretty much that story. At the point where he sells the ox I suddenly realized I was hearing something extraordinary. My spine shivered. I don't know if I knew at that moment that I was going to write about it, but I began the next morning and I took about a year making that little poem.

Of course, it's a yearly cycle poem, and I carried it through, originally. I went through boiling down the sap, shearing the sheep, planting the crops; but Louis Simpson said, "When they know how it's going to end, you've got to cut it off." I said, "Never," and then I did it. When you're running a circle, as a poem for grown-ups, you do the capital "C," and then the reader closes it up and makes it a circle. Otherwise, you're boring. But when I wrote it later for children in a children's book I could go full circle. The five-year-old wants you to fill the circle up.

OX CART MAN

In October of the year,
he counts potatoes dug from the brown field,
counting the seed, counting
the cellar's portion out,
and bags the rest on the cart's floor.

He packs wool sheared in April, honey
in combs, linen, leather
tanned from deerhide,
and vinegar in a barrel
hooped by hand at the forge's fire.

He walks by his ox's head, ten days
to Portsmouth Market, and sells potatoes,
and the bag that carried potatoes,
flaxseed, birch brooms, maple sugar, goose
feathers, yarn.

When the cart is empty he sells the cart.
When the cart is sold he sells the ox,
harness and yoke, and walks
home, his pockets heavy
with the year's coin for salt and taxes,

and at home by fire's light in November cold
stitches new harness
for next year's ox in the barn,

and carves the yoke, and saws planks
building the cart again.

MOYERS: What have you learned about children from their response to your books?

HALL: I love the constantly changing, constantly same audience of five- and six-year-olds who write me letters about the "Ox Cart Man." Every year I go to a good many schools and the questions that they ask about the "Ox Cart Man"—about his way of living, about his way of work, and about making books; the questions go all over the place—always thrill me. When I come out of the classroom or read their letters I feel exalted, made fresh again.

MOYERS: They *want* to create, don't they?

HALL: Again and again when you go to any classroom and start talking about a book or about books in general, kids'll start talking about *their* books. "How long does it take you?" they'll ask, and they want to hear, "It took me two days!"

MOYERS: And when you tell them that some of these poems took seventeen years?

HALL: I hold that back, with the five-year-olds.

MOYERS: Were you admiring of the simplicity and cyclical life of the ox cart man?

HALL: Yes. A life of productive work that sustains itself by expending itself is also the life of a perennial plant that dies down in the fall and comes up again in the spring. Somebody reminded me later of my advice to young writers, "Don't ever hold anything back. Put everything out that can possibly belong in that poem or story. Don't save anything for the next one." That's the only way to work. It's the only way to live, really.

Jane Kenyon, Donald Hall

Ultimately, a poem has an electrical force field which is love.

Joy Harjo

Joy Harjo, who was born to a Creek father and a French-Cherokee mother, grew up in Oklahoma. She says that when she writes, she is often guided by the voice of an old Creek Indian within her. She writes poignantly about her Native American culture—and the stereotypes that have defined it—but her concerns of personal survival and freedom have universal appeal. She often performs her poems—and plays the saxophone—with her band, Poetic Justice. She teaches at the University of Arizona in Tucson.

MOYERS: You told students earlier today that you discovered your language came from "some other place," that it was different from the language being spoken around you as you were growing up. What was that place?

HARJO: I guess you would call it that mythic place—that river ultimately—that is within all of us which is not tapped as often with the general public as it used to be in cultures which had living oral traditions and very vital heroes and heroines. In our time it's tapped by the artists—you could hear it today in the performances as people pulled on that incredible rich source.

MOYERS: How did you discover it?

HARJO: I guess painting first got me in touch with it. I have a full-blood Creek grandmother who was a painter and my aunt was a painter, so I started pulling on this river that way. From the time I was a child I always knew there was something very important that I was given to do, and although I didn't always have the words for it, I knew that I was going to be an artist. I would always say, "I'm going to be an artist when I grow up."

As a child, I had a very difficult time speaking. I remember the teachers at school threatening to write my parents because I was not speaking in class, but I was terrified. Painting was a way for me to do what I felt it was given to me to do. I won all the art awards at school, and I had my work on exhibit from a very young age. After grade school I went to the Institute of American Indian Arts, which at that point was an all Indian arts high school.

MOYERS: Tell me about the first time you wrote a poem.

HARJO: One day in the eighth grade the teacher came in and said, "All right, everyone's got to write a poem." We were dumbfounded—a poem? It turned out there was a state anthology she wanted her students to be represented in, so we all wrote poems. Mine was terrible—I don't remember it—but I did get an honorable mention for a story. The next time I consciously remember writing was at Indian school when I wrote acid rock songs for an all-Indian acid rock band in Santa Fe. I hope none of those survive.

MOYERS: Hardly an auspicious beginning for a poet!

HARJO: It wasn't until I was about twenty-two and a student at the University of New Mexico—I was majoring in painting after starting out in pre-med—that I started listening to poetry and writing my own poetry. It was at that time that I met Simon Ortiz and Leslie Silko and also went to hear Galway Kinnell read poetry—he was one of the first poets I ever heard, and a great love for poetry evolved from that experience.

MOYERS: You have said that when you write, an old Creek Indian enters the room and stands over you.

HARJO: Yes, that does happen sometimes. I think my muse takes different forms, but I have often felt this presence. Sometimes it seems to be a singular presence, and other times it seems to be multiple. I have a very old tie-in, of course, with my father's people—I feel they're behind what I do—but sometimes the presence seems something else entirely. I have a poem called "The Woman Hanging from the 13th Floor Window" that came out of my going to Chicago, the first huge city I had ever been in. I went to the Chicago Indian Center, which struck me as unusually angular and hard, and in the Indian Center I came across a rocking chair which was very round, and which actually *shocked* me in its roundness.

Over the next three years this rocking chair would appear at the edge of my vision. Sometimes I would see different people from the Indian Center sitting in it, and once there were a couple of little girls rocking and laughing and giggling, as little girls will. Another time it was an old man who sat and sang songs to himself in his native language. Finally, this woman came and sat—she had probably gone to Chicago on one of the relocation programs, or maybe her parents had—but she appeared in the rocking chair and she would not let me get up from my typewriter until I wrote the poem. So it's *her* story, and I also consider her a muse of sorts.

MOYERS: You must sometimes feel the presence of ancestors. In your imagination, I mean.

HARJO: Oh, sure I do. You might think I'm crazy, but I *do* feel the presence of such a world. In fact, I have a poem about the presence of those other worlds and the ways in which they interact. I have a sense of *all* those worlds as being very, very alive. In the beginning when I was writing poetry, a poem had definite limits. I started out knowing definitely what I wanted to begin and end with, or one particular image that I wanted to stay with. Now I feel that my poems have become travels *into* that other space.

MOYERS: Many worlds crowd your poems, and contrasting images are juxtaposed—horses and jazz, eagles and airplanes, busy cities and space stretching into the universe—I see *many* different worlds in your work.

HARJO: That's how it *is*. I don't see time as linear. I don't see things as beginning and ending. A lot of people have a hard time understanding native people and native patience—they wonder why we aren't out marching to accomplish something. There is no question that we have had an incredible history, but I think to understand Indian people and the native mind you have to understand that we experience the world very differently. For us, there is not just *this* world, there's also a layering of others. Time is not divided by minutes and hours, and everything has presence and meaning within this landscape of timelessness.

MOYERS: I am fascinated by the story of Black Elk, the Sioux boy who envisions the hoop of his nation and the hoops of other nations, interconnected and interlocking, moving out in a constantly expanding horizon.

HARJO: For me the *illusion* is that we're separate. *That's* the illusion. One of my favorite stories lately is of a phone call I had from a friend who was recently made an official of his tribe in the Southwest. He was ecstatic to be home because he had lived out in the world, and now he was taking part in the ceremonies of his people, praying outside in the moonlight on a wonderful night—very dark and very cold so the sky had that icy clarity that lets you see into it forever. Of course they were praying for their people; but what most Americans and most people don't understand is that they were praying not just for their people, but for *everyone,* for *all* people.

MOYERS: The young people today were obviously touched when you said this morning, "When you pray, open your whole self."

HARJO: There's an incredible relationship of guilt between native people and white Americans. It's an odd relationship. Many white Americans think native people have special spiritual knowledge or know certain tricks. Certainly there are some people who are more in touch with those things than others, but we *all* have prayer. Prayer was *not* just designated to native people, and there are *no* special spiritual qualities designated for native people. Of course, at one point we were *all* tribal people. Europeans were tribal people; all around the world the roots of all human beings were tribal.

MOYERS: That heritage seems particularly alive to you right now.

HARJO: The heritage *is* alive, but I always meet people who think that Indian people are dead. They don't see Indian people even if they are in a roomful of them because Indian people don't look the way they do on TV. Indian people often don't look real because real for many people is Hollywood real. We live in a reality that has been falsely created, and this is especially true for the younger generation. Many people assume that all Indian people lived a long time ago in a certain way and wore certain clothes, so if you don't look like that now, you're not really Indian people; but all cultures change. In our case, the change has certainly been abrupt and shocking, and we *have* had to struggle to maintain the heritage within that terrible upheaval.

Maybe *all* artists now must struggle to understand the connections between the world of heritage and the present world. These worlds certainly do converge and maybe poems are points of convergence or, in some sense, paintings of that convergence. Maybe the artist has always worked to find those connections, but I think the struggle is especially important in these difficult times when the illusion of separation among peoples has become so clear.

MOYERS: You said "illusion."

HARJO: Because I think it *is* an illusion. I think this is more the shadow world than it is the real world. But this shadow world is also *very* real. There are many wars going on all over the world and each of them is very real, and the losses people suffer because of them are very real. I don't mean to deny that at all.

MOYERS: And yet there is something underneath seen only by the artist.

HARJO: Yes, but I think artists always have to include what's apparent and real in that vision, even while we're always searching for what makes sense *beyond* this world.

MOYERS: Memories run all through your poems. The students really liked "Remember." What are *you* remembering?

REMEMBER

Remember the sky that you were born under,
know each of the star's stories.

Remember the moon, know who she is. I met her
in a bar once in Iowa City.
Remember the sun's birth at dawn, that is the
strongest point of time. Remember sundown
and the giving away to night.
Remember your birth, how your mother struggled
to give you form and breath. You are evidence of
her life, and her mother's, and hers.
Remember your father. He is your life, also.
Remember the earth whose skin you are:
red earth, black earth, yellow earth, white earth
brown earth, we are earth.
Remember the plants, trees, animal life who all have their
tribes, their families, their histories, too. Talk to them,
listen to them. They are alive poems.
Remember the wind. Remember her voice. She knows the
origin of this universe. I heard her singing Kiowa war
dance songs at the corner of Fourth and Central once.
Remember that you are all people and that all people
are you.
Remember that you are this universe and that this
universe is you.
Remember that all is in motion, is growing, is you.
Remember that language comes from this.
Remember the dance that language is, that life is.
Remember.

HARJO: Especially because I'm a person from a tribe in the United States of America, I feel charged with a responsibility to remember. I suppose *any* poet in *any* tribal situation feels that charge to address the truth which always includes not just the present but the past and the future as well.

MOYERS: Were you read poems and stories when you were growing up in Oklahoma?

HARJO: I have to recognize that one of my influences is country and western music. When I was very young I used to see my mother sitting at the table with an old typewriter, writing song lyrics for country western songs which she would then send out. Of course I also heard many stories about my family.

MOYERS: Tell me about your family.

HARJO: I suppose the person who influenced me the most was my Aunt Lois Harjo Ball. She was a painter, and I was always amazed by what she could remember. In fact, I've always been amazed at what native people can remember. Native people are generally from oral cultures—they may be able to read and write, sometimes even in their own language, but the expression of the culture is primarily oral. So they're incredibly gifted in memory and in telling stories.

For example, even though she wasn't there, my Aunt Lois Harjo could remember what people were wearing as they walked on the Trail of Tears. She had heard the stories of that terrible walk, and the story of Monahwee who fought against Andrew Jackson in the Redstick War—one of the Creek Wars fought against the move to Oklahoma, but we wound up having to move anyway. Many of the people who fought in that war went down to Florida and became part of the Seminoles, but he wound up going to Oklahoma. Anyhow, she had been with other older Creek people who, for example, described Monahwee's horse and a little black dog that someone else had, things that you would never find in history books.

MOYERS: This was in the 1950s and they were talking about events over a hundred years ago that had not been written down! Did these stories come down through the generations as a kind of poetry?

HARJO: Yes, they *are* a kind of poetry, and I greatly admire the speakers, those who keep the stories alive. My paternal grandfather was a Creek Baptist minister, and although he died long before I was born, I always recognize something of his life in what I am doing. I love the ability to tell a story and to tell it well. Traditionally, wealth was often determined by your gifts in this area. How many songs do you know? How many stories can you tell? And how *well* can you tell them? I think the skills which enabled the retelling of memory were seen as our *true* riches.

MOYERS: Did you think being born of mixed blood was a curse?

HARJO: Sure. There were times when I went through a period of really hating myself for being a mixture of both races. I wanted to be either all of one or all of the other because in some ways I think it would have been easier, but at the same time part of my lesson in this life is to recognize myself as a whole person and to recognize the possibility that because of this mixture I have something that no one else has. We each have our own particular gifts, but I've had to take what has been, to me, a symbol of destruction and turn it into creative stuff. Poetry has given me a voice, a way to speak, and it has certainly enriched my vision so that I can see more clearly.

MOYERS: Many of your poems begin with fear and end with love. Is writing the poem itself a process of reconciliation?

HARJO: I'm aware of being involved with transformation in my work. I spend much of my time with Indian people, and I love my people—I love human beings, period!—but because I've seen a lot of destruction and many of the effects of that destruction—the alcohol, the government programs, and so on—I know that I want to work with all that and encourage the incredible live spirit in my people. I want to have some effect in the world; I want my poetry to be useful in a native context as it traditionally has been. In a native context art was not just something beautiful to put up on the wall and look at; it was created in the context of its *usefulness* for the people.

MOYERS: So what do you hope your poems do?

HARJO: I hope that on some level they can transform hatred into love. Maybe that's being too idealistic, but I *know* that language is alive and living, so I hope that in some small way my poems *can* transform hatred into love.

MOYERS: Language has a healing capacity.

HARJO: It does and I understand that, but I also love *poetry*. I mean, I love what the *words* can do. I love the *language,* the *music* that happens. I'm not going at this because I want something in particular to happen. I do it because I love what I can *make* with it.

MOYERS: What can you tell me about the poem called "I Give You Back"? It's a beautiful poem.

I GIVE YOU BACK

I release you, my beautiful and terrible
fear. I release you. You were my beloved
and hated twin, but now, I don't know you
as myself. I release you with all the
pain I would know at the death of
my daughters.

You are not my blood anymore.

I give you back to the white soldiers
who burned down my home, beheaded my children,
raped and sodomized my brothers and sisters.

I give you back to those who stole the
food from our plates when we were starving.

I release you, fear, because you hold
these scenes in front of me and I was born
with eyes that can never close.

I release you, fear, so you can no longer
keep me naked and frozen in the winter,
or smothered under blankets in the summer.

I release you
I release you
I release you
I release you

I am not afraid to be angry.
I am not afraid to rejoice.
I am not afraid to be black.
I am not afraid to be white.
I am not afraid to be hungry.
I am not afraid to be full.
I am not afraid to be hated.
I am not afraid to be loved, to be loved, to be loved, fear.

Oh, you have choked me, but I gave you the leash.
You have gutted me but I gave you the knife.
You have devoured me, but I laid myself across the fire.

I take myself back, fear.
You are not my shadow any longer.
I won't hold you in my hands.
You can't live in my eyes, my ears, my voice
my belly, or in my heart my heart
my heart   my heart

But come here, fear
I am alive and you are so afraid
                              of dying.

HARJO: It's a poem that I wrote specifically to get rid of fear, and I've gotten more letters from people about this poem than about any other.

MOYERS: Your own fear?

HARJO: Yes, my own fear. Sometimes I feel that it's a fear linked up to generations and that we all carry it. I think of my mother and what she lived through in coming out of extreme poverty, and I understand what's been passed on to me and what was passed on to her and so on. Just as there is a love that gets transmitted, there's probably a fear that gets transmitted, too. So when I come up against it, I sometimes feel that it's a fear engendered in *many* of us. What I'm touching on in this poem is a fear or a force that includes generations of warfare, slaughter, and massacre. I'm thinking especially of America.

MOYERS: And does it work for you?

HARJO: I think it did, and it does. I guess what I'm having to learn is to make fear an ally instead of just an enemy. I'm trying to understand this destructive force and, in some way, to take it into myself. Otherwise, it's always going to be the enemy. If it's out there, it will always be your enemy and it will always be following you around.

MOYERS: I'm curious about poetic construction. In "I Give You Back" you say, "You can't live in my eyes, my ears, my voice / my belly, or in my heart my heart / my heart my heart." You repeat "my heart" four times. Why?

HARJO: Well, it mimics the heartbeat.

MOYERS: Bum, ba-bum, ba bum . . .

HARJO: Yes. I don't know if I did it consciously, but now I can look at it and say, "Well, that's what it does." In fact, you *don't* always know what you're doing.

MOYERS: You *really* don't?

HARJO: Not really. You may consciously do some things, including setting up forms, but when you're involved in the original construction of the poem, you're *not* in your left brain. The beginning of the poem comes out of the *right* brain.

MOYERS: Horses keep appearing in your poems. They're everywhere, horses of all shapes and sizes.

HARJO: They just showed up, and they're very much present. I finally linked their appearance to an experience I had when I was still an undergraduate at the University of New Mexico and Puerto del Sol Press, which was down in Las Cruces, was doing my first chapbook. I was driving my little red truck from Albuquerque to Las Cruces to help with the book and then to do a reading, and somewhere halfway between those cities a horse appeared to me.

I could smell the horse and I could see it at the edge of my vision, and this horse was a very old friend, someone I hadn't seen in a long time. This might sound crazy—I don't know any other way to explain it—but *that's* what happened. I had tears running down from my eyes because it was so good to see this horse whom I hadn't seen in years. I notice that for me certain forces seem to take two or three years before they come into being, and it took about that long before the poems with the horses began to emerge. Now I attribute this book to that horse.

MOYERS: I was intrigued this afternoon when you said, "Every poem is a love poem." In what sense did you mean that?

HARJO: Well, love isn't necessarily romantic. Sometimes love is just hard-core front lines; I don't want to say warfare, but it *can* be very gritty.

MOYERS: In what sense is *every* poem a love poem?

HARJO: You have to be feeling some sort of love to sit down and spend the time involved in the creation of poetry, especially when—as you said—the audience is not as large as it is elsewhere in the world; but I also mean that all poems are love poems in another sense which involves the power of language and the real nature of what a poem is. Ultimately, a poem has an electrical force field which *is* love. In one of my poems, "Day of the Dead," I have a line, "Love changes molecular structure," and that line describes something of what a poem does.

A poem may be about death or destruction or anything else terrible, but I somehow always want it to resolve, and in some manner I want the resolution of that poem to *be* love. When that doesn't happen it makes me nervous. I *do* have to be open for the poem to go its own way, but I think the natural movement of love is an opening, a place that makes connections.

MOYERS: Joseph Campbell said he felt a sort of cosmic energy flowing through those openings at such times.

HARJO: You have to be open in that way to write a poem that really works, and I think there's *always* love involved in the act of creation.

MOYERS: Do you give your students any advice about how to read poetry? I noticed today that faces of the audience would be occasionally bewildered, occasionally rapturous as they were not getting it and then getting it.

HARJO: First of all, it's important to read the poem out loud. Poetry is an oral art—it's *meant* to be spoken and to be read out loud. I have my students memorize at least two poems a semester, which they usually don't like doing, but they come to see why it's important. I've given thought to having everyone memorize a poem a week—for which I'm sure I would not be very popular—but there's such magic in doing that. Then it's important to be willing to let go of your immediate reality and enter the poet's world.

You also have to be able to let go of a particular kind of reason because I think poetry often involves a reasoning more akin to dream reason or nonlinear reason.

MOYERS: Dream reason?

HARJO: What I would call dream reason is a reasoning that I suppose has the shape of a mythic form, a shape that is not particularly logical in terms of Western thought.

MOYERS: Do you wake up and write your dreams down?

HARJO: I write my dreams down quite often because they tell me a lot. I don't usually say that I dreamed a particular image or sequence of events in a poem, but certainly that sensibility comes through. We spend nearly half our lives in that world, and I think we all draw on that material, whether consciously or not.

SHE HAD SOME HORSES

She had some horses.

She had horses who were bodies of sand.
She had horses who were maps drawn of blood.
She had horses who were skins of ocean water.
She had horses who were the blue air of sky.
She had horses who were fur and teeth.
She had horses who were clay and would break.
She had horses who were splintered red cliff.

She had some horses.

She had horses with long, pointed breasts.
She had horses with full, brown thighs.
She had horses who laughed too much.
She had horses who threw rocks at glass houses.
She had horses who licked razor blades.

She had some horses.

She had horses who danced in their mothers' arms.
She had horses who thought they were the sun and their
bodies shone and burned like stars.
She had horses who waltzed nightly on the moon.
She had horses who were much too shy, and kept quiet
in stalls of their own making.

She had some horses.

She had horses who liked Creek Stomp Dance songs.
She had horses who cried in their beer.
She had horses who spit at male queens who made
them afraid of themselves.
She had horses who said they weren't afraid.
She had horses who lied.
She had horses who told the truth, who were stripped
bare of their tongues.

She had some horses.

She had horses who called themselves, "horse."
She had horses who called themselves, "spirit," and kept
their voices secret and to themselves.
She had horses who had no names.
She had horses who had books of names.

She had some horses.

She had horses who whispered in the dark, who were afraid to speak.
She had horses who screamed out of fear of the silence, who
carried knives to protect themselves from ghosts.
She had horses who waited for destruction.
She had horses who waited for resurrection.

She had some horses.

She had horses who got down on their knees for any saviour.
She had horses who thought their high price had saved them.
She had horses who tried to save her, who climbed in her
bed at night and prayed as they raped her.

She had some horses.

She had some horses she loved.
She had some horses she hated.

These were the same horses.

MOYERS: You said today you didn't like to talk about "She Had Some
Horses." Why is that?

HARJO: I suppose because in some sense the material in that poem seems to me more unconscious than conscious. People always ask me, "What do the horses *mean*?" and "Who *are* the horses?" I see the horses as different aspects of a personality which are probably within anyone. We *all* have herds of horses, so to speak, and they can be contradictory. Those contradictions are a part of me: "She had some horses she loved. / She had some horses she hated. / These were the same horses." That ending probably comes out of dealing with the contradictory elements in myself, as I feel them. At times it's been warfare, sometimes *open* warfare, but other times you finally just have to say, "Hey, let's stop this. Let's see what we can do together."

MOYERS: One of my favorites, "Skeleton of Winter," seems different from those you read today. This is one of the first of your poems that I read, and the line I like most is "I am memory alive." Do we even know these voices that are speaking to us?

SKELETON OF WINTER

These winter days
I've remained silent
as a whiteman's watch
keeping time
         an old bone
empty as a fish skeleton
at low tide.
It is almost too dark
         for vision
these ebony mornings
but there is still memory,
the other-sight
and still I see.

Rabbits get torn under
cars that travel at night
but come out the other
side, not bruised
breathing soft
like no fear.

And sound is light, is
movement. The sun revolves
and sings.

There are still ancient
symbols
       alive
I did dance with the prehistoric horse
years and births later
near a cave wall
late winter.

A tooth-hard rocking
in my belly comes back,
something echoes
all forgotten dreams,
           in winter.

I am memory alive
           not just a name
but an intricate part
of this web of motion,
meaning: earth, sky, stars circling
my heart

       centrifugal.

HARJO: No, we don't, and I believe there's another whole way of education that can put us in touch with that world which, to me, is immensely rich. I mean, talk about wealth! That world is the source of real wealth, and people are so hungry for those voices and what they have to tell us. I think what Joseph Campbell was showing us in his study of myths is that those voices are who we *are*.

MOYERS: "I am memory alive." That's what *you* are.

HARJO: That's what we *all* are.

Joy Harjo, Mary TallMountain

MICHAEL S. HARPER

Michael S. Harper writes about the immediate circle of his family but enlarges the definition of *kin* to embrace personalities from the past as varied as Frederick Douglass and Bessie Smith. Long influenced by the oral traditions of jazz and the blues, his poems are rhythmic compositions intended for the voice. A native of Brooklyn and the first poet laureate of Rhode Island, he teaches at Brown University, and is a founding member of the African Continuum in St. Louis.

MOYERS: I enjoyed hearing you read poems to music last night. What is it like to do that?

HARPER: The first thing you have to do is catch the cadence. You better listen to the base line, to what the string instruments are doing, so that you can catch the rhythm and then you have to tune out some things. For example, the drums have a certain kind of prominence which can sometimes break your concentration. So what you're looking for is a space to enter, and you need the rhythmic line to figure that out. It's a matter of waiting for an opening rather than just rushing into what's happening. It's very much like a conversation.

MOYERS: Jazz is like that—back and forth—very often an exchange with yourself.

HARPER: Yes, very much so. When you're working with a group, you're never the only story, and the soloist always has a special responsibility to the group because the group is the cushion that allows you to improvise and to solo. The group gives you signals and the conversation is ongoing because musicians are always talking to one another. The problem is that sometimes people don't always understand what the *tone* of the conversation is, but that happens to all of us in life, too.

MOYERS: In the workshop yesterday morning you said that the most important thing in a poem is silence.

HARPER: Yes. You know, *all* voids are not to be filled. You have to learn when to lay out because some space has to be left there to resonate. It is often the *absence* of sound, what is *not* going on, that people hear because so much has to do with measure, with what is said and with what is not said.

The job of the poet is to tell the truth no matter what.

MOYERS: In poetry as well as music, rhythm itself becomes a kind of language.

HARPER: Yes, rhythm *does* become a kind of language for me. So much of jazz music in particular depends on phrasing, and I have a kind of inner dynamic in my own compositional time, so when I'm writing a poem I'm completely wide open as to what my options might be. At that point I'm not concerned about audience or anything else. It is strictly a compositional moment, where the phrasing itself is entirely prominent and you experience it as a certain kind of blossoming. I only have that when I'm composing, not when I'm performing.

MOYERS: Even in the improvisation, there is, of necessity, some loyalty to structure, to rule, to the underlying pattern.

HARPER: Always.

MOYERS: Many kids don't understand that. They think, "All I have to do is put sounds together."

HARPER: Yes, everyone needs experience. Musicians build up a repertoire, tunes they just know, and that knowledge allows you to improvise because you're never creating out of a vacuum. So respect is shown in the willingness and the ability to play in the idiom of a master person who has gone before you, and not to violate the trust. Music is dynamic, and it's always building on something. You're *never* starting at ground zero. Somebody took you to the place where you now are.

For example, today is John Coltrane's birthday—he was born in 1926 and he died in 1967—so when I got in the car this morning I said, "Turn on 90.1 in Philadelphia." The driver said, "What are we doing that for?" I said, "Because today's Trane's birthday and he spent a lot of time in Philadelphia." He turned it on and after two bars I said, "That's 'Naima,'" He looked at me: "You really *know* this music don't you?" I said, "I *live* this music."

MOYERS: You *live* this music. Art and entertainment—music and poetry— the stuff of life.

ELVIN'S BLUES

Sniffed, dilating my nostrils,
the cocaine creeps up my
leg, smacks into my groin;
naked with a bone for luck,

I linger in stickiness,
tickled in the joints;
I will always be high—

Tired of fresh air,
the stone ground bread,
the humid chant of music
which has led me here,
I reed my song:

"They called me the black
narcissus as I devoured
'the white hopes'
crippled in their inarticulate
madness,
Crippled myself,
Drums, each like porcelain
chamber pots, upside down,
I hear a faggot insult my
white wife with a sexless grin,
maggots under his eyelids,
a candle of my fistprint
breaks the membrane of his nose.
Now he stutters."

Last Thursday, I lay with you
tincturing your womb
with aimless strokes I could not feel.
Swollen and hard the weekend,
penitent, inane
I sank into your folds,
or salved your pastel tits,
but could not come.

Sexless as a pimp
dying in performance
like a flare gone down,
the tooth of your pier
hones near the wharf.

The ocean is breathing,
its cautious insomnia—
driven here and there—
with only itself to love.

FOR ELVIN JONES

HARPER: I talked this morning about the relationship between perform-
ance and entertainment with an illustration from a poem called "Elvin's Blues," which is
a dramatic monologue. Now, most people don't know it's a dramatic monologue because
they're assuming that something in a particular idiom associated with black speech
doesn't have any formal requirements. So I said in the introduction, "I learned this tech-
nique from Robert Browning—he's not my cup of tea, but he was a master technician."
Out of concern for the monologue and in the interest of mastering a certain kind of
tradition, I applied what I learned about this particular form to my subject manner: here
I allowed a musician, in this case a great drummer named Elvin Jones, to speak.

In speaking about his circumstance, he reflects on the tension for a great artist in
having to defer to the demands of entertainment in order to make a living. In the poem
I tried to get the inner aspect of his life in his own voice. I knew Elvin Jones very well,
and when I gave him a copy of the book *Dear John* and he saw this poem, dedicated to
Elvin Jones, he showed it to all his friends. He was proud to be recognized as an artist.

The point is, everybody has tutelage, everybody learns discipline in various ways,
and when you come to perform, all of that weighs heavily. None of this music and none
of this language comes out of nothing.

MOYERS: It doesn't just happen?

HARPER: No, it absolutely does *not*. I don't know where people get the idea
they're building on nothing, because it's not like that. However, you *can* give a sense of
originality to something that has happened before. Very seldom does a sixty-year-old
seasoned veteran say, "This never happened to me before." When such a person *does* say
that, you know this is a genuine epiphany because that person has had enough experi-
ence to really qualify him or her to know what is a high moment and what is not a
high moment.

MOYERS: You tell a story about John Coltrane in which he is searching for
the perfect reed because he wants to play a very difficult note. Finally, he gives up and
you say, "There was no easy way to get that sound; he played through it to a love
supreme."

DEAR JOHN, DEAR COLTRANE

a love supreme, a love supreme
a love supreme, a love supreme

Sex fingers toes
in the marketplace
near your father's church
in Hamlet, North Carolina—
witness to this love
in this calm fallow
of these minds,
there is no substitute for pain:
genitals gone or going,
seed burned out,
you tuck the roots in the earth,
turn back, and move
by river through the swamps,
singing: *a love supreme, a love supreme*;
what does it all mean?
Loss, so great each black
woman expects your failure
in mute change, the seed gone.
You plod up into the electric city—
your song now crystal and
the blues. You pick up the horn
with some will and blow
into the freezing night:
a love supreme, a love supreme—

Dawn comes and you cook
up the thick sin 'tween
impotence and death, fuel
the tenor sax cannibal
heart, genitals and sweat
that makes you clean—
a love supreme, a love supreme—

Why you so black?
cause I am

why you so funky?
cause I am
why you so black?
cause I am
why you so sweet?
cause I am
why you so black?
cause I am
a love supreme, a love supreme:

So sick
you couldn't play *Naima,*
so flat we ached
for song you'd concealed
with your own blood,
your diseased liver gave
out its purity,
the inflated heart
pumps out, the tenor kiss,
tenor love:
a love supreme, a love supreme—
a love supreme, a love supreme—

HARPER: I knew Coltrane a bit and he was having a hard time because of trouble with his teeth. There were certain changes that he would try to make that he couldn't make, and he was a very disciplined practicer—he would practice for eight or ten hours a day, every day. A craftsman in Indianapolis had made a specific mouthpiece for him, and he was trying to get that man to make another one just exactly like the first one because for some reason the one he had didn't give him the kind of resonance he wanted, and he needed to hear a certain kind of resonance. When he couldn't find that reed, finally he gave up looking for it and just played through the pain.

MOYERS: "Played through the pain." You're saying that jazz musicians *and* poets often have to go through pain to find inspiration?

HARPER: Absolutely. The musicians of my era taught me that you have to pay your dues willingly, and you have to pay them up front. Often this has to do with discipline. You have a particular technique which is required, and to achieve it you're going to have to put yourself in service to something else and practice for a week. And if you avoid it, then a month later you're going to have to put in *twice* the time.

The structural fundamentals of poetry, of art of all kinds, are always the same. When you come to understand that you have to pay your dues willingly—"I've really got to take a week out now and *do* this"—you're gaining time later, because once you've got the structural pattern in order, you can always draw on it—nothing gets more complicated and more demanding than the fundamentals.

MOYERS: You can draw upon that suffering as if it were a well?

HARPER: You can.

MOYERS: Speaking of dues, pain, and suffering, you make me immediately think of "Reuben, Reuben" and that image—"a brown berry gone / to rot just two days on the branch."

REUBEN, REUBEN

I reach from pain
to music great enough
to bring me back,
swollenhead, madness,
lovefruit, a pickle of hate
so sour my mouth twicked
up and would not sing;
there's nothing in the beat
to hold it in
melody and turn human skin;
a brown berry gone
to rot just two days on the branch;
we've lost a son,
the music, *jazz,* comes in.

HARPER: Reuben was my second son, and a branch is a metaphor for a line of continuity. A child is a promise—all parents want to see their children outlive them—and the business about fruit not picked is something that everybody knows, it's common; in fact, most of the fruit produced in the world is never seen—it's in forests, in woods, in meadows—only the best at the proper time is actually harvested. Since my son did not come to a life full of promise, I was trying to create a kind of bridge to the world he never knew.

But at the time that I wrote this, I wasn't trying to write a poem at all—I was just making some notes and trying to deal with my wife's grief. I had written these notes and those which became another poem on the back of an envelope which happened to fall into the crevice of a couch, and when I came upon the envelope months later—having dealt a little with my own grief and just having to function, because we had another child to care for—I looked at it and came to realize that in that instant I had written my closest approximation of how to deal with my pain. At the same time, you have to understand that I wasn't *consciously* trying to do that at all.

There was some living germ of the future in the writing of those notes, some kind of belief that there was going to *be* a future, because at the time I was just trying to get through the circumstances. Then later on when I found the notes and read them, I said to myself, "This is something I could not write now," but there it was, and because I had the evidence, I began to craft it as I would any other material. But if I had not made those notes, I would not have written the poem.

MOYERS: Get it down when you hear it, when you have it—before the poem comes.

HARPER: Yes, and this certainly *was not* a poem then.

MOYERS: Did you share this with your wife?

HARPER: Oh, yes, although there are some poems I do not read around her. Like, for example, "Nightmare Begins Responsibility."

MOYERS: Why?

HARPER: Because I think I'm more sentimental than she is. She's very tough-minded. She understands it as a poem, but I'm still reliving the *experience*. Men may not deal with tragedies as well as women do; men may not be prepared for the losses that women are prepared for. Women are just tougher than men in all kinds of ways. I think the reason may be that the preservation of human beings is in women's hands, finally—they're the caretakers.

If you look at the repertoire of musicians, you notice that there are two things they do over and over again: they play great ballads for women and they learn how to play up tempo. They have to play up tempo because there's an energy which is required to live in the world. When you see the full robustness and expression of musicians, they're playing up tempo, the life force is coming through them, and it is a wonderful thing to see; but the history of ballads, in this country particularly, is a history of the love for women.

For example, that's why I mentioned "Naima" in the Coltrane poem. "Naima" was the name if his first wife and it was a beautiful song. It's become part of everybody's repertoire, but as its genesis it was written to elevate Coltrane's wife—that was the impulse.

MOYERS: How did your second son die?

HARPER: He died of hyaline membrane disease, the same thing that President Kennedy's son died of, what they now call respiratory distress syndrome. The children who have that condition are born too early.

MOYERS: How old was he?

HARPER: Seven and a half months.

MOYERS: And it was around that event that you wrote "Reuben, Reuben"?

HARPER: Yes.

MOYERS: Why does nightmare begin responsibility?

HARPER: Because one has to transcend what one can't change, and one has to live in the world. I think we can live through much of the grief that is brought to us if we can accept it willingly and openly. If we try to defer or deflect it and not deal with it, then we're going to have to ascertain its meaning in an indirect way; but I don't think there's anything that's brought to human beings that we can't tolerate if we're willing to.

MOYERS: By playing through grief?

HARPER: Yes, by playing *through* it.

MOYERS: Have you been able to do that?

HARPER: I've tried. I can't say that it's all completely behind me, but this is a poem of retrospect—what's being described has already happened. Yeats said, "in dreams begin responsibility," and I take him to mean that one can envision something before it manifests itself, but the responsibility to live one's life in the face of what has been dreamed comes afterwards.

In other words, you get the image and then you find out in resonant life what life requires you to understand by it. Artists always see the image first, but actually getting to it is difficult. A poet can write the words down, but is it a poem? A musician can write the notes down, but when the notes are played are they music? In my case, my wife and I had five children, and our second and third sons died. So we now have three children—two sons and a daughter. Both of the sons who died have living siblings who are testaments to what they might have been. My first responsibility is to the living, but I also have a responsibility to give my children some sense of who they're connected to and who they might have been.

Ancestral inheritance and the line of family are always complicated. If you go back into families you find there are people who didn't survive but who are often talked about in some ways. As Etheridge Knight, a poet and a friend of mine, said in his poem "The Idea of Ancestry," "there is no place in my grandmother's Bible for whereabouts unknown." So I wanted to give people connected to them an awareness of those who had been here but who were not going to be *in* the world.

Nightmare Begins Responsibility

I place these numbed wrists to the pane
watching white uniforms whisk over
him in the tube-kept
prison
fear what they will do in experiment
watch my gloved stickshifting gasolined hands
breathe *boxcar-information-please* infirmary tubes
distrusting white-pink mending paperthin
silkened end hairs, distrusting tubes
shrunk in his *trunk-skincapped*
shaven head, in thighs
distrusting-white-hands-picking-baboon-light
on this son who will not make his second night
of this wardstrewn intensive airpocket
where his father's asthmatic
hymns of *night-train*, train done gone
his mother can only know that he has flown
up into essential calm unseen corridor
going boxscarred home, *mamaborn, sweetsonchild*
gonedowntown into *researchtestingwarehousebatteryacid*
mam-son-done-gone/me telling her 'nother
train tonight, no music, no breathstroked
heartbeat in my infinite distrust of them:

and of my distrusting self
white-doctor-who-breathed-for-him-all-night
say it for two sons gone,

say nightmare, say it loud
panebreaking heartmadness:
nightmare begins responsibility.

MOYERS: The word "distrust" appears time and time again in that poem. What's that distrust about?

HARPER: Well, it's about the distrust we *all* feel toward the medical culture. It's about people who are working to give assistance to your beloved when you haven't even *held* this child. People are fulfilling their roles through their institutional responsibilities—nurses, doctors, orderlies—and you're on the other side of a window looking in without even a chance to touch your own child.

There's also an awareness that they're doing all they can, but all they can is not enough, and you know that particularly when you lose a child. At the same time, you're in a state of suspension because you're deferring to people. Doctors are almost always very officious: they come in and give you the diagnosis, but there's no time to really talk about the emotional content of what they have given you. I'm not saying that they're unfeeling, but they *are* technicians.

You're hoping that your child is in the hands of an artist, and in a way they *are* artists, too. The man who breathed for my son all night was certainly an artist. I teach at Brown University, and because he taught at Brown Medical School I actually met him years later—we had a conversation, so life has a way of compensating in some ways—but at that particular time I felt great distrust, and there was also a racial distrust in it.

MOYERS: He was white?

HARPER: Yes, he was white and in that situation you're looking at people all dressed in white or pastel colors. Most of the technicians are white, and you're on the other side of things. The great divide of race always operates when one is in need and has to deal with the public. Anybody who has spent time in hospitals knows that if you don't have the right kind of coverage and the right kind of entrée you're not going to get certain kinds of care, and you want immediate and total attention for your child. So that anxiety was in my head and in my heart, but I didn't have any distrust in terms of what they were doing technically.

MOYERS: There's a lot of culture, a lot of history, and a lot of color in there.

HARPER: Very much so.

MOYERS: Did it help you to write that poem?

HARPER: Many mothers walk up to me and say, "Thank you for writing that poem." In fact, that poem and others on those themes have often been collected in anthologies, but I just wrote them to deal with my own circumstance. Then after they are published you find that there's a certain universality of loss that is shared by many, many people who have lost children. So when people come up and say, "Your poem helped me get through my own pain," you receive a certain wonderful succor.

MOYERS: So what is the job of the poet?

HARPER: The job of the poet is to tell the truth no matter what. As James Baldwin said, "Artists are here to disturb the peace" and by "the peace" he means our tendency to be vague and inactive and not attentive enough to the dynamism and the requirements of living. What I find more than anything else is that *you* do not choose art, *art* chooses you. I honestly can't imagine anybody *wanting* to write a poem and be a poet full time if one could be something which provides a more immediate return. *Nobody* writes poetry for money—I don't care whether they manage to win awards or not.

MOYERS: You don't write poetry to make a living?

HARPER: Absolutely not! That's what I meant when I said art chooses you. When I first declared that I wanted to write poetry, my parents looked at me and said, "Well, how are you going to support yourself?" They said, "Why don't you become a doctor like you're supposed to? What do you think we sent you to school for, so you can mess up like this and be locked into self-expression? This is *not* about self-expression!" What they didn't understand is that it is the job of the poet to make the reader cry. That's the job. And that's what happened to me. Those people who come up to me and say, "You know, that poem you wrote really helped me get through . . ." *That* was the intent, although I didn't know it at the time.

There's a sense in which poetry is not so much the writing of words as it is the movement of breath itself.

ROBERT HASS

Robert Hass has lived most of his life in his native California, and its landscapes have greatly influenced his poems and his quest to connect human language and the natural world. A versatile and influential writer, his poems move with humor, intelligence, compassion, and halting grace toward the benediction of tenderness, even when his subject is the dubious fate of Western civilization. Hass is a skilled translator of Japanese haiku and has incorporated Buddhist notions of balance into his own life and work. His many awards include a MacArthur Fellowship. He teaches at the University of California, Berkeley.

MOYERS: My favorite of your poems in *Field Guide* is entitled, "Concerning the Afterlife, the Indians of Central California Had Only the Dimmest Notions." Some title!

HASS: Isn't that wonderful? I found it in the first history of California by a late Victorian writer named H. H. Bancroft. What a confident sentence.

MOYERS: That's a spectacular image, "the whorled opalescent unicorn." But pray tell, what *is* a whorled opalescent unicorn?

HASS: It's a Pacific Coast snail. I think it was first identified by Ed Ricketts, who was Doc in the John Steinbeck books. He ran a marine lab down in Monterey. It's a tide pool snail. I don't know why it's called the unicorn, but you see the shells all over the place in California tide pools. The shell looks like an opal turban. It's very beautiful.

CONCERNING THE AFTERLIFE, THE INDIANS OF CENTRAL CALIFORNIA HAD ONLY THE DIMMEST NOTIONS

It is morning because the sun has risen.

I wake slowly in the early heat,
   pick berries from the thorny vines
   They are deep red,
   sugar-heavy, fuzzed with dust.

The eucalyptus casts a feathered shadow
on the house which gradually withdraws.

　　After breakfast
you will swim and I am going to read
that hard man Thomas Hobbes
on the causes of the English civil wars.
There are no women in his world,
Hobbes, brothers fighting brothers
over goods.
　　　　　　I see you in the later afternoon
your hair dry-yellow, plaited
from the waves, a faint salt sheen
across your belly and along your arms.
The kids bring from the sea
　　intricate calcium gifts—
　　black turbans, angular green whelks,
　　the whorled opalescent unicorn.

We may or may not
feel some irritation at the dinner hour.
The first stars, and after dark
Vega hangs in the lyre,
the Dipper tilts above the hill.
　　　　　　　　Traveling
in Europe Hobbes was haunted by motion.
Sailing or riding, he was suddenly aware
that all things move.
　　　　　　We will lie down,
finally, in our heaviness
　　and touch and drift toward morning.

MOYERS: There are wonderful images all through that poem—you describe berries as "deep red, / sugar-heavy, fuzzed with dust."

HASS: The image *must* have music, you know. You have to have the sound first. At least I do.

MOYERS: Do you hear that sound, or do you compose it?

HASS: I usually have a scrap. If I see people on the street corner and the phrase "nagged by wind" comes into my head, then I have a little bit of music and I can do something. But ideas almost never help. There's a famous story about Degas, the painter, who late in life fell in love with the idea of writing poetry and started writing sonnets. Then he got stuck, and when he ran into Mallarmé, the French poet, he said, "I have a million ideas, but I can't get anywhere." And Mallarmé said, "But Degas, poems aren't made out of ideas, they're made out of *words*."

MOYERS: But Thomas Hobbes appears in this poem, who said that life is—

HASS: "Nasty, brutish, and short."

MOYERS: Why does he make an appearance here?

HASS: Well, this poem was written during a period when I was trying to think about American politics and also raising a young family, so the first thing that struck me as I was reading Hobbes and the early thinkers who gave rise to our political and economic system was that they always imagined man in a state of nature. Man is always *solo*—he's Robinson Crusoe on the island—and that *isn't* a place to begin to imagine social life. Social life begins with men and women and kids. It begins in family groups. I was just terrified of an empty world that was only matter and motion, violent and abstract.

MOYERS: So that explains the last lines, "We will lie down, / finally, in our heaviness / and touch and drift toward morning." You and your wife. You and . . .

HASS: And *all* of us. The line that I actually liked best goes, "We may or may not / feel some irritation at the dinner hour." I didn't want to make this too idyllic.

MOYERS: What about the short poem a few pages later? "Bashō, A Departure."

HASS: Oh, yes. Bashō was the great seventeenth-century initiator of the haiku form. He was of the samurai class, a sort of middle-level gentleman farmer's son, who gave the form to this kind of little poem.

BASHŌ, A DEPARTURE

Summer is over and
we part, like eyelids,
like clams opening.

MOYERS: Is that a poem?

HASS: I think it is. This is my translation of a poem of his that's not translatable, actually. A more literal translation of the Japanese would be, "Summer is over and we part at Futami Bay." Futami is the name of the place where they actually were; Futami means "two views," and *futa* also means "lid." All the commentators have said that the lid refers to clam shells, but it also made me think of eyelids opening. There is a buried metaphorical pun in the Japanese that all Buddhist teaching is rooted in: all being awake is saying good-bye. Or, to put it another way, every time we say good-bye, we awake to the nature of things.

Because *futa* means "lid" and *mi* also means "meat," there's another pun in the poem—parting is the meat of the clam. When the shell opens, the sweetness, the meat can be devoured. Buddhism awakens one to the transitoriness of things. You can't translate the whole of the philosophy of one culture into the philosophy of another culture, but I wanted to get a little bit of the oddness of eyelids opening, clams opening, and parting.

MOYERS: There is a kaleidoscope of quick images in the poems included in *After the Gentle Poet Kobayashi Issa.*

HASS: Issa was a famous haiku poet later in the tradition. Some people have compared him to Robert Frost, saying that he was a sort of Japanese farmer poet, but others have said he's like a mini-Whitman because he was a miniaturist who loved all kinds of creatures. I think in his lifetime he wrote over a thousand poems about bugs and insects, and this is a kind of kaleidoscope, as you say, of my free use of his images.

Traditionally on New Year's, which was the first day of spring, all Japanese poets wrote a poem—it was a way of taking their pulse—and this first little poem is one of his.

New Year's morning—
everything is in blossom!
   I feel about average.

· ·

Blossoms at night,
and people
   moved by music

Napped half the day,
no one
   punished me!

> Fiftieth birthday:
>   From now on,
> it's all clear profit,
>   every sky.

> Don't worry, spiders,
> I keep house
>   casually.

This next one is Issa's response to a proclamation that went out during their time of chauvinist expansion encouraging all poets in Japan to write a patriotic poem. So far as I know this is the only patriotic poem he ever wrote.

> These sea slugs,
> they just don't seem
>   *Japanese.*

And this last one is called "Hell":

> Bright autumn moon;
> pond snails crying
>   in the saucepan.

MOYERS: I don't get that one.

HASS: It's very much a poem about the full moon of the harvest season. And I think he's just hearing the little mewling sound, like a cry of pain, of the air escaping from these pond snails that are being sautéed in a round pan—the round pan, the round moon. We're *all* cooking in what Allen Ginsberg called the "alphabet soup of time" here. We're *all* being sautéed in the dish of living, and Issa hears it in the word that I translated with "crying."

I didn't really know what the right word would be. I had a neighbor, a wonderful, quite brilliant Korean professor of computer engineering who as a boy had loved haiku, so I asked him how he would translate this word. He said, " 'Crying' is not bad." As I was brooding over these poems I would see him coming out of his house, and he would say, "What about 'whimpering'?" And I should say, "Oh, that's too long." Or, another time, he would say, "Well, the air is escaping, what about 'hissing'?" Finally I realized that I was trying to find the word for the little half cry, half song of pain at the middle of the universe, at the middle of living, and it started to give me the creeps.

Issa's poems often ask us to see the image as if it were the *whole* of reality. Writing it was a discipline that left him with no protection. I think he had a sort of thinness of the mind's skin because for so many years he wrote these poems in which there wasn't room to have ideas about *why* things suffer; he's just saying "is," "is," "is," over and over again. Here are a couple of examples:

> For you fleas too
> the nights must be long,
> they must be lonely.

> Don't kill that fly!
> Look—it's wringing its hands,
> wringing its feet.

One of the things I love about his work is that it's this completely undefended looking at joy and pain and suffering all together. In another one he says, in a sort of comic way.

> In this world
> we walk on the roof of hell,
> gazing at flowers.

So the poem called *"Hell,"* which we started with, just tries to catch this moment as if it were *all* the beauty and *all* the pain in the world.

MOYERS: The reality of the food chain.

HASS: Yes. I think it was Joseph Campbell who said that the beginning of all poetry is uneasiness about the food chain. One of the sources of myth was the need to sacralize the pain of the food chain.

MOYERS: To turn necessity into drama and into narrative so that we can accept it and go on?

HASS: Yes, and live at the center of it, at the center of reality.

MOYERS: How do you describe haiku to someone totally unfamiliar with it?

HASS: I did the book on haiku partly because when I was a young writer reading around in poetry the ideal of this poetry—to be able to look in such a way that you could live at the center of your own life—seemed so desirable to me. I started reading these poems and then got Japanese grammars and tried to find my way through them to get a little closer to the language.

MOYERS: What *drew* you to haiku—to these short Japanese poems?

HASS: Their brevity, but also their centeredness. These poets seemed to be alert every moment of their lives. I discovered, of course, that that wasn't true—they were like everybody else, though gifted artists. Except maybe for Bashō, who was really quite an amazing man, in some ways a figure as powerful in Japanese literature as Shakespeare is in English.

What I would say about the haiku is that it's a form of poetry that takes some absolutely traditional image of Japanese life—"bright autumn moon"—and then adds one other image to it, to bear down on a sense of reality.

> Bright autumn moon;
> pond snails crying
> in the saucepan.

The haiku form actually developed out of a practice of early Japanese poets playing around with something like a call-and-response form, like an African American work song. One poet might say the lines I just quoted and the second poet would then have to add the final two lines that would make a *real* poem—that is, a *tanka,* which was the classic five-line lyric poem. There would be the first little hit, which was called *hokku,* and then there would be second image that completed it.

So, this practice of alert transcription, this notation of the world, came out of a game of starting a poem, adding another part, then adding another part. Endless transformation—the heart of the Buddhist religion. So that the *hokku* would be this first little image, then it would be completed by another thought. Then someone would take the little uncompleted thought and start a new poem. And it went through a cycle. In the old days, it went through a cycle of a hundred poems. It was called a *renga,* linked verse. They would have *renga* parties, drinking parties, at which people did this as a form of socializing, but it also enacted a fundamental Buddhist ways of looking at reality as endlessly in motion. When the middle class, merchants and lawyers, got interested in the court games and wanted to be part of them, they developed a much more realistic form and it was called *haikai no renga,* which meant playful *renga.* So *haikai* meant playful. Then somebody put the two words together—*hokku,* starting verse, and *haikai*—and made the notion of the haiku. But it was always thought of in terms of this social practice.

MOYERS: Poetry as play.

HASS: Poetry as play. There's nothing exactly like it—people getting together and improvising endlessly on a theme as a form of play—in the Western literary tradition. The thing it's most like in our tradition is the twenties jazz band's skilled improvisation with a master. Louis Armstrong's improvising is probably the nearest thing in our culture to the circumstance the haiku came out of improvisatory play with language that depended on acute observation and a live sense of reality.

MOYERS: When you say *hokku*, you release a sudden burst of breath. And at the festival, I heard you working with kids talking about breath and playing that game with them. Remember that?

HASS: Yes. There's a sense in which poetry is not so much the writing of words as it is the movement of breath itself. To write it, you must pay attention to the breathing of poetry, to *all* speech as breath, to the relationship of our thoughts and emotions and the actual way they fill our bodies. This is the emotional, physical centering of the activity of poetry. The Japanese and Chinese make more of this than we do. But let me tell you about an experience I had.

I was doing a radio call-in show up on the Oregon coast, and all sorts of people called in to recite poems they'd written at one time or another in their lives. One old man called in with a poem that he entitled "Thinking About Cole Porter on Wake Island"—the only poem he'd ever written in his life he wrote when he was a Marine in the Second World War. And this prompted a guy from the local state prison to call and say: "I'll tell you what poetry is. If you say *anything* and *know* it's your breath and that you have this *one* life and this is the *only* time this breath is ever going to pass through your body in *just this way,* I don't care if it's a laundry list you read, it's *poetry.*" And I thought, that's pretty good: poetry is mortal breath that *knows* it's mortal. So getting the kids to sense that as they work on their poems can be a way of centering them and getting them beyond what spins out of their brain roof chatter.

MOYERS: In Buddhism one is taught to meditate by riding the breath into the inner life, to the habitat of the soul.

HASS: Yes. The connection between breath and spiritual practice is ancient, and it's there in our tradition in the pun on spirit—*spiritus* was breath in Latin. When you think about it, breath may be the way to feel yourself into the constant exchange that our lives involve, giving away the air and taking it back and giving it away and taking it back until we see that even our ideas and feelings are just that—a giving and taking back and giving and taking back.

MOYERS: I heard you tell the students that art occurs when you put the structure of breathing *into* other people's bodies. I need some help with that notion.

HASS: I was just thinking about the fact that when one says somebody else's poem aloud, one speaks in *that person's* breath. If I say, "Tomorrow, and tomorrow, and tomorrow, / Creeps in this petty pace from day to day / To the last syllable of recorded time, / And all our yesterdays have lighted fools / The way to dusty death," everything that's happening in my physiology Shakespeare quite literally put there. It's a very mysterious process. Probably he's writing in silence, but he's *hearing* all of these vocalizations, *hearing* these rhythms, and when you take them in, you take in the physiology of the phrases. Whitman says, "I lean and loaf at my ease observing a spear of summer grass." You have to let all the carbon monoxide up out of your lungs to say that line. I was urging the students to love and care about the rhythms and sounds of the language—you are going to be putting that inside other people, so you want to take some responsibility for it.

MOYERS: Do you have a favorite haiku?

HASS: I have *many*. This is a little poem of Bashō's about the cry of the cuckoo, which was associated with summertime. It was one of the first migratory birds to arrive in Kyoto.

> Even in Kyoto—
> hearing the cuckoo's cry—
> I long for Kyoto.

Even in the middle of what we want, we *want* it. We want the *ideal form* of it. I think of coming to New York for the first time when I was a kid—New York with all of those images of the romance of the city—and I could say, "Even in New York, sunlight on the brownstones, I long for New York." It's that kind of *ideal* desire.

Let's see, what are some others that I love?

> Having slept, the cat gets up,
> yawns, goes out
> to make love.

This is a famously cute one:

> Climb Mount Fuji,
> O snail,
> but slowly, slowly.

MOYERS: Wasn't Issa, one of the most famous of Japanese poets, a contemporary of Thomas Jefferson's? So wouldn't "All men are created equal" have been written at about the same time Issa was writing about this snail?

HASS: Yes. You know, Japanese culture was hugely class-conscious, but it also went through a period of democratization; and Issa belonged to a democratizing, populist sect of Buddhism. Jefferson, of course, was reading William Cowper and Robert Burns and the English poets of that time who also were advancing a similar sensibility. Robert Burns's little poem about digging up a field mouse contains that famous phrase, "The best laid schemes o' mice an' men / Gang aft agley." He begins, "Wee, sleekit, cow'rin, tim'rous beastie, / O, what a panic's in thy breastie!" There was a moment, it might be ending just now, when the whole liberal and reforming sensibility that gave rise to the term *liberalism*—which meant a philosophy founded in some notion of generosity—began with this poetry of sensibility and its awareness of the helplessness and undefended quality of *all* life.

MOYERS: Let's look at your poem "House," one of my favorites. In the beginning you seem so happy with your bacon and your coffee and your classical music and then something happens. What are those "old dusks" that break over you?

HASS: Remembered—and I suppose transformed by memory—dusks. I was twenty-six or twenty-seven and raising a family, and it felt like such an accomplishment to have a life with ordinary forms of happiness in it. Then whatever was frightening and disordered in my own childhood wells up as the underside in this poem.

HOUSE

Quick in the April hedge
  were juncos and kinglets.
I was at the window
  just now, the bacon
sizzled under hand,
  the coffee steamed
fragrantly & fountains
  of the Water Music
issued from another room.
  Living in a house
we live in the body
  of our lives, last night
the odd after-dinner light
  of early spring & now

the sunlight warming or
    shadowing the morning rooms.

I am conscious of being
    myself the inhabitant
of certain premises:
    coffee & bacon & Handel
& upstairs asleep my wife.
    Very suddenly
old dusks break over me,
    the thick shagged heads
of fig trees near the fence
    & not wanting to go in
& swallows looping
    on the darkened hill
& all that terror
    in the house
& barely, only barely,
    a softball
falling toward me
    like a moon.

MOYERS: What triggers that welling up?

HASS: At the time I would have said that this is just one of those moments when a poem veers off in a new direction. Now, however, I think the trigger is that my wife is asleep upstairs.

I had constructed this new domestic life against the confusion and fear of my child-hood. But somehow in the feeling moment of the poem I get to my wife asleep upstairs and, as Robert Bly might say, I get to material with my mother which I had not yet attended to, so everything I have been warding off with Handel and bacon comes rushing up in the poem. This is a case where you have caught the shape of a little tectonic plate fracture and rapid charge in the inner life of a poem.

MOYERS: Why the image of "a softball / falling toward me / like a moon"?

HASS: Perhaps I was remembering the hypnotic, trancelike pleasure of those early spring nights when you could play ball right up to and through dinnertime; you'd play until you couldn't field flies anymore except at your peril, let alone line drives. So I think I was remembering those moments that are moments of pure escape that we Americans still love and re-create by sitting around watching sports on television, avoiding reentering our lives as long as we possibly can. And the last thing that came to me was that sense of the looming softball in the twilight as it descends into your hands.

MOYERS: There's almost a dreamlike quality in the "softball / falling toward me / like a moon."

HASS: Yes. I think now that I didn't want to unpack "all that terror / in the house."

MOYERS: What *was* that terror?

HASS: I think it was my parents' difficulties. The troubles they had which sometimes made my house a scary place to be in. So, correspondingly, when I was a mature man it seemed like magic to me to get up in the morning and have the warm bodies of these happy little kids come in to breakfast, and music showering from another room.

MOYERS: How about "Song"?

SONG

Afternoon cooking in the fall sun—
who is more naked
                    than the man
yelling, "Hey, I'm home!"
            to an empty house?
thinking because the bay is clear,
the hills in yellow heat,
& scrub oak red in gullies
        that great crowds of family
should tumble from the rooms
                to throw their bodies on the Papa-body,
                I-am-loved.

Cat sleeps in the windowgleam,
            dust motes.
    On the oak table
    filets of sole
stewing in the juice of tangerines,
    slices of green pepper
        on a bone-white dish.

HASS: This is another of these poems that present what the eighteenth century used to call "domestic felicity."

MOYERS: How do you get from the disappointment in the first part of that poem to the serenity and peace of the last part of it?

HASS: No one's there when I expect a response. They're *not* there, but the world *is*. The last part for me is like haiku—a series of rapid notations of this given world, which is given and constructed since somebody has put the fish out to prepare.

MOYERS: "Slices of green pepper / on a bone-white dish."

HASS: Yes.

MOYERS: Still, there's an emptiness here. You come home. The family's gone.

HASS: That's interesting.

MOYERS: Well, you poets write but we readers interpret.

HASS: Oh, yes. No doubt. It's interesting your saying that because I felt a little unnerved by the reading of it. We *do* construct the world with our families but that emptiness is in it, too. I wanted the poem, even in its absences, to be full, but as I read it just now I felt the twinge of emptiness that's also in it. Or you did. And I caught it from you.

MOYERS: An empty house can be full of terror if you're not expecting it to be empty.

HASS: Yes. I think it's true. And it's true that poems belong to readers. That's why the old poets used to make that song: "Go, little book." Somebody said that all interesting works of art come very close to saying the *opposite* of what they *seem* to say, in the way that there's no "yes" without a "no." For example, a parent's "yes" is not credible if there's not a "no." And the "no" is not credible if there's not a "yes." If we make a poem of celebration, it *has* to include a lot of darkness for it to be real.

MOYERS: We need experience to be kept fresh. That's what poetry does for me. I can't write poetry, but when I hear it read, as you just did, your experience becomes fresh in me.

HASS: One hopes.

MOYERS: That's the power of art.

HASS: Yes, in the same way that you come out of a museum and suddenly see the world more vividly from looking at paintings and sculptures. *That's* what I hope happens with my poems.

I write for the ambition I have for myself—to be a voice that I can listen to, that makes sense and raises my own bereft and mundane consciousness, that speaks to me as if it were the elder I've always wanted.

—— GARRETT KAORU HONGO ——

Garrett Kaoru Hongo was born in Volcano, Hawai'i, and raised in Los Angeles. A fourth-generation Japanese American, he writes to uphold the tradition and emotional dignity of his ancestors. His poems preserve a suppressed history while examining the painful contradictions of culture in the United States for many ethnic Americans. *The Rivers of Heaven* won the Lamont Poetry Prize in 1987. Playwright and poet, he teaches at the University of Oregon, Eugene.

MOYERS: Why did you decide to write poetry?

HONGO: I wanted to explore the life of emotions. As a child in Hawai'i I remember not only having emotions, but they seemed authorized by the world and the family surrounding me. As an adolescent growing up in Los Angeles and the public schools there, emotions seemed to be under a tight reign even in sports. People seemed to want to deny them.

I didn't understand that as a Japanese American I was experiencing a social and historical sadness. Because my own family did not suffer relocation, they were trying to live it down and grow out of their own grief. So I had all these feelings which had no form of expression. My brother became a blues guitarist, and at first I was just angry, then I became a poet. Poetry and photography seemed to give me ways to explore and connect with the history that was repressed.

MOYERS: Repressed in what sense?

HONGO: There wasn't anything in my high school textbooks about Japanese in America. I knew that we weren't there when Lee surrendered to Grant. I knew we weren't there when Washington crossed the Delaware.

MOYERS: Or at the Alamo, on either side.

HONGO: Yes, and I wanted the words I was reading to belong to me, but there were no words for me, no words for my grandfather, no words for my grandmother. They simply weren't portrayed, so I felt that I didn't have an identity. Then I set about trying to learn that history and to put what did not exist for me on the page. Poetry was almost completely unwilled, I just had to have it.

MOYERS: Were these concerns shared within your family?

HONGO: With my grandfather, mostly. My own parents were immigrants from Hawai'i to the mainland and they had a lot to do just to survive and to provide for my brother and me. My father was an American soldier at the same time that my grandfather was imprisoned in Hawai'i. My grandfather was born in America in 1899 but was sent back to Japan for his education, so the day after Pearl Harbor he was arrested and taken down for questioning in Honolulu. In a sense he was disappeared for a short time, not an uncommon story among Japanese Americans. My grandfather was a community leader, the president of the Japanese language school, who sponsored Japanese citizens to come over and be schoolteachers in Hawai'i. So of course he was under suspicion. He would sit down after dinner every night with his bourbon and tell me, his oldest grandchild, the story of how he was arrested and questioned by the FBI and how they tried to trick him into betraying his true identity.

MOYERS: They thought he was a spy?

HONGO: That's right. And he was still angry about it. He'd tell me the story, and no one else would listen, they were embarrassed by his passion and by his giving me a responsibility for this story. I was told that he was senile, but he wasn't. He was obsessed with a wrong that he felt needed to be righted and he was also obsessed that the story had to be told. So he'd tell me the story every night. He said, "You learn the language good"—he spoke broken English, a Hawaiian kind of pidgin English because he was educated in Japan—"Learn speak like white Americans. You tell story." Kids remember that kind of thing. I remembered it.

I share with so many Japanese Americans of my generation a feeling that we have a story to tell, that we have a responsibility to that generation who suffered the humiliation and the loss and who did not have their presence in this country endorsed. I've been interviewing Japanese American lawyers and different people who've worked on redress, which is to say compensation for their relocation, and I've been more and more impressed with how this is a way for us to earn back what we all felt we lost during World War II.

MOYERS: When you were talking about that subject with the young people today, they responded to your poetry but not to your discussion about relocation. They didn't understand what the term means. It's not a part of their experience.

HONGO: Exactly, and that's why I needed to write the story of relocation into the books. I remember as a student in Los Angeles, we'd study World War II and there would be no mention of the evacuation, no mention of Executive Order 9066 that sent 120,000 Japanese Americans from the West Coast in the United States to the relocation centers all over the barren places of the West and Arkansas. I wasn't angry about it; I just couldn't believe that it wasn't spoken about so I would raise the question. I didn't understand that this caused a great deal of embarrassment to many of my classmates who were mainland Japanese Americans. I didn't understand that even the *nisei,* second generation, didn't wish to bring up the subject. It was very painful to them, and a source of humiliation. Congressman Robert Matsui from California said that when he was in school and World War II came up, he'd pretend to be sick so he didn't have to go. He was ashamed. But that's something I didn't feel myself.

MOYERS: You said a minute ago that you felt sadness.

HONGO: Yes. I felt everyone was sad, that there was this unspoken sadness all around me. I wanted to understand it and to bring it into language. What inspired me were things I read, like Greek tragedies. Here was Orestes full of action and Antigone standing up for a principle, so I said, "What the hell are *we* doing? We're not speaking to the issue. We're not articulating our emotions or our beliefs about the dead and about history." I was basically indoctrinated in a Western vision of articulation, of speaking to emotional and historical issues, but my experience was one of repression.

MOYERS: You didn't think that you could talk about this?

HONGO: I didn't feel that others could or would, and that caused a great frustration. And I didn't know it at the time but I think I unconsciously absorbed my grandfather's directive to me. He'd charged me every evening with this responsibility, so I'd bring it up and then it would be sort of silenced. There was a great social dissonance between my inner life and the exterior life, and I needed to make them come together somehow.

I had the feeling, as many of my generation did at the time, that the country was living a great untruth. This was during the time of Vietnam after the assassinations of JFK, Malcolm X, Robert Kennedy, and Martin Luther King and these also were subjects not addressed in my public life in schools. So this kind of idealism and that kind of social dissidence empowered some powerful desires and wishes, and the context of American universities and colleges provided so many of us with the opportunity to confront them and bring them into our lives.

MOYERS: You could reach far more people with a camera, with essays, with journalism. Why poetry?

HONGO: Poetry is primary. When I was in college the poets would come and speak and read. They were the truth-tellers, the passionate ones. When I was a freshman, just before the invasion of Cambodia by American troops, poets would come and speak about it. My faculty wouldn't speak about it, the American media didn't speak about it, as far as I knew, but the poets did speak about what was happening. There was something in their speaking that changed me. There was an integrity to it and also an incredible willingness to face difficult issues about both the failure of the society outside and the loss of human potential within. There was a greatness to it that impressed and stirred me.

MOYERS: You were talking earlier about two generations of your family laboring as field hands on the plantations of Hawai'i to buy your way out. Has poetry helped you to resurrect the images of your ancestors?

HONGO: Yes, I believe it has. I feel really fortunate that I was allowed to attain this level of literacy and the leisure to explore the development of an ideal of culture in my own education and in my own life. I feel very powerfully that my place in this country was earned by my forebears so that I could become expressive in a civilized way.

MOYERS: What did your forebears do?

HONGO: They emigrated from Japan, labored as field hands for two generations in Hawai'i, went to war in Italy and France, worked at menial jobs in industry and civil bureaucracy so that I could attain the leisure to be able to contemplate not just the body of knowledge that is literature but also the lives that they led in order to buy my way out of that kind of life. I feel privileged and I feel responsible to them.

MOYERS: There's so much of your father in these poems. Tell me a little bit about him.

HONGO: Well, it's hard for me to talk about him and our relationship.

MOYERS: Easier to write about?

HONGO: Much easier, but it's hard to write about it, too. My father lost a lot, he lost our place in Hawai'i, he lost his hearing, he lost even the power of speech because he was increasingly hard of hearing as he aged, so that we had to communicate in ways without words and still enjoy each other's presence. But he inspired me because he never seemed to become beaten down or embittered by his life and the difficulty of that life.

MOYERS: Were you close to your father?

HONGO: Yes and no. One of my teachers said to me that we're drawn to the parent we least understand. My father was a silent man—I mean he was hard of hearing and laconic. He was disenfranchised, in a sense, because the language that he spoke was Hawaiian pidgin English, and the language where we lived in Los Angeles was not that language. He'd been made, as many have been, to feel ashamed of his speech, but I loved his speech. To me it was a speech of love and intimacy and grandness and heroicism. However, as he got older he grew increasingly more hard of hearing and more quiet. I felt a great sadness and a great withdrawing from life there, but I knew that he was a grand person and I knew that he conquered a lot in his life. Somehow that inspired me and what he couldn't say or would not say I had to say.

MOYERS: Were you ever able to tell him that?

HONGO: Well, I wrote the poems and he read every one. But it was hard for us to say much to each other. For example, when I wanted to go away to college, we didn't have any money but he had a car, a BMW, amazingly. One day as we were driving in his BMW, I was telling him how I thought I should go to a school I wasn't interested in going to because it was less expensive and he said, "Well, this car is yours."

I had been telling him how I wanted to be a photographer or a writer, I didn't know which, and after I got the car into overdrive on the freeway going up to Santa Monica all he said was, "This car is yours. I give it to you." It didn't make sense right away, but later I put it together. I sold the car and had the first year's tuition. He never said anything except in that way. He was of a different generation and he believed you didn't show those kinds of feelings, but I always felt I had his blessing.

MOYERS: So a poem is a carrier of memory for you, almost like a photograph.

HONGO: I wanted to be a photographer. I was inspired by W. Eugene Smith. I remember his famous photographs of women weeping with a dead child in Baifra, of the mother holding her diseased daughter in Minamata, and of American men in industry in Pittsburgh working in the steel factories. These were lives I knew my people led, and I wanted to somehow bring that starkness and that immediacy and unequivocal presence into my life, but I also wanted to read. I just happened to find a good place to read when I went to college, so I began to write poetry and that was it. In the early 1970s people like Galway Kinnell, Philip Levine, and William Merwin would come to our school and they spoke so clearly, so eloquently, and with such authority I knew that if I could get close to that, I might be okay. I didn't think about making a living or doing anything else. I just wanted to be that close to passion, that close to the tactile reality of life. I felt they had it in a way that was just as powerful as any photographs I'd seen by W. Eugene Smith. So, you go on from that.

MOYERS: Some of my favorite lines are these: "I want the dead beside me when I dance, to help me / flesh the notes of my song, to tell me it's all right." What's all right?

O-Bon: *Dance for the Dead*

I have no memories or photograph of my father
coming home from war, thin as a caneworker,
a splinter of flesh in his olive greens
and khakis and spit-shined G.I. shoes;

Or of my grandfather in his flower-print shirt,
humming his bar-tunes, tying the bandana
to his head to hold the sweat back from his face
as he bent to weed and hoe the garden that Sunday
while swarms of planes maneuvered overhead.

I have no memories of the radio that day
or the clatter of machetes in the Filipino camp,
the long wail of news from over the mountains,
or the glimmerings and sheaths of fear in the village.

I have no story to tell about lacquer shrines
or filial ashes, about a small brass bell,
and incense smoldering in jade bowls, about the silvered,
black face of Miroku gleaming with detachment,
anthurium crowns in the stoneware vase
the hearts and wheels of fire behind her.

And though I've mapped and studied the strike march
from the North Shore to town in 1921, though I've
sung psalms at festival and dipped the bamboo cup
in the stone bowl on the Day of the Dead,
though I've pitched coins and took my turn
at the *taiko* drum, and folded paper fortunes
and strung them on the graveyard's *hala* tree;

Though I've made a life and raised my house
oceans east of my birth, though I've craned
my neck and cocked my ear for the sound of flute
and *shamisen* jangling its tune of woe—

The music nonetheless echoes in its slotted box,
the cold sea chafes the land and swirls over gravestones,
and wind sighs its passionless song through ironwood trees.

More than memory or the image of the slant of grey rain
pounding the thatch coats and peaked hats
of townsmen racing across the blond arch of a bridge,
more than the past and its aches and brocade
of tales and ritual, its dry mouth of repetition,

I want the cold stone in my hand to pound the earth,
I want the splash of cool or steaming water to wash my feet,
I want the dead beside me when I dance, to help me
flesh the notes of my song, to tell me it's all right.

HONGO: That they *are* the dead. That they're not the living. That these people whom I treasure and these lives which were exemplary and are exemplary to me, these presences which I don't enjoy as I enjoy yours, are still somehow present. It's a magical belief, a primitive religion, but it's something for me as a poet that's crucial. It's not intellectual, it's almost a *need* to believe. Maybe religion is not so much belief, as the *need* to believe.

MOYERS: But given that poetry is so personal and intimate and that your own poetry is a country populated by your own ancestors, people need help entering that country.

HONGO: I think poetry is about our most familiar need which we deny in order to lead more practical lives, but ultimately these lives are impractical because they do not have such presences in them. I think poetry can bring such presences back, whether they're the dead or evanescent feelings or insinuations, or glimmerings, or vanishings. These are the most essential things, and poetry turns to them in the way that many arts do. So I feel like a conduit for things other than myself—these vanishings, insinuations, glimmerings. I feel they're essential. I can't do without them.

MOYERS: What happens to you when you're writing poetry? Is there anything mystical in the experience?

HONGO: I suppose there are many faces and masks and voices that speak through the poet. The poet becomes all things, so it's a way for me to connect with things that I am not. It's also a way to communicate with the great poetic tradition of the dead—for example, Yeats, Blake, Li Po, Tu Fu, Homer. It's a long conversation, and five years ago I would have said, "I think we're keeping it alive," but today I say, "We poets *are* keeping it alive."

MOYERS: That appears to me both true and a problem. It's true that poetry is a conversation of all poets down through the ages, but it's a problem in the sense that many of us don't have an ear for that conversation. Not familiar with poetry, we can feel left out.

HONGO: That might be true of poetry as an elite practice, but one of my basic tenets as a poet is to try to write to the uninitiated. In fact, my poems are *always* addressed to the uninitiated. For instance, I always ask myself what my father would want to hear from me, my father who only finished high school and trade school, who never took a course in literature, who read only the papers. I'd try to imagine what he would want to hear from poetry and try to write him and his concerns. I feel that what's grand about the twentieth century in American letters is that we write to as many people as we can. They may not read us—we may not be heard—but we *want* to write to as wide an audience as possible, in fact, to as unacademic an audience as possible.

MOYERS: Do you believe the poets of our time are engaging society in a conversation?

HONGO: Well, I believe that I'm in a conversation with society. Maybe society's not talking to me, but I'm talking to it. I feel I'm true to the jerk I was in high school, I'm no less uncouth than I was twenty years ago, and I do feel that I'm an American. I want to write American English, and I want to reach American people.

MOYERS: American culture is changing so dynamically right now that you yourself have said that you're living in a cultural whirlwind.

HONGO: Yes, and I like that, it's how I grew up. I was born in Hawai'i, and I moved as an older child to a neighborhood in Los Angeles that was populated by African Americans and Hispanics and Japanese Americans from Hawai'i. All around us were other kinds of Americans—people from Beverly Hills, people from Hollywood, and people from Watts—and I saw them in the way that I was taught to see them as a child in Hawai'i, which is to say, with acceptance. We have so many different peoples in Hawai'i that you cannot reject anyone. Everyone is part of the family, and that's a great feeling.

MOYERS: Are you hopeful about America's cities? Many people write them off as third-world countries.

HONGO: Well, I think those cities are America's hope; we *are* a third-world country. America is *not* the melting pot, but a meeting place, and that inspires me. I can believe in Walt Whitman again when I go back to downtown L.A. and I hear all those sounds—Spanish, disco, rap, buses squeaking, barkers shouting, people arguing, knife fights breaking out—that's America to me. I hear a guy taking his girl out for a date on

Friday night, and I hear somebody else looking for a good deal on a boom box. It's okay, it's my world.

MOYERS: You said that despite the life he lived, your father felt no hate. Have you come to terms over the anger you felt over your separation from your own culture?

HONGO: I still don't know. I'm still exploring it, and that anger still sustains me. It might be over the loss of that feeling of security of knowing that one belongs, as I felt I belonged when I was a child in Hawai'i, and as my father seemed to belong when he was with his pals from back in the old days in Hawai'i.

MOYERS: You were born in Volcano, Hawai'i—aptly named, given all the upheavals both literal and metaphorical in the lives of your people.

HONGO: Yes, it's erupting now—Kilauea. The current vent is the newest place on the planet; it's still being made. I was born there and lived there for the first eight months of my life before we moved away from Hawai'i. I did not return until I was thirty-one, when my first book was published and the Hawaii Arts Council invited me back to give readings in the islands. When my aunt and uncle took me back to the place I was born I was astonished that a place like that existed and that I was from that place. It was a place as magical, as mythical, as surreal and beautiful as any spot I had ever read about. It was my own origin, and it was also a place of origin for the planet.

MOYERS: Did you write "Hilo: First Night Back" as a result of that trip?

HONGO: Yes, I wrote it the first night I got back to the Big Island, where I was confronted not only with the physical beauty of the place, but also with the great graciousness of my father's family in assembling to meet me. It was unspeakably moving.

HILO: FIRST NIGHT BACK

There are things tonight I've never known:
Aunt Lily's face like my father's, the glance
from a squealing child that seems my own,
a way of speech with echoes all the way
to the everlasting. My father's people like gifts
arranged around me for the first time;
and the last time 30 inarticulate years ago—
some infant bawling in blue blankets,

my mother's arms wrapped around him
like a coat of warm wind.

Revelations tonight:
my lost family of artists and entrepreneurs,
Aunt Charlotte's anthuriums and baby's breath
in twists of modish *ikebana* on the television,
and Bobby, my father's younger brother, is still far away,
the stories about him mounting,
cloned mysteries prolific in imagination.
We write our name this way,
as I suspected, with flourishes,
and my grandmother's still alive
teaching *odori* in Honolulu.

What's the news
of this world? The volcano I was born under?
All I had of my father's past a paling photograph,
small as a half-dollar
whirling in my memory. He stands in front of
the old store, dressed in a T-shirt and loose cotton pants,
skinny as DiMaggio and in dark glasses,
holding the baby squirming in his arms
to face the camera, sunlight and time
in cascades of white from the borders
erasing us year by year.

Proud to be back
under the navy wool of this night sky,
the angle Orion takes from here
to everywhere I've been. Silver giants slice
these heavens. A small crane
tumbles in its long flight home.

MOYERS: That moment is caught forever. Stories do that.

HONGO: Yes. But I didn't have them as a kid. The stories I wanted were stories which were forbidden, so I grew up with surrogate stories, making them up and adopting others which were not mine. What I love are not only the stories that haven't yet been told to me but the stories which I've yet to tell. I like that which is forbidden. There's probably a reason why they're forbidden, but somehow they empower me.

MOYERS: Like the Asian legend of the Milky Way.

HONGO: Yes. In Asian cultures—in China and Japan and throughout that part of the Pacific Rim—there is a legend about the River of Heaven, our Milky Way, which is seen as a river of stars separating two lovers: a goatherd and the weaver girl who has responsibility for making the raiment of beauty in the universe. Because her responsibilities are so important and so difficult to accomplish, she has to deny herself the love of her life, the goatherd boy. But because the universe feels pity for her, at least once a year it responds with an action which temporarily enables their love. Sometimes it's a flock of sparrows who feel her sorrow, sometimes it's starlings, sometimes it's just a single crow who spreads his wing across the river to make a bridge of flesh so that the lovers can cross and meet halfway. It's a great story. I love that story. In Japanese it's *Tanabata* and it's the source of the Tanabata festival on the seventh of July. It's also a festival in China, the Festival of the Weaver Girl. Both are so very close to the solstice. We know its origins because of Joseph Campbell.

THE LEGEND

In Chicago, it is snowing softly
and a man has just done his wash for the week.
He steps into the twilight of early evening,
carrying a wrinkled shopping bag
full of neatly folded clothes,
and, for a moment, enjoys
the feel of warm laundry and crinkled paper,
flannellike against his gloveless hands.
There's a Rembrandt glow on his face,
a triangle of orange in the hollow of his cheek
as a last flash of sunset
blazes the storefronts and lit windows of the street.

He is Asian, Thai or Vietnamese,
and very skinny, dressed as one of the poor
in rumpled suit pants and a plaid mackinaw,
dingy and too large.
He negotiates the slick of ice

on the sidewalk by his car,
opens the Fairlane's back door,
leans to place the laundry in,
and turns, for an instant,
toward the flurry of footsteps
and cries of pedestrians
as a boy—that's all he was—
backs from the corner package store
shooting a pistol, firing it,
once, at the dumbfounded man
who falls forward,
grabbing at his chest.

A few sounds escape from his mouth,
a babbling no one understands
as people surround him
bewildered at his speech.
The noises he makes are nothing to them.
The boy has gone, lost
in the light array of foot traffic
dappling the snow with fresh prints.

Tonight, I read about Descartes'
grand courage to doubt everything
except his own miraculous existence
and I feel so distinct
from the wounded man lying on the concrete
I am ashamed.

Let the night sky cover him as he dies.
Let the weaver girl cross the bridge of heaven
and take up his cold hands.

IN MEMORY OF JAY KASHIWAMURA

MOYERS: How did you come to connect this story to the killing of an anonymous Asian man on the streets of Chicago?

HONGO: It was given to me. At that time I was in graduate school, reading Western philosophy with people who had an analytic approach, what they call critical theory, and the approach stifled something in me. I felt the same way I had felt when I was in high school, which is to say there was a barrenness to my life. I happened to be in Chicago on a job interview, stuck in a motel room, when I saw something on TV about anonymous street violence, and in this case the person gunned down happened to be Asian. They didn't know if he was Cambodian or Thai—he was just vaguely Asian.

I remember carrying this experience back and then being asked by a magazine for a poem. Because I didn't have any new poems I just tried to sit down and write one—you don't want to give up the publication, you know—but I couldn't write anything. Then the next morning I woke up and started writing and it just appeared. I didn't will the poem, it just came together from that trip, and in the process of writing I recollected a memory, a story from my childhood that I never really understood. It was there in my subconscious, but it never found expression in my life in my own words. So that poem was just simply given because of my experience and because of the people who taught me. It was a flower, as they say in the Asian traditions.

MOYERS: A flower?

HONGO: Yes, the flowering of consciousness, something coming to fruition, something beautiful—*hana* in Japanese. I knew right away that it would be my polestar, it would guide the rest of my pursuits, so I decided not to do a dissertation and to write a book of poems instead.

ERUPTION: PU'U Ō'Ō

We woke near midnight,
flicking on the coat closet's bulb,
the rainforest chilled with mist,
a yellow swirl of gas
in the spill of light outside.
Stars paling, tucked high
in the sky's blue jade,
we saw, through the back windows
and tops of *ohi'a* trees,
silhouettes and red showers
as if from Blake's fires,
magenta and billows of black volleying.
Then, a burbling underground,
like rice steaming in the pot,
shook through chandeliers of fern
and the A-frame's tambourine floor,

stirring the cats and chickens
from the crawl-space and their furled sleep.
The fountain rose to 900 feet that night,
without us near it, smoking white,
spitting from the cone 6 miles away,
a geyser of flame, pyramids and gyres of ash.
Novices, we dressed and drove out,
first to the crater rim, Uwēkahuna
a canyon and sea of ash and moonstone,
the hardened, grey back of Leviathan
steaming and venting, dormant under cloud-cover.
And then next down Volcano Road past the villages
to Hirano Store on Kīlauea's long plateau
There, over canefield and the hardened lava land,
all we saw was in each other's eyes—
the mind's fear and the heart's delight,
running us this way and that.

MOYERS: Was "Eruption: Pu'u Ō'ō" also given to you?

HONGO: In a sense, yes. I brought my wife and young baby boy back to live in Volcano for a month when I was there the second time—I had a summer fellowship, and I wanted to bring my wife there to show her. About one o'clock in the morning on our third night in Volcano there was noise, the ground started rumbling, and things started shaking. I woke up, looked out, and through the windows I could see that everything was red. I figured "Eh, it must be an eruption"—we were eight or nine miles from the vent—and I went back to bed.

But my wife, who is from Oregon and whose idea of volcanoes is Mount St. Helens said, "Am I correct in assuming that you're going back to bed?" My idea of volcanoes is something else, more steady-state, the benign kind of thing we have in Hawai'i, so I said, "Yes," and did in fact go back to bed. Then my wife said, "I'm going to call the neighbors. I'm going to call the Coast Guard." I said, "Don't do that! You'll make us look stupid!" But she called the volcano watch to talk to the guy—who turned out to be a classmate of ours from college—and she said, "Where should we go?" He asked, "Where are you?" and when she told him, he said, "Just drive down Volcano Road till you get to Hirano Store. You can see it real good from Hirano Store." She said, "I don't want to *see* it! I want to get *away* from it!" He started laughing and said, "It's no danger." So it was just the twenty-fourth phase of the eruption of Kīlauea, 1985, and I wrote that poem in response to her fear and its grandeur.

MOYERS: ". . . the mind's fear and the heart's delight . . ." Language and landscape equal poetry.

HONGO: In his *Autobiography,* Yeats said that for a poet's words to live beyond his own time those words have to be wedded to the natural figures of his landscape. I think he actually might have said native landscape, which is a problem for many of us here, because for most of us nothing is native.

I had those words, but they didn't really reach me until I went back to my birthplace, to Volcano, and I saw that rainforest of *ohi'a* trees. When I could look up at the cloud line and beyond the cloud line I could see Mauna Loa rising up to fourteen thousand feet on one side and when I could stand on the crater rim of Kīlauea and look down into Halema'uma'u, the caldera, then I knew what his words and injunctions meant. I had to treasure the landscape, and I wrote my next book from that impulse. I'm grateful that when I was there at the crater rim I had the education and the words of the great poets to help me know what I was feeling and to help me evince the clarity of emotion needed to maintain the glimmering of consciousness I had at that moment.

MOYERS: Poetry and volcanoes keep remaking the world.

HONGO: Yes, I guess so. When you look into a volcano, at the lava pond, an acre and a half of living, molten flesh of the universe, your words feel like nothing. It's no wonder Hawaiians believe in Pele. Nothing feels the same after you have had an experience of the sublime.

© William Abranowicz

SHARON OLDS

Sharon Olds is greeted with zestful applause when she reads in public and bravely tests the frontiers of what a poet can write about in a poem. Her mission has been to enlarge the uses of poetry in society, and she has taught in many places, including five years at the Goldwater Hospital in New York City for severely disabled people. She currently teaches at New York University.

Poets are like steam valves, where the ordinary feelings of ordinary people can escape and be shown.

When I first wrote, I wrote in private. I never thought I would show my work to anyone. Then I got to where I wanted to send my poems out—to join in. I even worked on pseudonyms. And then I decided I did not want to join in but under my own name.

When I first gave readings, I had nightmares before the readings; I felt that the hearers were my judges. I had nightmares in which I was way down below and the audience was all the way up behind the judge's bench, and they were all saying, "To the lions!" But I don't feel that way anymore.

I Go Back to May 1937

I see them standing at the formal gates of their colleges,
I see my father strolling out
under the ochre sandstone arch, the
red tiles glinting like bent
plates of blood behind his head, I
see my mother with a few light books at her hip
standing at the pillar made of tiny bricks with the
wrought-iron gate still open behind her, its
sword-tips black in the May air,
they are about to graduate, they are about to get married,
they are kids, they are dumb, all they know is they are
innocent, they would never hurt anybody.
I want to go up to them and say Stop,
don't do it—she's the wrong woman,
he's the wrong man, you are going to do things
you cannot imagine you would ever do,
you are going to do bad things to children,
you are going to suffer in ways you never heard of,
you are going to want to die. I want to go
up to them there in late May sunlight and say it,
her hungry pretty blank face turning to me,
her pitiful beautiful untouched body,
his arrogant handsome blind face turning to me,
his pitiful beautiful untouched body,
but I don't do it. I want to live. I
take them up like the male and female
paper dolls and bang them together
at the hips like chips of flint as if
to strike sparks from them, I say
Do what you are going to do, and I will tell about it.

When I finished this poem I saw that it was a kind of manifesto in a way—
womanifesto in a way—and felt that I had said something that I hadn't said before.

I think people imagine that poets live a kind of exalted existence, which we don't. We have the same problems that everybody else has.

JANE KENYON

Jane Kenyon's poems are prayerful meditations on immediate human realities that simultaneously acknowledge the presence of mystery in human life. Through them, she confronts her experiences with depression, her husband's ordeal with cancer, and the trials and blessings of daily life. She and her husband, the poet Donald Hall, live on his ancestral New Hampshire farm, where she is devoted to poetry and gardening alike.

MOYERS: Your poems on moving—on leaving one place and arriving in another—rang true with me because they express a sense of being lost I have experienced even when I know where I am. How did you come to write these?

KENYON: I think that writing those was my effort to understand and control what was happening to me. For me poetry's a safe place always, a refuge, and it has been since I took it up in the eighth grade, so it was natural for me to write about these things that were going on in my own soul.

MOYERS: What *was* going on?

KENYON: I felt quite disembodied for a while. Someone said that when you move, it takes your soul a few weeks to catch up with you. Of course, this house is so thoroughly full of Don's family, his ancestors, their belongings, their reverberations, that when we came here, I felt almost annihilated by the "otherness" of it at times.

MOYERS: When I read "Here" I'm struck by the paradox that it was you who persuaded Don to come back to New Hampshire, it was you who imagined a future here.

HERE

You always belonged here.
You were theirs, certain as a rock.
I'm the one who worries
if I fit in with the furniture
and the landscape.

But I "follow too much
the devices and desires of my own heart."

Already the curves in the road
are familiar to me, and the mountain
in all kinds of light,
treating all people the same.
And when I come over the hill,
I see the house, with its generous
and firm proportions, smoke
rising gaily from the chimney.

I feel my life start up again,
like a cutting when it grows
the first pale and tentative
root hair in a glass of water.

KENYON: I did, strange to say. I guess I didn't know what I was saying when I said it. I was born in Ann Arbor, but my family lived outside the city limits and I went to a one-room school until I was in the fifth grade when the township was annexed into the Ann Arbor city schools, so I grew up in the country. The farm across the road was a working farm, and all the smells and sounds of country existence were familiar and dear to me. When I grew older, there was a gradual erosion of that existence as the road was paved and the town of Ann Arbor crept out to where my family was living. So coming here was like recovering something for me that was very, very dear.

MOYERS: And yet in the beginning you felt like a stranger.

KENYON: I did, but I think that's natural.

MOYERS: In "From Room to Room," how does the mind go from singing "the tie that binds" down the road at the church to the astronauts in the heavens?

FROM ROOM TO ROOM

Here in this house, among photographs
of your ancestors, their hymnbooks and old
shoes . . .

I move from room to room,
a little dazed, like the fly. I watch it
bump against each window.

I am clumsy here, thrusting
slabs of maple into the stove.
Out of my body for a while,
weightless in space . . .

                    Sometimes
the wind against the clapboard
sounds like a car driving up to the house.

My people are not here, my mother
and father, my brother. I talk
to the cats about weather.

"Blessed be the tie that binds . . ."
we sing in the church down the road.
And how does it go from there? The tie . . .

the tether, the hose carrying
oxygen to the astronaut,
turning, turning outside the hatch,
taking a look around.

KENYON: It's really a visual image of the astronaut floating out with his umbilical cord from the mother ship.

MOYERS: Women are always doing this, aren't they? They move from their place to their husband's place, from their ground to his ground. When I read these poems I think of my own wife, Judith, who moved with me from pillar to post, from Texas to Scotland to Washington to New York. I imagined her when I read "Finding a Long Gray Hair."

FINDING A LONG GRAY HAIR

I scrub the long floorboards
in the kitchen, repeating
the motions of other women
who have lived in this house.
And when I find a long gray hair
floating in the pail,
I feel my life added to theirs.

KENYON: It's funny how working in a place and perhaps changing it a little is a way of making it yours. I've patched and sanded and painted and scraped and raked and shoveled. That was the way I gradually came to feel that this was my place too. I think making my gardens—I have enormous perennial gardens—was probably the thing that finally really tied me to this place.

MOYERS: Why is the natural world so important to you?

KENYON: I love it so much. I always have. I think growing up in the country far from friends made me an inward child to begin with. I can remember playing long hours outside by myself.

MOYERS: Did you really know at the age of eight that you wanted to be a poet?

KENYON: Heavens, no!

MOYERS: When did that insight come to you?

KENYON: That's something that I almost feel spooky about saying. Even now calling myself a poet seems, somehow, to step out of line.

MOYERS: Why?

KENYON: I guess it's not for me to say somehow.

MOYERS: But you write poems.

KENYON: I guess I do.

MOYERS: You just got a Guggenheim Fellowship for your poems, and I've seen people respond to your poems at the poetry festival. But something holds you back from claiming what you've done.

KENYON: There *is,* and I don't know quite what it is. I mean, at a party if someone asks. What do you do?" I think, "Oh, dear," and say, "Well, I'm a writer." Then they say, "What do you write?" and I say, "I'm a poet." A funny look comes across their face at that point and they say, "Have you published?" When I say, "Yes, I have published," they tell me about *their* beginning efforts at poetry and how they no longer have time to read poetry, and we go from there.

MOYERS: What does it say that many of us want to be poets and yet, as a society, we scarcely honor poets, even dead poets?

KENYON: I think people imagine that poets live a kind of exalted existence, which we don't. We have the same problems that everybody else has. I don't know why people like to imagine that they could write poems. I think it's partly because everyone uses language.

MOYERS: We all have something to say.

KENYON: Yes. We all have something to say, and we all use language, so people think that they themselves could do this. It's like the mother who says, looking at Picasso's paintings, "My child draws better than that." People don't know how hard it is to write, what a struggle it is to know what you want to say and then to say what you mean.

MOYERS: How long does it take you to write a poem?

KENYON: Usually for me it's a process of at least three or four months. I work with several other writers. Of course, Don and I exchange work and help each other a good deal. But there are two other writers with whom I work very closely, and we meet two or three, sometimes four, times a year and go over everything we've written together.

We sit down and read and talk about every single line and then I go home and finish something. So if I've started something relatively close to workshop, I may be able to finish the poem within a month or two. But if there's a long break between workshops, then I'm kind of held up until I take it through workshop. I would never consider sending anything out until my friends have looked at it.

MOYERS: They're your first editors?

KENYON: Yes. I really have three first readers. Don's my first reader always. I listen to everything he says, as I listen to everything my friends tell me, and then finally I have to decide for myself what really needs to be changed and what really can't be changed.

MOYERS: You both gave up a lot when you moved to New Hampshire. Don gave up tenure, insurance, retirement, pension plan, all the amenities that come with an established university position. Does choosing the life of the poet require a vow of poverty?

KENYON: It requires a life of as much simplicity as possible, but far from being impoverished by coming here, we have both been incalculably enriched in our inner lives by becoming part of this community.

MOYERS: When did you know that you were at home here?

KENYON: I'd say I began to feel at home here within eight or ten months.

MOYERS: Did writing poetry help you to settle in?

KENYON: I'm sure it did. You see, when we moved here, I had absolutely unstructured time. I had twenty-four hours a day to do or not do what I wanted. So I really began to work seriously as a poet when we came here.

MOYERS: Long hours every day?

KENYON: Not long hours. Two or three hours of intensive work on poems are about as much as I can do. Writing poems is spilling your guts, and you can't sustain that over hours.

MOYERS: In talking to poets about their work I've noticed there comes a moment when their emotional exhaustion is evident.

KENYON: Yes. Poetry has an intensity about it, which is one of its loveliest qualities, but that's also the thing that fatigues you when you're working on it. There's a pitch of emotion in poems that you must rise to. Every time you work on the poem you must rise to it again.

MOYERS: It's such a way of remembering, and remembering what it is you want to hold on to is very difficult to do at times. I am reminded of "February: Thinking of Flowers." Is that poem a deliberate effort to break through the melancholy of winter?

FEBRUARY: THINKING OF FLOWERS

Now wind torments the field,
turning the white surface back
on itself, back and back on itself,
like an animal licking a wound.

Nothing but white—the air, the light;
only one brown milkweed pod
bobbing in the gully, smallest
brown boat on the immense tide.

A single green sprouting thing
would restore me. . . .

Then think of the tall delphinium,
swaying, or the bee when it comes
to the tongue of the burgundy lily.

K E N Y O N : Dreaming of gardens is something that always elevates my mood.

M O Y E R S : What do you mean by "greedy for unhappiness" in "Depression in Winter"?

DEPRESSION IN WINTER

There comes a little space between the south
side of a boulder
and the snow that fills the woods around it.
Sun heats the stone, reveals
a crescent of bare ground: brown ferns,
and tufts of needles like red hair,
acorns, a patch of moss, bright green. . . .

I sank with every step up to my knees,
throwing myself forward with a violence
of effort, greedy for unhappiness—
until by accident I found the stone,
with its secret porch of heat and light,
where something small could luxuriate, then
turned back down my path, chastened and calm.

K E N Y O N : Do you ever get into a state where you just need to let it go? I find that when I feel that way I do something. I desert myself physically in some way and that lets the steam off without hurting anybody I care about.

M O Y E R S : I know people who welcome melancholy.

K E N Y O N : Yes. Then they know where they are. There are moments, I think, when we all feel that. Depression is something I've suffered from all my life. I'm manic-depressive, actually, and I was not properly diagnosed until I was thirty-eight years old. In my case it's more like a unipolar depression. Manic-depression usually involves both poles of feeling. That is, when you're happy you're too happy, when you're sad you get too sad. Mine behaves almost like a serious depression only and I rarely become manic.

M O Y E R S : Depression is really the land of the living dead.

K E N Y O N : It surely is.

M O Y E R S : It must be hard to read poems about depression in public.

KENYON: It can be.

MOYERS: How do audiences respond?

KENYON: I find people are usually moved by them, and many people, even if they've never experienced such unhappiness themselves, know people who have. Either they have parents or siblings or spouses or friends who have been touched by mood disorders. I have found that when I've read any of these poems that really dwell on depression, people come up to me afterward and hug me. They say, for example, "My mother was manic-depressive, and I had a terrible childhood because of it." As I was reading "Having It Out with Melancholy" last week in Louisville, Kentucky, a man in the second row, who had been looking at me intently as the poem went on and it talks about unrelenting depression, took his hand and put it over his heart. Then he brought his hand to his heart over and over and just looked in my face. I knew that he also suffered.

FROM HAVING IT OUT WITH MELANCHOLY

If many remedies are prescribed
for an illness, you may be certain
that the illness has no cure.

A. P. CHEKHOV
The Cherry Orchard

1 FROM THE NURSERY

When I was born, you waited
behind a pile of linen in the nursery,
and when we were alone, you lay down
on top of me, pressing
the bile of desolation into every pore.

And from that day on
everything under the sun and moon
made me sad—even the yellow
wooden beads that slid and spun
along a spindle on my crib.

You taught me to exist without gratitude.
You ruined my manners toward God:
"We're here simply to wait for death;
the pleasures of earth are overrated."

I only appeared to belong to my mother,
to live among blocks and cotton undershirts
with snaps; among red tin lunch boxes
and report cards in ugly brown slipcases.
I was already yours—the anti-urge,
the mutilator of souls.

. . . .

3 SUGGESTION FROM A FRIEND

You wouldn't be so depressed
if you really believed in God.

4 OFTEN

Often I go to bed as soon after dinner
as seems adult
(I mean I try to wait for dark)
in order to push away
from the massive pain in sleep's
frail wicker coracle.

5 ONCE THERE WAS LIGHT

Once, in my early thirties, I saw
that I was a speck of light in the great
river of light that undulates through time.

I was floating with the whole
human family. We were all colors—those
who are living now, those who have died,
those who are not yet born. For a few

moments I floated, completely calm,
and I no longer hated having to exist.

Like a crow who smells hot blood
you came flying to pull me out
of the glowing stream.
"I'll hold you up. I never let my dear
ones drown!" After that, I wept for days.

6 IN AND OUT

The dog searches until he finds me
upstairs, lies down with a clatter
of elbows, puts his head on my foot.

Sometimes the sound of his breathing
saves my life—in and out, in
and out; a pause, a long sigh. . . .

7 PARDON

A piece of burned meat
wears my clothes, speaks
in my voice, dispatches obligations
haltingly, or not at all.
It is tired of trying
to be stouthearted, tired
beyond measure.

We move on to the monoamine
oxidase inhibitors. Day and night
I feel as if I had drunk six cups
of coffee, but the pain stops
abruptly. With the wonder
and bitterness of someone pardoned
for a crime she did not commit
I come back to marriage and friends,
to pink fringed hollyhocks; come back
to my desk, books, and chair.

MOYERS: I believe your poems help people to deal with depression.

KENYON: That is my hope, because if this is just personal, then I've been wasting my time. The unrelenting quality of depression really makes its impression on people. It's this thing that will not let you go, that comes when it wants and goes when it wants. You're like a chipmunk in the eagle's talons. There's nothing you can do. Well, that's not strictly true. There is something you can do if you have mood disorders. There are medications that help people.

MOYERS: And are you on medication?

KENYON: Oh, yes. I'm on a lot of medication. I'm on a combination of medications, and I jokingly call my psychiatrist my "mixologist." He's a good man.

MOYERS: When you write "I was already yours," you mean depression? Depression owned you?

KENYON: Yes. There is a genetic component to this. My father had it, and I believe his mother had it. I really take after my father's people. I'm sure that it came down his lines. I'm trying to explain to people who have never experienced this kind of desolation, what it is. It's important for people to understand that those with endogenous depression, melancholia, don't do this for the fun of it. I'm no more responsible for my melancholy than I am for having brown eyes. Unfortunately, it's taken me a long time to really believe that it's not my fault. It's like having heart disease or diabetes. I've decided that I want to increase people's understanding about this disease. I want to ease people's burdens.

MOYERS: Well, you do just that when you say, "I go to bed as soon after dinner / as seems adult / (I mean I try to wait for dark)." My own brother suffered from depression. I have had occasional bouts with it. How many times have we wanted to go to bed without being able to explain to anybody? When I read that, I thought, "She's got it."

KENYON: There are lots of people in public life who have had serious mood disorders. Abraham Lincoln was depressive.

MOYERS: Lyndon Johnson suffered bouts of melancholy.

KENYON: See, anybody who's anybody is manic-depressive.

MOYERS: I'll let the audience decide, but I appreciate the courage it takes for you to address it.

KENYON: Well, it's either courage or I don't know what.

MOYERS: Tell me about "Once There Was Light."

KENYON: I really had a vision of that once. It was like a waking dream. My eyes were open and I saw these rooms, this house, but in my mind's eye, or whatever language you can find to say these things, I also saw a great ribbon of light and every human life was suspended. There was no struggle. There was only this buoyant shimmering, undulating stream of light. I took my place in this stream and after that my life changed fundamentally. I relaxed into existence in a way that I never had before.

MOYERS: Relaxed into existence?

KENYON: Having had life-long struggles with depression, there have been long periods in my life when being in this world hasn't seemed like any great bargain, but after having this wave of buoyant emotion, my understanding was changed fundamentally.

MOYERS: What happens at the end of that poem?

KENYON: It's a kind of personification of the return of this awful feeling, in the midst of this joy that I was momentarily experiencing. I realize, in retrospect, that this was probably a manic swing followed by a crash, a bad one.

MOYERS: When you crashed, would drugs bring you back?

KENYON: Yes, very gradually. They take a long time to work, and there are sometimes false starts with drugs. Sometimes you begin on a course of treatment with a drug that ultimately you're just not going to be able to tolerate. They all have some nasty side effects, and it's always a question of balancing side effects against the good that comes of them. Sometimes a drug just doesn't work for you. There's no way of knowing except by trying. It can take months to get straightened around. I went off all drugs this summer for the first time in eleven years, because I thought to myself, "I need to find out if I really need this stuff, or if I'm just pouring money down the drain." I went off everything. I tapered off and by June I was off everything. Five weeks later I crashed and it took us seven months to find the right drug in the right dose. I didn't write for seven months. I couldn't concentrate. I couldn't read. I didn't answer my mail. I didn't want to see friends.

MOYERS: Was it only medication that brought you back? Is it only medication that keeps you going?

KENYON: We don't know. In the years before I used antidepressants, I would sometimes have a kind of spontaneous relief from depressions. Who knows what happens in the brain? But I really seem to need these drugs.

MOYERS: What else has helped you?

KENYON: My belief in God, such as it is, especially the idea that a believer is part of the body of Christ, has kept me from harming myself. When I really didn't want to be conscious, didn't want to be aware, was in so much pain that I didn't want to be awake or aware, I've thought to myself, "If you injure yourself you're injuring the body of Christ, and Christ has been injured enough."

MOYERS: What about the little church here in town? You and Don are regulars there.

KENYON: Oh, that's a long and complex relationship. We began going to church when we moved here, and I had not been to church since I was twelve years old. I was brought up in the Methodist Church in Ann Arbor, a large, rather rich suburban church, but my parents very much enjoyed the minister and so we went. Both of them had grown up in Methodist families. In fact, we have Methodist preachers on both sides.

MOYERS: Now there could be the cause of your depression!

KENYON: That could be! I have schoolmarms and Methodist ministers. But at the age of twelve I announced that I was too sophisticated for that kind of thing, whereupon the entire family stopped going to church. So I had not been in a church except for weddings, funerals, and baptisms since that time.

Then when we came here Don said, "Well, they'll be expecting us at church," and I thought, "Oh, this means putting on stockings and not lazing about reading the paper all day." Well, off we went. There was a wonderful minister who became a dear friend. That day he gave a shapely, intelligent, convincing sermon and I thought to myself, "I wouldn't mind going back and hearing him again." We got into the habit of going to church, and at first it was more a social act than a spiritual act. But within a short time I discovered that I had an enormous spiritual hunger that I knew nothing about. It had been stirred a little by Robert Bly in the late '60s and early '70s. I could sense in Bly the power of the sublime. He was in touch with some power that was thrilling. I began to see that the spiritual dimension that poetry could have, an almost priestly function for the poet, was the only spirituality I had known for a long time. Then we started going to church and, before I knew what had happened to me, I'd become a believer, which I really never was as a child. I dutifully said my prayers when I was a child, but I was afraid of that God. The God that our minister here talked about in his sermons was a God who overcomes you with love, not a God of rules and prohibitions. This was a God who, if you ask, forgives you no matter how far down in the well you are. If I didn't believe that I couldn't live.

MOYERS: Can you write a poem or think about faith when you're depressed?

KENYON: I do think about faith and I have been able to revise when I'm depressed, but I don't initiate things when I'm depressed. I can't call the plumber to come and fix the drain. I can't initiate anything. I can't move.

MOYERS: But you can think about your faith?

KENYON: Well, I can call out.

MOYERS: And do you get an answer?

KENYON: Sometimes I do. When you get to be my age and you've lived with depression for a number of years, you begin to have a context for believing that you will feel better at some point. You have been through it enough times so that you know, sooner or later, if you can just stick it out, it's going to lift. It's going to be better.

MOYERS: That might explain "Peonies at Dusk."

PEONIES AT DUSK

White peonies blooming along the porch
send out light
while the rest of the yard grows dim.

Outrageous flowers as big as human
heads! They're staggered
by their own luxuriance: I had
to prop them up with stakes and twine.

The moist air intensifies their scent,
and the moon moves around the barn
to find out what it's coming from.

In the darkening June evening
I draw a blossom near, and bending close
search it as a woman searches
a loved one's face.

KENYON: Gardening is something that has helped me. Gardening and hiking, exercise, being outside, that's all very important.

MOYERS: I know what you mean. When the claustrophobia of the city sets in and the darkness of winter is all around us, my wife and I begin to think of spring and her own flowers and plants. That's why I think this poem is one of my favorites. I really like that notion of concentrating on the blossom. It reminds me of meditation, paying attention.

KENYON: Yes. Being awake. I suppose that the men in the white coats would come and get me if they could hear me in my garden talking to my plants and saying, "What is it you need, my dear? Your leaves are turning yellow. Is the soil too alkaline for you? Do you need nitrogen? What's the problem?" When the roses are blooming and the peonies are blooming, I literally just say, "My beauties." I talk to them, I really do. It's nuts, but . . .

MOYERS: We should all be so nutty. So many people now live lives remote from "Peonies at Dusk."

KENYON: One of the functions of poetry is to keep the memory of people and places and things and happenings alive.

MOYERS: There's a curious passage perhaps related to this question in "The Bat." You're writing about this creature people habitually shun when suddenly the third person of the Trinity, the Holy Spirit, enters the poem.

THE BAT

I was reading about rationalism,
the kind of thing we do up north
in early winter, where the sun
leaves work for the day at 4:15.

Maybe the world *is* intelligible
to the rational mind;
and maybe we light the lamps at dusk
for nothing. . . .

Then I heard wings overhead.

The cats and I chased the bat
in circles—living room, kitchen,
pantry, kitchen, living room. . . .
At every turn it evaded us

like the identity of the third person
in the Trinity: the one
who spoke through the prophets,
the one who astounded Mary
by suddenly coming near.

KENYON: What I had in mind was being broken in upon, the way Mary was broken in upon by Gabriel. You think you're alone and suddenly there's this thing coming near you, so near that you can feel the wind from the brushing of its wings. Why this experience with the bat made me think of Mary and Gabriel, I don't know, but it did.

MOYERS: That's the point, isn't it? Inspiration occurs without explanation.

KENYON: There are times when I just feel I'm being *given* poems.

MOYERS: How do we cultivate that in ourselves?

KENYON: We have to get quiet. We have to be still, and that's harder and harder in this century.

MOYERS: Has it ever occurred to you, and I don't mean this as perversely as it sounds, that perhaps depression is itself a gift, a kind of garden in which ideas grow and in which experiences take root?

KENYON: That may be because—I never thought of it this way—depression makes me still.

MOYERS: All through history it's been the people in retreat, those who go into stillness, who hear that voice.

KENYON: Yes. I use a long portion of the 139th Psalm as a sort of epigraph to *Constance*. The psalmist says, darkness and light, it's all the same. It's all from God. It's all in God, through God, with God. There is no place I can go where Your love does not pursue me. The poems in this book are very dark, and many of them I can't read without weeping. I can't read many of them when I do poetry readings, but there is something in me that will not be snuffed out, even by this awful disease.

MOYERS: How did you receive the word of Don's cancer?

KENYON: Well, at first with disbelief. You know, Kübler-Ross's five steps. At first there was disbelief, then there was a lot of howling around here.

MOYERS: Howling?

KENYON: Yes. Not a Yankee trait, but there was a lot of howling around here. And, well, what we have is the present. That's all we ever had, really, except for memory. So we're trying to learn to live in the present.

MOYERS: You wrote "Pharaoh" after Don's experience. Why did you call him "Pharaoh"?

PHARAOH

"The future ain't what it used to be,"
said the sage of the New York Yankees
as he pounded his mitt, releasing
the red dust of the infield
into the harshly illuminated evening air.

Big hands. Men with big hands
make things happen. The surgeon,
when I asked how big your tumor was,
held forth his substantial fist
with its globed class ring.

Home again, we live as charily as strangers.
Things are off: Touch rankles, food
is not good. Even the kindness of friends
turns burdensome; their flowers sadden
us, so many and so fair.

I woke in the night to see your
diminished bulk lying beside me—
you on your back, like a sarcophagus
as your feet held up the cover. . . .
The things you might need in the next
life surrounded you—your comb and glasses,
water, a book and a pen.

KENYON: This was an actual visual perception. He was lying in bed with the covers over him and his feet were holding up the covers at the bottom. I could see the outline of his body dimly in the dark room. This was after he was home and recovering from his big surgery, and it suggested to me a pharaoh, a sarcophagus.

MOYERS: A sarcophagus? A tomb?

KENYON: Yes. It's odd but true that there really is consolation from sad poems, and it's hard to know how that happens. There's the pleasure of the thing itself, the pleasure of the poem, and somehow it works against the sadness.

MOYERS: We now know that grief can be a consolation if you work through it therapeutically, and a poem can help us do that, though not by sugar-coated optimism or denial.

KENYON: No. Certainly not by denial.

MOYERS: I admire your attitude toward denial and the notion of living in the present which comes with it. You catch both so beautifully in "Otherwise." Is this a late poem, written after Don's illness? But didn't you have cancer also?

OTHERWISE

I got out of bed
on two strong legs.
It might have been
otherwise. I ate
cereal, sweet
milk, ripe, flawless
peach. It might
have been otherwise.
I took the dog uphill
to the birch wood.
All morning I did
the work I love.

At noon I lay down
with my mate. It might
have been otherwise.
We ate dinner together
at a table with silver
candlesticks. It might
have been otherwise.
I slept in a bed
in a room with paintings
on the walls, and
planned another day
just like this day.
But one day, I know,
it will be otherwise.

KENYON: Yes. I had a cancerous salivary gland removed from my neck about seven years ago, and I believe I wrote "Otherwise" before we knew about his metastasis, before we knew about his liver cancer. After the first bout but before the second.

MOYERS: Well, the first was bad enough, wasn't it?

KENYON: Yes, the first was plenty bad. He's had two big surgeries, but he has enormous human vitality and sprang back very well.

MOYERS: Do you and Don talk about death?

KENYON: Yes, we've talked very openly about our fears and our angers and our sorrows.

MOYERS: Do you see new subjects, new horizons for your work?

KENYON: I have been going through a time of poor concentration. I think it's partly to do with the upheaval in our lives from Don's illness and his mother's illness, and then my mother had a bad fall in October. So there've been a lot of upheavals in my personal life that have broken my concentration. I'm not in a good rhythm of work. But I think that also happens to me when I'm getting ready to make some kind of leap, either in the subjects I undertake to talk about in my poems or some technical change, maybe longer lines or something else—I don't know. These silences often come over me before something new breaks in, but they're hard to wait out.

MOYERS: How did you come to write "Let Evening Come"? So many people say that's their favorite of your poems.

LET EVENING COME

Let the light of late afternoon
shine through chinks in the barn, moving
up the bales as the sun moves down.

Let the cricket take up chafing
as a woman takes up her needles
and her yarn. Let evening come.

Let dew collect on the hoe abandoned
in long grass. Let the stars appear
and the moon disclose her silver horn.

Let the fox go back to its sandy den.
Let the wind die down. Let the shed
go black inside. Let evening come.

To the bottle in the ditch, to the scoop
in the oats, to air in the lung
let evening come.

Let it come, as it will, and don't
be afraid. God does not leave us
comfortless, so let evening come.

KENYON: That poem was given to me.

MOYERS: By?

KENYON: The muse, the Holy Ghost. I had written all the other poems in the book in which it appears, and I knew that it was a very sober book. I felt it needed something redeeming. I went upstairs one day with the purpose of writing something redeeming, which is not the way to write, but this just fell out. I really didn't have to struggle with it.

MOYERS: Do you still believe what that poem expresses, given Don's cancer and your own illness?

KENYON: Yes. There are things in this life that we must endure which are all but unendurable, and yet I feel that there is a great goodness. Why, when there could have been nothing, is there something? This is a great mystery. How, when there could have been nothing, does it happen that there is love, kindness, beauty?

Jane Kenyon, Donald Hall

© William Abranowicz

STANLEY KUNITZ

Stanley Kunitz begins his ninetieth year with a new collection of luminous, life-affirming poems. Still wrestling with basic themes— "the world's wrongs and the injustice of time"—and still joyfully re-arranging the sounds of language as he does the flowers in his garden, Kunitz has received nearly every honor bestowed upon a poet, including the Pulitzer Prize in 1959 and appointments as consultant in poetry to the Library of Congress (now called poet laureate) and poet laureate of New York. He was a founder of the Fine Arts Work Center in Provincetown, Massachusetts, and of Poets House in New York City. He is also a chancellor of the Academy of American Poets.

MOYERS: Do you remember the first time you truly experienced words, somehow, as part of your being?

KUNITZ: I used to go out into the woods behind our house in Worcester, Massachusetts, and shout words, any words that came to me, preferably long ones, just because the sound of them excited me. "Eleemosynary," I recall, was one of my favorites. "Phantasmagoria" was another.

MOYERS: I grew up in the South where Lincoln was not as revered as he was elsewhere. I remember the sound of that language, even to this moment:

George Washington was a great big boss,
He rode himself around on a big white horse.
Abraham Lincoln was a goddamn fool,
He rode himself around on a skinny old mule.

KUNITZ: When I was in the fourth grade, my teacher, Miss McGillicuddy, had assigned us a composition on George Washington to celebrate his birthday. I still remember my sensational beginning: "George Washington was a tall, petite, handsome man." Whether or not I suspected what "petite" meant, I found it too elegant to resist. Miss McGillicuddy, whose French vocabulary may have been no better than mine, thought my composition was fabulous and every year from that point on into the next generation she used to read it to her new classes as a literary model. I spent a good part of my childhood exploring language, trying to find a new word every day in the unabridged Century Dictionary that was one of our household's prized possessions. And I

Poetry is the most difficult, the most solitary, and the most life-enhancing thing that one can do in the world.

haunted the public library. The librarian said sternly, "Five books. That's the limit you can take, Stanley. Five for the week." When I came back in a couple of days, she insisted I couldn't read that much so fast. I convinced her I had, and wangled permission to haul away five more. She was really a kind soul.

MOYERS: Were these books of poetry?

KUNITZ: Some were. Of course, my taste in poetry was indiscriminate. Tennyson and Whittier and Longfellow and James Whitcomb Riley and Robert Service all seemed to offer equal enchantments. When I was graduated from elementary school, as class valedictorian, the poem I chose to recite for the occasion was Kipling's "Recessional":

> Lord God of Hosts, be with us yet,
> Lest we forget—lest we forget!

By then I knew that language was tremendously important to me. I already felt drawn to the community of poets.

MOYERS: Once in East Africa on the shore of an ancient lake, I sat alone and suddenly it struck me what community is. It's gathering around the fire and listening to somebody tell a story.

KUNITZ: That's probably how poetry began, in some such setting. Wherever I've traveled in the world, I've never felt alone. Language is no barrier to people who love the word. I think of poets as solitaries with a heightened sense of community.

MOYERS: But, Stanley, is your community limited to other poets?

KUNITZ: I should be sad if that were true.

MOYERS: Have you ever changed a poem you wrote long ago?

KUNITZ: There are a few old poems I've tinkered with, correcting a word here or a phrase there that was obviously wrong, but I think it's foolhardy to attempt radical revisions of early work. You are no longer the poet who wrote those lines in his troubled youth. Time itself is stitched into the fabric of the text.

MOYERS: What has happened to the music of poetry? Why does poetry now simply lie there on the printed page, which you have called "a very cold bed"?

KUNITZ: One of the problems with poetry in the modern age is that it's become separated from the spoken word. When you ask students to read a poem aloud, you find they have no idea of the rhythm of the language, its flow, inflection, and pitch.

They do not understand that stress and tonality are instruments of meaning. Is the fault wholly theirs? Poetry has strayed far from its origins in song and dance. With its gradual retreat into print and, currently, into the academy, it is in danger of becoming a highly technical and specialized linguistic skill. It has already lost most of its general listening audience.

M O Y E R S : Is it possible that the rock musician is the poet of our day?

K U N I T Z : It's a commentary on the state of our culture that the vast audience for rock and other varieties of pop seems to be quite satisfied at that level of communication. It doesn't feel a need for poetry. That disturbs me because poetry explores depths of thought and feeling that civilization requires for its survival. What does it signify that the mass of our adult population cares as little for the poets of the great tradition as it does for the moderns? The consoling thought is that children are still impressionable and ready to receive poetry, ready to make it part of their lives. But that's before they are spoiled. Our educational system had failed us in that respect, among others.

M O Y E R S : I think back on the poems I read in high school—Shelley, Keats, and Byron. They rhymed. They had meter. That's not true anymore.

K U N I T Z : Certainly it's easier to remember verse that has a fixed rhyme scheme, a regular beat, and a standard length of line. Much of the pleasure we derive from the poetry of the past, regardless of its quality, is due to the fulfillment of expectations. But that's precisely the kind of aesthetic satisfaction that the most representative and seminal imaginations of this century taught us to question. Right now we seem to be entering a more conservative phase, but I'm not ready to greet the dawn of a neoclassical age.

M O Y E R S : Do people quote your poems?

K U N I T Z : Not by the tens of thousands, but I've heard of some who do. Perhaps it's relevant to note that I was trained in the metrical tradition or, rather, I trained myself, since there were no creative writing programs in those days. At a later stage I became a lapsed formalist, choosing to write by and for the ear, without preimposed conditions. I trust the ear to let my rhythms go where they need to go. The ear is the best of prosodists.

M O Y E R S : These lines of yours come to mind—I wish you'd comment on them.

> I dance, for the joy of surviving,
> on the edge of the road.

KUNITZ: That's the ending of "An Old Cracked Tune," a poem that had its origin in a scurrilous street song remembered from my youth. The butt of the song's mockery was a stereotypically avaricious and conniving Jewish tailor. The very first line—the one I appropriated—went: "My name is Solomon Levi." It didn't occur to me until later that Solomon was my father's given name and that he was a Levite, a descendant of the priestly house of Levi. When the line from that odious song popped into my head, I wondered, "Can I redeem it?" And so I wrote the poem.

AN OLD CRACKED TUNE

My name is Solomon Levi,
the desert is my home,
my mother's breast was thorny,
and father I had none.

The sands whispered, *Be separate,*
the stones taught me, *Be hard.*
I dance, for the joy of surviving,
on the edge of the road.

MOYERS: You must have been repelled by the anti-Semitism.

KUNITZ: It hurt me and left a scar. The bigotry of this country early in the century cut deep into our social fabric. And it persists to this day, as an ugly racist infection. I'm not implying that this was in mind when I started to write that poem. Poems don't tell you why you need to write them. Perhaps you write them in order to find out why. My driving impulse was to embrace a wounded name.

MOYERS: Why did you call the poem "An Old Cracked Tune"?

KUNITZ: I've never thought about it—the title came with the poem. "Old tune" must allude to the source of the poem, as well as to its being a sort of ancestral song. "Cracked" tells something about the speaker's age and voice and maybe about his state of mind.

MOYERS: Do you remember the original lyrics?

KUNITZ: No. Only the first line and "zip-zip-zip" out of the refrain. The one person on earth, to my knowledge, who remembers that song is Richard Wilbur.

MOYERS: The poet.

KUNITZ: Yes, and he can sing several stanzas of it—more, I guess, than I've ever wanted to remember. He may have heard it at Harvard years after I did.

MOYERS: Anti-Semitism cost you a teaching position at Harvard.

KUNITZ: According to the illustrious head of the English Department in 1927, the year of my M.A., Harvard's Anglo-Saxon students would resent being taught English literature by a Jew.

MOYERS: What did you do?

KUNITZ: I left Harvard in a state of rage and confusion. After a brief start as reporter for the *Worcester Telegram*, my hometown paper, I came to New York—this was on the eve of the Great Depression—and went to work for the H. W. Wilson publishing firm. There I became editor of the *Wilson Library Bulletin* and initiated a series of biographical dictionaries that are still standard works of literary reference. In 1930 Doubleday published *Intellectual Things*, my first book of poems.

MOYERS: What did you mean when you said you wanted to "redeem" the man in the poem?

KUNITZ: I hoped to restore his dignity by identifying with him. Like him, the poet in our society is a marginal character, dancing on the edge of the road, not in the middle where the heavy traffic flows. Maybe one of the secrets of survival is to learn *where* to dance.

MOYERS: You took something bitter and turned it into something joyous.

KUNITZ: Poetry has a great digestive system and can consume and recycle almost anything. It is the poet's persona that gives meaning to the process. For years I've been telling young poets that the first important act of the imagination is to create the person who will write the poems. And that's not the end of it. We have to invent and reinvent who we are until we arrive at the self we can bear to live with and die with. Art demands of the artist the capacity for self-renewal. Without it, art withers. And, of course, so does the life.

MOYERS: There is an erotic quality to poetry—creative and re-creative. Do you make love to the word?

KUNITZ: Every new poem is like finding a new bride. Words are so erotic, they never tire of their coupling. How do they renew themselves? In their inexhaustible desire for combinations and recombinations.

MOYERS: Is it hard work to write a poem?

KUNITZ: Is it *hard*? I think poetry is the most difficult, the most solitary, and the most life-enhancing thing that one can do in the world.

MOYERS: What makes it such a struggle?

KUNITZ: Because in our daily lives we enslave words, use them and abuse them, until they are fit for only menial tasks and small errands.

MOYERS: You have to kill a lot of clichés, don't you?

KUNITZ: You have to remove the top of your head and plunge into the deep waters of the buried life in order to come up with words that are fresh and shining. Poetry isn't written on schedule. A poem that occupies less than a page may take days, weeks, months—and still want more attention to set it right. You know, that's not very practical in the world's terms.

MOYERS: The world is so meagerly supportive of the poet. How do you keep going?

KUNITZ: A poet has to be cunning in the world's ways, too. Poets who flunk their lessons in the art of survival either drop out or die young. Above all, we need to buy time, meditation time, but not at the world's price. One of the strategies I've learned is to stay alive when the rest of the world is asleep. When I shut the door of my study, the clocks stop ticking. A few minutes seem to pass, and suddenly it's dawn.

MOYERS: On what are you meditating?

KUNITZ: *You* don't choose the subject of meditation, *it* chooses you. But you have to put yourself into a state of readiness. You have to move into areas of the self that remain to be explored, and that's one of the problems of maturing as a poet. By the age of fifty, the chances are that you've explored all the obvious places. The poems that remain for you to write will have to come out of your wilderness.

MOYERS: Wilderness?

KUNITZ: Yes, the untamed self that you pretend doesn't exist, all that chaos locked behind the closet door, those memories yammering in the dark. . . .

MOYERS: You have said that certain images are "key images." Are these memories of childhood?

KUNITZ: Usually so. I believe that at the center of every poetic imagination is a cluster of images associated with pivotal moments. That cluster is the key to one's identity, the purest concentration of the self. Poetry happens when new images of sensations are drawn into the gravitational field of the old life.

MOYERS: In "Three Floors," which is one of my favorite poems, you are remembering your childhood.

THREE FLOORS

Mother was a crack of light
and a gray eye peeping;
I made believe by breathing hard
that I was sleeping.

Sister's doughboy on last leave
had robbed me of her hand;
downstairs at intervals she played
Warum on the baby grand.

Under the roof of a wardrobe trunk
whose lock a boy could pick
contained a red Masonic hat
and a walking stick.

Bolt upright in my bed that night
I saw my father flying;
the wind was walking on my neck,
the windowpanes were crying.

KUNITZ: That poem is one of several stemming from the suicide of my father a few weeks before I was born. My mother kept just a few of his relics in a trunk in the attic, including a red Masonic hat and a walking stick, which figure in the poem. The time was World War I, when I was about ten. Another poem, "The Portrait," returns me to that attic, discovering a portrait of my father. When I brought it down to show to my mother, she tore it up.

MOYERS: And your mother slapped you for finding it, as the poem says?

KUNITZ: Yes.

THE PORTRAIT

My mother never forgave my father
for killing himself,
especially at such an awkward time
and in a public park,
that spring
when I was waiting to be born.
She locked his name
in her deepest cabinet
and would not let him out,
though I could hear him thumping.
When I came down from the attic
with the pastel portrait in my hand
of a long-lipped stranger
with a brave moustache
and deep brown level eyes,
she ripped it into shreds
without a single word
and slapped me hard.
In my sixty-fourth year
I can feel my cheek
still burning.

MOYERS: Do you think she slapped you because you found the portrait or because she held you responsible for your father's death?

KUNITZ: Her anger was directed at him, not at me. She wanted to expunge his memory. No mention of him ever crossed her lips.

MOYERS: For a long time you did not write about it.

KUNITZ: In "Father and Son," written in my mid-thirties, I pursue and ultimately confront his image. It was an act of liberation for me.

MOYERS: Of whom is the portrait a portrait? Your father, your mother, yourself? Or is it the portrait of an experience, a memory?

KUNITZ: You are perfectly right to imply that it is more than my father's portrait.

MOYERS: How do dreams play a role in the creating of poetry?

KUNITZ: In their fluidity and illogic, dream images readily translate into poetry. Everything in "Quinnapoxet," for example, came to me in a dream—not the words, but all the images.

QUINNAPOXET

I was fishing in the abandoned reservoir
back in Quinnapoxet,
where the snapping turtles cruised
and the bullheads swayed
in their bower of tree-stumps,
sleek as eels and pigeon-fat.
One of them gashed my thumb
with a flick of his razor fin
when I yanked the barb
out of his gullet.
The sun hung its terrible coals
over Buteau's farm: I saw
the treetops seething.

They came suddenly into view
on the Indian road,
evenly stepping
past the apple orchard,
commingling with the dust
they raised, their cloud of being,
against the dripping light
looming larger and bolder.
She was wearing a mourning bonnet
and a wrap of shining taffeta.
"Why don't you write?" she cried
from the folds of her veil.
"We never hear from you."
I had nothing to say to her.
But for him who walked behind her
in his dark worsted suit,
with his face averted

as if to hide a scald,
deep in his other life,
I touched my forehead
with my swollen thumb,
and splayed my fingers out—
in deaf-mute country
the sign for father.

MOYERS: Two people come into view, and a woman says, "Why don't you write?" The other is wearing a burial suit. Is he your father?

KUNITZ: That's the image.

MOYERS: You salute him. That is a reconciliation?

KUNITZ: The recognition of a bond. As if to say, we belong to each other.

MOYERS: And you dreamed this.

KUNITZ: From beginning to end. Then I began exploring what I had dreamed. In an illustrated article on sign language for the deaf I found the hand gesture I had made in my dream. It is the most reverential of all the signs for father.

MOYERS: Do you think there's special wisdom in dreams?

KUNITZ: Poets have always loved the language of dreams—it's so full of secrets.

MOYERS: Do you sometimes think you're carrying on a conversation with ancestors you never knew?

KUNITZ: The arts, by their nature, are our means of conducting that dialogue. Where is the history of the race inscribed, if not in the human imagination? One of my strongest convictions is that poetry is ultimately mythology, the telling of the stories of the soul. We keep asking Gauguin's famous set of questions, "Where do we come from? Who are we? Where are we going?" The echo that mocks us comes from the Stone Age caves. The poem on the page is only a shadow of the poem in the mind. And the poem in the mind is only a shadow of the poetry and the mystery of the things of this world. So we must try again, for the work is never finished I don't think it's absurd to believe that the chain of being, our indelible genetic code, holds memories of the ancient world that are passed down from generation to generation. Heraclitus speaks of "mortals and immortals living in their death, dying into each other's lives."

MOYERS: The other night, at your reading, young people were approaching, and they had very special applause for "End of Summer."

END OF SUMMER

An agitation of the air,
A perturbation of the light
Admonished me the unloved year
Would turn on its hinge that night.

I stood in the disenchanted field
Amid the stubble and the stones,
Amazed, while a small worm lisped to me
The song of my marrow-bones.

Blue poured into summer blue,
A hawk broke from his cloudless tower,
the roof of the silo blazed, and I knew
that part of my life was over.

Already the iron door of the north
Clangs open: birds, leaves, snows
Order their populations forth,
And a cruel wind blows.

KUNITZ: That poem came to me in mid-life when I was living in Bucks County, Pennsylvania. The occasion is still vivid in my mind. I was out in the field, hoeing down an old standard of corn. Suddenly I heard a commotion overhead. A flock of wild geese, streaking down from the north, rattled the sky with their honking. I stood in the field, gazing upward with a sense of tumult and wonder, for something had been revealed to me: the story of migration had become my story. At that moment I made one of the most important decisions of life. I dropped my hoe and ran into the house and started to write this poem. It began as a celebration of the wild geese. Eventually the geese flew out of the poem, but I like to think they left behind the sound of their beating wings.

MOYERS: Why did you use the word "perturbation" in the second line, "A perturbation of the light"? Why not "commotion" or "disturbance" or "flurry"?

KUNITZ: There's more wingbeat in "perturbation." I might add that the rhythm is intentionally persistent, relying largely on the interplay between open and closed vowels.

An agitation of the air,
A perturbation of the light
Admonished me the unloved year
Would turn on its hinge that night.

MOYERS: Did you speak the lines?

KUNITZ: I *always* speak the lines. That's how I write my poems.

MOYERS: You said that you heard the geese and looked up and responded instantly with a decision. That couldn't have been an intellectual decision. Your *body* said something to you which was triggered by the geese.

KUNITZ: I saw the writing in the sky. Don't forget that there were soothsayers in ancient times who practiced divination by studying the flight of birds.

MOYERS: I remember seeing your poem about the moonwalk, "The Flight of Apollo," in *The New York Times*

THE FLIGHT OF APOLLO

Earth was my home, but even there I was a stranger. This mineral crust. I walk like a swimmer. What titanic bombardments in those old astral wars! I know what I know: I shall never escape from strangeness or complete my journey. Think of me as nostalgic, afraid, exalted. I am your man on the moon, a speck of megalomania, restless for the leap toward island universes pulsing beyond where the constellations set. Infinite space overwhelms the human heart, but in the middle of nowhere life inexorably calls to life. Forward my mail to Mars. What news from the Great Spiral Nebula in Andromeda and the Magellanic Clouds?

2

I was a stranger on earth.
Stepping on the moon, I begin

the gay pilgrimage to new
Jerusalems
in foreign galaxies.
Heat. Cold. Craters of silence.
The Sea of Tranquillity
rolling on the shores of entropy.
And, beyond,
the intelligence of the stars.

KUNITZ: You have a long memory, for that was in 1969. The *Times* had asked me for a poem in tribute to man's first landing on the moon, and fortunately I had one at hand, having written it in the days before Apollo 11 was launched. When I saw the actual landing on TV, I felt I had already been there. There was no need to change a word. I've always been fascinated by space exploration, so that it seemed quite natural for me to imagine myself a stranger on earth seeking a new home in the skies. Eventually, I suppose, the human race will have to move from this planet and settle elsewhere in the galaxy, for this planet will die.

MOYERS: Beyond this planet, as you say in the poem, is "the intelligence of the stars."

KUNITZ: Simply on the basis of probability. I cannot believe that planet Earth is the only blob of dirt in the firmament that supports life.

MOYERS: There is a man in one of your poems who "carries a bag of earth on his back," and it reminds me that you are a gardener who likes to work with his hands. What does gardening have to do with poetry?

KUNITZ: It has *everything* to do with poetry. When I work in my garden I feel that it is myself being planted, nourished, reborn. I am enchanted with every step in the process of making things grow. In the grand view, I see gardening as a ritual drama, in which the whole cycle of death and rebirth is enacted annually. But that doesn't prevent me from undertaking the most lowly tasks and truly enjoying them, even weeding and grubbing. It strikes me that gardens and poems are equally unpredictable, given the vagaries of weather and imagination. A plant behaves beautifully one summer. The next summer it turns gross and invasive. Or languishes in the heat, disfigured and splotchy with mildew or succumbs to the voracious appetites of cutworms and beetles and slugs. In the civilization of the garden such specimens must be treated as outlaws. Out with them! The making of a garden requires the same kind of ruthlessness as the making of a poem.

MOYERS: I like the image of growing a garden as you grow a poem, as you grow a self. "Passing Through," the poem you wrote on your seventy-ninth birthday, implies a process of changing. In your later poems you write with much more simplicity and economy than in your early poems. Why is that?

PASSING THROUGH

—ON MY SEVENTY-NINTH BIRTHDAY

Nobody in the widow's household
ever celebrated anniversaries.
In the secrecy of my room
I would not admit I cared
that my friends were given parties.
Before I left town for school
my birthday went up in smoke
in a fire at City Hall that gutted
the Department of Vital Statistics.
If it weren't for a census report
of a five-year-old White Male
sharing my mother's address
at the Green Street tenement in Worcester
I'd have no documentary proof
that I exist. You are the first,
my dear, to bully me
into these festive occasions.

Sometimes, you say, I wear
an abstracted look that drives you
up the wall, as though it signified
distress or disaffection.
Don't take it so to heart.
Maybe I enjoy not-being as much
as being who I am. Maybe
it's time for me to practice
growing old. The way I look
at it, I'm passing through a phase:
gradually I'm changing to a word.
Whatever you choose to claim

of me is always yours;
nothing is truly mine
except my name. I only
borrowed this dust.

K U N I T Z : In a curious way, age is simpler than youth, for it has fewer options. In the beginning, life seems to offer us infinite choices, a bewilderment of opportunities. We have no certainties about our destination, or a path that will lead us there. We might become a scientist, or a theologian, or a farmer, or a poet. Who knows? Every time we make a significant choice—affecting, let's say, our education, or career, or involvement with others—we reduce, exponentially, the number of choices left to us. Finally, we arrive at the realization that the only remaining choice of any consequence, if it can be considered a choice at all, is between living and dying. This simplifies, as it purifies, the operation of the mind. What could be more natural than for the mature imagination at sunset to move toward economy of style and gravity of tone? When I read the late work of Hardy or Yeats, I get the distinct impression that the life of the poet is already passing into his poems.

M O Y E R S : You once said that you were living and dying at the same time, but when you reach a certain age aren't you dying faster than you're living?

K U N I T Z : I prefer to say, as I do in "Passing Through," that "gradually I'm changing to a word." The beauty of that transaction is that it involves a transfer of energy, not a loss. I'm conditioned to believe that the word is less perishable than its creator.

M O Y E R S : In another poem you ask, "What do I want of my life?" And you answer, "More! More!"

K U N I T Z : That's from an earlier poem—but I still subscribe to the sentiment.

M O Y E R S : Before we met today I was listening to Mozart's Piano Concert No. 21 and I thought, *that's* immortality. The musician has given way to the music. What about poetry?

K U N I T Z : I follow Coleridge in believing that the sense of musical delight, together with the power of producing it, is the gift that marks the poet born. When Keats wrote in one of his letters, "I am certain of nothing but of the holiness of the heart's affections and the truth of imagination," he was defining for all of us the ground of that music. Let me tell you about a twelfth-century Chinese poet named Yang Wan-li, one of the four masters of Southern Sung poetry. One day he gathered his disciples around him and addressed them in this fashion: "Now, what is poetry? If you say it is simply a matter of words, I will say, 'A good poet gets rid of words.' If you say it is simply a matter of meaning, I will say, 'A good poet gets rid of meaning.' But, you say, if words and meaning are gotten rid of, where is the poetry? To this I reply, 'Get rid of words and meaning and there is still poetry.'"

Scholars have been wrestling with that test for centuries. I think that Yang is telling us that poetry is more than a product of human intelligence and craft. It is an intrinsic element of the beauty and mystery of existence, something we take in with the air we breathe. We take it in and then we give back some semblance of it in our art.

In writing poetry, all of one's attention is focused on some inner voice.

LI-YOUNG LEE

Li-Young Lee was born in Djakarta, Indonesia, to exiled Chinese parents. His grandfather was the first president of the Republic of China, his mother was a member of the Chinese royal family, and his father was once personal physician to Mao Tse-tung. Fleeing persecution in Indonesia, the family wandered through Southeast Asia for five years before arriving in the United States, where his scholarly father became pastor of a small Presbyterian church. Li-Young Lee's poetry recaptures the stories that immigrants tell to preserve their history and identity. *The City in Which I Love You* won the Lamont Poetry Prize in 1990. Li-Young Lee lives in Chicago.

MOYERS: How do you answer when people ask, "Where are you from?"

LEE: I say Chicago, then I tell them I was born in Indonesia, but I'm adamant about insisting that, although I was born in Indonesia, I'm Chinese. I don't want them to think that I'm Indonesian—my people were persecuted by the Indonesians.

MOYERS: Your great-grandfather was the first president of the People's Republic of China.

LEE: Yes. He's my mother's grandfather and, of course, my mother's family—the House of Yuan—fell into demise during Mao's cultural revolution. Because my mother came from royalty and my father's father was a gangster and an entrepreneur, my parents' marriage was very frowned upon in China. When they got married they started traveling, and they finally fled to Indonesia, where my father had taught medicine and philosophy at Gamaliel University in Jakarta. Later on he was incarcerated by Sukarno because of his Western leanings. My father loved Western theology and Western literature. He was teaching the King James Bible there as literature, and when interest in Western culture fell out of favor he was locked up.

I was born in 1957, and he was locked up in 1958 and kept in prison for nineteen months. When he escaped we fled Indonesia and traveled throughout Indochina and Southeast Asia for several years before winding up in Hong Kong, where he became an evangelist minister and head of a hugely successful, million-dollar business. But he was driven almost solely by emotion and at one point got into an argument with somebody and simply left Hong Kong. We just left it all and came to America.

M O Y E R S: And what did he do then?

L E E: He took whatever money he had in his bank account, a couple thousand dollars, and my mother sold the jewelry off her body to get us through the first few years. We went from Seattle, where he was a greeter at the China exhibit at the Seattle World's Fair, to Pittsburgh, where he studied theology at the seminary there. He got his degree and became a Presbyterian minister at a very small church in Vandergrift, Pennsylvania.

M O Y E R S: What a story! From that rich, complex Oriental culture to a small American town.

L E E: Yes. I always thought there was something tragic about it, but he loved it. He loved the church and he loved the town we lived in. He loved being a pastor.

M O Y E R S: Why did the story of his life strike you as tragic?

L E E: He was a man of huge intellectual and artistic talents. He was reading and translating the Bible and Kierkegaard, and he loved Shakespeare and opera. Then he came to a basically working-class town where, although there were many beautiful and wonderful people, I think his intellectual life somehow stopped, or it wasn't fed. But he seemed not to mind—he told me when he was very ill that he was tired of running around so much, and that's why he loved being there.

M O Y E R S: Your journey—China, Indonesia, Hong Kong, Macao, Japan, Seattle, Pittsburgh—is a story of the twentieth century, the century of refugees.

L E E: In a way, I feel as if our experience may be no more than an outward manifestation of a homelessness that people in general feel. It seems to me that anybody who thinks about our position in the universe cannot help but feel a little disconnected and homeless, so I don't think we're special. We refugees might simply express outwardly what all people feel inwardly.

M O Y E R S: Do you feel yourself an exile?

L E E: In my most pessimistic moods I feel that I'm disconnected and that I'm going to be disconnected forever, that I'll never have any place that I can call home. For example, I find it strange that when I go to visit my father's grave I look down and there on his stone is the Chinese character for his name and, when I look up, there are all these American flags on the other graves. So I feel a little strange, but I don't know what it is. I don't feel nostalgic because I don't know what to feel nostalgic *for*. It's simply a feeling of disconnection and dislocation.

M O Y E R S : What is there about exodus and exile that gives some poets a special power?

L E E : I don't know. Exile seems both a blessing and a curse. A lot of my friends who are writers have said to me, "You're so lucky to have this background to write from," and I guess in a way I *am* lucky, but I wouldn't wish that experience on anybody. The literature I love most is the literature of ruins and the experience of exodus. I don't know why but, for example, the Book of Exodus is very important to me—the wandering of the children of Israel has profound resonance for me. I don't feel as if those stories are about a primitive tribe in some distant desert. That struggle for belief and faith in the face of humiliation, annihilation, apostasy—all of that seems to me really what I go through and what we *all* go through, finally.

M O Y E R S : How did you become a poet?

L E E : In my household my father read to us constantly from the King James Bible, and because he had a classical Chinese education, which meant he had memorized three hundred poems from the Tang Dynasty, he would recite those poems to us as well and we would recite them back to him. My memory was so bad I could never do very well, but I *did* learn to love poetry.

When I heard him read from the pulpit from Psalms and Proverbs, I would think, "My God, that's incredible! What power!" Then I would hear people in the congregation. I don't know if other faiths do this, but Presbyterians have a responsive reading where the minister reads a passage and the congregation responds by reading another passage—steelworkers, schoolteachers, all of us together saying, "Make a joyful noise unto the Lord, all ye lands." That seemed magical to me and entirely beautiful, but I never thought I could write it.

I thought poetry was some high and mighty thing of the angels and of the ancient dead in China. Later on, when I met Gerald Stern at the University of Pittsburgh, I read his poetry, and I suddenly realized that poetry could be written by living human beings. Then he became my teacher and I tried doing it myself.

M O Y E R S : Both of you write about exodus and ruins.

L E E : Yes. When I first opened his book *Lucky Life,* I expected small anecdotal poems—that's what we were taught to expect in modern poetry—but I suddenly thought I was reading something out of the Psalms or Lamentations. I walked around with *Lucky Life* in my pocket for two years—that book was just in tatters.

M O Y E R S : Well, the fact is that you were the son of a New Testament preacher and you were tutored by an Old Testament prophet—Gerald Stern is a prophet in shirtsleeves—so it's no surprise that I hear so much of the Bible in your poems.

LEE: Oh, I *love* the Bible. I adore it. I love it as literature—the stories, the drama, the largeness, the characters—and I love the wisdom in it.

MOYERS: So many of your early poems in particular deal with your father.

LEE: He was for me a huge character. He made it obvious early on that he was the template by which all his sons and his daughter were to measure our lives. He always set himself up as a goal for us, and he wasn't modest about it. He impressed upon us that we were supposed to speak seven languages, as he did; but I only speak two—Mandarin Chinese and English. He told us that we should be able to translate Kierkegaard and the Psalms. A few years ago I actually thought that I was going to study Hebrew and translate the Psalms before I realized that was merely another quarrel I was still having with my dead father.

MOYERS: Are you able to let go of your father as a subject? Do you think you've written your last poem about him? Have you settled that old quarrel?

LEE: I don't think I've settled that old quarrel, but I think for the good of my own writing, I have had to force myself to look beyond him, although in a way I'm being guided again by him to look at things that were important to him. I'd like to write about my *own* struggle with belief and disbelief, and I'd like to write my *own* experiences as an immigrant and refugee.

MOYERS: Did you ever feel devastated by him, as some sons do by a strong father?

LEE: No! You know, that's the one thing I have no doubt about. My mother once pointed to me and said, "*You* are the stone on which your father's patience broke." I realized that she was talking about a great deal of strength that I got from both my mother and father and that a part of him broke against me. Of course, she didn't tell me that until he was dead, but I realized that I had a lot of strength to be able to stand up against him. I never wanted to leave home. I always knew that I would only grow stronger by struggling against him, and I was never afraid of him. I was in awe, but I never feared him.

MOYERS: There's so much tenderness that comes through in your poems about him.

LEE: He was an infinitely tender man. I remember a day—I think we were living in Hong Kong at the time—when he came rushing home, very excited, with a small brown paper bag. He had discovered Worcestershire sauce. He had the servants move all of our living-room furniture out onto the lawn and cook a meal, then he doused everything with this sauce, and we are out on the lawn. He was an exuberant kind of wild man, and he was infinitely tender.

THE GIFT

To pull the metal splinter from my palm
my father recited a story in a low voice.
I watched his lovely face and not the blade.
Before the story ended, he'd removed
the iron sliver I thought I'd die from.

I can't remember the tale,
but hear his voice still, a well
of dark water, a prayer.
And I recall his hands,
two measures of tenderness
he laid against my face,
the flames of discipline
he raised above my head.

Had you entered that afternoon
you would have thought you saw a man
planting something in a boy's palm,
a silver tear, a tiny flame.
Had you followed that boy
you would have arrived here,
where I bend over my wife's right hand.

Look how I shave her thumbnail down
so carefully she feels no pain.
Watch as I lift the splinter out.
I was seven when my father
took my hand like this,
and I did not hold that shard
between my fingers and think,
Metal that will bury me,

christen it Little Assassin,
Ore Going Deep for My heart.
And I did not lift up my wound and cry,
Death visited here!
I did what a child does
when he's given something to keep.
I kissed my father.

M O Y E R S : I'm touched by "The Gift." Tell me why you wrote it.

L E E : I was with my wife in a hotel and I woke up and heard her sobbing. I looked for her and she was sitting on the edge of the bathtub, sobbing and holding her hand. I noticed that her hand was bleeding, and when I looked there was a splinter under her thumbnail. My father was dead at the time, but when I bent down to remove the splinter I realized that I had learned that tenderness from my father.

M O Y E R S : And the gift was?

L E E : I suppose it was a lesson, a gift of tenderness that he gave to me and that I was able to give to somebody else.

M O Y E R S : You've written that you really discovered most about your father when you opened his Bible after his death and read his notations in the margin.

L E E : I inherited all his books, and when I opened his Bible one day and began reading it, and also reading the marginalia—all the things he had written in the margins of the book—it was like experiencing his mind at work, and I realized it was a fierce, questioning mind. When he was teaching us he always seemed so sure—he never questioned anything; everything that came out of his mouth was spit out in hard, pithy statements—and then when I opened his Bible and saw there were questions and underlinings and references to other books I realized he was struggling to come to terms with his own belief, and I really grasped another dimension of him.

I also realized that basically I didn't know him, and that both of us were at fault. He put up a huge front, the front of a man who would not be questioned. He would *always* be right, he would *always* be sure. And I suppose that comes from his experience of imprisonment and wandering—he wanted his children to have faith in him. He didn't want us to be afraid, so he had to keep up that front.

But by the same token, it didn't make me ever feel I had a human being for a father. He was always right next to God. There was an hour each day when we had to be very quiet because he was praying in his study, and I remember thinking, "Jeez, he's in there convening with this Being Who is like no being that I know." So for an hour we had to observe this silence and tiptoe around him. That's the way it was in our house.

MOYERS: But when you opened the Bible the man you found there was less austere, less dogmatic, less cocksure?

LEE: Exactly. For example, he always talked to us about the Song of Songs as if it were a song between the church and God. Then when I read his Bible I realized he read it very explicitly as a poem about sexuality. He would refer to other poems about sexuality and he had underlined his favorite passages and written out little love poems in the corners of the pages. Finding all that was an incredible experience. I realized he was a man who was saying one thing but who was living another life.

EARLY IN THE MORNING

While the long grain is softening
in the water, gurgling
over a low stove flame, before
the salted Winter Vegetable is sliced
for breakfast, before the birds,
my mother glides an ivory comb
through her hair, heavy
and black as calligrapher's ink.

She sits at the foot of the bed.
My father watches, listens for
the music of comb
against hair.

My mother combs,
pulls her hair back
tight, rolls it
around two fingers, pins it
in a bun to the back of her head.
For half a hundred years she has done this.
My father likes to see it like this.
He says it is kempt.

But I know
it is because of the way
my mother's hair falls
when he pulls the pins out.
Easily, like the curtains
when they untie them in the evening.

MOYERS: What about your mother?

LEE: As I said earlier, my mother was the great-granddaughter of Yuan Shi-Kai, and she was classically educated, but she doesn't speak much English. She lives with us. It was a lifelong dream for all of us to live together, so my brother and sister and my mother and my family all live in one house. I think she's an incredibly resilient woman, though she's become very reclusive since my father has died. She's a beautiful woman, and there was a point when she had hair down to the back of her knees.

MOYERS: Does she ever talk about what it was like to have been a member of the Royal Family of China?

LEE: Occasionally she experiences a kind of nostalgia, but I think she has the feeling that we're in America now and that history is not going to help us. I grew up with the feeling that those stories about the House of Yuan and all the grandeur were simply stories. My father found it important to tell us stories about both families, but my mother was basically very reticent about her story. I don't know whether she was too sad about it or whether it didn't interest her, but even now when I ask her about what it was like growing up like that, she doesn't like to talk about it.

I ASK MY MOTHER TO SING

She begins, and my grandmother joins her.
Mother and daughter sing like young girls.
If my father were alive, he would play
his accordian and sway like a boat.

I've never been in Peking, or the Summer Palace,
nor stood on the great Stone Boat to watch
the rain begin on Kuen Ming Lake, the picnickers
running away from the grass.

But I love to hear it sung:
how the waterlilies fill with rain until
they overturn, spilling water into water,
then rock back, and fill with more.

Both women have begun to cry.
But neither stops her song.

MOYERS: Will you ever return to China?

LEE: I wonder about China, but I have no immediate plans to return there. My mother returned and found the family graves dug up, and she was told the bones were scattered—that happened during the Cultural Revolution—so in a way I feel there's nothing to return to. From what I understand, everything has been confiscated. They lived in a huge mansion, which has been turned into a small hospital, and certain parts of the land they owned have been turned into public parks, so I don't have any ruins to go back to, and it seems to me important that I should have ruins. I mean, shouldn't we? I have friends who have French, Spanish, or Italian backgrounds, and they go to Europe and I suppose they can connect. But if I go to Europe I would feel as if I'm going to look at somebody *else's* ruins, and if I go to China I'd *also* be looking at somebody else's ruins. I have the feeling I need to get back to Indonesia and yet, I don't know what I would look for there either. I'm not sure what I am supposed to look for anywhere.

I'm afraid to say that often my longing for home because a longing for heaven—instead of casting myself backwards, I take the impulse and cast it ahead—and yet, I question my own belief constantly. You know, I don't know if I believe in a heaven or a hell. But there's a longing in me for heaven. Maybe my longing for home comes from a longing for heaven.

MOYERS: What are your favorite books in the Bible?

LEE: I think the Book of Exodus is my favorite, but the books of poetry I most like would be The Song of Songs and Ecclesiastes. On gloomy days I tell myself, "I just want to write something like Ecclesiastes. And on happy days I think, "I'm going to write The Song of Songs. Whoever put those two books side by side was definitely wise. We go from one extreme to another—a celebration of sexual love and then a kind of diatribe about the futility of life in general—but those are my two favorite books. If I could pinpoint what I want to do in my writing, I'd like to write something someday that would own the kind of scope and grandeur and intensity of those two books.

MOYERS: When you read the Bible, what do you find out about yourself?

LEE: I identify with *all* the characters. For a while I was reading the Abraham and Isaac story, and I read that as my father as Abraham and me as Isaac. Then later on I read the story of Jacob and the Angel as a good metaphor for poetry, that somehow it's the struggle between the longing for heaven and the longing to stay on earth. I discover that there's a great longing in me to believe. I wouldn't say I believe, but I *want* to believe. I want badly to believe in a God, in a palpable God. I don't sense a palpable God, but as I'm reading the Bible, *that's* what I want.

MOYERS: There are a lot of "outsiders" in the Bible. Exiles, seekers, rejected and despised.

LEE: Exactly. For a while I began to really rebel against Christianity, but when I realized that it began as a slave religion and that Christ was an outsider, then it began to make more sense to me.

MOYERS: It seems to me that you are struggling in the same way your father was.

LEE: If I didn't know that he had struggled, I would always be questioning myself, asking, "Why aren't I as strong as he was?"

MOYERS: But what you found in the margins of his Bible were the tracks of his own doubt.

LEE: Which helps me. Doubt is okay. In a way, I guess I'm affirming God by my doubt. Is that possible?

MOYERS: Let's talk about the craft of writing poetry. How do you put a poem together?

LEE: For me, all the work *precedes* the actual writing of the poem and requires a kind of supplication, assuming a vulnerable posture, keeping open. It's like prayer. I think one has to do a lot of struggling before one actually kneels and says the words. Then after that, of course, there's a lot of revision; but I do a lot of reading and mental, spiritual, and emotional struggling before I actually come to the page.

When I *do* get to the page, it usually begins with a line that I can't make any sense of. Then I write to find out what that line means. I hate to sound as if language doesn't refer to something. In fact, I come to the page with certain experiences and intentions, but the poem begins to happen in a line, and I write to understand that.

MOYERS: I hear you are now writing about your own children. Are they growing up thoroughly American?

L E E : I can see that they're in a way headed for doom because they're crazily dislocated. They're growing up in a household where both Chinese and English are spoken. At this point, they only speak English but they understand Chinese. If they walk into a room and there's Chinese opera on the television, they'll sit down and watch these crazy antics, so they're already growing up dislocated. The older one said, "I'm Chinese, right?" I said, "Yes, you're *half* Chinese." He said, "And I'm half regular?" So there's Chinese and regular—he's already crazy with this stuff.

M O Y E R S : Do you tell them stories?

L E E : Yes, I tell them stories constantly, and they love to hear stories. I used to tell them the basic stories, and then I ran out of those, so I started making up stories in which the bad guy's name is Sukarno and the good guy's name is Yeh, which means grandfather in Chinese. Now they say, "Tell us the Sukarno stories."

A STORY

Sad is the man who is asked for a story
and can't come up with one.

His five-year-old son waits in his lap
Not the same story, Baba. A new one.
The man rubs his chin, scratches his ear.

In a room full of books in a world
of stories, he can recall
not one, and soon, he thinks, the boy
will give up on his father.

Already the man lives far ahead, he sees
the day this boy will go. *Don't go!*
Hear the alligator story! The angel story once more!
You love the spider story. You laugh at the spider.
Let me tell it!

But the boy is packing his shirts,
he is looking for his keys. *Are you a god,*
the man screams, *that I sit mute before you?*
Am I a god that I should never disappoint?

But the boy is here. *Please, Baba, a story?*
It is an emotional rather than logical equation,
an earthly rather than heavenly one,
which posits that a boy's supplications
and a father's love add up to silence.

MOYERS: Do you tell them the story of your own family's fugitive travels?

LEE: Those are in fact the stories that I tell them. I make them sound more fairytale-like for them, but those stories are the only ones I know.

MOYERS: Stories are crucial to the memories of exiles. They tell these stories over and over again. The stories often become scripture.

LEE: Yes. And that's the beauty of the Bible too—it's insistence on the importance of memory. The injunction *Zakhor* occurs more than one hundred times in the Bible, so that is important to me. Part of the problem refugees encounter is that as those stories are told again and again, from generation to generation, sometimes they're changed, so each time we're getting farther and farther away from factual reality, but I think the stories still adhere to an emotional and spiritual reality.

MOYERS: What's the spiritual reality of your own family's journey.

LEE: Ah, God. I don't know. I'm sad to say this, but I think we all feel dislocated, and that's why we want to live together. I think the spiritual reality of my family is dislocation, disconnectedness.

MOYERS: Yet there's a lot of joy in your poems.

LEE: I hope there is. I wouldn't want to think that I write poems that make people sad.

MOYERS: Your family will find themselves in your poems and in this new book, *Rose,* in particular.

LEE: Actually, I really dislike the poems in that book.

MOYERS: Why?

LEE: I don't know. I think that's my father. There's the answer to your question. Nothing I do is going to be good enough for him, so everything I write I hate a week later. My poet friends tell me, "I hate the poems in my first book too, but I like the poems I'm writing now." But I hate the poems I'm *working* on. As I'm writing them, I'm realizing this is not Ecclesiastes, this is not *The Song of Songs,* and yet I realize I have a duty to finish those poems, and I know that they're going to help me get to the next poem.

MOYERS: Why do it?

LEE: Maybe I'm obsessive by nature—my father was obsessive by nature—but it's probably really a love of a state of being. I think when a person is in deep prayer, all of that being's attention is focused on God. When a person is in love, all of that being's attention is focused on the beloved. I think in writing poetry, all of the being's attention is focused on some inner voice. I don't mean to sound mystical, but it really *is* a voice, and all of the attention is turned toward that voice. That's such an exhilarating state to be in that it's addictive.

MOYERS: It's like rapture?

LEE: Yes, a kind of rapture and a joyful sorrow and a mixture of other things as well.

MOYERS: So you can't *not* write.

LEE: Correct. At this point in my life, I can say I can't *not* write. It might change, you know?

MOYERS: You're thirty-one now. Are you suggesting you might not be a poet for the rest of your life?

LEE: Even now I don't consider myself a poet. I get very nervous when people say, "Oh, you're a poet." I don't *feel* like a poet. David, the Psalmist, was a poet. Milton was a poet. Li Po was a poet. I'm working hard to be a poet; that's the way I like to think of it.

MOYERS: But if you've published a book of acclaimed poems and you're not sure you're a poet yet, how *will* you know when you're a poet?

LEE: I have no idea. I guess my father is going to have to materialize and tell me, "You're okay now. I think you're a poet now." I simply have the sense that I'm not there yet.

Poetry allows one to speak with a voice of power that is not, in fact, granted to one by the culture.

LINDA MCCARRISTON

Linda McCarriston writes about women, children, animals—and healing. The poems in *Eva-Mary,* 1991 winner of the Terrence Des Pres Prize, deal with the domestic violence she saw and experienced growing up in a working-class family in Lynn, Massachusetts, and with her later disconsolation as a wife and mother. Her capacity for joy in daily life and her reverence for the ordinary facts of nature are the sources for enduring portraits of a woman who has moved beyond victimization. She teaches at the University of Alaska, Anchorage.

MOYERS: You tell students that poetry is about "Saying what we don't want known; it's saying the unsayable." And you write often about the brutalities of domestic violence in your own childhood. How do you decide to write about such painful experiences?

McCARRISTON: Someone once asked me why I didn't choose to write about the unsayable in prose, and my answer was that I believe I'm a poet—I think *that's* a given. I had stopped writing for many years for various personal reasons, then when I returned to it, I began to write poems that were modeled on the great poems—the canon—not on the voices of common people—men or women—and not about the anguish of the private lives of those at the bottom of various heaps. At the same time I felt driven to attempt to write poems from these very difficult experiences of my childhood.

The material was hard to handle, but in some ways a more difficult problem was that many people actively tried to discourage me from writing these poems. They felt that if I were to write them, the poems would be shrill or I might be identifying myself as a feminist or a radical. Because I knew that these experiences told in this first person woman's voice of outrage were not supposed to be poetry, I tried to write these poems in a way that was veiled. But when I veiled the voice or the experiences I put the fire out in them.

I tried again and again and again to write these poems, and I was really driven a little bit wild by the *necessity* to write them. I didn't know why I felt so compelled to write them, but when I finally found that I was beginning to write poems about these experiences that were standing on their own, that were good poems, I realized that I simply had to speak back to the culture that I saw as creating and sustaining the ideas that led to this violent situation in the first place. I really don't feel I had a choice. That *was* my material, and the difficulty was simply in waiting and leaning on the material long enough until a way came to me by which I could speak.

MOYERS: What is it about poetry that enabled you to do this?

McCARRISTON: That's a very difficult question. Those who argue that poetry says the unsayable generally mean the unsayably beautiful or the unsayably profound, but the unsayable can also mean what people simply don't want said, ever. That's why poetry is extremely radical—poetry allows the individual experience to strike like lightning through the collective institutional consciousness and to plumb the depths of actual communal experience so that what people don't want said in fact gets said, and in a way that is unignorable. Poetry does this through the stature of utterance which characterizes it.

MOYERS: Utterance?

McCARRISTON: Utterance. The simplest definition for poetry that I have is *heightened speech*. I think that poetry is truly inspired, truly vatic or bardic. It is extraordinary speech that at times comes through a poet with extraordinary power. It allows one to speak with a voice of power that is not, in fact, granted to one by the culture. In other words, as a woman in this culture I did *not* have the stature from which to speak those poems. I was simply a common woman—I was not authorized to speak in any institutional way, I was not a judge, I was not a priest; I was not a psychiatrist; I was simply a housewife—and yet the stature and authority of poetry *itself* visited me, permitted me, enlivened me, enlarged me, and those poems were written *by* me. If I had been a novelist, I think I might have been able to do something similar, but the fact that poetry is not a respecter of institutional power and that it comes to all sorts of people meant that I was permitted to assume a voice of stature to utter these poems.

MOYERS: Even women who have never been physically or sexually abused relate to your poems—they know what you are describing is true.

McCARRISTON: I think the poems seem true and *are* true to many readers, even those who've not experienced the circumstances of the poems, partly because they know this experience exists all around them—it really *is* a common occurrence—and also because I think that each of the poems earns the ground it stands on in terms of its aesthetic making. The poems do not rest on any outside assumptions. Each poem builds its own case in the particular details of the situation so the conclusions that I draw are earned right there in the very poems in which they occur.

A CASTLE IN LYNN

In the hometown tonight,
in the quiet before sleep,
a man strokes himself in the darkened
theater of memory. Best old

remembrance, he gets to play it
as slow as he needs, as his hand,
savvy tart of a million reruns,
plays the tune, plays the parts:

now hand is the hard bottom
of the girl. Now hand is full
of the full new breast. Now hand
—square hand, cruel as a spade—

splits the green girlwood of her body.
No one can take this from him now
ever, though she is for years a mother
and worn, and he is too old

to force any again. His cap hangs
on a peg by the door—plaid wool
of an elderly workingman's park-bench
decline. *I got there before*

the boys did, he knows, hearing
back to her pleading, back to her
sobbing, to his own voice-over
like his body over hers: laughter,

mocking, the elemental voice
of the cock, unhearted, in its own
quarter. *A man is king in his own*
castle, he can still say, having got

what he wanted: in a lifetime
of used ones, second-hand, one girl
he could spill like a shot of whiskey,
the whore only he could call *daughter.*

MOYERS: One woman told me she was struck by how often the word "castle" surfaced in your poetry. Are you conscious of that?

McCARRISTON: I wasn't at the time, though I knew that word was a key for me, and I think in this book it may occur two or three times. "A man's home is his castle" was a very real phrase in my childhood and a *very* real phrase for the father in these poems, *my* father. It was an informing idea over the years for me as I attempted to understand how the conditions of our life in that home came to be.

MOYERS: In your home your father was the king, the law?

McCARRISTON: He *was* the king. He *was* the law. He answered to *no one*. And the forces outside the home agreed that a man's home *was* his castle—he was free to do as he wanted in that castle.

MOYERS: The "forces outside" being?

McCARRISTON: The church, the state, the schools, the doctor, the lawyer. There are several other poems in *Eva-Mary* that refer to efforts to speak or to get help from the priest, from the doctor, from the lawyer, those in positions of power and authority.

TO JUDGE FAOLAIN, DEAD LONG ENOUGH: A SUMMONS

Your Honor, when my mother stood
before you, with her routine
domestic plea, after weeks
of waiting for speech to return
to her body, with her homemade
forties hairdo, her face purple still
under pancake, her jaw off just a little,
her *holy of holies* healing,
her breasts wrung, her heart
the bursting heart of someone
snagged among rocks deep
in a sharkpool—no, not "someone,"

but a woman there, snagged
with her babies, *by* them,
in one of hope's pedestrian

brutal turns—when, in the tones
of parlors overlooking the harbor,
you admonished that, for the sake
of the family, the wife
must take the husband back to her bed,
what you willed not to see before you
was a woman risen clean to the surface,
a woman who, with one arm flailing,
held up with the other her actual

burdens of flesh. When you clamped
to her leg the chain of *justice,*
you ferried us back down to *the law,*
the black ice eye, the maw, the mako
that circles the kitchen table nightly.
What did you make of the words
she told you, not to have heard her,
not to have seen her there? Almost-
forgiveable ignorance, you were not
the fist, the boot, or the blade,
but the jaded, corrective ear and eye
at the limits of her world. Now

I will you to see her as she was, to ride
your own words back into light: I call
your spirit home again, divesting you
of robe and bench, the fine white hand
and half-lit Irish eye. Tonight, put on
a body in the trailer down the road
where your father, when he can't
get it up, makes love to your mother
with a rifle. Let your name be
Eva-Mary. Let your hour of birth
be dawn. Let your life be long
and common, and your flesh endure.

MOYERS: You placed a curse on Judge Faolain at the end of "To Judge Fao-
lain, Dead Long Enough: A Summons" because he let your father get away with such
brutality?

McCARRISTON: Yes, that's why. I refer to his "almost-forgiveable" igno-
rance in not hearing what my mother had to say when she tried to divorce my father,
and that is why I fling the curse.

MOYERS: And the curse is "Let your life be long/and common, and your
flesh endure." Why common?

McCARRISTON: Well, first of all, I curse him back into being as a woman
and as a girl infant, Eva-Mary. At the time I wrote that poem, which is one of the first
that really worked in this book, I was unconscious of a lot of themes that later developed,
but by "common," I wanted him to be powerless. I wanted to strip him of all privilege
and power.

MOYERS: As you had been as a child?

McCARRISTON: Yes, so that he would experience life as my mother had
experienced it, as I had experienced it, and as my brother had experienced it—although
my brother didn't suffer the sexual violations that the women in my family suffered. I
curse him back to life as a "common woman" because I felt that in his courtroom he was
willfully ignorant of the common women who were before him attempting to find safety
and justice in him.

MOYERS: So you call his spirit back divested "of robe and bench," because
you want him to be as vulnerable and as weak as you and your mother were?

McCARRISTON: Yes.

MOYERS: He sent your mother back into the home, didn't he?

McCARRISTON: Yes, he did.

MOYERS: If his flesh endures, what do you hope will happen to his spirit?

McCARRISTON: I didn't mean to make a curse that would destroy his
spirit, and yet that's implicit in that line. I think I need to have his spirit in some way
broken into knowledge of all that he did not see and of all that he does not know of the
suffering of those less privileged and less safe who have depended upon him. If you
believe in reincarnation, you believe that we go through these lives until we get it right,
and I've often wondered whether I was some Judge Faolain in a past life. One of the
interesting things about this poem is that it led me to think, "This is perhaps how I got
here in the first place; I must have been some male tyrant in a past life and now I'm
learning my lessons." So in a way I curse him into consciousness.

MOYERS: Consciousness of what was happening to the woman standing before him, consciousness of what pain awaited her back in her husband's "castle"?

McCARRISTON: Yes.

MOYERS: What do you mean "you clamped/to her leg the chain of *justice,*/you ferried us back down to *the law,*/the black ice eye, the maw, the mako . . ."?

McCARRISTON: Earlier in the poem I say: "what you willed not to see before you/was a woman risen clean to the surface,/a woman who, with one arm flailing,/held up with the other her actual/burdens of flesh." This is a woman in a sea of sharks, and she rises to the surface flailing with one arm to stay up and with the other holds up her baby to call for help. And instead of plucking her out of the shark pool, the judge, metaphorically, puts a chain on her leg that drags her back to the depths which contain the mako. These were visions that came to me very quickly once this poem opened up.

Interestingly enough, I had written a lot about sharks when I was young, and the image recurred even though I had not written any poems with images of sharks or the ocean. But I had, and have, this image of a room that is really underwater, and in this room the mako circles the kitchen table nightly. This image of a great shark in a little room, moving around the kitchen table every night, suggests exactly what it was like to be in that kitchen with my father and his constant potential madness and violence. That's what it felt like—the mako that circles the kitchen table nightly. There you are.

MOYERS: The law is the force of your father? His power in his own castle?

McCARRISTON: Yes and, also, law in terms of the courtroom. The judge was the arbiter of law, and the courtroom was the place where law was enforced. The judge was Irish Catholic, and he told her to go home for the sake of the family. This was the 1950s and, while women are still being told to go back home for the sake of the family, back then it was said much more commonly.

MOYERS: And the priest in the poem?

McCARRISTON: In *Eva-Mary* I have a poem called "Grateful" which is about my brother who was off studying to be a priest, and in it I describe trying to tell the priest in confession about my abuse at home and I give his response. "He told me to mind my father./To obey./So I put my soul to bed by itself,/so far away that as a woman I still can't/find it, and waited to grow up, to be/a person in the Great World, where men/would be as safe to know as dogs."

MOYERS: And have you reached that place?

MᴄCARRISTON: Yes, I have. It took some doing, but I have.

MOYERS: Your soul's awake again, and not in bed alone.

MᴄCARRISTON: Yes, to both questions. It's been a very deliberate journey, and poetry has been the avenue down which those things were sealed and hidden and that had no usefulness in my life were able to walk and find expression, validation, and truth—from which I really have built a life.

MOYERS: What are you doing now?

MᴄCARRISTON: I've been teaching for many years, but I am beginning to teach this fall at the University of Alaska, at Anchorage, and I'm delighted to be there. I live in a log house built in 1953, and I have my two horses—my mother horse and her baby horse.

MOYERS: Animals appear throughout your poems. Were you conscious of that?

MᴄCARRISTON: I *wasn't* at the time I wrote the poems, but I am now. I'm aware of the mantle, as people have said, that the horse in particular wears in my poems. I think some of my very best poems are about animals, in fact.

MOYERS: Why is that?

MᴄCARRISTON: I can say that as a child, when this family presented itself to me not only as violence but as a set of ideas, I kept asking myself: What does it mean to be human? What does it mean to be alive? What does it mean to be good? What does it mean to be evil? And finally, What power do I have over *any* of it?

It was very crazy-making to be a child in that brutal environment, and people have written a lot about that, but it was particularly so at the time when I became aware of gender, when I became aware that I really *had* to make a choice—"the maiming choices of adolescence" as they have been called.

I decided early that if the choices were to be like my father—abuser—or abused, I would choose to be myself, I would choose to be the victim, rather than occupy his shoes because I felt that he had lost his soul. Even as a young girl I knew that his soul wasn't working right, and I felt mine *was*. I also felt that he couldn't contaminate my soul, so if the world was going to turn out to be those choices in their extreme form, I would choose to be *me,* not him. I knew I didn't want to be a man if being a man was to be like him, and I certainly didn't want to be a woman if being a woman was to be like my mother.

At the same time I could see all around me this pretty consistent sanity in the lives of animals. Animals seemed to be physical, at home in their bodies, and relatively predictable—if you treated them a certain way they responded in a certain way. So in some spiritual sense I became a person who identified with animals, which is sometimes seen to be a failure of human development, or at least it has been seen that way in the past. But in thinking about St. Francis and in reading Martin Buber's *I and Thou,* I've come to realize that it was a very healthy thing for me to do at that point in my life. In a way I was saying, "I'm just going to take a step to the side here, folks, and continue my spiritual development in the company of dogs and horses and cats and birds and worms and anything else like them because you guys don't have it—the way you're doing it isn't the way it's supposed to be or the way it has to be—so if you'll excuse me, I'm going to do some psychic maneuvering here, off to the side, and ally myself with the animals."

At some level, I *did* that and I think that strand remains unbroken. This was a very important strand of healing for me especially when, in my forties, I was going through much of the work on this material and I finally got a horse for the first time. In some of the poems that people have quoted—"Healing the Mare," for instance—I think I was doing a lot of work in a ten-year-old's psyche around those animals.

MOYERS: You have said that "Healing the Mare" isn't one of your favorite poems, but it seems to be the favorite of nearly everyone else around this festival.

HEALING THE MARE

Just days after the vet came,
after the steroids that took
the fire out of the festering
sores—out of the flesh that in
the heat took the stings too
seriously and swelled into great
welts, wore thin and wept, calling
more loudly out to the green-
headed flies—I bathe you
and see your coat returning,
your deep force surfacing in a
new layer of hide: black wax
alive against weather and flies.

But this morning, misshapen
Still you look like an effigy,
something rudely made, something
made to be buffeted, or like
an old comforter—are they both
one in the end? So both a child

and a mother, with my sponge and
my bucket, I come to anoint, to
anneal the still weeping, to croon
to you *baby poor baby* for the sake
of the song, to polish you up,
for the sake of the touch, to a shine.

As I soothe you I surprise wounds
of my own this long time unmothered.
As you stand, scathed and scabbed,
with your head up, I swab. As you
press, I lean into my own loving
touch, for which no wound
is too ugly.

MᶜCARRISTON: A lot of people like it, and it's been quoted in different places. It says a great deal that people resonate to and recognize, but when I think of it as a poem, I see that it's held together with Scotch tape and bailing twine and little bits of coat hangers and Band-Aids. It doesn't have that strong, muscular, seamless, inevitable, complex, multifaceted feel that the poems I admire most have; but it certainly works. It serves a purpose in this book, and many people to respond to it.

MOYERS: It's suffused with healing—just the sound of your voice when you read it is a healing experience.

MᶜCARRISTON: I think that's what people respond to, that it *is* possible for the people who are damaged to deal. Many, many people suffer cruelly tragic childhoods, and many others who don't suffer cruelly tragic childhoods suffer painful childhoods, but they're all encouraged by the future just to grow up and get over it. So they have all this experience which they can't get over very easily, and it continues to be painful. At times when they begin to confront it, they feel that they're going to be stuck in it forever, and they don't want to be stuck in it forever. Then they begin to ask: *Is* there a way out? *Can* one heal? How *does* one heal? I think it's the possibility of healing in that poem that people have responded to.

MOYERS: Your mother was so cruelly abused—did she heal?

McCARRISTON: No. I don't think so. She's still alive, and I don't think she has changed much.

MOYERS: What does she think about these poems?

McCARRISTON: She said that she's happy that I wrote them. Her exact words were, "I knew I didn't go through all that shit for nothing." She feels that both her life and mine involved great suffering, but it was not for nothing if this special baby, me, that she wanted for a long, long time—she had many interrupted pregnancies before I was born—could do this work and touch and move other people.

MOYERS: Have you and your brother ever talked about "Billy," the poem in which he figures so prominently?

BILLY

As though a bare bulb hung
over your head as it does in
movie scenes of interrogation,
you are the single vivid thing
in the shades-of-gray memory,
the white center, out from which
the whole dank tenement
cellar—the dirt floor, the boulders
that formed the old foundation,
the three fat coal-burning
furnaces, one for each of the three
stories, the coal bins punky
across from each, the mud-thick
little windows above that were
coal shutes when the truck came,
the new table-saw, the new
table-saw overhead worklight,
and even our father,
who stood beating you with his fists

where he'd stuck you into
a barrel, as a mountaineer might plant
a banner into a peak, to keep your
skinny thirteen-year-old self erect
till he was finished—the whole
rest emanates and fades.
It was winter. You had driven
your homemade go-cart into a door
that he was saving for something,
I can see the little v's you made
in the paint. I see his upper body
plunging up and down like one
of those wind-driven lawn ornaments,
the one that is pumping.
The barrel reaches your bottom.
You must be holding onto it.
It must be braced against
his table saw. There are no words.
The barrel bangs and scrapes.
Your body sounds different than
a mattress. The noises he makes
are the noises of a man trying to
lift a Buick off the body of
a loved child, whose face he can
see, upturned, just above the wheel
that rests on her chest, her eyes right
on his eyes, as yours were on mine.

McCARRISTON: Yes. My brother came to see me in Vermont because he was concerned about me—he felt that I was too caught up in the past. I was so glad to see him, and I said: "Billy, I just want to sit down with you and cry in your presence. I want to tell you what it was like to be that little girl, standing at the foot of the cellar stairs, watching you being beaten that particular time when I could do nothing to save you. And that was not the only time, but I feel strongly about that particular time."

However, my brother didn't really want to enter into a lively reliving of that memory with me. He has a spiritual life and a way of dealing with these things that says, basically: "The father I had on earth was not my real father. My real father is a spiritual father. We aren't going to cry now—pat, pat—that's all in the past."

I wanted desperately just to hold him and say, "This is thirty-five years too late, but I love you so much and it was so horrible to watch that happen to you and to be a little girl and useless." But he would not permit that—it was too dangerous—so he left. He didn't fling his cape over his shoulder and leave—we visited and stayed within the perimeters he set—but then he left, and I was really wrought up.

Then, bam! I wrote that poem, just like that! I was shaking but I kept at it until the manuscript was complete. Then after it was accepted by the publishers and was going to come out in a book, I sent it to my brother and said, "I want you to see this; this is going to be hard for you" because, of course, he hadn't even seen the poem. At that point I think he knew that I was not going to be able to resolve all of this experience as he had done—by just putting it aside and leaving it behind and pretending that our parents were really our heavenly parents and that our earthly parents weren't quite as good as our heavenly parents. So the poem was difficult and very challenging for him. And yet when the book came out, and I went to Chicago to read at the awards ceremony, bless his heart, he drove from the Upper Peninsula to be there. And I said, "Billy, I want to read that poem while you're here; I want to read it to you, but only with your permission, only if you allow me to." And he said he would allow it.

So he *stood* there, and I mean it was an agony!—he wanted so much to have the indignity of that life behind him, and *my* necessity to transform the indignity of that life into indignation and public speech and art. Feeling all that he felt, he so bravely and generously and lovingly—in his best suit and with a face that was a cross between pain and awe and love—stood in public while I read that poem. So he finally came to know how it was for me, loving him at that moment when he was so damaged.

MOYERS: Is he still a priest?

McCARRISTON: No. He left the seminary after several years and is married with sons of his own.

MOYERS: In "Grateful," you write, "looking back I'm grateful/for what kept you away from *the game the whole/family can play*." And that game was?

McCARRISTON: Incest. That particular poem uses several common popular sayings and it refers to an incident in Vermont, a terrible rape and murder—one girl child survived and one did not. The two boys who were finally discovered to be the murderers were boys in families where there had been a great deal of sexual violence in the home. It had been perpetrated on the little sisters, and the fathers and sons were involved together which is sadly very common in incestuous families. So I incorporate a couple of common phrases in the poem—I heard one of them the day the news broke on this terrible crime in Vermont. I went to the village to buy the paper and I heard someone say, "What makes a woman beautiful?" And the answer was, "Jelly doughnuts and incest." Then someone else referred to incest as, "The game the whole family can play."

There's widespread knowledge of the reality of this kind of domestic abuse which, up until very recently, the culture has simply denied, which is like the culture's denying that it eats a particular brand of breakfast cereal, an activity that's about as common statistically. I tried to weave into this poem an indictment of some of these practices that are protected by silence.

MOYERS: It occurs to me that when you were a child in Boston there was a Society for the Prevention of Cruelty to Animals, but no Society for the Prevention of Cruelty to Children or Women.

McCARRISTON: That's right, and as a child in the torment of this life I was aware of that. There are other poems that are not written yet, and which may in fact never be written as poems, about other instances in that home of simply egregious cruelty that involved animals as well.

MOYERS: As you look back at your father, how do you see him?

McCARRISTON: He was crazy. He was one of six children of a family that fled Northern Ireland just before the civil war. The whole family was alcoholic, and there was a great deal of madness and violence of every kind. He was himself an abused child. I have a poem to my father called "October 1913" about a family story in which his older brother prevented their mother from throwing my father into the fire when he was five days old.

This was a time of civil war, starvation, people living in mud hovels; and it was not very far away and not very long ago. These were extreme historical and political conditions, and to imagine that infanticide was not practiced in Northern Ireland or in the early twentieth century is probably naive. It was difficult for me to imagine those historical conditions, but it was only by coming to terms with them that I could even imagine how my father could have become as profoundly disturbed as he clearly was.

MOYERS: Knowing what you know about all this suffering, how is it that at the end of a new poem you can "dance on/the lawn of what's left of summer . . ."?

McCARRISTON: I am blessed by my life. I am blessed by consciousness. I am, at root, a profoundly joyful person. I know great sadness, which is often with me, but I feel as if I wanted so much to get in, and I'm one of the lucky ones who knows that *I got* in. And, of course, it's optional whether you're going to get in. This is all very wild sounding but . . .

MOYERS: To get in?

McCARRISTON: Into the field of time. *Here.* Briefly. In the garden. *Here.* It's just so beautiful, it's *so* beautiful.

MOYERS: Even though you were abused and beaten you can still celebrate the moment, the garden?

McCARRISTON: Oh yes, but *that* violence isn't the garden. That's evil.

MOYERS: The evil in the garden?

McCARRISTON: The evil in the garden, yes—our human capacity for blindness to our own cruelty. So much of the art I admire seeks to illuminate this. There's a wonderful phrase in something Jim Haba has written for this festival—"the anonymous river of poetry." Poetry can be so much about ego and the individual—you know, "I *the poet!*"—but I look to science as a model because scientists are content to spend a life contributing one little brick, a single discovery, to the edifice of some branch of knowledge.

Human blindness to human cruelty does *not* come from the hand of God, it is *not* just human nature, it is definitely *not* inevitable. It is learned. So I feel that if by making my poems beautiful my work can contribute one little stone to this generation's efforts to illuminate and enlarge our understanding of evil and human suffering, that would be a great joy.

MOYERS: After *Eva-Mary* you must want to write poems about daisies and rain on the pond and clouds in the sky and the landscape of Alaska. You don't want to get stuck in the success of these violent themes, do you?

McCARRISTON: No, I *don't.* Robert Hass was my first teacher when I came back to writing in 1976, and we were just talking about how difficult it can be when a book is successful. *Eva-Mary* is in its fourth printing, and it's taken me all over the place in a couple of years. I've read in all sorts of circumstances and to all sorts of groups of people—for example, I've done a lot with literacy among rural people partly with this book. It's been really wonderful, but it holds you in the past and my life has really moved beyond it. I'm still passionate for being honest and open about the situation of domestic violence and for understanding how it's the DNA of a violent culture—it really *isn't* incidental to other things we suffer; it's where we learn the basic stuff of the culture, and some of us get a more concentrated dose than others.

I didn't want *Eva-Mary* to be a book for a women's press—and I very much admire women's presses—I wanted that book to go to the judge. I didn't want it just to go around women's kitchen tables where they would pass it secretly among themselves. I wanted that book to go before people of power, *men* of power; and it *has*. It's really quite amazing, quite wonderful—but now I do want to go beyond it.

I have a long poem in process which is actually very sexual, in a way. It's big and abundant and outrageous and funny and sassy. It's struggling through a keyhole much the same way that *Eva-Mary* did. I feel as though being in Alaska with all this new material for poetry will help. I don't know what I'll find there, but I don't *feel* grim, and I don't want to *be* grim.

I do actually have a little house on a pond. Rain does fall on the pond and, in fact, I've even written about the rain on the pond. And about the water lilies and the sitka spruce and the great mountains and the firewood and the amazing beauty and otherness of that place—these twenty-hour summer days like big nectarines. Just so beautiful. *So beautiful!*

© Lynn Saville

Robert Hass, Linda McCarriston, Gary Snyder

SANDRA MCPHERSON

Sandra McPherson honed the unsentimental exactness that characterizes her poetry working as a technical writer for a defense contractor in California before she began to teach. McPherson was adopted at birth, and her poems—praised for their fusion of the visual and the literary—treat the complexities of searching for an identity; chronicle her evolution as daughter, wife, and mother; and reveal the poignancy of her relationship with her high-functioning autistic daughter. She teaches at the University of California, Davis.

MOYERS: Women appear to be claiming new territory in their poetry. One of my favorites of yours is "Pregnancy." Would you read that for me?

McPHERSON: Certainly.

PREGNANCY

It is the best thing.
I should always like to be pregnant,

Tummy thickening like a yoghurt,
Unbelievable flower.

A queen is always pregnant with her country.
Sheba of questions

Or briny siren
At her difficult passage,

One is the mountain that moves
Toward the earliest gods.

Who started this?
An axis, a quake, a perimeter,

I have no decisions to master
That could change my frame

Though life may be painful, there is a joy and a power in writing, even when you're dealing with something that is hard to live through day by day. You're trying to understand what you're living through by using the tools of words and images and the beautiful inner structure of language.

Or honor.
Immaculate. Or if it was not, perfect.

Pregnant, I'm highly explosive—
You can feel it, long before

Your seed will run back to hug you—
Squaring and cubing

Into reckless bones, bouncing odd ways
Like a football.

The heart sloshes through the microphone
Like falls in a box canyon.

The queen's only a figurehead.
Nine months pulled by nine

Planets, the moon slooping
Through its amnion sea,

Trapped, stone-mad . . . and three
Beings' lives gel in my womb.

MOYERS: "and three/Beings' lives"?

McPHERSON: The daddy's and mine and my daughter's.

MOYERS: I suppose this is a poem just waiting for a woman to write it.

McPHERSON: Yes. I would love to be pregnant continuously, but I would like to give birth to things like endangered species and not humans.

MOYERS: Why?

McPHERSON: At this point we need more animals of particular sorts than we do people, and while I love pregnancy, the condition of it, I don't want any more children.

MOYERS: Why did you qualify "Immaculate" with "Or if it was not, perfect"?

McPHERSON: "Immaculate" means that at least you're married, doesn't it? And I was not. But conception *is* perfect—the meeting of two people which forms a third *is* a perfection.

MOYERS: There's another way in which women appear to be claiming new territory in their poetry. Men have always written about women's bodies, but women haven't often written about men's bodies. Yet here you are with a poem called "His Body."

HIS BODY

He doesn't like it, of course—
Others, who don't wear it but see it, do.
He's pale, like a big desert, but you can find flowers.
No, not entirely pale:
Between shin and ankle the twin sun marks;
And where his shirt (now draped from a chair back)
Was, he contrasts with dark hands
And neck/face
Like a rained-on street where a car has just been driven
Away.
Don't picture a beer paunch.
And he is a smooth animal, or soft where he isn't smooth,
Down to his toadskin testicles.
He lies prone on clean bedsheets.
There is a single light in the room.
Now run your hand down his back, its small, and up
The hips and over. Their sheen's like that
On blue metal music boxes made to hold powder.
But the rest of him is sprouted with black down-going hair,
His whiskers in so many foxholes,
Eager to out.
Are they in any order?
Age has so far
Remained locked inside.
I'm not a doctor
And glad not to have a doctor's viewpoint.
I'm glad I haven't the petite,
Overwhelmed sight of an antibody.
And yet I'm not just anybody perusing his body—
I have a reason to like it better than I like other bodies.
Someone else can praise those,
Each lonely and earthly, wanting to be celestial.

McPHERSON: Exactly so. I realized there was a gap in literature, and I wanted to begin to fill it.

MOYERS: What inspired that?

McPHERSON: A body!

MOYERS: Not an act of the imagination?

McPHERSON: No. This is one for which I had already done the research. This was my first husband in the second year of our marriage, and I set about describing him from head to toe. You can't tell, but I was actually angry at him at the time. I didn't intend the anger to come through—it just intensified my seeing.

MOYERS: Why were you angry?

McPHERSON: Why is *anybody* angry? Everybody gets angry at everybody. I can't remember, or I don't *want* to remember. I want the poem to survive, as an act of respect. Also, I was thinking of how prevalent the nude is in paintings and in sculpture; what does it take to create a nude with words? That was a challenge to me, too.

MOYERS: Do you see a difference in the way women are writing about men's bodies from the way men have written about women's bodies?

McPHERSON: You know, I don't see much difference. Personally, I just want to appreciate the human form by observing it in detail, much the way that in the Bible it is written that "God did this, God did that; He created this bird, this tree, this animal, and He's wonderful because He did this and this and this." The more details you accumulate, the more you have praised God.

MOYERS: By looking at the details, you're not idealizing the body.

McPHERSON: I'm always working *against* the sentimental tradition, but there also is a tradition, around Shakespeare's time, of men parodying their own descriptions of women's bodies. There are some very funny poems that inventory from head to toe the woman that they claim to love while really making fun of every single part of the body. I always include humor in the most serious of my poems. I think everything has to be whole and everything has a comedic side. Or, if you're not laughing out loud, everything has at least a smile side.

MOYERS: You've been including the blues in your poems, too.

McPHERSON: Yes, but that doesn't mean sadness. That's a joy of creation, and of singing strong and loud, saying, "This is my life, share this."

MOYERS: You seem to find such pleasure in writing.

McPHERSON: It's great fun. The words themselves are fun, one at a time, and the images are fun. Though life may be painful, there *is* a joy and a power in writing, even when you're dealing with something that is hard to live through day by day. You're trying to understand what you're living through by using the tools of words and images and the beautiful inner structure of language.

MOYERS: When you start do you know how a poem is going to end?

McPHERSON: Oh no. I don't do well if I know that. I have to *not* know where I'm going. I have to feel almost lost at the beginning, and ignorant—but *full* of curiosity: Where is it going to go? What am I going to learn by the end?

MOYERS: I suppose if you're lost, you're looking; and if you're not lost, you don't ask questions.

McPHERSON: Yes. I have a poem about being lost. I got lost twice in the mountains in the Northwest—why one would get lost a second time after getting lost once makes no sense to me—but each time I was lost in the mountains, I saw very fine details: mushrooms and elk scat and little insects and so on. When you're looking for *any* sign to find your way forward, you see each detail along the way as if it's a clue.

MOYERS: Some of your poems have different voices in them. How do you decide which character will tell this story?

McPHERSON: I'm a truth teller. I can't make stories up at all. I can't make *anything* up, except one lie I keep using in my poems which is that I drive, and I don't drive.

My daughter is one of my characters. I now have twenty-seven years of poems about her—each poem over those years concentrates on something quite odd and wonderful that she did—and as she grows older I try to capture that. Now I'm trying to capture my in-laws who are great characters.

MOYERS: Do they know it?

McPHERSON: Yes. They *want* me to. In fact they have wanted me to for ten years! They would always say, "Why don't you write a poem about *me*?"

MOYERS: How do you go about doing that?

McPHERSON: Recently I have been putting interviews with them in the middle of poems that are set in their house.

MOYERS: So one thing young poets could do is to start taping interviews with their relatives, right?

McPHERSON: Yes, *if* people are willing to talk!

MOYERS: In one poem, you write that orange is the single perfect color. How so?

McPHERSON: It has a singleness of purpose. It knows where it's going. It is not distracted by green or purple or any other colors. It does not even have shades of light and shadow within it, or at least that's the way I perceive it. I remember thinking of orange that it was always just coming forward toward you. Then I began to think of a line of poetry as a two-tone line or a three-tone line or a four-tone line, like the old cars that were two-toned. And recently I've been collecting quilts, which have many colors shocking against each other and patterns that don't usually go together.

MOYERS: Quilts have been prominent in so many of your poems.

McPHERSON: I became curious a few years ago about the aesthetic of a certain kind of African-American quilt that was improvisational. The women took ribbons or strips of fabric and arranged them off beat, changing the pattern a bit in each block, unlike the quilts that I grew up with which take the same pattern and repeat it exactly the same twenty-five times on a quilt. I was very excited by the African-American quilts that enjoyed asymmetry and enjoyed surprises in the way a writer enjoys being surprised by her lines and images as they come up unexpectedly. "Quilt of Rights" started with a quilt like this which had lots of tiny pieces in it.

In this case, one of the squares started out with a medium blue going with a light blue and a dark blue, and the squares get progressively wilder and more experimental with juxtaposing materials—patterns that are not usually together—until it's very busy and it's completely alive. There are maybe twenty-five little one-inch by one-inch pieces put together in each block, so the energy never stops. The quilt never stops talking. You never wholly get to know that quilt—you could look at it for the rest of your life. It's *still* talking. The individual squares that are put together are talking to each other, and in an unpredictable way. As if the quilter herself was surprised as she pieced each one, instead of planning it out all in advance.

MOYERS: Is the quilter the poet?

McPHERSON: I identify with the *method*. That *is* how I write. I know people who are afraid of scraps, afraid to write anything down. They're afraid to keep a diary or they keep it and then they burn it. Those are the scraps of your life. But to write a poem you have to acknowledge *all* those little scraps, and *no* scrap is too small. In a quilt are the parts of your life. I've had quilts that have long underwear inside for batting when they didn't have regular batting. All the parts of your life—all the clothing you've ever worn—can make this quilt that is beautiful and warm and bigger than you are. And the poem ends up bigger than you are, too. It is *always* more than I think I am.

QUILT OF RIGHTS

Yes, I do see many of us afraid of scraps,
afraid of their big design.
But once, every quilter knew she had a right
to color and shape, even if she believed in
no known meaning of *pretty*.

It is that maker whom I ask to teach me.

In the Muskogee Flea Market this soul's claim
to color passes to anyone.
She built cloth skylights
and for a while trusted herself
to fit just blue ones,
clear around a weather of small forms—
birds' eyes, pollen.
But then she guessed her right to sun in windows;
she colored her way to coral panes;
and finally directed all her vistas
to be plaid: plaid elms, plaid storm,
all shoppers and all dogs
tartan and clashing
as was her right.

No shadings between the frenzied and the cool.

But listen, I tell my rocky soul:
the normality of this—
For it is not done with moods.
It is given with a right to color.

M O Y E R S : The quilt of rights—the bill of rights? Was that in your mind at the time?

McPHERSON: Yes. I guess this is a feminist poem because it is discovering a power from the small details which are the leftovers of our lives, and it is not wasting anything. As a poet, I have a right to words. I have a right to acknowledge what I've lived through, as peculiar as it may be, and as embarrassing as it may be to people that I know. I have a right to acknowledge those parts of my experience and put them together in this beautiful poem, or in this beautiful quilt.

MOYERS: Women always made the quilts. They always had the right to the quilt but not the right to the word.

McPHERSON: They *didn't* have the right to call their quilt art, and these particular quilts, in fact, were completely ignored by the quilting shows and the county fairs. The books on quilting completely ignored the quilts that fall into this particular aesthetic. Only in the last ten or fifteen years have they been honored and now they are being preserved.

And also, you see, women for the most part did not put their names on their quilts— they're unsigned. So there's an anonymous quality to a lot of quilts, and I want the names on them.

MOYERS: How did you get interested in quilts as poems?

McPHERSON: I started collecting quilts almost accidentally by going to Chicago to hear bluesmen. When I heard the blues and met some bluesmen, I discovered they would put their first names in their songs. They would speak of themselves by their own name, and I thought what an interesting contrast to the quilters whose names are not on the quilts—they let the colors and patterns speak for them. So I wrote a poem that has men putting their names in their songs and the women who left their names off their quilts. I supplied a lot of the women's names straight out of the Chicago phone book which, if you had to go to a desert island and take one book, would be an excellent book to take.

MOYERS: The Chicago phone book?

McPHERSON: Yes, the Chicago phone book. It's magnificent reading. There's every kind of name you could imagine in there. Just gorgeous names that have a life of their own.

MOYERS: Names and the naming of things are very important to you in your poetry, right?

McPHERSON: Yes. Because at one time *I* had another name. I had another name for about one day. I was adopted at birth, and on the adoption papers, my birth parents had to supply a name for me, even though my adoptive parents would later give me my name. So for about one day I was Helen Todd.

MOYERS: And you wrote a poem—

McPHERSON: And I wrote a poem wondering who I would have been if I had been raised with that name. I do believe that if you changed as much as one syllable in the pronunciation in your name, you would be different.

MOYERS: Read "Helen Todd."

HELEN TODD: MY BIRTHNAME

They did not come to claim you back,
To make me Helen again. Mother
Watched the dry, hot streets in case they came.
This is how she found a tortoise
Crossing between cars and saved it.
It's how she knew roof-rats raised families
In the palmtree heads. But they didn't come—
It's almost forty years.

I went to them. And now I know
Our name, quiet one. I believe you
Would have stayed in trigonometry and taken up
The harp. Math soothed you; music
Made you bold; and science, completely
Understanding. Wouldn't you have collected,
Curated, in your adolescence, Mother Lode
Pyrites out of pity for their semblance
To gold? And three-leaf clovers to search
For some shy differences between them?

Knowing you myself at last—it seems you'd cut
Death in half and double everlasting life,
Quiet person named as a formality
At birth. I was not born. Only you were.

McPHERSON: I'm speaking to Helen. I can't say I *am* Helen, only that she is who I *would* have been.

MOYERS: Helen is the name you had for one day?

McPHERSON: Yes. It was actually my birth grandmother's real name on my father's side, and I found out when I met my birth parents that she was a poet—she had published poems in the *Christian Science Monitor* and in some seniors publications.

MOYERS: You're addressing this other child who was named briefly and disappeared?

McPHERSON: Yes.

MOYERS: Was it important to you over the years to imagine the life of that other child?

McPHERSON: I didn't imagine my own life. I imagined my birth parents' life as I grew, as they were before I found them. I only imagined my own life once I found out I had a name. Then I realized that I was that shadow person living alongside, and not too far from where I actually was raised.

MOYERS: And the poem helps unite the two?

McPHERSON: Yes, it does.

MOYERS: "At birth. I was not born. Only you were."

McPHERSON: Yes. Sandra McPherson was never born. Helen Todd *was* born.

MOYERS: And is Sandra McPherson real?

McPHERSON: Oh yes. I'll *never* get rid of her.

MOYERS: What can you tell me about the images in "Wings and Seeds"?

WINGS AND SEEDS

Hiking a levee through the salt marsh,
My birthmother and I. She is not teaching
Me to read and write but to believe
The hummingbird mistrusts its feet,
Weak below its feisty wings.

We trample brass buttons and chamomile,
As if to concern ourselves no more
With clothing and tea.
We twine hands, we trade heavy binoculars.
The clouds are coming from far out on the sea
Where they'd only the fetch to ruffle.

Separately our lives have passed from earthy passion
To wilder highliving creatures with wings.
With our early expectancies
Did we come to think ourselves a flight of nature?

Terns flash here, four dolled-up stilts in a pool,
Dozens of godwits a thick golden hem on the bay—
You'd think we too knew how to find
Our way back to this home ground.

I was a child of pleasure.
The strong pleasurable seeds of life
Found each other.
And I was created by passion's impatience
For the long wait till our meeting.

McPHERSON: When I met my brith parents about thirteen years ago, I discovered that we had very similar interests. They were amateur naturalists. They knew the names of plants, birds—anything that comes alive—and they wanted to show me those things when I first went to their part of the country and visited them. The very first day I met them we went out into a salt marsh, and my birthmother began identifying some of the plants there in the marsh, and telling me why we don't very often see a hummingbird perching, things like that.

Also in this poem is the fact that my birthmother, myself, and my daughter were all surprise pregnancies, whereas I was raised almost out of immaculate conception in a very fundamentalist Christian pure, virginal home. So I thought of these two—my mother who raised me and my birthmother—as being two parts of a whole.

MOYERS: So the seeds in the title refer to those "strong pleasurable seeds of life" that had brought you into the world?

McPHERSON: Yes, that and literal wings—the marsh birds—and real seeds of marsh plants, and something else, something transcendent.

MOYERS: You and your birthmother now discovered taking flight together?

McPHERSON: Perhaps we were very much a part of the ecology of the marsh which was home ground. I found my way back to where she was when I was born.

MOYERS: If this is a question you don't want to answer, I'll understand. But I'm curious. How do your poems about your adoption affect both your birthmother and your adoptive mother?

McPHERSON: My birth family and my adoptive family have met. We have Christmas together. I wanted my adoptive family to know I was not seeking for other parents. Two are usually enough, you know. I was seeking the people they were. I wanted to know them. And I did not want either family to feel that they were competing against each other. I knew that I was raised with much love, and I did not want my adoptive mother to feel deprived of her motherhood. Similarly, I wanted my birth parents to know that I loved them and always thought positively of them.

I never felt at all bad about being given up for adoption. I thought that proved to me that they had strong interests in life, interests that they perhaps wanted to pursue for many years before they had any children, if they would want children at all.

MOYERS: A wonderful example of the healing power of poetry.

McPHERSON: Yes. In this instance, poetry *was* healing to everyone. My birth parents had lived for thirty-seven years with the fact that they had given up a child for adoption, and keeping the secret had been a bit of a burden on them.

MOYERS: And when they read the poetry?

McPHERSON: They said, "We knew you would write about us."

© Lynn Saville

If poetry gets too far towards the realm of the aesthetic, the formal, and the beautiful and doesn't acknowledge the other side of existence—the history that we live in, the changes and the darkness of history—then the life goes out of poetry, and it becomes an escape.

DAVID MURA

David Mura was born in Great Lakes, Illinois, to parents who had been placed in U.S. internment camps during World War II. In poetry and nonfiction prose he traces themes of racial discrimination and betrayal as well as his own struggles as a third-generation Japanese American to reconcile conflicting notions of sexual and social success. A member of The Loft and the Asian-American Renaissance Conference, he is a popular performance poet. He teaches at St. Olaf College.

MOYERS: How do you arrive at metaphors like those in "The Colors of Desire"? You write that "the sidewalk's rolling, buckling, like lava melting."

MURA: That line happened largely through sound. When I talk about writing poetry with students, I tell them not to go in a straight line and not to think what they would logically think. Then the question becomes, "How do you proceed in a non-logical way which lets your imagination and your unconscious out?" One way is simply by associating through sound. For example, in that particular line I think I got to "rolling" fairly straightforwardly, but then I start associating simply by sound, so "buckling" takes the "l" from "rolling" and the "k" from "sidewalk" and combines them together.

MOYERS: Such poetry is written for the tongue, the lips.

MURA: Yes, and reliance on sound releases your unconscious because those associations are happening through rhythm and music and not through any type of logic. So your unconscious, what is really creative inside you, is bubbling up.

MOYERS: There's still a bias in this country that says unless it rhymes, it's not poetry.

MURA: I write in many different forms—some poems are in free verse and some may look like free verse, but they actually have the ghost of blank verse in them. I also write some poems which are very long-lined and which have a much more prosy rhythm. I find that I can achieve different tones and voices by working in various forms. For instance, at times I can get a more meditative abstract language in long lines which I can't get in short lines because for me such language just doesn't fit into the small line.

Sometime, instead of placing the rhyme at the end of a line, I'll bury it in the middle of a line, but the music is still there. An example is my poem "Open & Shut":

> Here is the rose of history. Pull the petals apart.
> A faint murmuring starts, then shouting, shrieking,
> an interminable roar. So you close the rose, call it
> simple, a rose without history, innocent, eternal.

The rhymes between "simple" and "eternal" are buried within the line. As I'm writing, I'm hearing those rhymes, but I'm slightly fiddling against the form to fight the feeling of monotonous regularity.

MOYERS: "The rose of history"—what is that metaphor saying to the reader?

MURA: Well, I think of it as two poles between which my poetry exists—the tension on the one hand between the moment of the aesthetic and the beautiful, the concern with form and the timeless, the lyrical moment, and on the other hand, the process of history which is often brutal and unjust, and also filled with stories and lives which go neglected and unrecorded.

The process of history is often permeated by a darkness that people don't want to look at, but I want my poetry to be a combination of those *two* things. I think that if poetry gets too far towards the realm of the aesthetic, the formal, and the beautiful and doesn't acknowledge the other side of existence—the history that we live in, the changes and the darkness of history—then the life goes out of poetry, and it becomes an escape.

MOYERS: The rose in the rubble. The rose is innocent, but history is not. Throughout your poetry you grapple with what it means to be neither black nor white. You seem to live in a country in between.

MURA: There is a moment in my poem "The Colors of Desire" when my father gets on a segregated bus while he is in the internment camp in Jerome, Arkansas, during World War II—the Japanese American internees were allowed to get out of the camps on weekend passes—and the question he faces is, "Where do you sit?" When I asked my father where he sat, he said that the whites urged the Japanese American internees to sit in the front of the bus while the blacks urged them to sit in the back of the bus.

The Japanese Americans tended to sit in the front of the bus, and one of the ways I talk about this is to say that America has often offered Asian Americans honorary white status, but that status is predicated on a deal—you get to sit in the front of the bus and to be an honorary white, but you don't get to sit at the *very* front of the bus. Also, you don't *ever* get to drive the bus. Also, you must pay *no* attention to what's happening to the people on the back of the bus. You must claim *no* relationship to the people in the back of the bus. You must absolutely *never* do anything to change the status of the people in the back of the bus. And if you agree to *all* of these conditions, we will consider you an honorary white.

When I came to that image of my father stepping on a segregated bus, I realized that Asian Americans—and in my case, Japanese Americans—often think of our identity simply in relation to our own community or in relationship to white society. But in actuality, when my father gets on that bus his identity is already formed against the matrix of black-white relations, and the decision that he makes to sit in the front of the bus is an historically understandable decision because he's sitting where the power is.

But in 1994 that's a decision we have to reconsider. I think much of the mistrust that many African Americans feel toward Asian Americans arises from the historical fact that many of us have settled for this honorary white status. And yet, as an Asian American and as a Japanese American, I've learned a lot about who I am from writers like James Baldwin, Alice Walker, Toni Morrison, black poets like Amiri Baraka, and the black West Indian psychologist Franz Fanon.

MOYERS: What is something you learned from them?

MURA: I learned about my own identity. When Franz Fanon writes that the black school child in the French West Indies reads about our ancestors the Gauls and then about how the great white hunter went into Africa to civilize the savages, Fanon says the child learns self-hatred, self-alienation, and identification with the oppressor. I read that and I said, "Oh. That's what I've been doing."

MOYERS: Your people weren't on the *Mayflower*.

MURA: That's right, and because I grew up under the assimilation model of the 1950s when you were encouraged to lose your ethnic heritage, I actively tried to blend in and assume a middle-class white identity. Even when I was a very young poet, the poets with whom I identified were Robert Lowell and John Berryman.

MOYERS: Both white.

MURA: Yes, both white upper class . . .

MOYERS: And established.

MURA: Yes, established and Ivy League educated. At that time I was in a sense saying, "Don't call me an Asian American poet. Don't call me a Japanese American poet. Don't call me a poet of color. I don't want to be in a literary ghetto. I don't want to be part of some literary affirmative action. I want to be a *writer*!" But I was really just feeling uncomfortable about who I was; I was internalizing the racial hierarchy that I had learned growing up, and I wanted to put a distance between myself and other Asian Americans.

FROM THE COLORS OF DESIRE

1 Photograph of a Lynching (circa 193__)

These men? In their dented felt hats,
in the way their fingers tug their suspenders or vests,
with faces a bit puffy or too lean, eyes narrow and close together,
they seem too like our image of the South,
the Thirties. Of course they are white;
who then could create this cardboard figure, face
flat and grey, eyes oversized, bulging like
an ancient totem this gang has dug up? At the far right,
in a small browed cap, a boy of twelve smiles,
as if responding to what's most familiar here:
the camera's click. And though directly above them,
a branch ropes the dead negro in the air,
the men too focus their blank beam
on the unseen eye. Which is, at this moment, us.

Or, more precisely, me. Who cannot but recall
how my father, as a teenager, clutched his weekend pass,
passed through the rifle towers and gates
of the Jerome, Arkansas camp, and, in 1942,
stepped on a bus to find white riders
motioning, "Sit here, son," and, in the rows beyond,
a half dozen black faces, waving him back,
"Us colored folks got to stick together."
How did he know where to sit? And how is it,

thirty-five years later, I found myself sitting
in a dark theater, watching *Behind the Green Door*
with a dozen anonymous men? On the screen
a woman sprawls on a table, stripped, the same one
on the Ivory Snow soap box, a baby on her shoulder,
smiling her blond, practically pure white smile.
Now, after being prepared and serviced slowly

by a handful of women, as one of them
kneels, buries her face in her crotch,
she is ready: And now he walks in—

Lean, naked, black, streaks of white paint on his chest
and face, a necklace of teeth, it's almost comical,
this fake garb of the jungle, Africa and All-America,
black and blond, almost a joke but for the surge
of what these lynchers urged as the ultimate crime
against nature: the black man kneeling to this kidnapped
body, slipping himself in, the screen showing it all, down
to her head shaking in a seizure, the final scream
before he lifts himself off her quivering body . . .

I left that theater, bolted from a dream into a dream.
I stared at the cars whizzing by, watched the light change,
red, yellow, green, and the haze in my head from the hash,
and the haze in my head from the image, melded together,
        reverberating.
I don't know what I did afterwards. Only, night after night,
I will see those bodies, black and white (and where am I,
the missing third?), like a talisman, a rageful, unrelenting release.

▪ ▪

3 MISS JUNE 1964

I'm twelve, home from school
with a slight fever. I slide back the door
of my parents' closet—my mother's out shopping—
rummage among pumps, flats, lined in a rack,
unzip the garment bags, one by one.
It slides like a sigh from the folded sweaters.
I flip through ads for cologne, L.P.'s, a man
in a trench coat, lugging a panda-sized Fleischman's fifth.
Somewhere past the photo of Schweitzer
in his pith helmet, and the cartoon nude man
perched as a gargoyle, I spill the photo
millions of men, white, black, yellow, have seen,
though the body before me is white, eighteen:

Her breasts are enormous, almost frightening
—the areolas seem large as my fist.
As the three glossy pages sprawl before me,
I start to touch myself, and there is
some terror, my mother will come home,
some delight I've never felt before,
and I do not cry out, I make no sound . . .

How did I know that photo was there?
Or mother know I knew?
Two nights later, at her request,
father lectures me on burning out too early.
Beneath the cone of light at the kitchen table,
we're caught, like the shiest of lovers.
He points at the booklet from the AMA
—he writes their P.R.—"Read it," he says,
"and, if you have any questions . . ."

Thirty years later, these questions remain.
And his answers, too, are still the same:
Really, David, it was just a magazine.
And the camps, my father's lost nursery,
the way he chased me round the yard in L.A.,
even the two by four he swung—why connect them
with years you wandered those theaters?
Is nothing in your life your own volition?
The past isn't just a box full of horrors.
What of those mornings in the surf
near Venice, all of us casting line after line,
arcing over breakers all the way from Japan,
or plopping down beside my mother,
a plateful of mochi, pulling it like taffy
with our teeth, shoyu dribbling
down our chins. Think of it, David.
There were days like that. We were happy. . . .

4

Who hears the rain churning the forest to mud,
or the unraveling rope snap, the negro

plummet to rest at last? And what flooded my father's eyes
in the Little Rock theater, sitting beneath the balcony
in that third year of war? Where is 1944,
it snows sweeping down Heart Mountain,
to vanish on my mother's black bobbing head,
as she scurries towards the cramped cracked barracks
where her mother's throat coughs through the night,
and her father sits beside her on the bed?
The dim bulb flickers as my mother enters.
Her face is flushed, her cheeks cold. She
bows, unwraps her scarf, pours the steaming
kettle in the tea pot; offers her mother a sip.
And none of them knows she will never
talk of this moment, that, years later,
I will have to imagine it, again and again,
just as I have tried to imagine the lives
of all those who have entered these lines . . .

Tonight snow drifts below my window,
and lamps puff ghostly aureoles
over walks and lawns. Father, mother,
I married a woman not of my color.
What is it I want to escape?
These nights in our bed, my head
on her belly, I can hear these thumps,
and later, when she falls asleep,
I stand in our daughter's room,
so bare yet but for a simple wooden crib
(on the bulletin board I've pinned the sonogram
with black and white swirls like a galaxy
spinning about the fetal body),
and something plummets inside me,
out of proportion to the time
I've been portioned on this earth.
And if what is granted erases nothing,
if history remains, untouched, implacable,
as darkness flows up our hemisphere,
her hollow still moves moonward,

small hill on the horizon, swelling,
floating with child, white, yellow,
who knows, who can tell her,

oh why must it matter?

MOYERS: You write "Father, mother, / I married a woman not of my color. / What is it I want to escape?" Have you answered that?

MURA: No, that's a question I'm constantly investigating because one of the things my work is about is the conjunction between race and sexuality, and I think that is an area which American culture has not investigated nearly enough. I believe there is a conjunction between those whom you hire and those whom you desire. People think that the realm of individual sexual desire ought to be kept separate from the public question of affirmative action—who is hired, quotas, things like that—but even as a young person, it became very apparent to me that there were standards of white beauty and of masculinity to which I, an Asian American male, couldn't ever relate.

I didn't really understand any of this until I began to read Franz Fanon's discussion about how black men who are fascinated by white women have really bought into the racial hierarchy because they think that sleeping with white women will make them equal to white men. I read that and, again, I said, "Oh. That's what I've been doing."

So when I addressed the question of my love for my wife in "The Colors of Desire," I knew it was a very complicated matter, and I did not want to bury any aspects of it under the table. My wife is three quarters WASP, one quarter Austrian Hungarian Jew, and her WASP side goes all the way back to the *Mayflower*. A lot of people want to say that love is color blind, but that has not been my experience. I think that idea makes people less interesting and less complicated than they actually are.

MOYERS: What does poetry do that helps you cope with these desires and fears that you haven't been able to reconcile?

MURA: Poetry allows me to bring them together, to combine and compress the complexity of my experience so I can comprehend it, and at the same time, understand my relationship to the past and to the world around me. T. S. Eliot said that a poet is "constantly amalgamating disparate experience," and in my poems I'm often bringing together *very* disparate experience. "The Colors of Desire" starts off with a lynching, then my father is getting on a segregated bus, then the poem goes to an incident where I'm fighting with my brother in our bedroom when I'm a child, then to the discovery of a *Playboy* in my father's closet, then to my mother in Hart Mountain internment camp, and finally to myself listening to my wife's belly when she's pregnant with our first child.

In the poem all of these things are connected, so the poem helped me to see *how* they are connected, and I think it also helped me to go on with my life.

I should say here that my early poems were often about Japanese and Japanese American subjects, so even while I was saying, "I'm just a *writer*. Don't label me!" my creativity was already pulling me toward that material. Had I not been a writer, had I not been pushed by what I feel is a writerly duty to look for the truth of your life in the world around you, to dive into those complexities and contradictions, I think I might have ended up so messed up that I could conceivably be dead now; and that's not just melodramatic because there was a point in my late twenties where my identity simply fell apart. I indulged in a lot of self-destructive behavior—drugs and drinking and promiscuity—all of which I think was fueled by self-hatred and rage that I didn't understand.

MOYERS: Does poetry take you back into the past, help you to discover the origins of your present confusion and rage?

MURA: Yes, poetry does do that for me.

Writing is how I hear my own voice confronting me, saying that you're trying to excuse yourself with all these explanations—you're trying to say, "It's my family. It's history. It's race," when you know it's actually your *own* nature. It's who you *are—your own nature* is where this lust and perversions reside. There is something in me which does believe in original sin—I don't believe we're ever born innocent and I think that's okay.

MOYERS: You write about addiction to pornography. You're asking some challenging questions about your own nature.

MURA: In my second book, *The Colors of Desire,* I have a poem called "Pornography Abandoned" about a man abandoning pornography, and in my first book, *After We Lost Our Way,* I have another poem, "The Bookstore," about a man going to a pornographic bookstore. The rhetoric of *Playboy* or *Oui* or *Penthouse* takes for granted that consuming pornography is a natural and pleasurable hedonistic activity, but in a poem like "The Bookstore" I show a detailed examination of somebody going to one of those book stores, and it's really a re-creation of some private hell—a man sitting in a booth watching a pornographic film and masturbating.

It's a picture of *extreme* alienation, of being cut off from any real human communication with other people. After reading the poem I think you have to ask, is this man's experience pleasurable? In his experience something that anybody would logically want to undergo?

MOYERS: When I read that poem I felt the sadness in it.

MURA: Yes, but the problem is that the man involved in that activity can't express that sadness. I also think that beneath his experience there's an anger at being alienated and an anger at not being able to communicate what he most deeply yearns for.

MOYERS: He's feeling inadequate?

MURA: Yes, and you have to ask where that inadequacy comes from. Is it something that's natural? When I was a member of several men's groups and therapy groups I saw that, in general, this was learned behavior that came through dysfunctional family systems in which people could not communicate about their sexuality and where the men grew up feeling shameful about their bodies.

Nobody gave them a language to talk about their own feelings, and therefore they grew up incredibly angry and sad but without any way of expressing that. So pornography comes to be used almost like a drug to deaden feelings and to enter this reverie, but when the reverie ends, where are you? You're in the same place where you started.

MOYERS: Pornography is very public now. It's not kept off the street, in cubbyholes, it's *everywhere*. What does this say to you about our society?

MURA: Well, it's a very sad state and, in certain ways, I think it's a logical progression of capitalism. I mean, what *is* the logic of capitalism? If you can sell it, sell it. There's no morality there. There's no boundary. We don't say, "Here's something we *don't* sell." It's *all* about making a profit, and with pornography you have something which is consumed like a drug, which can be consumed over and over again, and which always leaves you feeling that you need another fix—that's the perfect engine for a capitalist society.

MOYERS: So you think the market is driving pornography?

MURA: Yes, but we are only in a very incipient stage. I think women have been a lot more articulate about the harm that pornography does towards them than men have been about the harm that it does towards men. I think women have, in general, obviously been much more articulate about the ways that traditional sexual roles and traditional ways of looking at sexuality have damaged them. Men have been damaged as well, but they have barely begun to articulate the damage that has been done to them.

MOYERS: It strikes me that in your own story you are suggesting that this inadequacy and your transient addiction to pornography issued from a conflict of family history and alienation.

MURA: Yes, I think it *does* go back to the image I had of myself as an adolescent boy, feeling incredibly inadequate and going, for instance, to my first boy/girl party and suddenly realizing when they played spin the bottle that I was different. I was the lone Japanese American amid a group of white kids, and suddenly there was a barrier there, and I couldn't quite articulate what the barrier was.

MOYERS: The poem about your wife's grandfather intrigues me.

GRANDFATHER-IN-LAW

It's nothing really, and really, it could have been worse, and of course, he's
    now several years dead,
and his widow, well, if oftentimes she's sometimes distracted, overly
    cautious when we visit—
after all, Boston isn't New York—she seems, for some reason, enormously
    proud that there's
        now a writer in the family,
and periodically, sends me clippings about the poet laureate, Thoreau, Anne
    Sexton's daughter,
        Lowell, New England literary lore—
in which I fit, if I fit at all, simply because I write in English—as if color of
    skin didn't matter
        anymore.
Still, years ago, during my first visit to Boston, when we were all asleep,
he, who used to require that my wife memorize lines of Longfellow or Poe
    and recite them on
        the phone,
so that, every time he called, she ran outdoors and had to be coaxed back,
    sometimes with
        threats, to talk to Pops
(though she remembers too his sly imitations of Lincoln, ice cream at
    Brighams, burgers
        and fries, all the usual grandfatherly treats),
he, who for some reason was prejudiced against Albanians—where on earth
    did he find them I
        wondered—
who, in the thirties, would vanish to New York, catch a show, buy a suit,
    while up north,
the gas and water bills pounded the front door (his spendthrift ways startled
    me with my
        grandfather's resemblance),

who for over forty years came down each morning, "How's the old goat?"
    with a tie only his
                wife could knot circling his neck,
he slipped into my wife's room—we were unmarried at the time—and
    whispered so softly she thought
he almost believed she was really asleep, and was saying this like a wish or
    spell, some bohunk
                miscalculated Boston sense of duty:
"Don't make a mistake with your life, Susie. Don't make a mistake . . ."
Well. The thing that gets me now, despite the dangling rantings I've let go,
    is that, at least at
                that time,
he was right: There was, inside me, some pressing, raw unpeeled
    persistence, some libidinous
                desire for dominance
that, in the scribbled first-drafts of my life, seemed to mark me as wastrel
    and rageful,
                bound to be unfaithful,
to destroy, in some powerful, nuclear need, fissioned both by childhood
    and racism,
                whatever came near—
And I can't help but feel, forgiving him now, that it she had listened, if she
    had been awake,
if this flourishing solace, this muscled-for happiness, shared by us now, had
    never awakened,
he would have become for me a symbol of my rage and self-destruction,
    another raw, never
                healing wound,
and not this silenced grandfatherly presence, a crank and scoundrel, red-
    necked Yankee who
                created the delicate seed of my wife, my child.

MURA: I married into an old WASP family, on my wife's mother's side—they go all the way back to the *Mayflower*—and when we met, my wife told me that her grandfather was prejudiced against Albanians. That was a new one to me! I think this poem is about that confrontation with an old WASP family which, in many ways, was probably even more familiar to me than a Japanese American family because when I was growing up that's what I read about and those were also the images that I'd seen in movies and on TV.

I read about the Pilgrims and the *Mayflower,* but in my history books I didn't read about Japanese American immigrants coming to America. So in certain ways, it was ironically natural for me to be in that family, even though the grandfather had misgivings about his granddaughter's being with me; but the poem is really about forgiveness. I think it's about forgiving him for who he was and for his prejudice against me; and it also deals with the irony that when he says, "Don't make a mistake with your life, Susie. Don't make a mistake," in certain ways he was right because, in the early parts of our relationship, I was not faithful. A lot of that unfaithfulness was fueled by my own sense of inadequacy about issues of race that I couldn't articulate and, from one point of view, my wife probably should have left me then.

M O Y E R S : You confess that her grandfather may have been right in saying to her, "Don't marry David Mura."

M U R A : Yes, but he was *not* right in the way that he thought he was right. He thought she shouldn't marry somebody of another race, and in the poem I'm saying she shouldn't marry somebody who is being a real jerk to her. This poem was written after a period when my wife and I both entered therapy to deal with all these issues, and in dealing with them we had to take apart our relationship and put it back together. The poem expresses my gratitude for her acceptance of me and for her willingness to go through that process of rebuilding our relationship which led to her ultimately forgiving me, and it is also about my work to forgive myself and to go on with my life.

M O Y E R S : Forgive yourself for what? What *was* this demon?

M U R A : The demon was rage, rage at racism and rage at the fact that nobody recognized the racism. I would try to talk about it, and people would look and say, "What are you *talking* about?" That still happens—*Miss Saigon* is a Broadway hit, but most Asian American artists think it's an abomination that perpetuates racist stereotypes. Thousands and thousands of people go to see it and millions and millions of dollars are made off what I perceive as a racist musical. When I talk about it to certain people, they have no idea what I'm talking about. It's as if I've come from outer space.

As enraging as this response is, it's understandable because those people have never been given any context to understand who I am or how I would interpret what's up there on that stage. They just think, "Oh, *Miss Saigon,* it's a sweet story about love and death." They don't think about how it perpetuates a very constant image in our culture of a white male with an Asian female who is in various ways submissive and pining for him. That image goes all the way back to *Madama Butterfly,* and it's deeply embedded in popular culture. For instance, when Alan Parker wants to make a movie about the internment camps, who's going to be the hero of the internment camp film? Is it Sab Shimono? Is it James Shigeta? No. It's Dennis Quaid! In the film *Come See the Paradise,* Dennis Quaid is an Irish American married to a *Nisei* woman. And I have to ask, "Why do *that?* Why can't you center the story on a Nisei couple, especially since almost all my parents' generation *did* marry other Japanese Americans?"

The argument many people make is that you need a white entry into the world of Japanese Americans, but *I've* been seeing films with white faces since I was born and I had no trouble entering *those* films. When I went to Japan for the first time in 1985, I had a curious experience which I think is very telling—Japan was my first experience of being surrounded by a culture where everybody looked like me, even all the images on TV looked like me, and it felt wonderful! While I was there I went to see *Out of Africa* in which Meryl Streep plays the Danish author Isak Dinesen. When Streep arrives at her Kenyan plantation and all the black hands come out to greet her, I found myself watching this white face in the center of the film and suddenly saying, "I'm bored with this!" I've seen the white bwana in Africa over and over again, but what I'm really interested in is what is happening in the minds of the Kenyans because I know that in twenty or thirty years they're going to form the Mau Maus and kick the Europeans out. Something is changing their consciousness, and *that* is what I'm really interested in.

I felt I was withdrawing affection, attention, curiosity—which I naturally gave to the Meryl Streep face in the center of the film—and giving it instead to those black faces on the margins. Suddenly the world looked different to me, and I realized that that's part of what racism is. Discrimination is not just shouting insults, or jobs; it's how you react emotionally when you see a face: Are you curious about that face? Do you feel affectionate towards that face? Do you feel a desire to understand and to know what's going on in that person's interior life? Does that face seem a blank? Do you even *see* that face? Do you just put that face to the margins?

MOYERS: Subdued rage runs through "A *Nisei* Picnic: From an Album." That's your uncle's story.

A *NISEI* PICNIC: FROM AN ALBUM

Here is my uncle, a rice ball in his mouth,
a picnic basket (ants crawl in the slats) at his side.
Eventually he ballooned like Buddha,
over three hundred pounds. I used to stroke
his immense belly, which was scarred by shrapnel.

It made me feel patriotic.
Once, all night, he lay in a ditch near the Danube,
shoved in his intestines with his hands.
When he came back, he couldn't rent an apartment.
"*Shikatta ga nai,*" he said. *Can't be helped.*

Turning from her boyfriend, a glint of giggle
caught in the shadows, my aunt never married.
On the day of her wedding, sitting in the bath,
she felt her knees lock; she couldn't get up.
For years I wanted to be her son.
She took me to zoos, movies, bought me candy.
When I grew up, she started raising minks
in her basement—"To make money," she said—
Most of them died of chills. She folded each one
in a shoebox and buried it in her yard.

My father's the one pumping his bicep.
(Sleek, untarnished, he still swims two miles a day.)
I can't claim that his gambling like his father
lost a garage, greenhouse or grocery,
or that, stumbling drunk, he tumbled in
the bushes with Mrs. Hoshizaki, staining
his tuxedo with mulberries and mud. He
worked too hard to be white. He beat his son.

Shown here, my head like a moon dwarfing my body
as I struggle to rise. Who are these grown-ups?
Why are they laughing? How can I tear
the bewilderment from their eyes?

MURA: Yes. He was a member of the famous 442nd Infantry Division, and he was injured. I looked at him as a hero, as a Japanese American John Wayne. It was only later that I learned that internment politics were much more complicated than that.

MOYERS: He fought for the U.S. against the Nazis, yet when he came back from the war and couldn't find an apartment, he wasn't angry. How do you explain that?

MURA: There's a Japanese expression which I quote in the poem, *shikatta ga nai,* which means "It can't be helped." It's like our expression "What can you do?" You can either rage and rage against it or you can just live with it. I think people make that decision constantly about things that happen in their lives. All of us experience various injustices, and at times for our own sanity and peace of mind we decide, "What can you do? It can't be helped." But there are points in history when that attitude snaps, and suddenly it *can* be helped, we *can* do something about it.

Not getting an apartment is wrong. I *can* protest against that, and it's worthwhile for me to get angry about it. It's worthwhile for me to work to change it, and the means exist by which I *can* change that situation.

MOYERS: In "An Argument: on 1942" your mother says, "I know, it's all / part of your job, your way . . ." What does she mean?

AN ARGUMENT: ON 1942

—FOR MY MOTHER

Near Rose's Chop Suey and Jinosuke's grocery,
the temple where incense hovered and inspired
dense evening chants (prayers for Buddha's mercy,
colorless and deep), that day he was fired . . .

—No, no, no, she tells me. Why bring it back?
The camps are over. (Also overly dramatic.)
Forget *shoyu*-stained *furoshiki, mochi* on a stick:
You're like a terrier, David, gnawing a bone, an old, old trick . . .

Mostly we were bored. Women cooked and sewed,
men played black jack, dug gardens, a *benjo.*
Who noticed barbed wire, guards in the towers?
We were children, hunting stones, birds, wild flowers.

Yes, Mother hid tins of *tsukemono* and eel
beneath the bed. And when the last was peeled,
clamped tight her lips, growing thinner and thinner.
But cancer not the camps made her throat blacker.

. . . And she didn't die then . . . after the war, in St. Paul,
you weren't even born. Oh I know, I know, it's all
part of your job, your way, but why can't you glean
how far we've come, how much I can't recall—

David, it was so long ago—how useless it seems . . .

M U R A : I think she knows that it's part of my job as a poet to dig up the truths that everybody wants to bury under the table, but she wants to say, "Look how far we have come. The past is past." I want to honor that viewpoint by having her voice in the poem, because what I finally believe is that it's not *my* viewpoint which is true. We require *both* viewpoints, which is the reality of the Japanese American experience.

I love to write poetry instead of essays because I don't have to argue a point in poems. In a way, I do argue points in poems, but in "The Colors of Desire," for example, I get to give my father's voice, his version. In "An Argument," I get to give my mother's version of the past, and in each case readers have to deal with the complication of these two different voices and two different interpretations of the past—my parents' and mine.

M O Y E R S : Who is speaking in "Letters from a Tule Lake Internment Camp (1942–45)"?

M U R A : An *Issei*—first-generation Japanese American—man who's been separated from his wife. Often the leaders of the Japanese American communities were taken away first—before the official camps were set up at the beginning of World War II—so he's writing to his wife who is in another camp.

The position of the *Issei* was very complicated. They were put in camps and then asked to sign a loyalty oath. "Do you forswear allegiance to the emperor and swear allegiance to the United States? And will you serve in the armed forces?" Even the women were asked to sign this oath. But the *Issei* by law were not allowed to become U.S. citizens, so if they signed the loyalty oath they were left without a country—they had no citizenship. Yet many of them signed anyway. So in that poem the man asks what country he's in because he's almost stateless.

He was accused of no crime, there was no trial, there was no habeas corpus, so he asks, "Where am I?" He's lost his nursery, which he worked all his life to build up, he's lost his house, his possessions. Most of the *Issei* never recovered economically after the war. One of my grandfathers owned a nursery, the other owned a thriving produce store; and they both lost everything. After the war the best they could do was that one grandfather was hired as a janitor in a hotel. That was it!

M O Y E R S : How do you come to terms with the moral idealism of America and these brutal realities in your family history?

M U R A : I have faith on some level in the promise of America, but I want to hold America and all of us to that promise. I believe it's important to have that ideal out there—it's one of the terrific things about this country—but, at the same time, the only way we're going to reach that ideal is by seeing the ways in which we failed in the past because the past explains what's here now. I think when you change the telling of the past, you actually change the present. Poets here at the festival like myself and Marilyn Chin and Michael Harper and Sekou Sundiata and Naomi Shihab Nye and Victor Hernández Cruz and many, many more throughout the country are layering all sorts of other histories on the history that has been allowed into the schoolbooks. I think we are creating a fuller and more complete picture of what America always was so that history can help us to recognize what is happening in America today. Suddenly the people no one paid attention to are here with their stories. Suddenly, a tremendous world-class novelist like Toni Morrison and a whole array of other black authors compel our attention, and we realize there *is* a history of African Americans and a present for African Americans as well, and we have to pay attention to *all* of it.

MOYERS: A poem is fact, history, and fiction. What makes it true?

MURA: First of all, I would say the poem is my subjective vision, and it is up to readers and listeners to take in the subjective visions of each poet and to weave those visions into their understanding of what the world is.

When the readers and listeners do that, suddenly there's more information available, other voices are coming in, and they have to listen to those voices. Some of what those voices say may be true, some of what those voices say may not be true, but the readers and listeners certainly have to deal with the presence of those people whose voices they have absorbed.

So if I am able to write poems with a certain beauty and resonance, and if that beauty and resonance has truth, then the readers and listeners have no choice but to reckon with that truth.

David Mura, Jimmy Santiago Baca, Claribel Alegría

NAOMI SHIHAB NYE

Naomi Shihab Nye, the daughter of a Palestinian father and an American mother, grew up in St. Louis, Old Jerusalem (then in Jordan), and Texas. Her poetry reflects this textured heritage, which endowed her with an openness to the experiences of others and a sense of continuity across borders. "In the alchemical process of purification," one reviewer wrote of her poems, "Nye often pulls gold from the ordinary," including pulleys, buttonholes, and brooms. She lives with her family in San Antonio, Texas, and teaches at the University of Texas, Austin.

MOYERS: I heard you tell a group of young people today that this festival is like Woodstock.

NYE: Well, actually I was quoting Linda McCarriston who said that when we drove up and saw the hordes of school buses and tents. I said that when I was here before I felt that the Dodge Festival was like a circus to which people come with animated hopes, anticipating whatever magical feats will be performed. I love the dynamics of this festival—its huge scale and being outside and attracting the kind of audience it attracts. I think this festival is very important.

MOYERS: Does this festival say something about what's going on in our society today?

NYE: I definitely feel there are many listening ears in our society and many people eager to use their voices in ways that lead to questioning and wonder. I feel that hunger every place I go, and I feel a receptivity in our culture *to* that hunger. I think teachers and poets who have worked in schools have contributed greatly to this growth of interest in and desire for poetry so evident over the past twenty or thirty years in our country.

MOYERS: This morning you were talking about energy in poetry—what can you tell me about energy and poems?

NYE: The older I get, Bill, the more I think energy is everything. If we have it, feel connected to it, we are rich. If we don't have it, we are forever searching. High school students frequently say that emotion is the key to life—and at their age it might be—but the older I get the more that key, that source of all living, seems to be energy.

Poetry is a conversation with the world; poetry is a conversation with the words on the page in which you allow those words to speak back to you; and poetry is a conversation with yourself.

Energy comes from many places including juxtaposition and contradictory things, elements, experiences, impulses coming together.

The energy that comes from rubbing one image up against another in poems is quite surprising and majestic, and I think our brains are *desperate* for that energy. A poem is a place where we can put things together maybe momentarily and maybe only for ourselves—that energy may not be there for someone else reading or hearing the poem, but I think energy is a primeval, basic aspect of poetry.

MOYERS: When you sit down to write, do you know why you're doing it?

NYE: I know why I'm *hungry* to do it. My first hunger of every day is to let words come through me in some way, and I don't always feel that I succeed in doing it—sometimes I feel that I am just an audience for words floating by and through. But the possibilities seem inexhaustible: I don't know what story will rise up out of that deep well of experience, and I'm always fascinated by how there's something there to work with every morning.

MOYERS: Do you wait, or is it work to bring that story up from its source?

NYE: Sometimes you wait, but the more receptive you are on a regular basis, the more easily things are given to you; so it's not as if you wait for hours with nothing going on. You may not get anything that goes anywhere, but many possibilities are always generated. There is great energy released just by the act of being receptive to words. The poet David Ignatow has talked about keeping the door open—it could be a door in a relationship or a door between the poet and words so that words can come through—and I believe that when you regularly sit down to write, when you regularly make yourself available to words, they come through more readily for you.

MOYERS: But you're not being passive.

NYE: Not at all. As you rub these words together they spark and whole new combinations happen. The unpredictable quality of writing always fascinates me. An image comes to you and you think you might know what it's about or where it wants to take you, and invariably the poems which matter to you turn out to be those poems which took you somewhere other than where you thought you needed to go.

MOYERS: Poetry is a form of conversation for you, isn't it?

NYE: Absolutely. Poetry is a conversation with the world; poetry is a conversation with the words on the page in which you allow those words to speak back to you; and poetry is a conversation with yourself. Many times I meet students and see a little look of wariness in their faces—"I'm not sure I *want* to do this or I'm not sure I *can* do this"—I like to say, "Wait a minute. How nervous are you about the conversation you're going to have at lunch today with your friends?" And they say, "Oh, we're not nervous at all about *that.* We do *that* every day." Then I tell them they can come to feel the same way about writing. Writing doesn't have to be an exotic or stressful experience. You can just sit down with a piece of paper and begin talking and see what speaks back.

M O Y E R S : Talking out loud? When you're alone?

N Y E : Well, sometimes. I often begin talking out loud, whether I'm alone or not. My son will say, "You were talking to yourself right now." And I say. "That's what I was doing; but I was so comfortable with you that I didn't notice it." I often just repeat a phrase I've heard or some words I want to write down so I won't forget them. In our culture especially I think we need to talk to ourselves more, and we also need to *listen* to ourselves more.

M O Y E R S : Some people think there's so much talk in America—the talk shows, call-in shows, interviews, C-Span, CNN, press conferences, TV commercials— that it's all just a babble.

N Y E : Maybe what I mean is a different kind of talk, because the kind I'm thinking about is a very slow and deliberate, delighted kind of talk. My favorite quote comes from Thailand, "Life is so short we must move very slowly." I think that poems help us to do that by allowing us to savor a single image, a single phrase. Think about haiku—those little seventeen syllable poems—how many people have savored a single haiku poem over hundreds of years? Reading a poem slows you down, and when you slow down you are likely to read it more than one time. You read it more slowly than you would speak to somebody in a store, and we *need* that slow experience with words, as well as those quick and jazzy ones.

M O Y E R S : When you read "The Art of Disappearing" this morning, young people visibly responded as you confessed to walking around feeling like a leaf that "could tumble any second." They got it. They knew what you were talking about.

THE ART OF DISAPPEARING

When they say Don't I know you?
say no.

When they invite you to the party
remember what parties are like
before answering.

Someone telling you in a loud voice
they once wrote a poem.
Greasy sausage balls on a paper plate.
Then reply.

If they say We should get together
say why?

It's not that you don't love them anymore.
You're trying to remember something
too important to forget.
Trees. The monastery bell at twilight.
Tell them you have a new project.
It will never be finished.

When someone recognizes you in a grocery store
nod briefly and become a cabbage.
When someone you haven't seen in ten years
appears at the door,
don't start singing him all your new songs.
You will never catch up.

Walk around feeling like a leaf.
Know you could tumble any second.
Then decide what to do with your time.

N Y E : I think high school students have a keen sense of the fragility of life and the precariousness of relationships. When I commented that young writers need to be sturdy, one boy said, "I think I need to be the opposite because I need to be emotional." But I think emotion is *part* of being sturdy—to become sturdy you don't have to become cold—I just meant that you have to grow confident in yourself and of yourself. This vocation *matters.*

M O Y E R S : How is it that daily and mundane objects—gloves and forks and onions and buttonholes and pulleys—find their way into so many of your poems?

N Y E : These tangible small objects are what I live with. I'm attracted to them. Gravity points. Since I was a small child I've felt that little inanimate things were very wise, that they had their own kind of wisdom, something to teach me if I would only pay the right kind of attention to them. William Stafford's poems and the poems by so many other poets which I've loved through my life take us back to the things of the world, the things which often go unnoticed—these poems all say: "Pause. Take note. A story is being told through this thing."

I don't look at anything as being insignificant. I think that's another overlooked gift of poetry. Many times people imagine that poets wait for some splendid experience to overtake them, but I think the tiniest moments are the most splendid. This is the wisdom that all these small things have to teach.

MOYERS: Where did you get this gift to appreciate what so many of us take for granted?

NYE: I'm sure that the love of my parents, both very particular people, had a lot to do with it. I lived in a very nurturing household—both my mother and my father paid a great deal of attention to little things, and they still do. That gave me a certain appetite for how things were, the particulars of things. When I go into somebody's house, I always look to see what's there. What have they chosen to save? What's on the book-shelf? What's on the windowsill? For me, these are little clues I can pick up about ways to live. These things all tell stories.

MOYERS: You say of the man who makes brooms that he finds "holiness in anything/that continues, dream after dream." Holiness in what?

THE MAN WHO MAKES BROOMS

So you come with these maps in your head
and I come with voices chiding me to
"speak for my people"
and we march around like guardians of memory
till we find the man on the short stool
who makes brooms.

Thumb over thumb, straw over straw,
he will not look at us.
In his stony corner there is barely room
for baskets and thread,
much less the weight of our faces
staring at him from the street.
What he has lost or not lost is his secret.

You say he is like all the men,
the man who sells pistachios,

the man who rolls the rugs.
Older now, you find holiness in anything
that continues, dream after dream.
I say he is like nobody,
the pink seam he weaves
across the flat golden face of this broom
is its own shrine, and forget about the tears.

In the village the uncles will raise their *kefiyahs*
from dominoes to say, no brooms in America?
And the girls who stoop to sweep the courtyard
will stop for a moment and cock their heads.
It is a little song, this thumb over thumb,
but sometimes when you wait years
for the air to break open
and sense to fall out,
it may be the only one.

                                        JERUSALEM

NYE: In his case—a Palestinian in the old city of Jerusalem—he finds holiness in continuing to do a task so particularly and well, so beautifully under very difficult daily circumstances of occupation. To me this is a political poem just as, to me, it was a political act to continue doing one very small thing with elegance and firmness—the way he knotted the string, the way his shop was arranged with straws in the buckets, everything ready. He was a *master* broommaker.

In many of what I consider to be my more political poems about Palestine and Palestinians, I feel I have focused on their relationships with daily life. Even under the most pressing, terrible circumstances, they have retained the dignity of continuing, day after day, "dream after dream."

MOYERS: You call it a political poem. It seemed to me a personal poem bestowing upon the seemingly insignificant a transcendent beauty and purpose.

NYE: Thank you, I appreciate that comment. People have sometimes asked me, "Why don't you write more political poems?" And I always answer, "Oh, but I *do. These* are my political poems." The most political poem I could ever write is a poem about a Palestinian gardener planting his garden and loving his garden and knowing his garden intimately.

MOYERS: Why?

NYE: Because he is doing this even under very difficult, unsupportive circumstances. He is not going off into theories about how terrible the governments are or talking about how his situation is so oppressed. He is simply doing what he knows and what he loves doing, day after day. He is putting himself into the ground that he and his family have lived on for hundreds of years, and that is a very political act.

MOYERS: So politics is not only a matter of revolution or legislation?

NYE: Not at all! Politics also involves the dignity of daily life. To me politics is how somebody carries himself or herself, regardless of the surrounding situation.

MOYERS: What about the line "no brooms in America"?

NYE: My relatives in Jerusalem were laughing at me because they could not understand why I would buy brooms and carry them as hand luggage in a plane across the ocean. For me they were emblematic of the dignity of my father's people and their quest for simple daily civil rights. Brooms by which we may sweep away all the ideology that engulfs us. Those brooms were tangible—you could hold on to them. Of course Palestinians know how to do many more things than make brooms—and I'm sure this man had many more things to talk about other than brooms—but the broom was *my* focus because he did it better than anyone else.

MOYERS: In the last part of that poem, "It is a little song, this thumb over thumb,/but sometimes when you wait years/for the air to break open/and sense to fall out,/it may be the only one." What is the sense that falls out there?

NYE: The sense of a large, ongoing struggle finally coming to positive fruition. This doesn't apply only to Palestinians; it applies to so many places in the world where people are struggling for recognition or for self-determination or simply for acknowledgment. I want us to recognize and remember the dignity of daily affirmation, whatever one does—the mother speaking to the child is *also* a poem; the story one woman is telling to one person is an *important* story. I am loyal to those domestic impulses that want to acknowledge all the little parts of our lives.

MOYERS: In several of your poems there's this pining for another reality, a yearning that there's more meaning, order, and happiness somewhere else. The teacher in "New Year" envisions "every future which was not hers." Over and over there is a sense of a life not chosen, a path not traveled. Are you conscious of that?

NYE: Doesn't that seem to be the universal human experience? Lots of times students imagine that other people, like writers, have more interesting lives than they themselves do, to which I say, "It's not that a writer's life is more interesting; it's just that writers have a different way of *looking* at our lives."

People look with longing at other experiences that they imagine as being more real, more true, more deep than their own; but I think people are also riveted by a kind of great human longing for something, whether it's better or other or different, that is deeper than whatever they have at that moment. I think that's almost a universal condition.

MOYERS: Do you think this is more so for women who have, for biological reasons, more difficult choices in their lives than it is for men, for many of whom the world seems to offer infinite paths and opportunities?

NYE: No, I think women are often luckier, because in many cases we have a closer relationship with domestic detail which is very sustaining. When I would observe my grandmother who just died at the age of 106 in her West Bank village, and the other women of the family, for example, I might see them going out to pick something in the field, or smelling the mint, or making the fresh lemonade, while the men were talking politics. Well, which group would *I* rather be with? It's *not* hard to chose. I've always felt very happy to be a woman, with immediate intimate access to a whole world of objects and details. Of course many men sustain this closeness too. My husband, a photographer, often speaks of "inquiry" as being at the heart of his artistic process. Many people come at this from many directions.

MOYERS: I see now why I liked your poem "Famous." You write of wanting "to be famous in the way a pulley is famous,/or a buttonhole . . ." Wait a minute, I thought—buttonholes and pulleys are obscure little items, while fame has to do with celebrity.

FAMOUS

The river is famous to the fish.

The loud voice is famous to silence,
which knew it would inherit the earth
before anybody said so.

The cat sleeping on the fence is famous to the birds
watching him from the birdhouse.

The tear is famous, briefly, to the cheek.

The idea you carry close to your bosom
is famous to your bosom.

The boot is famous to the earth,
more famous than the dress shoe,
which is famous only to floors.

The bent photograph is famous to the one who carries it
and not at all famous to the one who is pictured.

I want to be famous to shuffling men
who smile while crossing streets,
sticky children in grocery lines,
famous as the one who smiled back.

I want to be famous in the way a pulley is famous,
or a buttonhole, not because it did anything spectacular,
but because it never forgot what it could do.

NYE: I think it's energy again. You trust a buttonhole don't you? Don't you trust a pulley to know what it is intended for? A pulley is a discreet, subtle, but very useful and important implement. That poem is simply reexamining the word "famous." Many times when I visit an elementary school and the student ask questions, the first question they'll ask is, "Are you famous?" I wrote that poem in response to their question. I said, "Everything is famous if you notice it. This leaf right here is famous if you picked it up."

MOYERS: What *is* fame to you?

NYE: Whatever we pay attention to becomes famous to us. I have many heroes in the world of poetry, and their poems are famous in my mind. They resonate and return to me when I need them. They're given back to me. That makes them famous for me.

MOYERS: "The Traveling Onion" is one of my favorites. What is it that makes the onion a "small forgotten miracle"?

THE TRAVELING ONION

"It is believed that the onion originally came from India. In Egypt it was an object of worship—why I haven't been able to find out. From Egypt the onion entered Greece and on to Italy, thence into all of Europe."

BETTER LIVING COOKBOOK

When I think how far the onion has traveled
just to enter my stew today, I could kneel and praise

all small forgotten miracles,
crackly paper peeling on the drainboard,
pearly layers in smooth agreement,
the way knife enters onion
and onion falls apart on the chopping block,
a history revealed.

And I would never scold the onion
for causing tears.
It is right that tears fall
for something small and forgotten.
How at meal, we sit to eat,
commenting on texture of meat or herbal aroma
but never on the translucence of onion,
now limp, now divided,
or its traditionally honorable career:
For the sake of others,
disappear.

NYE: An onion is ubiquitous, showing up in many places and different reci-
pes. That quote which the poem starts with was from the *Better Living Cookbook*. I liked
the way it exalted the onion's history. It made it seem that the onion had traveled far and
wide to get into all the countries that it's in now; the history of the onion seemed like
one of these things that nobody ever really mentions. People talk about food when they
have a lovely meal, but how often do they praise the onion?

Then look at how an onion is constructed—its magnificence, its layering—I've read
many wonderful poems in which poets use the onion as an exquisite metaphor for hu-
man beings, for life, for time and yet it is almost a forgotten thing in and of itself. The
onion disappears to become a part of our food, but we don't just sit down and eat an
onion or pay attention to it.

MOYERS: And yet it leaves its savor—it makes its contribution.

NYE: It contributes, but it also disappears. I guess I have an obsession with
disappearing.

MOYERS: Yes, you do.

NYE: Maybe that's why I love the subtlety of Japanese poetry so much. I love
that understatement which is a powerful part of Japanese culture. I think most poets

would prefer not to be present in a notorious or a flamboyant way, but in a quietly observant way.

MOYERS: In "Yellow Glove" you write, "There were miracles on Harvey Street." You got me to thinking about the "miracles" on East Austin Street in Marshall, Texas, and miracles on Nathan Street, and miracles on Shipman Lane and Fourth Street.

NYE: There are miracles on *every* street.

MOYERS: And by "miracles" you mean . . .

NYE: The small transactions of spirit, the small ways that things connect and become indelible. I feel miracles all the time on Main Avenue in San Antonio, where I live now. I feel miracles of remembrance. For example, you might see something that's no longer there, but it's still there in your mind. A voice emerges and someone very old says, "Well, you know what he said once standing here . . ." and I feel a miracle happening, or that tree falls and fire goes down the pole and a sizzle enters the air, or a little boy picks up a stone, or the pecans tumble down at our feet year after year—so *many* miracles! They're all around us wherever we are. A student just asked me if I thought travel was necessary for writing. I would also adhere to Thoreau's idea that you can stay in your own backyard all your life and have plenty to write about. Travel just seems to have been a recurrent theme in my own life.

MOYERS: When you begin to write poems like "The Traveling Onion" or "Yellow Glove," have you made a decision about what you're going to say before you actually put pen to paper?

YELLOW GLOVE

What can a yellow glove mean in a world of motorcars and governments?

I was small, like everyone. Life was a string of precautions: Don't kiss the squirrel before you bury him, don't suck candy, pop balloons, drop watermelons, watch TV. When the new gloves appeared one Christmas, tucked in soft tissue, I heard it trailing me: Don't lose the yellow gloves.

I was small, there was too much to remember. One day, waving at a stream—the ice had cracked, winter chipping down, soon we would sail boats and roll into ditches—I let a glove go. Into the stream, sucked under the street. Since when did streets have mouths? I walked home on a desperate road. Gloves cost money. We didn't have much. I would tell no one. I would wear the yellow glove that was left and keep the other hand in a pocket. I knew my mother's eyes had tears they had not cried yet and I didn't want to be the one to make them flow. It was the prayer I spoke secretly, folding socks, lining up donkeys in windowsills. I would be good, a promise made to the roaches who scouted my closet at night. If you don't get in my bed, I will be good. And they listened. I had a lot to fulfill.

The months rolled down like towels out of a machine. I sang and drew and fattened the cat. Don't scream, don't lie, don't cheat, don't fight—you could hear it anywhere. A pebble could show you how to be smooth, tell the truth. A field could show how to sleep without walls. A stream could remember how to drift and change—the next June I was stirring the stream like a soup, telling my brother dinner would be ready if he'd only hurry up with the bread, when I saw it. The yellow glove draped on a twig. A muddy survivor. A quiet flag.

Where had it been in the three gone months? I could wash it, fold it in my winter drawer with its sister, no one in that world would ever know. There were miracles on Harvey Street. Children walked home in yellow light. Trees were reborn and gloves traveled far, but returned. A thousand miles later, what can a yellow glove mean in a world of bankbooks and stereos?

Part of the difference between floating and going down.

NYE: I may have a sense of the story or the image, the glove or the onion, but you basically have to let it happen on the page. The story is given to you through the *process* of writing. I always encourage students to trust the process of writing. It *will* take them somewhere, and it may not be where they thought they were going. "Yellow Glove" was a story that I carried around for twenty-five years before I wrote it, and during that time I never told anybody about it. I didn't even think about it all the time, but when, as an adult, I lost something that I really cared about, that story rose up out of the well and was given back to me.

MOYERS: Given back to you?

NYE: Given back to me just by writing it. I had this image of the glove returning to me and then the whole story came with it. The story began connecting to the present and to other things as almost an emblem when I started to write it. I think that will happen for everybody who opens that writing door. First there is one thing—and then there's always more.

MOYERS: What about the lines "If you don't get in my bed, I will be good. And they listened. I had a lot to fulfill." It's a sort of perfect example of a child's . . .

NYE: Well, that was spoken to roaches. I was very scared of roaches and spiders as a child—so I had little conversations with them: "Please don't get me. I won't get you." Our lives are full of those little conversations.

MOYERS: That's what you mean by talking to yourself?

NYE: Right, talking to *everything*. I hope we can encourage one another to engage in conversation with *everything* in the world. Sometimes when people talk about what's lost in the modern world, I think—but we still have so *much* in our daily lives! We travel so quickly, and there's so much that deserves to be communicated with . . . so much around us. Perhaps our ancestors who lived in one village or one town had all their lives slower, more intense, ongoing relationships with the same things, but we still need to engage with things around us in that same quiet, conversational way. I think poetry is one way we can do that.

MOYERS: When I hear "New Year" I am curious about how much of your poetry is autobiographical and how much is invented for the pleasure of the words. What can you tell me about this teacher looking wistfully out the window?

New Year

Maybe the street is tired of being a street,
They tell how it used to be called Bois d'Arc,
now called Main, how boys in short pants
caught crawdads for supper at a stone acequia
now covered over.
Sometimes the street sweeper stops his machine
and covers his eyes.

Think of the jobs people have.
The girl weighing citron in the basement
of H. L. Green's, for a man who says
he can't wait to make fruitcake

and she says, What is this stuff anyway
before it looks like this? and he leaves
on his cane, slowly, clutching the bag.
Then she weighs garlics for a trucker.

Think of the streams of headlights
on the Houston freeway all headed somewhere
and where they will be headed after that.
After so long, even jets might be tired of acceleration,
slow-down, touching-ground again,
as a child is so tired of his notebook
he pastes dinosaurs on it to render it extinct.
Or the teacher, tired of questions,
hearing the anthem *How long does it have to be?*
play itself over and over in her sleep
and she just doesn't know. As long as you want it.

What was this world? Where things you never did
felt more real than what happened.
Your friend's dishtowel strung over her faucet
was a sentence which could be diagrammed
while your tumbled life, that basket of phrases,
had too many ways it might fit together.

Where a street might just as easily have been
a hair ribbon in a girl's ponytail
her first day of dance class, teacher in mauve leotard
rising to say, We have much ahead of us,
and the little girls following, kick, kick, kick,
thinking what a proud sleek person she was,
how they wanted to be like her someday,
while she stared outside the window at the high wires
strung with ice, the voices inside them opening out
to every future which was not hers.

NYE: That came from a tiny episode when I accompanied someone picking
up a child at a dance class. I caught a glimpse of the incredibly beautiful teacher, and
thought, "What a graceful human being." She seemed like the person we might all like
to be. Then I encountered her a few days later and heard her bemoaning her fate as the
teacher of little children, doing the same thing season after season.

I was struck by these two different images and wondered if that discrepancy might be a part of everyday life. We observe others and admire them, while their own longings may or may not be fulfilled at all. "More than meets the eye"—a large part of the human experience.

MOYERS: What about yourself? What about the things you will never do, the future that will never be yours?

NYE: Oh, I'm sure there are *many* futures that will never be mine, but I feel very, very grateful in my life, Bill. I've been given a relationship with writing and reading since I was a small child, and there have been so many writers whom I love to read. Because I feel very nurtured by them and have had a chance to do the work I love, I don't feel much longing for any other life; but I certainly recognize that longing in other people.

MOYERS: When you write about the places you've been, I think of my own culture in East Texas and its particularities and peculiarities, all its mundane details. The universal is in the particular.

NYE: Absolutely! That you can connect with those details and those places even though you've never been there is a great gift that you as a reader bring to the work. If we are open to the poems, that's a gift we can all feel when we read about places we've never been to.

That gift of understanding extends our lives and makes them bigger. Reading opens us up so we can live *everywhere*.

© Lynn Saville

ADRIENNE RICH

Adrienne Rich has been a major figure in American letters for a generation. As poet, feminist thinker, and political activist, she addresses the dislocations of our world, especially the divorce of the private and the public, and so begins the slow labor of healing these rifts by first imagining them whole. She is both controversial and celebrated for her activism—and the recipient of many awards for poems and essays that bring a piercing candor to human relationships. She was a Fellow of the Academy of American Poets, and is a MacArthur Fellow. In 1992 she received the Frost Silver Medal for distinguished lifetime achievement awarded by the Poetry Society of America.

MOYERS: Listening to you and the other poets read here at the festival, I wanted the whole country to be gathered here so everyone could feel this music, share these ideas, perceive these images, witness these revelations. Relatively few experience what many would enjoy. Why do you think poetry has such a hard time getting a hearing in this culture?

RICH: Well, that's a huge question, and I'd want to divide it into a number of parts. First of all, we're a country of *many* cultures, and in many of those cultures poetry has never had a problem getting a hearing—for example, in original American culture, in African American culture, in the cultures of many of the recent immigrant groups.

MOYERS: Until now they have not been exposed to our dominant pop culture, which is driven by the mass media that invade every corner of our society today. It's so noisy in America it's hard for quiet voices to be heard.

RICH: Well, I think we're at a very interesting watershed, because I have been seeing and noting a tremendous renaissance of poetry in the United States over the past ten to twenty years nourished by the voices of many groups which had been largely silenced before that—by the voices of women, the voices of people of color, the voices of gay men and lesbians, the voices of working-class, white Americans. There is a seething, burgeoning poetry out there, but it's *many* poetries, and it's coming from many cultures and many communities. I live in California, where in both the San Francisco Bay area and Los Angeles there's an incredibly rich poetic culture. Those are two big, urban cen-

Poetry can bring together those parts of us which exist in dread and those which have the surviving sense of a possible happiness, collectivity, community, a loss of isolation.

ters, but all over the country I see community groups generating their own poets, many of whom we see here today.

MOYERS: What do you think when you look around this festival and you see Japanese American poets, Chinese American poets, Puerto Rican poets, poets from the white working class?

RICH: I feel enormous joy and exhilaration. This is so different from the poetry world into which I was growing up in the 1940s and 1950s. That was a world dominated by a few major figures, mostly from a certain class and of course male: Pound, Williams, Eliot, Stevens. I was saying to a young man, a poet working here, "Your generation doesn't have to look at the field of poetry as a hierarchy. You can draw from this enormously rich cluster of poetries, and you can enrich yourself from so many kinds that this is a wholly different situation than we had in the 1940s and 1950s."

IN THOSE YEARS

> In those years, people will say, we lost track
> of the meaning of *we*, of *you*
> we found ourselves
> reduced to *I*
> and the whole thing became
> silly, ironic, terrible:
> we were trying to live a personal life
> and yes, that was the only life
> we could bear witness to
>
> But the great dark birds of history screamed and plunged
> into our personal weather
> They were headed somewhere else but their beaks and pinions drove
> along the shore, through the rags of fog
> where we stood, saying *I*

1991

MOYERS: That was a more affirmative response than I had anticipated. Reading some of your recent work, I think of these concluding lines from "In Those Years": "the great, dark birds of history screamed and plunged / into our personal weather / They were headed somewhere else but their beaks and pinions drove / along the shore, through the rags of fog / where we stood, saying *I*." Your sense of the decadence of modern culture appears over and over in your recent essays and poems.

RICH: Yes, and there's a real contradiction here because I see poetry in the United States as coming out of the points of stress in our society. As I was saying to the teachers yesterday morning, we have at least a thousand points of stress and we see poetry emerging, not only from those places, but certainly from those places—as if the stress in itself creates a search for language in which to probe and unravel what is going on here. The moral and ethical confusion, the confusion of values, the whole question of our putative democracy and what is happening to it, how it is being eroded, these are questions which I know press on many, many people; and some of them turn to poetry.

MOYERS: Is there another contradiction in that these voices you talk about are being produced by the ferment of democracy itself? These voices may be arising from points of stress, but they are giving us points of life, as you and all the other poets here are doing. Our democracy is creating a cornucopia of voices and sounds and expressions and celebration, yet you see it as a troubled democracy.

RICH: It is *more* than troubled. I mean, it may be sliding out of our grasp. It goes without saying that this has never been a full democracy. It has always been a selective democracy, offering a few people the full enjoyment of a democratic society, but it has always been repressive toward certain groups, and I don't think that it is less so now. I think we're seeing a failure of the democratic dream and a cynicism toward that dream, so that the dream becomes mere rhetoric in the mouths of politicians and corporations. When people encounter a program like the one you are trying to create here on a television dominated by the messages of corporate capitalism, which has a kind of contempt for humanity, which represents humanity in the most gross and belittling forms, I have to tell you frankly that I feel skeptical about how the content and the substance of what you and I are trying to do here will be affected by this general context. I was looking at the Weather Channel this morning and there was a commercial which I thought summed it all up. It was a commercial for a book issued by some insurance company—the title of the book was *Die Rich: How to Avoid Estate Taxes*—and I thought, this is what it has come to. It's not about quality of life, it's not even about preserving the society unto the seventh generation. It's about the preservation of wealth, perhaps, but it's not about the quality of our children's lives or our grandchildren's lives.

MOYERS: What does poetry say to that?

RICH: Well, I believe that poetry asks us to consider the quality of life. Poetry reflects on the quality of life, on us as we are in process on this earth, in our lives, in our relationships, in our communities. It embodies what makes it possible for us to continue as human under the barrage of brute violence, numbing indifference, trivialization, and shallowness that we endure, not to speak of what has come to seem in public life like a total loss on the part of politicians of any desire even to appear consistent, or to appear to adhere to principle.

MOYERS: Do you see the possibility for new life?

RICH: Something has to die in order for us to begin to know our truths. Perhaps we have to lose our national fantasies.

MOYERS: You put your finger on part of the problem in your poem "In Those Years" where it seems that the sense of the republic—"We, the People"—has become just a welter of individuals isolated and fragmented, struggling for their own survival, and yet you seem critical of our trying to live a personal life in the midst of all this. What's wrong with trying to lead a personal life in these times?

RICH: There's nothing wrong with it. It's incredibly important, and one of the themes of the poetry that I've been trying to write in the last few years has been the necessity to keep hold of what I call in my own thinking "radical happiness." I think I got that phrase from Hannah Arendt, who was talking about public happiness, the happiness of the citizen participating in a civil compact that's really working. That was the right to the pursuit of happiness that the framers of the Constitution presumably intended. In another poem I say, "Take what's still given," because it's those moments in a personal life that give us a sense of the value of life and that give us a sense of what could be aspired to for the common life, for the common weal of us all.

To the Days

From you I want more than I've ever asked,
all of it—the newscasts' terrible stories
of life in my time, the knowing it's worse than that,
much worse—the knowing what it means to be lied to.

Fog in the mornings, hunger for clarity,
coffee and bread with sour plum jam.
Numbness of soul in placid neighborhoods.
Lives ticking on as if.

A typewriter's torrent, suddenly still.

Blue soaking through fog, two dragonflies wheeling.

Acceptable levels of cruelty, steadily rising.

Whatever you bring in your hands, I need to see it.

Suddenly I understand the verb without tenses.

To smell another woman's hair, to taste her skin.

To know the bodies drifting underwater.

To be human, said Rosa—I can't teach you that.

A cat drinks from a bowl of marigolds—his moment.

Surely the love of life is never-ending,

the failure of nerve, a charred fuse?

I want more from you than I ever knew to ask.

Wild pink lilies erupting, tasselled stalks of corn

in the Mexican gardens, corn and roses.

Shortening days, strawberry fields in ferment

with tossed-aside, bruised fruit.

Rosa Luxemburg (1871–1919): one of the most influential and controversial figures in European revolutionary socialism. Besides her political essays she left hundreds of vivid letters to friends and comrades. Imprisoned during World War I for her internationalist and anti-capitalist beliefs, she was murdered in 1919. On December 28, 1916, from prison, she wrote to friends: "Then see to it that you remain a *Mensch*! [Yiddish/German for 'human being'] . . . Being a *Mensch* means happily throwing one's life 'on fate's great scale' if necessary, but, at the same time, enjoying every bright day and every beautiful cloud. Oh, I can't write you a prescription for being a *Mensch*." (See *The Letters of Rosa Luxemburg*, ed., transl., and with an introduction by Stephen Eric Bronner. N.J.: Humanities Press, 1993.)

MOYERS: I hear that determination to value life in your poem "To the Days." At the end of the first stanza, after "the knowing what it means to be lied to," you take that sudden turn away from the evening news and the world's follies and find your escape with your lover, so the poem ends in a very sweet, quiet, and deeply satisfying way. I admire you for your struggle to affirm, but here you're able to affirm only in the personal, in the relationship with your beloved.

RICH: Well, yes. But each of us has to find those moments in relation with others, and I see nothing wrong with that. I see it as that which then gives us the power and the energy to try to work to create a different kind of society. It gives us the power and energy to go back into the public area.

MOYERS: Give me a clearer grasp of what "radical happiness" is for you.

RICH: It's something that I keep as a key phrase in my mind, that I write out of rather than try to define, and when I say "radical" I mean *at the root,* real. Real social transformation, real change has to come out of a love of life and a love for the world, not hatred of the world. Increasingly what I fear and what I see is a movement of people on the right who are moving from a hatred of human beings, a hatred of the other, a hatred of life. That's why I say there is nothing wrong with personal happiness if you can take it and use it as a key, a measure, a standard.

WHAT KIND OF TIMES ARE THESE

There's a place between two stands of trees where the grass
    grows uphill
and the old revolutionary road breaks off into shadows
near a meeting-house abandoned by the persecuted
who disappeared into those shadows.

I've walked there picking mushrooms at the edge of dread, but
    don't be fooled,
this isn't a Russian poem, this is not somewhere else but here,
our country moving closer to its own truth and dread,
its own ways of making people disappear.

I won't tell you where the place is, the dark mesh of the woods
meeting the unmarked strip of light—
ghost-ridden crossroads, leafmold paradise:
I know already who wants to buy it, sell it, make it disappear.

And I won't tell you where it is, so why do I tell you
anything? Because you still listen, because in times
    like these
to have you listen at all, it's necessary
to talk about trees.

             1991

MOYERS: "What Kind of Times Are These" seems to pick up this same concern. What is our country's "truth and dread" in that poem?

RICH: When I read that poem to teachers yesterday I talked about the fact that the title comes from a poem by the German Communist poet and playwright Bertolt Brecht who wrote—I'm paraphrasing—"What kind of times are these, when it's almost a crime to talk about trees because it means keeping silent about so many evil deeds?" Our country has many truths, but certainly one of them has to be that although this was never a democracy, this *was* an enormous hope for true democracy; but it failed many people from the outset, and it's failing more people now.

MOYERS: And what is its dread?

RICH: Well, I think there are many different kinds of dread for many different kinds of people. I think that more and more people feel uncared for, feel that their lives are not only unvalued but meaningless, feel that though *they* may care for their lives, no one else will, feel that the only way that they can protect their survival and interests is by the gun. I'm afraid that many people feel an enormous desperation which plays into the propaganda of hate.

MOYERS: You can say these often bitter things calmly and succinctly, and yet your poem doesn't reflect that bitterness. There's an affirmation in it, despite the fact that you're writing about these dreads. Where does that come from in your own story?

RICH: If poetry is forced by the conditions in which it's created to speak of dread and of bitter, bitter conditions, by its very nature poetry speaks beyond that to something different. That's why poetry can bring together those parts of us which exist in dread and those which have the surviving sense of a possible happiness, collectivity, community, a loss of isolation.

MOYERS: How do we reassert the "we" from this position of fragmented and isolated individual selves? I felt this "we," in a sense, when you were reading and all those people in that tent were joined in an emotional response to what was being said there. It can be joy, as you said last night, it can be tears, it can be deep concentration in response to one of your poems. A sense of community seems to arise out of the word.

RICH: Well, that's true. I believe that. I think that's one of the reasons that communities of poetry, and I don't just mean communities of poets, but communities of poetry—of people reading poetry, listening to poetry, coming together around poetry—are becoming everywhere in this country so widespread. It's as if this gathering around the word occurs in response to worsening conditions.

MOYERS: You were talking earlier about commercials on television designed to make us think happiness is not radical, and the political language of which you spoke is a language that more often conceals than reveals. If the corruption of language is behind the hunger that one senses, the very hunger being fed here at this festival, people need more than ever what poetry offers. Is your poem "Dedications," and especially its last line, addressed to this question?

FROM AN ATLAS OF THE DIFFICULT WORLD

(DEDICATIONS)

I know you are reading this poem
late, before leaving your office
of the one intense yellow lamp-spot and the darkening window
in the lassitude of a building faded to quiet
long after rush-hour.   I know you are reading this poem
standing up in a bookstore far from the ocean
on a grey day of early spring, faint flakes driven
across the plains' enormous spaces around you.
I know you are reading this poem
in a room where too much has happened for you to bear
where the bedclothes lie in stagnant coils on the bed
and the open valise speaks of flight
but you cannot leave yet.   I know you are reading this poem
as the underground train loses momentum and before running
              up the stairs
toward a new kind of love
your life has never allowed.
I know you are reading this poem by the light
of the television screen where soundless images jerk and slide
while you wait for the newscast from the *intifada*.
I know you are reading this poem in a waiting-room
of eyes met and unmeeting, of identity with strangers.
I know you are reading this poem by fluorescent light
in the boredom and fatigue of the young who are counted out,
count themselves out, at too early an age.   I know
you are reading this poem through your failing sight, the thick
lens enlarging these letters beyond all meaning yet you read on
because even the alphabet is precious.
I know you are reading this poem as you pace beside the stove
warming milk, a crying child on your shoulder, a book in your
              hand
because life is short and you too are thirsty.
I know you are reading this poem which is not in your language
guessing at some words while others keep you reading

and I want to know which words they are.
I know you are reading this poem listening for something, torn
         between bitterness and hope
turning back once again to the task you cannot refuse.
I know you are reading this poem because there is nothing else
         left to read
there where you have landed, stripped as you are.

                          1990–1991

RICH: Well, that line is multi-layered. Even as I was writing "Dedications," I wanted the poem to speak to people as individuals, but also as individuals multiplied over and over and over and over: the mother or father, as the case may be, warming milk by the stove with the infant over the shoulder; someone reading a book because she or he, too, is thirsty late at night; the office worker still in the office after rush hour. As part of a collectivity.

And then, in this last line, I thought first of all of someone dying of AIDS. I thought of any person in an isolate situation for whom there was perhaps nothing but a book of poems to put her or him into a sense of relation with the world of other human beings, or perhaps someone in prison. But finally I was thinking of our society, stripped of so much of what was hoped for and promised and given nothing in exchange but material commodities, or the hope of obtaining material commodities. And for me, that is being truly stripped.

MOYERS: Then you go on to say, "I know you are reading this poem which is not in your language/guessing at some words while others keep you reading . . ." Something like this happens to me when I read a poem: One minute I'm puzzling over some word or image, but the next line carries me forward beyond my misunderstanding into another realm of discovery.

RICH: Yes, and I had in mind an even more literal case as well—someone reading a poem in American English the way I would read a poem in Spanish or French or some other language that I know slightly, or used to know better, but of which I have forgotten a lot of the vocabulary, guessing at some words, yet struggling, and carried on by something in that poem. But what *is* that? And why do I want to know what it is? I want to know because whatever it is in my poem that keeps you reading is some kind of bond or filament between us, something that I've been able to put there that speaks even to this other person, whose language this is not.

MOYERS: How important is your audience when you are actually writing the poem? Do you picture the audience?

RICH: I write for whoever might read. I recently saw a very interesting distinction made by the African Canadian writer Marlene Nourbese Philip. She speaks of the difference between community, audience, and market. I believe that I write for a community. Obviously, I write for a community of other poets, people whom I know, people with whom I have already connected in some way, but I also write for whoever will constitute a new and expanded community audience.

MOYERS: What inspired "Dedications"? For whom were you writing it?

RICH: "Dedications" is the final section of a long poem, "An Atlas of the Difficult World," which reflects on the condition of my country, which I wrote very consciously as a citizen poet, looking at the geography, the history, the peoples of my country. I started writing "An Atlas of the Difficult World" just before the Gulf War, so I was writing it during and after the Gulf War, and "Dedications" came to me as a way of creating a personal dialogue with many different kinds of readers who might have read this whole poem and connected with it here or there. But I wanted "Dedications" to be there at the end, waiting for the reader.

MOYERS: So you *did* have the audience in mind, even though you couldn't picture the particular reader or listener.

RICH: I made up some readers and listeners, but I also remembered and recognized actual people, as a fiction writer might, in that section and throughout the poem. The poem is full of voices: they're not all my voice, they're not all women's voices, some of them are men's voices, but, yes, I certainly had an audience in mind. The distinction between community, audience, and market is a really important distinction for an artist of any kind. There is a community of those whose work and whose lives you respect and love and cherish, a community that gives you the strength to create, to push boundaries, to take risks, a community that perhaps challenges you to do all that.

There is an audience of those unknown to you but whom your words are going to reach. You can't know them in advance, but you can hope for them, desire them. Market, on the other hand, is all about packaging and buying and selling, and the corresponding group would be the consumer. I don't want my poetry to be consumed in that sense. I *do* want it to be used.

I was very moved by Robert Bly's just now reading Neruda's "Ode to My Socks," which ends with the poet's saying that something beautiful is twice beautiful, something good is doubly good, when it is a pair of socks—warm socks in winter. It's an ode to a very beautiful pair of socks that someone had made for Neruda. I think that what is beautiful is doubly beautiful and what is good is doubly good when it can be truly used, not consumed, but used in lives, and probably used in ways that, as an artist, you could never fully know or anticipate.

MOYERS: So much of your poetry helps people to cope with their own conflicts and with the stresses of modern life. I've heard a number of people here talking about your poem "From a Survivor," how it helped them to manage their own survival. Do people stop you and tell you that a poem like that actually helped them save their lives?

FROM A SURVIVOR

The pact that we made was the ordinary pact
of men & women in those days

I don't know who we thought we were
that our personalities
could resist the failures of the race

Lucky or unlucky, we didn't know
the race had failures of that order
and that we were going to share them

Like everybody else, we thought of ourselves as special

Your body is as vivid to me
as it ever was: even more

since my feeling for it is clearer:
I know what it could and could not do

it is no longer
the body of a god
or anything with power over my life

Next year it would have been 20 years
and you are wastefully dead
who might have made the leap
we talked, too late, of making

which I live now
not as a leap
but a succession of brief, amazing movements

each one making possible the next

1972

RICH: Well, I know that happens from my own reading of other poets, Bill. I have to tell you that I have survived many things through poetry. In short, it's helped me to live my life, and from a very young age.

MOYERS: Were you that young when poetry spoke to you down there in the South?

RICH: Yes. Well, you can't really call Baltimore the South. It *was* the South, in a sense, because all my family was southern. My mother played the piano and sang folk songs to me. My father would sing to me with the guitar. So that kind of poetry, folk poetry, was in my head, but also a lot of other things—Blake and Keats, the Victorians, the Iliad and Odyssey. I grew up in a house full of books and was encouraged to read poetry and to write it. In that sense, I've been privileged. But from a very young age poetry was always a sustenance for me. It was a way of going deeper into things, it was never escapism. It was a way, as a very young child, of finding out about life.

MOYERS: And it told you . . .

RICH: Many things. And they contradicted each other, of course, but it was a way of reflecting on and maybe testing out emotions and feelings that I had no words for myself.

MOYERS: Did you have a favorite poem?

RICH: No, I've always had many favorites.

MOYERS: Do you remember the first poem that touched you deeply, that awakened you somehow?

RICH: I think it was Blake's "The Tyger." I was given poems to copy, that was how my father taught me to do handwriting. "The Tyger" was one of them and it was so musical and mysterious. The wonderful image sank very deep very early.

MOYERS: Help me understand a little more clearly why you are writing politically even when writing personally, because if everything personal becomes political, it seems to me we have really lost something in the private realm.

RICH: Well, I guess I don't feel that way. For me, connectedness to the public realm could be a joy. I feel that participation with others in creating a way of life that would give all of us respect, and the joy of creativity in all senses, need not be a burden.

I think politics can seem a burden when we feel alone and powerless against enormous and impersonal forces out there in the public realm. The late years of the Vietnam War when a lot of poets were giving antiwar readings was a very crucial time for me. In the 1960s, when poetry was very much part of public life, I began trying to make connections for myself between the havoc being wreaked by my government on a small country thousands of miles away, which I and so many of my friend were protesting, and the relations between human beings within my country, especially the relations between women and men. That kind of synthesis really wasn't happening yet in the public sphere, but I was trying to make that synthesis in my poetry—which was the only way I knew how to do it.

MOYERS: Poetry did join a large social moment then, but not now. What's happened between then and now?

RICH: But I think it *is* doing that now. In my own small community we have a great many public poetry readings. We had a reading against the Gulf War, sponsored by the National Writers Union, and in the last couple of years we had Poets for Economic and Social Justice raising money for the homeless in our community. I think this goes on in communities small and large, all over the country. It may not be on the scale of the big demonstrations during the Vietnam period, but traveling around the country, I see it happening everywhere.

MOYERS: You are a prolific writer. What explains it?

RICH: I've been extremely fortunate in my life. I've had a lot of opportunities and a lot of support for my work. I've been given spaces of time—that very, very precious substance—to write in. What it takes internally to try to continue writing, above and beyond those spaces of time which are so important for an artist, and which so many artists just aren't given, is the sense that *that is what I can do*: this is how, in whatever infinitesimal way, I can make a difference. That possibility is a tremendous spur. Also, I have to say again that the kinds of support and the kinds of challenge that I receive from the lives of others around me—poets, non-poets, other kinds of artists, and activists—carries me. I don't feel like a solitary person in my lonely room at all, even though I have to spend hours alone in a room to do what I do.

MOYERS: What do you get from those people listening to you here? What happens between you and the audience at a reading?

RICH: I believe that a poem isn't completed until there's a reader at the other end of it. It can't just be produced, it also has to be received. And so, yes, I feel that the poems are being completed in so many different ways by so many different minds and consciousnesses.

MOYERS: As I watched each intent face as you were reading, I imagined that each face was receiving differently, weaving your story into her story, his story, their story.

RICH: Yes. Absolutely.

MOYERS: Do you lose control of it in a sense at that point?

RICH: Yes, but that's all right. I've often said to students, you have to understand that you let go of the poem when you publish it. When you put it out, you let go of it. I've also seen my own work wrenched out of context and quoted in ways which I deplore, but you have to let go. You have to believe that you've put it together as faithfully and as passionately as you can and that it's going to survive, not precisely as you put it out, but not in a totally mutilated form either.

MOYERS: Why do you say "You have to know these things" when you're talking about braiding a woman's hair in "North American Time"?

FROM NORTH AMERICAN TIME

V

Suppose you want to write
of a woman braiding
another woman's hair—
straight down, or with beads and shells
in three-strand plaits or corn-rows—
you had better know the thickness
the length   the pattern
why she decides to braid her hair
how it is done to her
what country it happens in
what else happens in that country

You have to know these things

RICH: Because I think that the truth of art allows us to take a microcosm, a tiny thing like one woman braiding another woman's hair, and let it stand for so much else. But the artist needs to know a great deal more than she or he is necessarily going to put into the work of art. The artist needs to have reflected on things that may not go into that poem. There's a work of constant reflection on one's own consciousness and on the conditions of life that surround the words and images that go on the page. When I was talking about trying to connect, as I said in those days, "the war in Vietnam and the lovers' bed," I was already trying to do that.

MOYERS: How do you go about connecting seemingly disparate metaphors to create a new truth, a new vision? It must be hard work.

RICH: It *is* hard work, and it's constant work. Yet it's so interesting to me. It seems to me that it is the responsibility of an artist to move out from our own necessarily circumscribed lives into the experience of others whom we don't know and might never know, and in doing this to experience what we could never have experienced ourselves. Being aware of the diverse lives around us and the conditions in which they are being lived is not just one way of making art. I think that it's also a responsibility and a source of strength. It's a tremendous resource.

MOYERS: In one of your poems you write a letter to yourself, asking "what you intend to do / with the rest of your life?" What's your answer?

FROM CONTRADICTIONS: TRACKING POEMS

6.

Dear Adrienne:

I'm calling you up tonight
as I might call up a friend   as I might call up a ghost
to ask what you intend to do
with the rest of your life.   Sometimes you act
as if you have all the time there is.
I worry about you when I see this.
The prime of life, old age
aren't what they used to be;
making a good death isn't either,
now you can walk around the corner of a wall
and see a light
that already has blown your past away.
Somewhere in Boston   beautiful literature
is being read around the clock
by writers   to signify
their dislike of this.
I hope you've got something in mind.
I hope you have some idea
about the rest of your life.

In sisterhood,

Adrienne

RICH: I intend to go on making poetry. I intend to go on trying to be part of what I think of as an underground stream—of voices resisting the voices that tell us we are nothing, that we are worthless, or that we all hate each other, or should hate each other. I think that there is a real culture of resistance here—of artists' and of other kinds of voices—that will continue, however bad things get in this country. I want to make myself part of that and do my work as well as I can. I want to love those I love as well as I can, and I want to love life as well as I can.

MOYERS: You have written, "I have a responsibility to keep looking for teachers." Why do you need teachers, after all the experiences of your life and with all you know?

RICH: Because I need to know about those other experiences that I was talking about. I've lived one kind of life, in many ways a very privileged life with my white skin and my middle-class background. I have also been exceptionally privileged to be able to think of myself as a creative person. There is so much creativity I believe in every infant born and yet so few of us get to develop it, so few of us even get to think about having an audience for our words. So, with the kind of audience that I now have, I want to speak responsibly and for that I need teachers.

MOYERS: Where do you find them?

RICH: In people—of every age, color, gender.

MOYERS: How do they teach? How do you learn from them?

RICH: Sometimes from their art. Sometimes from conversation. Sometimes from their actions.

IN A CLASSROOM

Talking of poetry, hauling the books
arm-full to the table where the heads
bend or gaze upward, listening, reading aloud,
talking of consonants, elision,
caught in the how, oblivious of why:
I look in your face, Jude,
neither frowning nor nodding,
opaque in the slant of dust-motes over the table:
a presence like a stone, if a stone were thinking
What I cannot say, is me. For that I came.

1986

MOYERS: Your poem "In a Classroom" starts with teaching poetry, then the teacher suddenly looks into the face of one of her students, Jude, who is neither frowning nor nodding. He's just there. What does the teacher *see* in Jude?

RICH: In writing that poem I was thinking of so many students I've had who were capable of becoming poets but who had not even been given the opportunity to write an English sentence. I used to teach basic writing at City College in New York, and in the writings of my students, however "incorrect" their English, I found so many images, so many leaps of the imagination, so much passion. I wrote that poem thinking of them. The teacher in that poem, who's been talking about poetry, immersed, I think I say, in the "how" and oblivious of the "why," suddenly *sees* the person who comes speechless into the class. Perhaps in that moment of recognition the teacher learns something. Perhaps the teacher learns that intelligence is not limited to those who are fluent in standard English.

MOYERS: So the teacher learns from the student?

RICH: Yes.

MOYERS: I don't know when you were in New York the last time, but did you know that your poem "Delta" wound up on the New York subway?

RICH: Yes, I did know that. A series of poems by a lot of poets have been up in the New York subway. The head of the Transit Authority is a lover of poetry and he decided he wanted "poetry in motion." I was very happy to see that. The same thing has been done in the bus system in San Diego, California, and I think it should be happening everywhere. I think the question of "how do we get people to read poetry?" might be to some extent resolved if people saw more poetry out in the world, places where they go, in just the ordinary public places where everybody has to stand on line, or hang from the strap, waiting, because people would be reading poetry. They would find themselves reading it and absorbing it.

DELTA

If you have taken this rubble for my past
raking through it for fragments you could sell
know that I long ago moved on
deeper into the heart of the matter

If you think you can grasp me, think again:
my story flows in more than one direction
a delta springing from the riverbed
with its five fingers spread

1 9 8 7

MOYERS: "Delta" is so full of multilayered experience and learning that it sounds to me like the life of Adrienne Rich. It is autobiographical, isn't it?

RICH: Well, it reflects the lives of many. I hope many people who saw that poem in the subway thought, "Yes—you can't wrap me up in the story of my life. I am more complicated than you can know."

Adrienne Rich, James Haba

GALWAY KINNELL

Galway Kinnell writes about the terror and wonder of human beings: the terror, because we know we must die; the wonder, because we are so capable of love. Awarded the Pulitzer Prize in 1983 and a MacArthur Fellowship in 1984, he has twice been a Fulbright Scholar. He currently teaches at New York University.

It might have been better if I had gone down to the frog pond and really listened to the frogs. Perhaps I could have recognized in myself what they were feeling.

In an early poem, "First Song," I wrote that the frogs were calling to the boy "with what seemed their joy." I'm not sure about it now. I may have settled on "joy" because of the need to maintain the rhyme with "boy" and "Illinois." It might have been better if I had gone down to the frog pond and really listened to the frogs. Perhaps I could have recognized in myself what they were feeling. If the theory of evolution means anything, it means that the poems of other creatures, even though in languages we don't know, may sometimes also speak for us.

FROM WHEN ONE HAS LIVED A LONG TIME ALONE

8

When one has lived a long time alone,
one likes alike the pig, who brooks no deferment
of gratification, and the porcupine, or thorned pig,
who enters the cellar but not the house itself
because of eating down the cellar stairs on the way up,
and one likes the worm, who by bunching herself together
and expanding works her way through the ground,
no less than the butterfly, who totters full of worry
among the day lilies, as they darken,
and more and more one finds one likes
any other species better than one's own,
which has gone amok, making one self-estranged,
when one has lived a long time alone.

10

When one has lived a long time alone,
and the hermit thrush calls and there is an answer,
and the bullfrog head half out of water repeats
the sexual cantillations of his first spring,
and the snake lowers himself over the threshold
and disappears among the stones, one sees
they all live to mate with their kind, and one knows,
after a long time of solitude, after the many steps taken
away from one's kind, toward the kingdom of strangers,
the hard prayer inside one's own singing
is to come back, if one can, to one's own,
a world almost lost, in the exile that deepens,
when one has lived a long time alone.

The earliest hominid being we can touch comes out in poetry. It's the way natural systems work.

GARY SNYDER

Gary Snyder, who won the Pulitzer Prize for poetry in 1975, is an unabashed lover of the natural world. Born in San Francisco, where he would eventually become a member of the Beat movement, his early experiences in the mountains and wilderness of the West afforded him extended, often solitary communion with nature. For the past twenty-five years he has made his home in the Yuba River watershed of the northern Sierra Nevada. His poetry often reflects his practice of Zen Buddhism. He teaches at the University of California, Davis.

MOYERS: Forty years ago you and Allen Ginsberg, among others, were responsible for bringing poetry readings back into the American landscape. Have you been pleased with what's happened since then?

SNYDER: Certainly. For millennia, the oral tradition was the way poetry was shared around the world, but in the fall of 1955 poetry readings were not a very large part of the American cultural landscape. And you're referring, of course, to some of those readings we gave in San Francisco in October of 1955?

MOYERS: Yes.

SNYDER: Literally—no kidding, Bill—from the night when Allen and I and others first read our works at the Sixth Gallery in October of 1955, there has not been a night without a poetry reading in the Bay Area. It started just like *that,* and then it moved out across the whole country, to coffeehouses and cultural centers and then into the academy where including a poetry reading series became part of the annual agenda of the university. It's one of the few success stories of the twentieth century. I'm delighted by it.

MOYERS: When five Poet Laureates recently read at the Cathedral of St. John the Divine in New York City on a wet and miserable day, over two thousand people turned out, standing room only, and there was not a single word about it in any local press, including *The New York Times.* The mainstream press has been missing this revolution.

SNYDER: They certainly have. For years I've been asking, "Why don't some people start reviewing poetry readings? Why don't we develop a language of criticism, a language for evaluating readings, and have a few poetry reading critics who did at least a paragraph?" It's really interesting how the mainstream press has averted its eyes or been unable to see the depth with which the American public truly does respond to poetry.

MOYERS: What is it about a poetry reading that creates so much electricity, so much intensity? Here at the Dodge Poetry Festival, the air crackles. People got as excited as if they were at a rock concert, or as engaged as if it were a religious service.

SNYDER: Real community is happening, for one thing. People are not reading a book or watching the TV in solitude. They're with each other. And something happens with a poem when it's experienced in the company of others different from what happens with the same poem experienced in private, which is not to deny that the experience of a poem in your own solitude can be remarkable and powerful. But at a reading another thing happens: it's communal, it's community spirit, it's convivial. And art as a convivial experience is just marvelous.

MOYERS: That happened when you were reading with Paul Winter last night, and yet some people may have been surprised to find your poems in the context of music.

SNYDER: For me the joining seems completely natural. I've always thought of poetry as a variety of song, and I know from my own studies and travels that through so much of the vernacular world of India and the Far East, and in Native American tradition, poetry is sung and accompanied by a little drum or a little string instrument, often also by dance. So I take the joining of music and poetry for granted as a desirable possibility.

And then, of course, in the 1950s, our music was jazz, cool West Coast jazz. San Francisco was the home of a lot of that, so my poetic teeth were sharpened during the Beat Generation in the streets and alleys of North Beach. We went right down into the jazz clubs and did poetry with jazz groups, improvising as we went. Sometimes it worked, sometimes it didn't. Paul remembers that, and I remember that. So it was completely natural when ten years ago Paul suggested we play together, improvise together. We've done it a number of times around the country.

MOYERS: You and Paul seem a natural duo.

SNYDER: We pay attention to each other. As I was saying to the group just the other night before we performed, "Let us think about this poem as music, as part of the music." I'm not afraid that the music will overpower the words or that the words will overpower the music. They can slide in and out of each other. If the audience loses some of the language, let's not worry about it. Let's play the words and the music against each other and be very open to what we hear, going back and forth between the two. The musicians were wonderful. They were listening to the poems, I was listening to them, and we were collaborating as we went.

MOYERS: Does something new happen that was not in the original poem or music?

SNYDER: Yes, it's an entirely new experience and very physical. It belongs in its own place—I just love that—and I think it's really a wonderful way to work.

MOYERS: I'm curious about how your description of the communal quality of poetry relates to your poem "How Poetry Comes to Me." What is it that you go to meet at the edge of the light?

HOW POETRY COMES TO ME

It comes blundering over the
Boulders at night, it stays
Frightened outside the
Range of my campfire
I go to meet it at the
Edge of the light

SNYDER: I go to meet that blundering, clumsy, beautiful, shy world of poetic, archetypal, wild intuition that's not going to come out into the broad daylight of rational mind but wants to peek in.

MOYERS: Poetry is like a wild animal?

SNYDER: You bet. Claude Lévi-Strauss, the great French anthropologist, said that the arts and poetry in the twentieth century are the "national parks of the imagination." I love that metaphor—the wilderness areas of the mind.

MOYERS: Did it occur to you forty years ago that you were in a way unleashing a kind of wild animal of the imagination on the body politic?

SNYDER: Yes, I had a sense of that. But I definitely perceived something hearing Allen Ginsberg read "Howl" for the first time when I also clearly felt the energy that was in the audience, which was surprisingly large. We held that poetry reading ourselves because we all had a lot of unpublished work which had been rejected everywhere we sent it, so we thought at least we could read it to each other and also send out some postcards, not expecting a big turnout.

We were just surprised, first of all, by the turnout, and then by the response. Looking at it, I couldn't help but feel that some little historical corner had been turned, particularly hearing "Howl" read aloud the first time. And it was true, a corner was turned there.

MOYERS: "Howl" raises the hair on my neck. What was going through your mind when Paul Winter and the Consort did "The Wolf"?

SNYDER: It made me think about howls actually, and it took me back to thinking again about howling. It made me recall that I have neglected practicing howling lately and that I've got to get out and keep practicing it some more, because I used to be a pretty good howler.

MOYERS: Well, I tried to howl in response to Paul last night, but it sort of trickled out as you might expect from a citified fellow who's been too long from the wilderness.

SNYDER: You *do* have to keep it up, and I like to think of howling not as perhaps Allen intended with his title—a cry of anguish, a cry of pain, a cry of rebellion. I like to think of wild animals as models of sanity, as models of music and as a statement of full presence in the world. When they hear the word "wild" animals, too many people think of "wild" as meaning chaotic, uncontrolled, and violent, whereas "wild" means self-maintaining, self-governing, totally balanced.

MOYERS: There's a difference between wilderness and wild.

SNYDER: Wild is the process of wilderness.

MOYERS: You spent some time, many years ago, as a lookout for the Forest Service and you wrote a poem about it, "Mid-August at Sourdough Mountain Lookout." Where is Sourdough Mountain?

MID-AUGUST AT SOURDOUGH MOUNTAIN LOOKOUT

Down valley a smoke haze
Three days heat, after five days rain
Pitch glows on the fir-cones
Across rocks and meadows
Swarms of new flies.

I cannot remember things I once read
A few friends, but they are in cities.
Drinking cold snow-water from a tin cup
Looking down for miles
Through high still air.

SNYDER: It's just south of the Canadian border, in the Northern Cascades of Washington State, in what is now the North Cascade National Park, headwaters of the Skagit River System.

MOYERS: How did that experience affect your life as a poet?

SNYDER: As a poet—and I didn't know it at the time—it gave me this large landscape view, this sense of the space of the planet and what it was like to look at range after range of mountains, through changing light day after day after day, and to see on different days different mountain ranges come forward and retreat, according to the light. That experience led me ultimately to the project I'm working on now which is called "Mountains and Rivers Without End." I'm finally trying to come to terms with the landscapes of the planet and to speak for them in some small way. I see this whole forty-year project as a little haiku for the planet.

MOYERS: A haiku—

SNYDER: A haiku is a seventeen-syllable poem.

MOYERS: What happened to you when you were alone with only your memories, your own thoughts, and the landscape?

SNYDER: Well, of course, I was called on to keep an eye out on the landscape for forest fires, and I was surprised at how much there is to see day after day in the changing light. I also realized that large-scale landscapes are a rare opportunity and not something that everyone is given to see easily, especially not whole mountain ranges for three months in solitude.

MOYERS: Then the solitude was broken.

AUGUST ON SOURDOUGH, A VISIT FROM DICK BREWER

You hitched a thousand miles
              north from San Francisco
Hiked up the mountainside   a mile in the air
The little cabin—one room—
              walled in glass
Meadows and snowfields,   hundreds of peaks.
We lay in our sleeping bags
              talking half the night;

Wind in the guy-cables   summer mountain rain.
Next morning I went with you
                    as far as the cliffs,
Loaned you my poncho—   the rain across the shale—
You down the snowfield
                    flapping in the wind
Waving a last goodbye   half hidden in the clouds
To go on hitching
                    clear to New York;
Me back to my mountain   and far, far, west.

SNYDER: A friend from San Francisco, a painter, came to visit me, and he only stayed overnight. Then he left for New York. I went to Japan.

MOYERS: The time you spent studying Japanese culture has really influenced your work. I mean, those descriptions of the vistas you see are like some Japanese paintings.

SNYDER: Yes, like the landscape scrolls. Actually there is some interesting feedback there. When I was about eleven years old, my parents and I went into Seattle on weekends from our dairy farm up north, and on one of those weekends we went into the Seattle Art Museum where I wandered around into the Chinese painting room and saw marvelous landscape scrolls. I didn't even know such things existed. All I could think was, "These people really knew mountains." They knew how to see them. Then later, I went out as a mountaineer and as a forest service worker, and I said to myself, "These mountains really know how to be mountains." Those two things weave together through the rest of my life. I've become a great lover of Chinese painting.

MOYERS: And what about the haiku? There are times in your poetry when those little flecks of thought just appear.

SNYDER: Oh, well, haiku is also part of the teaching of contemporary poetry in American life. It came to me through the images of Ezra Pound and Amy Lowell. Even as I was learning to read Japanese haiku in translation, I was studying the early Imagists and Ezra Pound's wonderful little statement, some notes for an Imagist on how to write poetry. So haiku became part of the poetics of the mid-twentieth century.

MOYERS: The poetics?

SNYDER: The sense of economy and visual directness, the call for clarity and the call for staying away from cliché—as a part of twentieth-century poetry. Those values came through Asia, through Fenellosa's essays on No to Ezra Pound, and to us.

MOYERS: How do you achieve that clarity and economy?

SNYDER: Work and play—you have to let loose the idea of correctness, of doing any more than you have to do. You have to be relaxed with language and goofy with it, loose as a goose, and then you have to throw away the excess.

MOYERS: Get it down to the haiku?

SNYDER: Yes, or the image.

MOYERS: Do you sometimes see the image before you find the word?

SNYDER: I never find words right away. Poems for me always begin with images and rhythms, shapes, feelings, forms, dances in the back of my mind. And much of the poem is already dancing itself out before I begin to look around for the words for it. So I'm not a language poet in the sense that some people say all poetry starts with language. For me, language comes *after* imagination. My imagination is pre-linguistic, pre-verbal.

MOYERS: In what sense?

SNYDER: In the sense that when you roam around in the spaces of your mind, you're not forming sentences and reeling out vocabulary, you're just looking. You're looking at the landscape of your mind, and you're solving problems. For example, how do you know where your socks are in your drawer? You don't make a sentence, "My socks are in the corner of my drawer." You pull the drawer out, look around, and you see all the socks are kept here. That's how we get dressed in the morning.

MOYERS: And that's how you write poetry?

SNYDER: Yes.

MOYERS: Rummaging in the socks?

SNYDER: Rummaging around in the various places in my mind, and looking at what's there.

MOYERS: When and how does it come together?

SNYDER: It comes together by itself, by my letting it come together and not interfering too much until it begins to pull together. Now all of this is not to say that after a poem is written down it's finished. By no means. There comes a further exercise, which is tuning—fine tuning, revision, listening to it many times and touching it up a bit—and when one comes to that, of course, language is of great importance. So I was just talking about the roots, the origins. Both exercises are real.

MOYERS: You talk about work a lot in your poems, including one of my favorites, "Hay for the Horses."

HAY FOR THE HORSES

He had driven half the night
From far down San Joaquin
Through Mariposa, up the
Dangerous mountain roads,
And pulled in at eight a.m.
With his big truckload of hay
     behind the barn.
With winch and ropes and hooks
We stacked the bales up clean
To splintery redwood rafters
High in the dark, flecks of alfalfa
Whirling through shingle-cracks of light,
Itch of haydust in the
     sweaty shirt and shoes.
At lunchtime under Black oak
Out in the hot corral,
—The old mare nosing lunchpails,
Grasshoppers crackling in the weeds—
"I'm sixty-eight," he said,
"I first bucked hay when I was seventeen.
I thought, that day I started,
I sure would hate to do this all my life.
And dammit, that's just what
I've gone and done."

SNYDER: That is my most anthologized poem, the poem all the high school kids know, and I'm delighted with that. It's another poem that comes out of working as a laborer up in the Sierra Nevada.

MOYERS: When you read it last night I saw many heads—young folks—nodding. It's their favorite too.

SNYDER: Well, I hope they all have a glint of humor in their eye like that old guy did, because he wasn't whining and slacking off.

MOYERS: Oh, no—in fact, in the opening of that poem you say, "He had driven half the night." He was determined to do his job.

SNYDER: He had to get there early so we could get it all unloaded so he could get back by nightfall.

MOYERS: This poem reminds me of another favorite in which you talk about work, "I Went into the Maverick Bar." What's the story behind that one?

I WENT INTO THE MAVERICK BAR

I went into the Maverick Bar
In Farmington, New Mexico.
And drank double shots of bourbon
            backed with beer.
My long hair was tucked up under a cap
I'd left the earring in the car.

Two cowboys did horseplay
            by the pool tables,
A waitress asked us
            where are you from?
a country-and-western band began to play
"We don't smoke Marijuana in Muskokie"
And with the next song,
            a couple began to dance.

They held each other like in High School dances
            in the fifties;
I recalled when I worked in the woods
            and the bars of Madras, Oregon.
That short-haired joy and roughness—
            America—your stupidity.
I could almost love you again.

We left—onto the freeway shoulders—
                    under the tough old stars—
In the shadow of bluffs
                    I came back to myself,
To the real work, to
                    "What is to be done."

SNYDER: In the early 1970s, I had finally come back to live in the United States, and I had a family and a little place up in the Sierra Nevada. Friends called me to join in on the Black Mesa issue down in New Mexico.

MOYERS: That's when they were trying to build the huge energy complex at the Four Corners, right?

SNYDER: Exactly. Doing open-pit strip-mining on Navajo and Hopi land. There was a group called The Black Mesa Committee, and some of us went down there to see it firsthand and to think about what we could do in the way of writing about it and so forth. We had to pass through Farmington, which is right near the Four Corners plant and which is not a New Mexican town. It's a Texan town full of Texan coal and oil people, and it was considered at that time a pretty heavy town to go through. So we went through it, and not only did we go through it, we stopped at a bar, which was maybe a mistake. Stopping was kind of bold.

MOYERS: Nothing is a mistake that produces a poem like this. What do you mean when you say at the end of the poem, "I came back to myself, / To the real work, to / 'What is to be done.' "

SNYDER: I've been working on that question ever since.

MOYERS: That happens to poets. It takes a long time to discover what you meant.

SNYDER: Oh, I believe so, yes. If you're honest. You might die without knowing, and that's okay, too. Keats said that we must be open to confusion and darkness and doubt, without an irritable grasping after reason. He called that "negative capability." It's part of what a poet has to be capable of. Actually, I brought out a volume of essays some years later called *The Real Work* explaining that question further, and what I would say in one sentence is that, for Americans, the real work is becoming native to North America.

MOYERS: Meaning . . .

SNYDER: The real work is becoming native in your heart, coming to under-stand we really live here, that this is really the continent we're on and that our loyalties are here, to these mountains and rivers, to these plant zones, to these creatures. The real work involves developing a loyalty that goes back before the formation of any nation state, back billions of years and thousands of years into the future. The real work is accepting citizenship in the continent itself.

MOYERS: The Indians called this continent Turtle Island. It expressed their notion of kinship with nature.

SNYDER: The Native Americans talk about being concerned with "all my kin," all my brothers and sisters. Think of the community of Turtle Island as including all the nonhuman beings as well as the human beings, and then let's talk about the neighborhood. What are we going to do with the neighborhood? Well, let's see what the trees want. You know, that's the approach to big-scale family values—including the nonhuman with the human, and in a very convivial way.

MOYERS: How did it come about—this conviviality between you and the natural world?

SNYDER: Well, I have to say it happened to me because I felt it so deeply. It was really a gift to me from childhood.

MOYERS: Growing up outdoors?

SNYDER: Growing up on a dairy farm in northern Washington on the edge of a clear cut where some of the largest conifer forests in the world had been. Right back of our cow pasture there were stumps twelve feet high and twelve feet across, the giant Douglas fir and western hemlock and western red cedar of Puget Sound, and I played among them as a kid. I became so tuned in and, in a certain sense, radicalized so early that I like to think that the ghosts of those giant trees were whispering to me as a kid, "Do something about this."

MOYERS: Was there a moment when you realized that poetry would be your response to that call?

SNYDER: There was a moment in college when I was doing my best to write good academic papers in anthropology and English and so forth, learning how to get it out with footnotes and documentation, and I was still not able to say what I wanted to say. So then I turned to poetry. There are things that you cannot say except in poetry, and those are the things I need to say.

MOYERS: What is it about poetry that makes it such a fitting vehicle for those things?

SNYDER: There's a freedom of mind, imagination, language, spirit that is granted you in poetry. It's the singing voice. It's the dancing body that is not in prose. It's ritual, it's ceremony, it's magic. The earliest hominid being we can touch comes out in poetry. It's the way natural systems work.

MOYERS: Many of us aspire to be poets, but most of us never succeed at it. Are there ways we can work on that?

SNYDER: Yes. I'm really glad you're saying that because I don't want people to think there are uniquely gifted people with the capacity to speak in some special way and that nobody else can do it. I don't believe that's true. Another way of looking at it comes from my practice of Buddhism and meditation. There, poetry is a mode of expression, but the mind that explores the world before you put it into words can find many ways to express the experience of the world, and poetry is only one of the ways.

You can move through those realms and see those connections and be delighted by those energies and then speak it out in dance or painting or cooking or childcare or fixing cars or managing offices. With a full heart, you can find your expression in the work you do, and this is really the truth of the world.

MOYERS: *Zen and the Art of Motorcycle Maintenance*? So that whatever one does—plumbing? carpentry? cooking?—is a form of art?

SNYDER: Yes. Zen and the art of being a human being.

MOYERS: Well, now I think I see why so often you return to the work people do with their hands. Your poems express such respect for craftspeople and tradespeople and ordinary workers—people like my father. I think of him when I read "Why Log Truck Drivers Rise Earlier Than Students of Zen."

WHY LOG TRUCK DRIVERS RISE EARLIER THAN STUDENTS OF ZEN

In the high seat, before-dawn dark,
Polished hubs gleam
And the shiny diesel stack
Warms and flutters

Up the Tyler Road grade
To the logging on Poorman creek.
Thirty miles of dust.

There is no other life.

SNYDER: Yes. In the summertime up where I live in the foothills of the Sierra Nevada a little group of people practice *zazen*—a Buddhist-style, cross-legged Zen meditation—in the early morning. We go up and we sit on the pine needles on a little ridge in the five a.m. light. But even then, starting at three-thirty a.m. or so, the log trucks were already on their way into the high country. The paved road is four miles away, but you can hear them because those big diesels really wrap it up when they head up the hill. So the working people are up as early as the spiritual people and the question is, "Who is more spiritual?"

MOYERS: And you knew people like this in your own life.

SNYDER: Yes. I grew up in the Depression in a working-class family. All my uncles were loggers or fishermen. My father was hand-splitting cedar shakes to make a few bucks when I was a kid during the Depression, so I grew up with it.

MOYERS: My father worked most of his life as a truck driver, often getting up early in the morning. He would have liked your friend Burt Hybart.

REMOVING THE PLATE OF THE PUMP ON THE HYDRAULIC SYSTEM OF THE BACKHOE

FOR BURT HYBART

Through mud, fouled nuts, black grime
it opens, a gleam of spotless steel
machined-fit perfect
swirl of intake and output
relentless clarity
at the heart
of work.

SNYDER: Burt Hybart was a true wizard with a backhoe. In fact, he was a wizard with any kind of heavy equipment. As a younger man, he'd been in charge of heavy equipment over at Pacific Lumber on the coast in the redwood logging. I wrote this poem for Burt when his backhoe broke down on a job at my place. He pulled in his welding torch, and he went to work on it and fixed it right there in front of me.

MOYERS: "Relentless clarity." He knew what he was doing, didn't he?

SNYDER: Yes, and he knew all tasks present within the task he was performing. A relentless clarity which is just wonderful.

MOYERS: How do we pass that on? How does one generation pass on to the next that sense of value inherent in honest work? I think you raise that question in "Axe Handles," right?

AXE HANDLES

One afternoon the last week in April
Showing Kai how to throw a hatchet
One-half turn and it sticks in a stump.
He recalls the hatchet-head
Without a handle, in the shop
And go gets it, and wants it for his own.
A broken-off axe handle behind the door
Is long enough for a hatchet,
We cut it to length and take it
With the hatchet head
And working hatchet, to the wood block.
There I begin to shape the old handle
With the hatchet, and the phrase
First learned from Ezra Pound
Rings in my ears!
"When making an axe handle
        the pattern is not far off."
And I say this to Kai
"Look: We'll shape the handle
By checking the handle
Of the axe we cut with—"
And he sees. And I hear it again:
It's in Lu Ji's *Wên Fu*, fourth century
A.D. "Essay on Literature"—in the
Preface: "In making the handle

Of an axe
But cutting wood with an axe
The model is indeed near at hand."
My teacher Shih-hsiang Chen
Translated that and taught it years ago
And I see: Pound was an axe,
Chen was an axe, I am an axe
And my son a handle, soon
To be shaping again, model
And tool, craft of culture,
How we go on.

SNYDER: Yes. Of course this is a poem of a father showing something to his son. Kai's my son. He's now twenty-six.

MOYERS: And you were actually doing this?

SNYDER: This is a true story, as we say.

MOYERS: What *about* fathers and sons?

SNYDER: If not fathers and sons, younger people and older people, daughters and mothers, or daughters and aunties, or sons and uncles, or sons and some big guy. They all need each other. The craft of culture is literal, it's a craft. If you don't have the tools in your hands as a kid, the little tools, even a hammer or a wrench, and somebody to show you how you tighten a nut and how you loosen a nut, you're in trouble. That's where, on the most fundamental level, our society *is* in trouble because we're not passing on how you do the details, how you literally handle the tools and how you put them away when you're done. Of course, when fathers and sons and mothers and daughters do this, it's great. There are also many societies in which aunties and uncles and friends do it, but somebody has to do it. I feel that so strongly now.

MOYERS: We still have workers and craftspeople, but we're no longer a society where most of the people make a living with their hands, producing something.

SNYDER: You can fix your own sink. I mean, the house itself is a little ecosystem. The house and the yard in any suburban or semi-suburban world is an ecosystem which can be studied and loved and maintained with intelligence and awareness and poetry. Or you can let it slide or hire somebody to take care of it. There's some territory in there where we have an opening that we're not using.

MOYERS: And we have to do this with nature too?

SNYDER: Exactly. Yes. That we are illiterate about nature is a very deep problem in American society. If we are going to talk about literacy and cultural literacy, which is great, we might also talk about nature literacy. Nature literacy assumes that any educated person, not necessarily a "bird lover" or a "conservationist," but any even moderately aware person would want to know some of the flowers, birds and grasses, would want to be attentive to the weather cycles. Nature literacy assumes that any educated person would want to have a notion that at certain times of the year these birds come, and at other times of the year they're gone. In other words, any educated person would make their neighborly and community consciousness extend outward and know what this world is doing around us.

MOYERS: Most of us live crowded around cities and megalopolises, far from nature.

SNYDER: We're surrounded by the largest of all wilderness areas, called the universe, and the vast cycles of climate pass over us daily. Huge watersheds are bringing the flow down the Hudson at every moment. Migratory waterfowl and hawks are going right over New York City.

An immense variety of spiders live in the alleys of Wall Street. This is what we call urban bio-regionalism. Right now people are leading nature walks in Manhattan and in San Francisco to help people understand that and to help them realize that the parks, the rivers, the open lands that are near them are full of richness and are available for study. It's just like going to an art museum like the Metropolitan or to the Museum of Natural History, all this land around us has that potential. You can stand in the engine room of nature, so to speak, and look around and see it all happening.

MOYERS: So loyalty to nature still survives.

SNYDER: It's on the rise. It's growing. Right now nature writing is one of the most vital parts of American creative writing. The new young natural historians like Gary Paul Nabhan, for example, or Richard Nelson are writing beautiful poetic prose grounded in direct experience and practice. It's a vital part of American literature right now. In the summers, I participate in a series of classes on teaching nature writing, and we have to turn people away. We had ninety people last summer up in the Sierra Nevada at a program called "The Art of the Wild." We say to them, "You must not write about nature without knowing what you're talking about. You've got to get in touch with it. You've got to be literate about it before you have any power to write about it." Then we send them out there.

Looking over the last forty years of American political history, I think we can say that the environmental movement has been an amazing success story of a movement that rose from the grass roots, with no spiritual or historical constituency in the American ideology and no original support from big money and big business, to become a force to be reckoned with in national politics. Now that's amazing. So that's my positive outlook on it.

MOYERS: Do you still believe that poetry is a part of the power of a sane people?

SNYDER: It *is* sanity. It is the voice of sanity, in the large picture. Which is not to say that sanity does not sometimes require you to be a crazy, nutty rebel. That's a larger sanity.

MOYERS: Is that larger sanity the crazy poet in the attic writing a poem like "What Have I Learned"? How did you come to write this poem?

WHAT HAVE I LEARNED

What have I learned but
the proper use for several tools?

The moments
between hard pleasant tasks

To sit silent, drink wine,
and think my own kind
of dry crusty thoughts.

    —the first Calochortus flowers
and in all the land,
       it's spring.
I point them out:
the yellow petals, the golden hairs,
      to Gen.

Seeing in silence:
never the same twice,
but when you get it right,

    you pass it on.

SNYDER: Yes, it is. Well, I was teaching my kids the flowers and thinking, it's enough to have been able to live this long to know enough to teach a kid a flower in the spring. What have I learned except to be able to do that? The rest is, in a sense, irrelevant.

MOYERS: Pass it on?

SNYDER: Yes, pass it on. And don't pass it on until you get it right!

Robert Bly, Gary Snyder

© Lynn Saville

GERALD STERN

Gerald Stern has been called "a poet of exile and ruins," laying claim to places and things other people have abandoned and investing them with new value through his incandescent imagination. His poems explore human beings' relationship to the past, time, and heritage, and especially his own roots as a nonpracticing and spiritual Jew. His first book of poetry was published when he was forty-six, and his second book, *Lucky Life,* was the Lamont Poetry Selection in 1977. He has taught at many colleges and universities, most recently at the Iowa Writers' Workshop.

MOYERS: *Lucky Life* is the title of one of your collections of poems. Is it autobiographical?

STERN: "Lucky" is a strange word. I like it because when I was a kid in Pittsburgh I would listen to the fights on the radio, and after Joe Louis would knock somebody out the announcer would say to him, "Joe, that was a fantastic night, just fantastic!" and Joe would always say, "Lucky night, lucky night, lucky night." I adored Joe Louis, and I used to listen, rapt, to the radio broadcasts of his fights.

There's also deep irony in the title because I am a poet partly of grief; so it's an ambiguous title, but it had a certain resonance and attraction for me. Some people have said that they didn't get the irony when they read the book, but they could see it in my performance.

MOYERS: I watched the students yesterday as you were reading. Your performance carried them from deep solemnity to boisterous laughter. At one time weren't all poems performed?

STERN: Exactly, and even when you sit in a room like this and you're reading alone, in your mind's eye you are performing, you are declaiming.

MOYERS: Poets acted out poetry to their clans and tribes.

STERN: Not only that, but they also composed it to be sung because there probably wasn't any distinction between music and poetry and maybe not even between music and poetry and dance. Not all poems are obviously melodramatic—some are very, very quiet—but even what seem the quiet ones contain drama and action, color. Emily

It's the poet's job to remember.

Dickinson, for instance, is not a quiet little piccolo. She's a trombone. She's a tuba. Emily Dickinson is a raging tuba!

MOYERS: And you're a whole orchestra. I watched you "playing" yesterday, and every string was strung, every pipe tuned, every bell chimed, and every note struck as you took us from sadness to hilarity and back again.

STERN: Well, that's what life is. If I could do what I have always wanted to do as a poet, I would just talk, literally just talk, and that would be poetry. I believe that as we walk about and do the things we do we're all in fact playing in that orchestra.

MOYERS: It's been said that you write about the darkest drama in the midst of tricycles and kittens.

STERN: That perception may result partly from my embarrassment at the heaviness of my subject. There may also be tenderness involved, but most important, the tricycle and the kitten are *there*. I mean, that's the life I lead—I'm always tripping over bicycles and kittens. I lead a disconnected, scattered life, but like everyone else I dream of a pure place, an unencumbered study with every book in its place, where I can press a button and up comes this poem or that poem, or this story. It has never happened, and now I am content that it never will happen for me in this life.

MOYERS: But you keep your eyes open, as in "Cow Worship." You see things I would never think of as being the stuff of poems.

COW WORSHIP

I love the cows best when they are a few feet away
from my dining-room window and my pine floor,
when they reach in to kiss me with their wet
mouths and their white noses.
I love them when they walk over the garbage cans
and across the cellar doors,
over the sidewalk and through the metal chairs
and the birdseed.
—Let me reach out through the thin curtains
and feel the warm air of May.
It is the temperature of the whole galaxy,

all the bright clouds and clusters,
beasts and heroes,
glittering singers and isolated thinkers
at pasture.

STERN: I love cows. At the time I wrote that poem I was living in Pennsylvania and my wife and I would drive three or four miles to pet the cows—that's what we did in the evening at just about this time of year, in late April or early May. We'd drive up and these cows would come rushing over to the fence—they'd want the weeds and the grass that grew on our side—and we would feed them. They would nibble and we would pet them. To me, that was the sweetest thing in the world, the sweetest thing.

MOYERS: Unthreatening creatures often occupy your poems—fleas, mosquitoes, moles . . .

STERN: Yes, and opossums and dogs who are not behaving in a threatening way. I never thought of it that way, but it's absolutely accurate: there are no wolves—not that I don't love wolves, we all adore and are mystified by wolves—there are no tigers, hyenas, or eagles. There *are* lots of doves, but I'm not fooled by doves—they're greedy and they fight with each other. I do love them, though.

MOYERS: None of these are creatures automobile companies are likely to name new models after.

STERN: The Opossum! Imagine Chrysler coming out with the *Opossum!*

MOYERS: Why do these little creatures turn up so frequently in your poems?

STERN: Maybe I identify with them because they're somewhat helpless and at the mercy of others. Partly I'm like them in that, as a human being and as a Jew, I have lived for so many years economically on the outside and at someone else's mercy. Is that why we have pets—to show that we *do* have kindness and mercy, or even a little justice in us?

MOYERS: Sometimes it's easier to love a pet than it is to love a human being.

STERN: It sure is, and of course many of us remember the stiff Englishman who loves his pet or even the Nazi who loved animals but didn't pay a lot of the right sort of attention to humans. I guess that's why I'm attracted to those animals. They're like weeds. I love weeds, they're outsiders too. They're exiles.

MOYERS: And you—

STERN: Yes, I *am* in exile. I'm in exile from the Christian world insofar as I'm a Jew and I'm in exile from the Jewish world insofar as I've broken away from Judaism. I'm in exile from the burgeois Jewish world from Pittsburgh that I was expected to flourish in because when I was nineteen or twenty I rented a room and started to read books and became a crazy poet, to the embarrassment and shame and possibly even a little to the delight of my parents. And I feel I'm in exile from the connection or communion that I had with my sister—she was about eleven months older than me and she died when I was eight. So I often feel that I'm writing for her and about her, and that my life is a debt I owe to her. I'm also in exile from the six million Jews who were killed. Now, at my age, I'm studying Yiddish, which is an expression of that exile and an attempt to redeem that exile simultaneously.

MOYERS: The farther you seem to get away from your origins, the more you seem to be trying to get back to them.

STERN: That's right. Life is short, even centuries are short. After a while you realize that I long for . . . maybe my longing is partly sentimental, and it's always schmaltz. I love it. I glory in it. I weep. I love the schmaltz. Schmaltz—chicken fat. My mother was eighty-nine three days ago, and we were talking about the food we used to eat after school when we came home. I reminded her that I'd get home at three or four o'clock in the afternoon and make a sandwich on cheap white Ward's bread. It was like rubber. I'd put ketchup and mayonnaise on it and eat that gunk. Without blinking an eye, she said she used to put schmaltz—chicken fat—on bread and eat it. Imagine how it clogs the veins! But she's made it to eighty-nine and she's in good shape. So that's schmaltz, Jewish sentimentality. I identify with it, but I'm ashamedly schmaltzy because I have other parts of the orchestra that can cut through the schmaltz.

MOYERS: During your performance yesterday you said that poets have the job of remembering. I thought of Czeslaw Milosz's observation that our age is so inundated by the mass media that it's characterized by the refusal to remember.

STERN: Absolutely. Of course, every older teacher is always shocked that young people do not remember what he or she remembers, but what we have now is way beyond that. Memory is not a part of our culture; it's almost as if we want to efface memory partly for political and partly for economic reasons.

Economic because it seems our main business is to sell products, and the producers don't want us to remember old things. Because they don't want us to save old things, we are taught to be ashamed of having anything that's two years old—it's partly a question of style.

Political because it is probably to the benefit of politicians and the controllers of institutions if people do not resist them through memory. I suspect the very first thing dictators do is to efface memory.

MOYERS: George Orwell talked about flushing memories down the memory hole so that the history which those memories preserved could then be freely rewritten.

STERN: The poet's main job might be to preserve memory. The Irish poets had to memorize the entire body of literature—they had to know it by heart—so I think it's dangerous when poets don't remember.

MOYERS: What do you feel obsessed to remember?

STERN: The obsession to remember is a loyalty to something, isn't it? It's often a loyalty to things that in and of themselves may seem insignificant, like a shirt, an old car, maybe even particular people. It may be the words of parents or grandparents, or the words of older poets. And while there is a very ambiguous attitude about nostalgia, there are different kinds of nostalgia. There is good and bad nostalgia. Nostalgia really means the desire to go home, so isn't memory ultimately a desire to go home?

MOYERS: Li-Young Lee called you a poet of ruins.

STERN: For the longest time I've been interested in ruins for their own sake. I once was offered a job in your state—at the University of Texas in Houston—which has a wonderful writing program, one of the best in the country. I loved the college and the people I met there, but I had mixed feelings about Houston. When they offered me the job, I said to the chairman of the English department and the poet who was there at the time, Edward Hirsch, that I thrive on old things, so what could they show me that was old? Well, before I went to the airport, they took me to see the old part of the city. They said, "Look at that building! It was built in 1945!"

Now I'm sure there are a few things older than that in Houston, but I own a house in Easton, Pennsylvania, which was built in 1790, and that's nothing special to a European, for whom a thing has to be fifty years old before it even has a taste, a smell, a life. It takes time for the soul to grow. It doesn't just emerge in a second or two.

MOYERS: You've said that ruins help you to stray, to enter the stream of your own life.

STERN: Yes. Somehow ruins give me delight in a crazy way. Maybe the straying that ruins help with is a way of finding the holiness in the thing that existed, the soul in the thing. I was recently in Miami, where they were tearing buildings down that were built only five or six years ago, and I was shocked. It's like killing someone when he's eight. They didn't give it a chance. It's bad enough that they tear it down when it's two hundred years old! It seemed not only a waste—forget about its being a waste, and forget about its being stupid—it seemed shocking. I was embarrassed. It seemed immoral.

MOYERS: Tearing down hotels and landmarks is one thing, but an old army barracks? There you are "On the Far Edge of Kilmer" at the old barracks before that blackened door. What are you trying to restore *there*? Why does *that* ruin appeal to you?

On the Far Edge of Kilmer

I am sitting again on the steps of the burned out barrack.
I come here, like Proust or Adam Kadmon, every night to watch the sun
    leave.
I like the broken cinder blocks and the bicycle tires.
I like the exposed fuse system.
I like the color the char takes in the clear light.
I climb over everything and stop before every grotesque relic.
I walk through the tar paper and glass.
I lean against the lilacs.
In my left hand is a bottle of Tango.
In my right hand are the old weeds and power lines.
I am watching the glory go down.
I am taking the thing seriously.
I am standing between the wall and the white sky.
I am holding open the burnt door.

STERN: Isn't it weird that it was the ruin of an old army barracks? But what it had been was not in fact the issue. The issue was just that it was an old building. There were these old bottles bums had left—bottles of whiskey called Tango—and it was the place of weeds. I don't altogether know the answer to your question, and if I did I would probably stop writing, but I'm attracted to these pockets, these secret places, to these places of escape, to the places that are ignored. I'm sure that barracks' ruin has been cleaned up and there's something else there now, but for a moment maybe it became its true self. Maybe the ruin was what that thing really was.

Maybe that's what our fancy buildings really are underneath. They're just these two-by-fours and wallboard or plaster cleaned up a little bit—a skin put on for show, for civilization. Maybe it's a question of the relationship of civilization with the other: uncivilization. Maybe civilization is show, so maybe there was a secret joy in experiencing a kind of brotherhood of destruction, and in declaring this is what a thing really is. This is what all things finally come to. You see it in *Revelations*. There's got to be some kind of joy—and it sounds horrible to put it this way—in destruction, where everything is leveled out. Not for the sake of destruction itself, because that's terrible, but where things finally are defined in a different way. I don't really totally understand this, but *I'm* alive and it's a victory to *be* there and to describe it. It's a victory to have gone through and to survive, but there's also a certain sadness in seeing the narrative of a thing from its beginning to its end and then just describing its existence.

MOYERS: You're alive, but you never stop reminding us, in one way or the other, of people who are not—those who have suffered and perished.

STERN: Right, and sometimes, of course, I disguise them as animals, but I'm really talking about people.

MOYERS: What moved you to write "The Faces I Love"?

THE FACES I LOVE

Once and for all I will lie down here like a dead man,
letting the socialists walk over my face, letting the fascists
crawl through my veins, letting the Krishnas
poison me with their terrible saffron.

Once and for all I will lie here helpless and exhausted.
I will let dishonor rise from me like steam
and tears fall down on me like oily rain.

In the end my stillness will save me;
in the end the leopard will walk away from me in boredom
and trot after something living, something violent
and warm to excite him before his death.

In the end I will have my own chair.
I will pull the blinds down and watch my nose and mouth
in the blistered glass.
I will look back in amazement at what I did
and cry aloud for two more years, for four more years,
just to remember the faces, just to recall the names,
to put them back together—
the names I can't forget, the faces I love.

STERN: As I reread it now all sorts of things are happening to me. And again, I don't always know what happened when I wrote a poem. Sometimes I start just technically, musically, writing lines down, and I don't know why I'm writing them down or where they're going. Finally it's as if the poem is a puzzle that will give me a secret about life itself, so that each poem is a journey that I must make to find out something— for myself, first, and then I pass it on to the next person, to the reader or to the listener. I notice here that, as always, I am sitting; and I guess Zen Buddhism and Judaism share sitting together. I don't know why I'm always sitting—though readers and poets do sit, you know—but I'm always sitting in a chair and I'm always absolutely still; it's my place of stillness.

I recently heard somebody talk about reading as a form of meditation—in the fullest sense of the word and not just metaphorically—and whatever else it is, I think writing for me is also meditation. I do most of my writing early in the morning. I get up, make coffee, and sit in the chair. Sometimes I sit there for two hours. Sometimes the phone will ring and I'm shocked back into the world. So it's a poem about stillness, about waiting, about joy in watching the whole thing come to an end, the whole process.

I look back in amazement. I'm full of happiness about myself—I hope this doesn't sound awful; I *like* what I do—and I will look back in amazement at what I did, and then of course I will want two more years or four more years. In this case, not to do more things, but just to relish things in memory, just to remember the faces, just to recall the names. To put them back together—"the names I can't forget, the faces I love." It's as if in its concept of a second world, of a second chance, religion itself is part of a larger process. Maybe that's what art and religion have in common.

Isn't art, after all, doing it a second time? Having a second opportunity to live it through again? And maybe in a more delightful and peaceful way. It's not purgatory. It's being born again, and that's what that poem is about.

To be bold about it, my poetry is a kind of religion for me. It's a way of seeking redemption for myself, but just on the page. It is, finally, a way of understanding things so that they can be reconciled, explained, justified, redeemed. I guess that's what it's about for me, so I think this is serious business. You've got to laugh when you're at the Gates, you know.

MOYERS: "I am taking the thing seriously" is, in fact, one of the lines in "On the Far Edge of Camp Kilmer."

STERN: But, finally, it's a wonderful game. It's life itself I'm talking about, and that's what the ruin is. It's an emblem of life. Life is not something that persists forever; life is something that grows, flourishes, and then falls into ruin.

MOYERS: So that's why you write about doomsday in the midst of joy.

STERN: Because that's what is really on our minds, and maybe it's a way of holding the ghost at bay. It's better than swimming a mile a day; if you keep writing you'll live forever. Maybe that's why Michelangelo lived so long—he painted *and* he wrote.

MOYERS: Read me "Behaving Like a Jew." The young people here were fascinated when you read it yesterday.

BEHAVING LIKE A JEW

When I got there the dead opossum looked like
an enormous baby sleeping on the road.
It took me only a few seconds—just
seeing him there—with the hole in his back
and the wind blowing through his hair
to get back again into my animal sorrow.
I am sick of the country, the bloodstained
bumpers, the stiff hairs sticking out of the grilles,
the slimy highways, the heavy birds
refusing to move;
I am sick of the spirit of Lindbergh over everything,
that joy in death, that philosophical
understanding of carnage, that
concentration on the species.
—I am going to be unappeased at the opossum's death.
I am going to behave like a Jew
and touch his face, and stare into his eyes,
and pull him off the road.
I am not going to stand in a wet ditch
with the Toyotas and the Chevies passing over me
at sixty miles an hour
and praise the beauty and the balance
and lose myself in the immortal lifestream
when my hands are still a little shaky
from his stiffness and his bulk
and my eyes are still weak and misty
from his round belly and his curved fingers
and his black whiskers and his little dancing feet.

STERN: I was moved by the opossum itself. I wrote that poem while I was taking my former wife to a hospital for, I think, some minor procedure on her wrist—you know how we're always frightened when we go to hospitals because anything could happen—and as we were driving through the country there was a dead opossum. Well, there are dead opossums all the time—of course, I know that—but I *saw* the opossum. His body was perfect, there was no blood, and, as I recall, there was just a simple clean bullet hole in the back of his head.

I got out of my car and touched him. It was silly and a crazy thing to do, but I pushed him off the side of the road so he would not be crushed and mutilated and made ugly. Then as I looked at his body with the bloated stomach and the hairy face, somehow that opossum became a representative Jew; but it was *the opossum* that moved me. I was in a state of fear, and I was in a state of sadness.

That his body wasn't crushed and that we were—really my former wife was—about to be put into somebody else's power to be victimized, albeit she was going to be helped, reminded me again of the Jew as an ethnic group put into this special situation: operated on and victimized. I'm not altogether sure why I wrote it and I don't remember if I gave it the title later. I may have started writing that poem and not realized till I was most of the way through that it was the Jewish experience I was writing about. Just the accident of having recently run across an old article by Charles Lindbergh in a *Reader's Digest* could have gotten me started. In all fairness to Charles Lindbergh, the article may have been about his own death and his way of handling it, but I saw it at that time as a glorification of death, a way of accepting death that I was not taught to accept.

One level of me understands and even appreciates that death is part of life, that death is even in some way the *goal* of life, but I want to go down kicking and protesting. That may be a human trick, it may be a particularly Jewish trick, but I want to go down protesting and kicking . . . maybe even thumbing my nose.

MOYERS: But Lindbergh symbolizes even more than that for you in this poem. He urged the United States to remain neutral toward the Nazis before World War II.

STERN: Oh, absolutely, and he visited Germany. He talked to Göring, who was head of the German Air Force, and he praised the German Air Force for its efficiency and its diligence. Lindbergh said that the West was no match for Germany, and at the same time his other connections were politically right-wing, even fascist. So that was the Lindbergh generated by my reading that article in the *Reader's Digest*.

"Behaving Like a Jew" is well-liked, but to a certain degree it's a failure for me because all these things that I'm talking about don't seem available in it. I don't know how much can be made available in a few words on a page, but I feel I have to explain a lot of this.

MOYERS: When you saw that opossum you saw a weak creature killed by a willful machine—in this case a gun. The Jews were slaughtered by a powerful machine—the German state fully armed.

STERN: My experience was an act of total identification.

MOYERS: So what do you mean when you say, "I am going to behave like a Jew"?

STERN: I'm declaring an act of mourning. In staring into that opossum's eye, I *became* that opossum and, identifying with him, I became a Jew. I identified with his whiskers, his round belly, his little dancing feet. Maybe I'm also claiming something for Jews that shouldn't be claimed for them, but for all good people, all thinking people, all feeling people. Maybe I'm claiming feeling for the Jew even though there are as many unfeeling Jews as there are unfeeling gentiles. I'm sensitive about arrogating feeling to Jews, but at that point in that poem, I was claiming feeling, tenderness, elegy, love, memory—memory for that absurd little animal.

MOYERS: In another poem you tell us "Don't flinch when you come across a dead animal lying in the road / . . . slow down with your radio off and your window open . . ."

STERN: ". . . to hear the twittering as you go by." I can't remember which pre-Socratic philosopher it was—maybe Democritus—who talked about immortality in the sense that when you broke a body up into pieces each piece would then assume its own soul. I think that notion was partly in my mind, that as these pieces were being broken up by a car there would not be one soul, there would be many souls. In the poem those souls are birds circling around because gradually, through the caress of the car—at first a bump being smoothed into the road and then complete disappearance—the animal is buried into the highway. That's what happens, literally, as hundreds of cars drive over it.

And I say, "Slow down with your radio off and your window open . . ." But nobody drives in the summertime with the window open anymore because we all have air conditioning. I'm one of the few monsters of the past who refuse to give it up! But the point is—in the midst of all this noise and all this energy and all this civility and all this anger—to stop for a minute. I say, "with your radio off," which is kind of archaic. It should be, "with your television off, with *everything* off." I'm asking that you stop for a minute to hear the twittering as you go by. Every religion and every work of art requires you to stop so you can listen and take in the full world around you.

MOYERS: In this case, to take in a dead animal.

STERN: Yes, in this case, a dead animal which has become immortal because now it's turned into all these birds. That animal still lives in the "twittering" you hear as you go by. It's a victory, a joyous victory. But it may be incorrect technically and, again, therefore a form of sentimentality: The animal *is* a dead animal. So what is this dance I'm doing in pretending that it's something else? But maybe Democritus was right, maybe there are a lot of spirits born from that dead animal, and each one will inhabit another animal or plant.

THE DANCING

In all these rotten shops, in all this broken furniture
and wrinkled ties and baseball trophies and coffee pots
I have never seen a post-war Philco
with the automatic eye
nor heard Ravel's "Bolero" the way I did
in 1945 in that tiny living room
on Beechwood Boulevard, nor danced as I did
then, my knives all flashing, my hair all streaming,
my mother red with laughter, my father cupping
his left hand under his armpit, doing the dance
of old Ukraine, the sound of his skin half drum,
half fart, the world at last a meadow,
the three of us whirling and singing, the three of us
screaming and falling, as if we were dying,
as if we could never stop—in 1945—
in Pittsburgh, beautiful filthy Pittsburgh, home
of the evil Mellons, 5,000 miles away
from the other dancing—in Poland and Germany—
oh God of mercy, oh wild God.

MOYERS: At the end of "The Dancing" you say, "as if we could never stop—in 1945—/ in Pittsburgh, beautiful filthy Pittsburgh, home / of the evil Mellons, 5,000 miles away / from the other dancing—in Poland and Germany . . ."

STERN: The concentration camps. The destruction of the Jews.

MOYERS: The Hasidim dancing on those open graves?

STERN: Yes, but "dancing" is a gory word there because in part it was, forgive me, those Jews dancing in the showers and at the end of gallows and as they were shot and as they were tortured. That's a kind of hideous dancing, Hieronymus Bosch dancing, but as you indicate, it also was a victorious dancing coming from a Jewish, though not just a Jewish, tradition. So it was partly joyous and party hideous. I remember my own dancing in Pittsburgh and I'm also remembering that other dancing.

Then, of course, in the last line I take the turn I do. I had no idea when I wrote that poem that I was going to write about anything else but my father playing his instrument and the three of us dancing around our little apartment in Pittsburgh. I didn't know the poem was going to include the other dancing or that it was going to take that turn in the last line. These were gifts. Terrible gifts. Sad gifts. Good gifts. I wrote and suddenly, "oh God of mercy, oh wild God."

I call Him "God of mercy," and there's irony there because what mercy was shown? But the wildness—I'm just realizing this because I've never examined that word before you prodded me into doing it—is a prayer and it's also a statement of praise for God. I call Him "wild God" as a way of almost forgiving Him because He is wild, because He's on another mission, because He wasn't paying enough attention, because He said, "I'll be back in a minute. I've got to do this wonderful thing. I'm creating a universe over here."

He's wild and He's unconnected, and He didn't pay enough attention so that horrible thing happened. Of course, that's my metaphor in the poem; I'm not talking about this philosophically or logically or literally. I was being ironic and not ironic when I called Him "God of mercy," because He is a God of mercy.

And I was being ironic, but I was mostly praising, when I said "oh wild God . . ." It was an act of forgiveness which I hadn't realized until you asked me. I think that's what I was doing—forgiving God. I should not have the right to forgive God for others, but for my own self I was partly doing that, and maybe to a degree for others as well. I don't know if it's right for me to do that, but the words seem to work, so maybe it is right.

MOYERS: A poet will do what a poet can do.

STERN: Many who have talked about what has come to be called the Holocaust say you can't write about the Holocaust, and that poetry is no longer possible after the Holocaust. But I don't agree with that. I don't believe you can't write about it. You can cheapen it and you can trivialize it. A bad poem can do it injustice, and most poems are bad poems, but American Jews—American non-Jews, too—are in a difficult place because of the Holocaust. What is their debt? What is their duty? Where were they?

We were saving ourselves. We were forgetting. We were not remembering. We were not identifying. We believed the government and the lies it told us. Even some of the more powerful Jews—there were two Jewish Supreme Court Justices at the time—half-believed the things that they were told. It's a complicated story, of course—I feel guilty about it—and I'm trying to pay my debt in the ways that I can.

MOYERS: "In remembrance is the secret of redemption." Or so the Rabbi said.

STERN: Wonderful. Memory is all. Memory is everything. We aren't going to let them make us forget.

MOYERS: What are you remembering in "Pile of Feathers"? It seems joyful.

PILE OF FEATHERS

This time there was no beak,
no little bloody head, no bony
claw, no loose wing—only a small
pile of feathers without substance or center.

Our cats dig through the leaves, they
stare at each other in surprise,
they look carefully over their shoulders,
they touch the same feathers over and over.

They have been totally cheated of the body.
The body with its veins and its fat
and its red bones has escaped them.
Like weak giants
they try to turn elsewhere.
Like Americans on the Ganges,
their long legs twisted in embarrassment,
their knees scraping the stones,
they begin crawling after the spirit.

STERN: I remember we had a lot of cats when I wrote that poem, which is about a dead bird. As is almost always the case with my poems, this one starts with a literal thing. When it moves me, I like to start with the thing in front of me, but I'm not always moved—thank God, or life would be hell! Anyway, this pile of feathers was there and the cats were disappointed and embarrassed. Cats can seem to be embarrassed and they try to get out of it. They back out. They say, "Oh, I was just *kidding, I know* it's not a bird."

But they seemed awkward, and they did have the long legs. Why did I call them "weak giants"? I guess because compared to the birds they *were* weak giants. The felt awkward and they tried to escape, they tried to turn elsewhere. They pretended none of it had happened. I really think they were embarrassed.

"Like Americans on the Ganges . . ." The way you dip into the holy water of the Ganges to become redeemed, but in this case Americans are doing it with their long white legs twisted in embarrassment, their knees scraping because they are not used to crawling with hundreds of other fellow humans down the banks of the River Ganges to be redeemed.

The cats also aren't used to having to crawl after the spirit this way. The bird has somehow escaped. His body is gone, there is "only a small / pile of feathers without substance or center"—there is "no beak, / no little bloody head," nothing for them to hang on to. The only thing left is a kind of spirit, so the cats are looking for the body, and in a certain sense the cats become the supremely sensual image here of everything that wants to connect with what is physical. They become my Americans because there is nothing here *but* spirit, so they have to become humble. They have to start crawling after the spirit.

And, of course, I do too.

MOYERS: It seems to me you're always tracking the human spirit in your poems.

STERN: Yes, I guess that's true, though I'm always a little embarrassed and nervous about the word "spirit." I use "spirit" and "soul" fairly freely in various guises, but I want to make sure when I use these words that I have earned the right to do so and that I don't do it too glibly.

But for God's sake! What are we here for, if not to track the spirit?

Gerald Stern, Lucille Clifton

Sekou Sundiata

Sekou Sundiata describes himself as a recording and performing poet. He frequently takes his poetry on tour in the United States and abroad with musician Craig Harris and the Black Coalition Orchestra. He was born in the housing projects of East Harlem, and his work owes much to the "oralizing" tradition of Africa and to the call-and-response rhythms of the black church in America. He teaches at the New School for Social Research in New York City, where he was the first writer-in-residence. A former fellow at the Sundance Film Institute, he wrote the script for an upcoming film based on his performance piece, "The Circle Unbroken Is a Hard Bop."

MOYERS: Watching you perform here at the Festival, and sensing that visceral response from the audience, I realized, he's *asking* them for something. What do you want from the audience?

SUNDIATA: I want to know if they're really in the house at that moment—call and response, question and answer, some kind of sustained interaction.

MOYERS: What accounts for your desire to experience the audience that way?

SUNDIATA: My practice of poetry is rooted in my experiences in black culture, and more specifically in the black Baptist church in New York and in the South. I was born and raised in East Harlem, but I always had one foot in South Carolina, and I also have relatives in Florida. So the culture of the black Baptist church both in the North and in the South greatly influenced my fascination with language, with drama, with theater, with music—all of it.

MOYERS: What were you hearing as a child in those churches?

SUNDIATA: I think the first thing I heard was language—which I had a love for anyway—and more accurately the whole idea of the text that existed between the spoken word from the pulpit and the music. Somehow or other, although they were separate, the spoken word and the music came together to form a sort of living text. Of course, I couldn't name it in that way as a child, but I knew the preaching styles of each of the ministers and I could imitate them. I'd listen to the cadences—where they

There's poetry in the language I speak.
There's poetry, therefore,
in my culture, and in this place.

breathed and where they paused—then I'd listen to the relationship between the choir and the piano player or the organist and the preacher's sermon.

MOYERS: What relationship?

SUNDIATA: For example, the preacher would say something, and then the organist might comment on it by playing a chord or just a few notes. Or the choir might comment in some way. There was *always* a vocal response from the audience, someone testifying as to the felt truth of the word, of that text. I think all those elements are still alive in what I do now.

MOYERS: When I was growing up in East Texas, I would occasionally visit a black church. The enthusiasm and passion were striking. The music rose from some deep vein of inner experience.

SUNDIATA: Yes. I think the passion has to do with the way people come to those churches to experience God at *that* moment in *that* church. Somehow that experience is itself a way of knowing. The aim there is actually to create a ritual that allows one to experience God, and that's how I think of poetry and performance. What's important for me is the *experience* of the poetry. Reading print-based poetry provides another sort of experience which may be more personal and which is not necessarily less powerful, but it is very different.

MOYERS: So when you broke out into singing last night, that wasn't just the entertainer in you.

SUNDIATA: Well, no. We call it oralizing, you know. That's part of my reference point and part of my ground. What I do is music, in particular, jazz, improvisational music. One of the things I learned in listening to that music and studying that music is how important it is for each instrumentalist to develop his or her own sound.

Once you get past the level of technical proficiency, or even virtuosity, there's the question of how you sound. For example, you can hear two musicians playing the same instrument and the same song, but after a while, once they have reached full mastery and once you know their tone, then you can tell which one is playing at any moment. In poetry, developing the sound that is mine means *everything* to me. So what you referred to as singing, and what I'm calling oralizing, is a part of that.

MOYERS: Which jazz musicians most influenced you?

SUNDIATA: Charlie Parker and Jimi Hendrix and John Coltrane and his sound on his particular instrument, the tenor saxophone. Having had both these northern urban and southern rural experiences is interesting because one of the things I heard and could not name when I first heard Coltrane—I think I was fourteen or fifteen years old—were these rural agricultural sounds like the sounds of a rooster in the morning. I didn't understand that music; I just knew there was something deeply familiar about it. If you live in that situation, those associations are just ingrained.

As I began to read the literature of jazz, I started to understand that they were intentionally developing these sounds, and that, in fact, there was a period of time when you could listen to those sounds and make clear connections between rural and urban experience. Somehow all of this was being drawn together in jazz, and metaphorically that meant everything to me as a poet because I was being given ways to connect the fact that this city boy can also feel very much southern and rural. I was one generation out of being born and raised in the South, so a lot of my feelings about the earth and about nature and about being outdoors were really based on that dual link.

MOYERS: As you perform, are you improvising as you go?

SUNDIATA: My poems are completely written out, then I add the oralizing aspect, using different rhythmic patterns or musical ideas grounded in the culture I've been talking about. For example, last night—I forget which piece we were doing—but I said something, and then Darryl Grant, who was playing piano, sort of answered me. I heard him and I said something else, and I found myself pointing toward him, without looking, and he answered again. For a brief moment we had set up this completely unplanned interplay. Sometimes I'll say a line and then I'll say, "Huh?" Or I'll say a line and then say it again as if I'm answering myself. That sort of thing *only* happens in the moment.

MOYERS: And sometimes you change a line after you've done it?

SUNDIATA: Yes, that's part of working with the living word in poetry. Poetry is this live thing, so there is always a process of revising and editing. Oftentimes I do poems that I don't feel are complete yet, but I can work them out on the bandstand. Whether I'm going to perform a poem or not, I always have to hear it out loud, over and over and over and over. My feeling for the poem is never satisfied on the page. So at home when I'm working in my studio I do the same thing the kids do who walk around practicing their raps. For me there's always something about poetry that just *has* to be heard.

MOYERS: What was your first experience with poetry?

SUNDIATA: My first experiences with poetry as such were in elementary school and junior high school in the 1950s and 1960s, and I was not interested. Even at that age I felt very much an outsider in school. I loved to read. I loved the library. But, although I was a reader, the stuff we were reading and hearing in school was not interesting to me.

I don't even remember the poems. I just remember that it was an assignment and it was work. It was about memorization more than anything else, so it didn't speak to me in any way or capture my imagination. When I first heard poetry that I thought about as *poetry* was toward the end of the 1960s. I started hearing poets like Amiri Baraka and Victor Hernández Cruz who, in fact, is here at this festival.

I just spoke to him a little earlier and told him how much it meant to me when I started hearing his poems that spoke this language that I'd come to love and that spoke about this culture I'd come to know and to love and in some cases to hate. His poems made sense to me.

My experience of my humanity first came through black culture—through the language, through the church, through the neighborhood, through all of that—and when I started hearing those poets, they spoke to that. Amiri Baraka had a poem called "With Your Badd Self." I didn't know you could say that in a poem. I mean, we said that all the time in the neighborhood, but he was saying that in a poem.

MOYERS: What did it say to you?

SUNDIATA: There was a hit song by James Brown which had that line, so it was a slang term, but this man made literature out of it and that really enabled me. It opened up a door and said, "Wait a minute! There's poetry in the language I speak. There's poetry, therefore, in my culture, and in this place."

I grew up in the projects and we never reflected on the projects, we just lived in them, but Victor Hernández Cruz and other poets started writing about the projects and people in the neighborhood. So here was some reflection, some introspection. Their poems named the world in particular ways and foregrounded things that in school were in the background or in the margins or even outside. That's how I discovered that there's poetry in the language I know and the culture I know.

MOYERS: Did you ever attempt poetry as a kid?

SUNDIATA: I only wrote imitative stuff. We used to write love letters, and many times we'd imitate lyrics we heard on records.

MOYERS: And the love letters were important?

SUNDIATA: They were *very* important. When a girl wrote me a letter, I would use a little quote sometimes, or not even quote, just plagiarize, just take a line to make my reply good. One of the most popular groups at that time was Smokey Robinson and the Miracles, and nobody could sing about romance the way Smokey could. You could cop lines for yourself and then play off them. I didn't realize until much later, as a beginning poet, how much that method had to do with learning poetry, how in fact I started with the poets I considered to be masters, in much the same way musicians do. Every guitar player, for example, has to come through Jimi Hendrix. If you want to play alto, you've got to cop Charlie Parker. You've got to listen and find out what they were doing.

MOYERS: Did Smokey Robinson influence you?

SUNDIATA: Bob Dylan said Smokey Robinson was America's greatest poet. But I think Smokey Robinson was the greatest singer *and* poet.

In his songs the loss is so deep and then he had a genius for begging to get back into good graces. We didn't do it last night, but we do something which is in the tradition of what we call the Almighty Beg. In that tradition, you see how noble and honorable it is to beg and how important it is not to be too proud to beg. So it's the use of language and sentiment that really came across to me in Smokey's music.

MOYERS: How have you been affected by the poems of Victor Hernández Cruz?

SUNDIATA: He talks about the community, and the names he uses come right out of the neighborhoods. For example, I knew someone named Little Man, one of the names he uses, and these were not names that I saw in the poetry presented in school. Therefore when I discovered this poetry, it validated the idea that poetry could be outside school and a little beyond the law as well. There's something lawful and authoritative about school curriculum, you know.

MOYERS: So you were moving beyond one culture that you didn't feel a part of and legitimating another one.

SUNDIATA: Yes, but I want to take your comment and almost switch the order, because the first thing was to assert our *own* culture—our experience and our emerging identity—and doing *that* meant rejecting something else. I came to this whole spirit of rebellion by trying to *assert* and trying to *affirm,* and finding myself not able to in certain quarters. It didn't start by rejecting something. It started as an impulse to *affirm.*

MOYERS: How did you come to write "Blink Your Eyes"?

BLINK YOUR EYES

(REMEMBERING STERLING A. BROWN)

I was on my way to see my woman
but the Law said I was on my way

thru a red light red light red light
and if you saw my woman
you could understand,
I was just being a man.
It wasn't about no light
it was about my ride
and if you saw my ride
you could dig that too, you dig?
Sunroof stereo radio black leather
bucket seats sit low you know,
the body's cool, but the tires are worn.
Ride when the hard time come, ride
when they're gone, in other words
the light was green.

I could wake up in the morning
without a warning
and my world could change:
blink you eyes.
All depends, all depends on the skin,
all depends on the skin you're living in

Up to the window comes the Law
with his hand on his gun
what's up? what's happening?
I said I guess
that's when I really broke the law.
He said *a routine, step out the car*
a routine, *assume the position.*
Put your hands up in the air
you know the routine, like you just don't care.
License and registration.
Deep was the night and the light
from the North Star on the car door, deja vu
we've been through this before,
why did you stop me?
Somebody had to stop you.
I watch the news, you always lose.
You're unreliable, that's undeniable.
This is serious, you could be dangerous.

I could wake up in the morning
without a warning
and my world could change:
blink you eyes.
All depends, all depends on the skin,
all depends on the skin you're living in

New York City, they got laws
can't no bruthas drive outdoors,
in certain neighborhoods, on particular streets
near and around certain types of people.
They got laws.
All depends, all depends on the skin
all depends on the skin you're living in.

SUNDIATA: Actually, that poem presents a common experience for males of color—African American and Latino males. Their encounters with the police and their being judged on the basis of skin color and the things that can happen as a result of that are entirely common. "Blink Your Eyes" comes out of that experience of being stopped by the police and not being given the benefit of the doubt, as a citizen *should* be, and having an unjust encounter come out of that. That's the source of the poem. And I also wanted to testify against the deforming experiences that have transformed so many lives and how many of those men have somehow managed to transcend those experiences.

If we just go back to the days of slavery when it was illegal for the slave to bear witness against the slave master, then you can see that in this case I wanted to make *that kind* of testimony too. I wanted to call out against the injustice of that kind of treatment. I wanted to bring testimony, to bear witness to the importance of that injustice.

MOYERS: There's a line in one of your poems that says the truth will not be told by the battles you win or lose, but by the stories we believe in. What kind of stories do you believe in?

SUNDIATA: That line refers to the mythic dimensions of poetry, of this narrative that I'm creating and that other poets create. For example, I have a poem about Jimi Hendrix which really creates a story about his life and the meaning of his life. That he lived and died is a fact. The meaning that we make of that fact becomes the story and the thing that people believe and invest in.

MOYERS: A repetition runs throughout "Blink Your Eyes." Why is that?

SUNDIATA: The line is, "All depends, all depends on the skin, / all depends on the skin you're living in." Part of it is just musical pattern, a rhythmic pattern, but the repetition also drives home the fact. Each time the line repeats it should add something to its meaning. We need to understand as fully and as deeply as possible just how much race—the color of one's skin—in this country and in the world is destiny. In many cases, you could say that skin color determines *everything*.

MOYERS: The audience loves your *"Dijerrido."* Tell me about the *dijerrido*.

SUNDIATA: Craig Harris introduced that instrument to me. He was the band leader last night, and he was the composer of that music. We work and collaborate together a great deal. Craig encountered that instrument on tour in Australia. He met some Aboriginal folk who introduced it to him and taught him about its ritual use and how to play it. What fascinated me about it is not only its deep sound but also the circular breathing technique that you need to play it. When played with masterful technique, so that one plays while both inhaling and exhaling, the sound is continuous.

This technique challenges your notions of what breathing is. If you don't know anything about this technique, you wonder how anybody can possibly exhale for two or three minutes, so this really magical thing happens because it's beyond what I know to be human capability. My fascination with that instrument has to do with this magic that's taking place.

DIJERRIDO

In your right mind
you say it can't
be done: *the highwire walk*
without the wire.
You exhale and breathe-in
without pause,
for as long as you can feel
one seamless stream.
The music never breaks,
it stops when you stop.
The word for this is dijerrido
and circular breathing,
the switching point
between what you hear
and what you can be led

to believe: wind
moving through wood,
the pressure of blood
against the walls of veins,
the pull of ovum and sperm,
the dreamy mantra of the Interstate
turning into a drowsy hum.
You could like being lost
once you've come this far
what you dream up is deeper
than what you know.
Like the sound the mind makes
at the root, only lower
below habits of thinking, below
the unseen motion
of synapse and hook, of a sigh, of a gaze.
What story does it tell?
Wood and lung and air
at the end of breathing
as we know it to be,
things we cannot explain,
the spells we want to be under.

MOYERS: "You could like being lost / once you've come this far . . ." Come from where and lost in what?

SUNDIATA: To me the sound of the *dijerrido* transforms the space and transforms your presence for the moment—you sort of trip; you go in directions and to places that maybe you didn't intend—it really *does* allow you to do that. So the sound helps you to get lost in your imagination. That's why I say, "You could like being lost"— you could like being out of your right mind under these conditions.

MOYERS: You mean the mind that only thinks logically? Sometimes a poet must be "out of her mind" in that sense?

SUNDIATA: Absolutely. And you've *got* to hear voices, from wherever they come. Sometimes I guess my own voice is coming in different kinds of ways, and I have to trust that there *is* something there.

MOYERS: That's the challenge young poets and writers—all artists—face: to learn to trust their inner lives.

SUNDIATA: One of the interesting things to me about the present time is this whole resurgence and revitalization of poetry that is going on. I think part of it has to do with the way in which people have really been beaten up and abused by language, to the point where they've become deeply distrustful. Much of language has gotten to the point where people don't feel they can trust it anymore. Advertising, for example, doesn't mean what it says. You think it means one thing, but it's really about something else. I think the cumulative effect is that the language has been denatured in a way. In many cases it's become a manipulative tool.

So I think people come to poetry now and expect at least to hear honest language. Whether you feel some alignment with the poet or not, I believe the sense is that this man or this woman is going to tell you what is in his or her heart and mind, and he or she is going to be as authentic and as up front about that as possible. This person before you is going to take a stand. He or she is not going to try to manipulate you but will speak about his or her life and times as it has been actually experienced. That's worth everything to me now.

MOYERS: What about those lines "what you dream up is deeper / than what you know" from *"Dijerrido"*?

SUNDIATA: That's my way of talking about the power of the imagination, and the other side of that is how estranged I feel we as a culture have become from our imaginations, from trusting the realm of dreams. Often we think that dreams are something that happened *to* us, when in fact the dreams *are* us. Those dreams come out of our deepest being, out of our innermost lives.

MOYERS: "Everything in the dream is the dreamer."

SUNDIATA: Yes. So, I wonder if it's enough to rely simply on what we know on a conscious level when there is a deeper area, a wellspring below that which is resourceful, regenerative, and useful.

That's where the sound of the *dijerrido* takes us, and really quickly. The sound is so visceral and so deep that it really takes us to that place at the root of mind, below habits of thinking. It's at that level that we know as much as we can ever know about anything. That is the level at which we truly love, at which we truly exist, at which we truly form friendships, and it's at that level that we experience human solidarity.

Wherever I can find a place to sit down and write, that is my home.

MARY TALLMOUNTAIN

Mary TallMountain was born in Nulato, Alaska, to a Koyukon-Atha-baskan mother and a Scotch-Irish signal corpsman. At age six, when her mother died, she became the first village child to be adopted out by an Anglo American couple. Her spiritual connection to her birthplace, her family, and her native culture inspired much of her poetry. Mary TallMountain died on September 2, 1994. The Mary TallMountain Circle in San Francisco now produces, promotes, and distributes her work and continues her support for Native American and Tenderloin writers.

MOYERS: You have written that you spent most of your childhood in violent revolt. Against what?

TALLMOUNTAIN: Against being taken out of my own society, my own culture. I was six at that time. My mother, Mary Joe, had tuberculosis—which was rampant in the Arctic region—and because my mother was terminally ill, the government doctor and his wife asked to adopt me. It caused quite a furor in the village because it hadn't been done before in that little village.

MOYERS: What was the population?

TALLMOUNTAIN: A hundred people. On the Yukon River, a hundred miles south of the Arctic Circle, and a hundred twenty miles west of Fairbanks. If I had been a boy, they *definitely* would not have given me up; but being a girl, they could do it.

MOYERS: And they voted to do it? The council?

TALLMOUNTAIN: Yes, the council did. Finally.

MOYERS: And so you did go with the couple who adopted you?

TALLMOUNTAIN: Yes. I was really sad, because I was leaving my home, but we came in the outside passage to Seattle on a steamer called the *Victoria,* and I thought the new country around Seattle was beautiful.

I made a few friends just before school started. Then in school I was put on stage, as described in a poem called "Indian Blood"—I was dressed in my parka and my mukluks and my velvet mittens and a knit cap. It was summertime, but they had me in winter dress on stage, and the white children laughed at me and pointed. I just rebelled. I got very angry. They thought I was a thing of humor.

INDIAN BLOOD

On the stage I stumbled,
my fur boot caught
on a slivered board.
Rustle of stealthy giggles.

Beendaaga' made of velvet
crusted with crystal beads
hung from brilliant tassels of wool,
wet with my sweat.

Children's faces stared.
I felt their flowing force.
Did I crouch like *goh*
in the curious quiet?

They butted to the stage,
darting questions; pointing.
        Do you live in an igloo?
        Hah! You eat blubber!

Hemmed in by ringlets of brass,
grass-pale eyes,
the fur of *daghooda-aak*
trembled.

Late in the night
I bit my hand until it was
pierced
with moons of dark
Indian blood.

beendaaga'	mittens
goh	rabbit
daghooda-aak	caribou parka

MOYERS: You were no longer in your native culture and you were not accepted in your new culture.

TALLMOUNTAIN: That's right. And when I went back to my village, fifty years later, I was not really accepted there either.

MOYERS: Fifty years later . . .

TALLMOUNTAIN: Yes, I can't blame them. Fifty years later *is* a long time! And I must have looked pretty white to them, just as I looked very Indian to the children outside. It took me a while to realize that I am a bridge between both cultures.

MOYERS: I've heard that when you were young you were so full of such anger that you once bit your own hand.

TALLMOUNTAIN: Until the blood ran.

MOYERS: You were . . .

TALLMOUNTAIN: Six. When these children began to laugh at me—yes, I was six.

MOYERS: And you bit like a wolf?

TALLMOUNTAIN: Yes.

MOYERS: Has poetry helped you live between two worlds, and to deal with anger?

TALLMOUNTAIN: Yes. It helped me to see that I just did not hate anyone and to write about these things without any bias.

MOYERS: How did poetry help you reconcile these two people living inside of you, the Indian and the white?

TALLMOUNTAIN: First of all, I started writing letters to the little girl who lived inside me. And I keep journals, intensely long journals, and I used those journals to write to this little girl.

MOYERS: This little girl?

TALLMOUNTAIN: My little child, me.

MOYERS: But which "me"? The Indian—or the white?

TALLMOUNTAIN: The Indian. I was a white woman speaking to the little Indian child whom she had neglected so long.

MOYERS: And what did you talk about?

TALLMOUNTAIN: We talked about how beautiful she was, and how sad it was that we had to part. For so long. I spent a lot of time apologizing to that little girl in me because I had neglected her so long.

MOYERS: How did this conversation start?

TALLMOUNTAIN: I think the poetic muse gave me that start.

MOYERS: The poetic muse?

TALLMOUNTAIN: Yes, my spirit guide I don't know just exactly where she lives, but she lives in my imagination and she comes to see me. She's like my wolf.

MOYERS: You also write about talking with your grandmother, your mother, and two aunts.

TALLMOUNTAIN: Every morning we talk about each other. We talk about me, what I'm doing right now, and how my spirit is doing—what is happening to it, here, in this place—and I lay my problems before them. They're the women that I speak with mostly.

MOYERS: Those women from your past are a powerful part of your life.

TALLMOUNTAIN: They *are* the powerful people to whom I owe my life and my power. And I am a powerful person too.

MOYERS: I like very much this poem about your grandmother, "Matmiya." Your grandmother's name was Matmiya?

MATMIYA

FOR MY GRANDMOTHER

I see you sitting
Implanted by roots
Coiled deep from your thighs.
Roots, flesh red, centuries pale.
Hairsprings wound tight
Through fertile earthscapes
Where each layer feeds the next
Into depths immutable.

Though you must rise, must
Move large and slow
When it is time, O my

Gnarled mother-vine, ancient
As vanished ages,
Your spirit remains
Nourished,
Nourishing me.

I see your figure wrapped in skins
Curved into a mound of earth
Holding your rich dark roots.
Matmiya,
I see you sitting.

TALLMOUNTAIN: Yes, Matmiya.

MOYERS: What does it mean in English?

TALLMOUNTAIN: Mountain. She's as strong as a mountain. She is a powerful woman. She controlled six sons and their father. She really did. So I called her my "mountain grandmother," Matmiya.

MOYERS: And there's one I also like addressed to your aunt. It enabled me to understand how you could indeed have a conversation such as you describe with the women from your past.

TALLMOUNTAIN: Oh, yes. You know there is no word for goodbye in our original tongue. When the Athabaskans parted company they didn't say goodbye, they said, "Tłaa!" Like that. "Tłaa!" Almost an expletive. Very sharp. So I wrote this poem.

THERE IS NO WORD FOR GOODBYE

Sokoya, I said, looking through
    the net of wrinkles into
    wise black pools
    of her eyes.

What do you say in Athabaskan
    when you leave each other?
    What is the word
    for goodbye?

A shade of feeling rippled
> the wind-tanned skin.
> Ah, nothing, she said,
> watching the river flash.

She looked at me close.
> We just say, Tłaa. That means,
> See you.
> We never leave each other.
> When does your mouth
> say goodbye to your heart?

She touched me light
> as a bluebell.
> You forget when you leave us,
> You're so small then.
> We don't use that word.

We always think you're coming back,
> but if you don't,
> we'll see you some place else.
> You understand.
> There is no word for goodbye.

> *sokoya:*   aunt (mother's sister)

MOYERS: And that's how the conversation goes on over the years. You never say goodbye to the past.

TALLMOUNTAIN: Tłaa!

MOYERS: Yet you went back to this village after you had been gone fifty years, and they didn't greet you heartily, did they?

TALLMOUNTAIN: No. A few greeted me heartily, but the others seemed to be a little bit angry somehow. They thought that maybe after being in the white world I was stuck up.

MOYERS: So when you got home, it wasn't home?

TALLMOUNTAIN: No. Only the land was home. The land and the animals. You see, those dogs howl at night. They're like my wolf. They howl during the night, and it's haunting. That's what I remember.

MOYERS: Tell me about the wolf.

TALLMOUNTAIN: About the wolf? Oh, you mean how did I find the wolf?

MOYERS: Yes.

THE LAST WOLF

the last wolf hurried toward me
through the ruined city
and I heard his baying echoes
down the steep smashed warrens
of Montgomery Street and past
the few ruby-crowned highrises
left standing
their lighted elevators useless

passing the flicking red and green
of traffic signals
baying his way eastward
in the mystery of his wild loping gait
closer the sounds in the deadly night
through clutter and rubble of quiet blocks

I heard his voice ascending the hill
and at last his low whine as he came
floor by empty floor to the room
where I sat
in my narrow bed looking west, waiting
I heard him snuffle at the door and
I watched
he trotted across the floor

he laid his long gray muzzle
on the spare white spread
and his eyes burned yellow
his small dotted eyebrows quivered

Yes, I said.
I know what they have done.

TALLMOUNTAIN: Oh, he came to me in the hospital. I had been having a very bad bout with cancer, and I was sitting in the half-dark night and all of a sudden I realized that there was a wolf somewhere here. I looked around and the wolf was under my bed, one of those tall hospital beds. I quickly got pencil and paper and I scribbled this poem. He shuffled his feet—I felt his paws shuffle down there under the bed—and I'm sure he helped me write the poem. You see, he's here now. He's *always* here. He's right here between us, or at my side.

MOYERS: The muse comes as the wolf.

TALLMOUNTAIN: Yes.

MOYERS: Is the wolf like the ones you remember as a child in the village?

TALLMOUNTAIN: Yes, like the dogs. The dogs were cousins to the wolf.

MOYERS: Do people say, "Oh, Mary, you're—you're—"

TALLMOUNTAIN: Crazy? No one ever has. No one even ever laughs. So I believe that they believe me.

MOYERS: The wolf, the dogs—all were part of that village.

TALLMOUNTAIN: Of course. It was my roots. It still *is* my roots. The river. I could close my eyes this moment and be sitting on the bank of the river. I can see that river going by. I can see the clouds, the way they were, great immense white clouds making shadows on the river, and the long land that just stretches out and out and out.

MOYERS: And why were the people angry at you?

TALLMOUNTAIN: I guess they didn't want to be reminded of the terrible things that happened when I was adopted out. That was considered something not to be done at that time because children were an asset, you see. A little boy was a particular asset and, as a matter of fact, the doctor and his wife wanted to take both children, but the council said no—they could take the little girl, but not the little boy because he'd grow up and be a hunter.

MOYERS: He would gather food for the tribe?

TALLMOUNTAIN: Yes. So I had to begin my life without my brother.

MOYERS: What do you remember most vividly about your mother, Mary Joe?

TALLMOUNTAIN: Her hands.

MOYERS: Because . . .

TALLMOUNTAIN: Because they dealt with fish, which are a holy creature. And she used a tłaamaas, a stone knife—now they're made of metal—but at that time they were stone. She had salmon laid on a table, with its belly up, and she just drew a line down there. Then there were the eggs. I did a poem about this.

THE HANDS OF MARY JOE

Her hands lift and tend King Salmon
Cherish the skin of her child
Light as willow-buds
Thread a needle's invisible eye
In dim flickering lamplight
Fingers weave patterns
In violet and amber beads

The brown-pearl hands
Etched with tiny lines
Curled into little cups
Stiffened, yet with
Delicate touch
Draw a comb of tortoise shell
Through dark-silvered hair

Hands that flowed in rhythms
Smooth as riverdrift
Attuned to daily music
Of her hidden life
Now lie folded in her lap
Trembling minutely
The hands of Mary Joe
Await
The approaching silence

for my mother,
an Athabaskan Woman

MOYERS: You said your mother honored the holiness of all things.

TALLMOUNTAIN: Of *all* things. She believed that. She lived by that, and I live by that.

MOYERS: You were baptized a Christian, were you not?

TALLMOUNTAIN: Yes. Yes, I'm a Christian, but I follow much of the ritual of the Indian. We have only one God—and we know that—but we follow two paths. Why not? Why not worship Him twice. Him or Her.

MOYERS: Why did you wait until you were fifty-five to publish poetry?

TALLMOUNTAIN: I was too busy fighting cancer and making my living in between. And I was still fighting, fighting the new culture.

MOYERS: All these years later.

TALLMOUNTAIN: All these years later I was still fighting it. Until I started writing, really. When I started writing that made my whole life. Then I felt I was someone and I could say what needed to be said.

MOYERS: When you read poems about your natural mother's hands, I can see her gift to you, but what about your adopted mother? What was *her* gift to you? She was the wife of the doctor in the village, the white doctor.

TALLMOUNTAIN: Yes. She gave me this language and she gave me my first poems. We talked poetry back and forth, over and over and over again. She introduced me to Wordsworth and other poets. She had me read aloud to her.

MOYERS: Well, where do you find home now, spiritually? Is it in that little village? Is it in this culture? Is it in your first mother's world? Second mother's world? Where is home?

TALLMOUNTAIN: It's wherever I am with them. They are with me wherever I am, so that's my home. I'm in the place where I need to be writing. Wherever I can find a place to sit down and write, that is my home.

QUINCY TROUPE

Quincy Troupe is the reigning "World Heavyweight Poetry Champion," a title he won at the 1994 Taos Poetry Circus. Born and raised in the city of jazz, St. Louis, his poetry has been deeply influenced by the improvisational brilliance of jazz. He frequently reads his poems in places where poetry is not often heard, including bars and prisons. He teaches at the University of California, San Diego.

MOYERS: The simplest of all questions: Why do you write poetry?

TROUPE: I write poetry because I *need* to write poetry. I need the music of language and the instant communication that I feel I get in writing poetry.

MOYERS: Interesting phrase—"the music of language."

TROUPE: I think every language has a musical core. I call our language the American language rather than English because the sounds of the American language come from *all* our different ethnic communities, and these sounds are beautiful to me. As a poet, I try to get the music that's underneath all of that. I come from the Midwest, from St. Louis. I grew up listening to blues and to the old African American people talking in bars and churches and walking the streets and in funeral homes and barbershops and in beauty parlors and in parks, and I especially loved to listen to jazz musicians talk. So all that musical language that I grew up listening to is what I try to make *my* language.

MOYERS: Your words often hang out there—apart from any apparent meaning, existing just for the experience of the sound of them.

TROUPE: I think that's what poetry is *supposed* to do, because one of the things we have to remember is that poetry at first was song—it was the troubadours, the griots, the singers.

MOYERS: "The griots"?

TROUPE: The griots were African troubadours, men who sang and brought songs to the villages. I look at myself as that kind of person because I want the words to sing.

MOYERS: Why?

I don't think poetry can be dead—it can only be alive.

TROUPE: When you read to diverse audiences—white Americans, African Americans, Asian Americans, Hispanic Americans—you find that song cuts across all these categories. If the language is rhythmic, if it's musical, then it touches people directly.

MOYERS: What do you think is the source of the power of language?

TROUPE: Language is evocative. It evokes something that I think is there in every human being. Sometimes sound alone—the beauty of the wind in the mountains, the beauty of the wind in trees—touches some secret place inside you, and I want my *words* to do that. I want them somehow to approximate that feeling.

MOYERS: But isn't music more accessible to the untutored than poetry?

TROUPE: Yes, I think that's true. Music doesn't have any meaning beyond what it is, and poets are trying to do that with words which have dictionary meanings; but poets are often after the connotation rather than the literal meaning of words. Language can be used so that it is seamless and also healing. Poetry has the power of healing the spirit and, like music, poetry can calm you. Certain music can make me feel calm at the core, and I would like to see poetry evolve to that same state so it can also be soothing and healing.

MOYERS: Healing for whom?

TROUPE: I'd like to say the entire American audience, because I think America needs healing as a nation. I would like to think that my work could serve that purpose. I would at least like to think that everybody could identify with some of what I write, and that some of it could be healing. We need to talk about certain things that afflict us as a nation, and this is really serious for me because I know that as an African American, I am *wholly* an American.

African Americans have no place to go back to—we were brought here from Africa and we can't go back. The metaphor that Alex Haley gave us was that every African American could go back to Africa, but, in fact, we *can't* do that. We can't, like John Kennedy, trace our roots back to a place in Ireland a thousand years ago. One of the most jealous moments of my life was when I saw Kennedy stand and say, "I have ancestors who grew up here a thousand years ago." I said, "Jesus, I wish I could do that!" But I *can't*. So I must think of *this* place as *my* place, and I need to see everyone here come together in some way. As a poet, that is one of my primary commitments.

MOYERS: I suspect that's why you so often go home to your old neighborhood in St. Louis.

TROUPE: Yes. It's important for me to return because language comes out of a place—in my case, St. Louis. You're from Texas, and when you go back to Texas I know you hear certain things that just automatically wake something up in you.

MOYERS: I do begin to speak differently. Here people say, "You don't have a Texas accent," but when I go home, I *do*.

TROUPE: When I go back to St. Louis, people come up to me and say, "Quincy" or whatever nickname they called me, and right away I'm *back* there; and the language that I hear there even now is the language that I grew up listening to. I think it's important for a writer to use the ear as well as the mind and go back to where he or she came from and listen to the words, the cadences, the sentences, the paragraphs, because I think we begin to drift away from those beginnings.

MOYERS: What are you hearing now when you're there?

TROUPE: I hear pretty much the same rhythms, but the words change. For example, we would say something like "Be cool," but now they say, "Take a chill pill." Language changes. Language is living. It gets old. You renew it. You try to make it better.

MOYERS: How was it you became a poet?

TROUPE: It was odd. I always read—my mother was a great reader who always had all kinds of books around the house and she got me into the Bookworm Club, which is how I discovered Faulkner, Richard Wright, Langston Hughes, Sinclair Lewis—but in the neighborhood I grew up in we didn't have a lot of readers. People thought you were a sissy if you read, so we used to have to put our books in our back pockets, and that's why I wear my shirt out still—so my shirt can hang down over my books. We used to wear clothes with big pockets for our books, or we used shopping bags and put something on top of the books so we could come home without getting into fights.

MOYERS: When you read those books, did you think, "*I'm* going to do this one day"?

TROUPE: No, I never thought about it like that. I used to read Jack London a lot because Jack London took me out of St. Louis and let me escape—for example, along the trails with the Eskimo dogs—but I never thought about writing myself. When I would come back to school in the fall and the teacher would say, "Tell me what you did for the summer," I would write long detailed descriptions, but because I was just a kid and an athlete I didn't know what they were leading to.

MOYERS: How did jazz and blues influence your poetry?

TROUPE: They shaped it in very important ways because both jazz and blues have distinct languages and, of all the cultural contributions that the United States has made to the world, those two have been the most profound. The blues is constructed close to the way Americans, and especially African Americans from the Midwest and the South, speak. We tend to speak in circles—we come back and say things over and over again, just for emphasis—and there you have the whole repetition of lines coming back like refrains. Jazz, on the other hand, can be notated. Total improvisation without notation, which you find in a lot of African music, is at the other end of the spectrum, but jazz is someplace in between—it's notated with room for improvisation. So jazz provides the model for taking a text and improvising on it in a performance. That's why performance is part of the whole concept of poetry for me.

MOYERS: Does a poem sometimes have a meaning for you when you read to an audience that is different from the meaning you intended when you wrote it? Does the experience with each audience create a new sensation?

TROUPE: When I work with musicians, I have the text in front of me, but as I read it I start to improvise on it—I take out some lines, and I might make up others as I go, and sometimes I might chant. I also might do something off whatever the musician is doing. So the poem changes, but I always try to come back to the text. What is happening here is that I become a conduit, a vessel through which language flows at the point of creation, and if I'm working with a musician, we are creating a different text as we go. It's creation happening right at that moment.

MOYERS: Language changes you, and you change the language. That's why language is life.

TROUPE: That's exactly right. You *are* life. *Language* is living. *You* are living. *You* change it at that moment.

MOYERS: Perhaps that's why I get more pleasure out of hearing you read than I do reading the poem myself. You are turning the language around right at the moment of creation and sending it in a whole new direction.

TROUPE: It's very important to touch the audience where they are. There's a debate going on right now about poetry in the United States between those who think that it should be performance and those who think it should be more academic. I happen to be in the academy, but I also think that, in order to get into people's blood and into people's consciousness and into people's lives, poetry has to sing.

MOYERS: You sometimes visit prisons to read your work to inmates and help them with creative writing. Why?

TROUPE: They're in prison, but they live lives that are real. They hunger to understand themselves and to understand what put them there.

MOYERS: How does poetry help them with that?

TROUPE: I'm not exactly sure how it helps them, but I've gone into enough prisons to know there are certain kinds of works that touch them, and it doesn't make any difference whether they're black or white or Hispanic or whatever. Prisoners want to hear something that's real, and they want to hear things that relate to them. Most of them have come through a hard life.

When I go into a prison, I like to read "River Town Packin House Blues" because of the violence that happened in the life of the man in that poem. I knew him and he was stripped of all kinds of feelings by his experience working in that packing house and killing every day. He was only killing cows and pigs, but after a certain point nothing had any meaning to him except his own breath. If you did something to him, he would *kill* you. *That* was his answer to everything and he had no feeling about it. To me he was a person who had been stripped of his humanity. I think a lot of prisoners have lost touch with their humanity, and they're trying to regain it, so they almost always respond to that poem.

RIVER TOWN PACKIN HOUSE BLUES

FOR STERLING BROWN

big tom was a black nigga man
cold & black
eye say, big tom was a black nigga man
black steel flesh
standin like a gladiator
soaked in animal blood, bits of flesh
wringin wet
standin at the center of death
buzzards hoverin
swingin his hamma called death
260 workdays
swingin his hamma named death

big tom was a black packin houseman

thirty years

eye say, big tom was a black packin houseman

loved them years

& swang his hamma like ol john henry, poundin nails

swang that hamma twenty years

crushin skulls

of cows & pigs, screamin fear

the man underneath slit their throats

twenty years

the man underneath slit their throats

big tom was a 'prentice for ten long years

watchin death

eye say, big tom was 'prentice for ten long years

smellin death

was helper to a fat, white man

who got slow

eye say, was helper to a fat, white man

who swang a hamma

till he couldn't do it no mo

so he taught big tom how to kill

with a hamma

eye say, he taught big tom how to kill

& twenty years of killin is a lot

to bring home

eye say, twenty years of killin is a lot

to bring home

& drinkin to much gin & whiskey can make

a gentle/man blow

don't chu know

eye say, drinkin to much gin & whiskey

can make a good man sho nuff blow

don't chu know

big tom beat his wife, after killin all day

his six chillun, too

eye say, tom beat his wife, after killin all day

his young chillun, too
beat em so awful bad, he beat em right out they shoes
screamin blues
eye say, he beat em so awful bad
he made a redeyed, hungry alley rat
spread the news, bout dues these black-blues people was payin
couldn't even bite em, cause of the dues these
black-blues people was payin

big tom killed six men, maimed a couple of hundred
& never served a day
eye say, big tom killed six men, maimed a couple a hundred
never in jail one day
the figures coulda been higher
but the smart ones, they ran away
eye say, the number that was maimed, or dead, coulda been higher
but the smart ones, they ran away
saved from the graveyard
another day
the smart ones
they ran away

big tom workin all day, thirty years
uh huh, sweatin heavy
eye say, big tom swingin his hamma, all right
twenty summers, outta love
eye say, big tom killin for pay, uh huh
twenty autumns, outta need
eye say, big tom dealin out murders, like a houseman
in the painyards, outta false pride
eye say, big tom drinkin heavy, uh huh
laughin loose, in taverns
eye say, big tom loose, in black communities
death fights cancel light
& big tom? he just keeps on
stumblin, all right

& twenty years of killin
is to much to bring home to love

eye say, twenty years of killin
is to much to bring home to love
& drinkin heavy gin & whiskey
can make a strong man fall in mud
eye say, drinkin to much gin & whiskey
can make a good man have bad blood
don't chu know
can make a strong man
have bad blood

big black tom was a cold, nigga man
strong & black
eye say, big black tom was a cold nigga man
hard steel flesh
& he stood, like a gladiator, soaked in animal blood
bits of flesh, soakin wet
stood, at the center, in the middle of death
sweatin vultures
swingin his hamma called death
260 workdays, for twenty years
like ol john henry, eye say
swingin his hamma named death

TROUPE: I think violence kills the spirit. We're such a violent country—our violence goes all the way back to what we did as a nation to the Native Americans and killing is just something that we do—killing is our way of responding to our problems—so when you find people whose spirits have been brutalized, I think the only way that you can connect with them is through a process of empathy, and sometimes you can't connect even then.

MOYERS: When we were filming your appearance the other day one of the prisoners said he was afraid both of tapping into his pain and also of letting that pain go. What was going on there?

TROUPE: I'm not sure about this because we didn't have a long conversation, but I think the only real emotion he knew was rage, and rage is something that consumes. In order to get rid of it, you have to push it down. Many African Americans, especially men, have had to push their rage down in order to live even the semblance of a normal, balanced life. In order to live anything like a normal life in this country you have to forget some things.

MOYERS: "Especially men"?

TROUPE: Black men and white men have had this problem for years in this society. It's about power and the ability to control. All of a sudden black men found themselves here, stripped of language, stripped of culture, on plantations working from can't-see to can't-see, and we were brutalized and told that we were less than human. There is great rage in that memory, and even after trying to do what we can and after telling our sons that if they go to school and graduate they will be able to move into the larger society and become bank presidents, we know *none* of it is true. People would rather hire a black woman than a black man in this country—at least that's what I and a lot of other black men sense.

MOYERS: Did *you* ever feel that rage? And could you have wound up like that guy in prison?

TROUPE: Oh, of course. I was very close to it many, many times; but I think I was helped by the whole idea of writing and of being an artist, someone who is compassionate and who also understands the psyche of this country. I also think that African Americans understand this country deeply, so I had some early help in seeing more.

MOYERS: Please explain.

TROUPE: We understand what this country *is*. We understand that it's a mélange of people. I call it a mestizo society, meaning that it is mixed or mulatto, but at the top we have white males who would like to keep it European. However, it's *not* European; it's this mélange, and that confusion is a major cause of our problems.

You have to remember that African Americans worked for whites in their houses and brought up the babies, worked in the kitchens, and really watched closely. White Americans never came to *our* houses and checked *us* out, so we know whites very well, and at this point they *don't* know us. If they *did* know us well, we wouldn't have the problems we have.

MOYERS: What would you like the country to hear?

TROUPE: First, I hope people hear the healing quality in the music of the language, and then I hope that some of the political and social and spiritual problems we face might become clear to them. Some people in the academy say poets shouldn't address political issues, but most of the greatest poets in the world have addressed political issues.

MOYERS: How do we learn to *listen* to poetry? For example, you had some difficulty at first connecting with those kids in that high school in St. Louis when we were with you. How can you help them, and me, to *hear* the poetry?

TROUPE: Let's talk about the high school kids first. High school kids are the *most* difficult to get to. You need more than one or two hours with them because they're thinking about how hip they look or what they really want to be doing, and they have also begun to buy into the system enough to think they want to move away from art. Little kids, on the other hand, dive right into metaphors, music, and imagination. But in high school, kids start to lose their imagination because all these rules and regulations are weighing them down, and they also probably see me as another teacher.

In order to listen to language people have to lose *whatever* perceptions of poetry they hold—that's what I had to do. I thought poetry was just something about dried roses and violets until I discovered that it could be about my shoestrings, about the neighborhood, about the sky, about my mother, about being a basketball player or a musician. I never thought that you could do *any* of that from reading the poetry I was given in school. Often, high school has really turned kids off to poetry because the poetry that was historically given was a poetry that had no connection to the kids' real lived lives.

For example, T. S. Eliot was writing about the Mississippi River, but because he wanted to be an Englishman, he made the Mississippi River the Thames River, and he made the bridge that goes over the Mississippi the London Bridge. What connected me to T. S. Eliot was the music in the language, so I wondered, "What *is* this music?" Then I read that he used to go down on the Mississippi River and listen to Scott Joplin, and I said, "Ragtime!" I read *The Waste Land* again and it *was* ragtime in the music of the language, but nobody told us it was ragtime and the poem is not talking about ragtime; it's talking about something else.

MOYERS: So lesson number one for understanding poetry—discover to whom the poet's been listening?

TROUPE: Yes. I think it's important to know what a poet likes and what a poet listens to. If you get close to that, maybe you can get close to what a poet is trying to do.

MOYERS: That's what you meant when you told the kids in St. Louis that if they want to write they've got to write from their *own* lives?

TROUPE: Yes. You have to make what you're coming from *live*. You have to find your central metaphor and your central meaning, and you have to make your language *live*—going back to the whole idea of language as being alive—so that when you read your poems you can become something else, a force.

MOYERS: "A force"?

TROUPE: Yes. When you're creating, you become a force. You become a conduit for the spirit to flow through, which might sound mystical but that's what it is. You become the conduit for the spirit of language to flow through. At that point you become a musician or an actor. You almost become possessed in the same that the world flows *through* you, *becomes* through you. It is healing, it is spiritual, and it is uplifting.

The whole idea of a poem as being totally academic is absurd to me. I always tell my academic friends who argue in that direction: "That's all well and good, but you're going to be talking to yourself. Don't complain that you're only talking to twenty people and that no one is buying your books. Don't walk around saying poetry is dead." I don't think poetry *can* be dead—it can *only* be alive.

MOYERS: Take a poem that is anything but mystical, the poem about Magic Johnson. I never thought I'd hear a poem about a basketball star.

A POEM FOR "MAGIC"

FOR EARVIN "MAGIC" JOHNSON, DONNELL REID & RICHARD FRANKLIN

take it to the hoop, "magic" johnson
take the ball dazzling down the open lane
herk & jerk & raise your six feet nine inch
frame into air sweating screams of your neon name
"magic" johnson, nicknamed "windex" way back in high school
cause you wiped glass backboards so clean
where you first juked & shook
wiled your way to glory
a new style fusion of shake & bake energy
using everything possible, you created your own space
to fly through—any moment now, we expect your wings
to spread feathers for that spooky take-off of yours—
then shake & glide, till you hammer home
a clotheslining deuce off glass
now, come back down with a reverse hoodoo gem
off the spin, & stick it in sweet, popping nets, clean
from twenty feet, right-side

put the ball on the floor, "magic"
slide the dribble behind your back, ease it deftly

between your bony, stork legs, head bobbing everwhichaway
up & down, you see everything on the court
off the high, yoyo patter, stop & go dribble, you shoot
a threading needle rope pass, sweet home to kareem
cutting through the lane, his skyhook pops cords
now lead the fastbreak, hit worthy on the fly
now, blindside a behind the back pinpointpass for two more
off the fake, looking the other way
you raise off balance into space
sweating chants of your name, turn, 180 degrees
off the move, your legs scissoring space, like a swimmer's
yoyoing motion, in deep water, stretching out now toward free
flight, you double pump through human trees, hang in place
slip the ball into your left hand
then deal it like a las vegas card dealer
off squared glass, into nets, living up to your singular nickname
so "bad," you cartwheel the crowd towards frenzy
wearing now your electric smile, neon as your name

in victory, we suddenly sense your glorious uplift
your urgent need to be champion
& so we cheer, rejoicing with you, for this quicksilver, quicksilver
                                        quicksilver
moment of fame, so put the ball on the floor again, "magic"
juke & dazzle, shake & bake down the lane
take the sucker to the hoop, "magic" johnson,
recreate reverse hoodoo gems off the spin,
deal alley-oop-dunk-a-thon-magician passes
now, double-pump, scissor, vamp through space
hang in place & put it all up in the sucker's face, "magic"
johnson, & deal the roundball, like the juju man that you am
like the sho-nuff shaman man that you am
"magic," like the sho-nuf spaceman, you am

TROUPE: That poem is about a game and one of the game's greatest players—he's tall, he's fast, he's graceful, he's innovative, he controls the game, and he's a champion. Basketball is about speed and quickness—when you watch it you're always asking, "Where's the replay?"—so my challenge as a poet was to re-create in motion a player playing.

Therefore, it had to be a very fast poem, but it had to start slow because basketball games start slow, then they pick up momentum before becoming a blur. The poem had to be very quick and have the momentum of a locomotive, but it also had to imitate the life that was happening there: these huge basketball players making pivots, moves, turns. All the images had to be fast, but they also had to be precise. In other words, I was trying to write that poem not as someone looking at a basketball game objectively, but as a former basketball player *from the court* in the hope that you would feel the kind of energy on the court from the inside.

MOYERS: What possessed you to write a poem about basketball in the first place?

TROUPE: I had tried to write a couple of poems about basketball, but there was always something that I couldn't get to. Then I saw Magic Johnson play, and I said to myself: "This is the greatest basketball player I've ever seen because not only is he a champion who is six feet nine and moves very fast and rebounds and scores, but he can also pass and, in fact, he would *rather* pass. Beyond that, though, he makes *everybody else* better—when they play with him, he makes everybody else better because he makes them alert."

You were asking me how to listen to a poem. Maybe you should listen to a poem the way you play when you play with Magic Johnson. When you play with him, you have to be alert at *all* times because he'll hit you in the eye with the ball if you're open and you're looking up at the basket thinking, "I know *he's* going to shoot," because he's constantly seeing *you*. He sees *everything* on the court. Like a magician, he makes you more alert and more intelligent by making you pay attention to what he's doing, because if you don't pay attention, he's going to bounce the ball off your head. If you don't pay attention he's going to make you look bad, *very* bad. Everyone knows that if they get in place, their spot, he's going to give them the ball, unselfishly, every time so they can shoot it. *That's* how you listen to a poem.

When I saw him play, I said, "I have to do something about this guy, but I don't know what I can do about him." Then one day the idea came to me to write that poem, and this is how I got the language at the end of the poem. One day during the period that I was writing it, I got on the elevator coming up to my apartment and this old lady who was already on the elevator said to me, "You sho' am dressed up today." I said, "I *what?*" She said, "You sho' am dressed up." I thought, "Sho' am?" I hadn't heard that phrase in a long time because you're supposed to say, "You sure are clean today" or "You sure are properly dressed," but she said, "You sho' am dressed up." I said: "Sho' am? Yes, Ma'am. I *sho'* am."

Now in the South, some people were juju men and witch doctors, and when Magic

Johnson played he was that kind of magic person for me; so I connected that feeling with the language of this eighty-year-old black lady on the elevator. When I came in I went straight to the typewriter thinking, "I'm going to use, 'I sho' am,'" that language given to me by that old lady come from the Old South. I wanted to celebrate that old lady whose spirit came to me and whose spirit I see in Magic, because although he's still young, he's also very old and very wise in a lot of ways.

MOYERS: He's doing some poetry himself out there on that court. That one was a favorite when you read it to the prisoners.

TROUPE: Yes. They love it. *Many* people have loved it. When I went back to St. Louis I had just finished my reading and a guy said, "You've *got* to read that Magic Johnson poem!" I get that in many places, because people have some kind of attachment to this poem. I haven't figured out what it is yet, but sometimes when people connect to a particular work of art you don't know why they do. So when somebody connects to something like that, I just say it's a part of them, because it's no longer altogether mine. When somebody howls out from the audience, "Read the Magic Johnson poem!" there's something compelling him to do that. *I* didn't say I was going to read it. *He* said it. I am just grateful at that moment that he thought enough of the poem to request it. I don't analyze the request, I just read the poem because somebody requesting something is one of the greatest honors you can receive.

MOYERS: When you're reading at a prison, does it ever occur to you that *you* could have been there?

TROUPE: In *many* instances I've thought of myself there. I was lucky growing up because, in fact, I did a lot of things that got these men into prison. I lived that same kind of life in the neighborhoods where I've lived in St. Louis, so I know what they went through. I knew what they wanted, and I understand their rage and their disappointment because I had those same feelings. I was just a little lucky—I played basketball and I was able to get out of it. I was able to move out of it and get to a safe harbor and look back and say, "Wow, that was a *terrible* sea out there! That was a *terrible* sea." What I have now might not be what I want, but it's *not* a raging sea—it hasn't got twenty-five-foot waves, and I can even swim a little bit.

MOYERS: What about the kids you teach, the affluent white kids in particular? How do they respond to the poetry that grows out of the blues and jazz? To poems about Magic Johnson?

TROUPE: I think at first they look at me askance as if they are putting up a wall and saying, "What is this guy talking about? Why is he telling me this? What does he expect from me? I'm from Connecticut. My family is wealthy. I'm white."

But I'm trying to tell them that, first of all, they're American, so we have *that* to share—we are *all* Americans—and the most essential American art birthed in this country has been jazz and blues; and they *have* to connect to that in order to understand themselves, because if they don't there's something missing. For example, if you hear an absolute racist walking down the street humming Stevie Wonder, you know there's something wrong there—there's something he's not connecting to.

I want those kids to understand that it's possible to get past a certain thing, like I got to that safe harbor. I got to that harbor but *they're* out there, too, those white kids. They think they're in a safe harbor, but they're *not*. They don't think they're out there, but they surely are, and in order to get to a real harbor, they have to go over that water—those raging seas—and they have to understand some things about themselves and about our country. They have to understand what a lot of other people have understood who have gone out and made it across those raging seas.

MOYERS: And poetry can take us across?

TROUPE: Poetry *can* take us across. Great art can take us across because it reveals our humanity and puts us in touch with it. That's what *all* great art is supposed to do.

Lucille Clifton, Quincy Troupe, Jimmy Santiago Baca

DAISY ZAMORA

Daisy Zamora was active in the National Sandinista Liberation Front that overthrew the dictator of her native Nicaragua in 1979. When the revolution was over she served as vice minister of culture and returned to writing poetry about family relations, in particular the life of women in her country. Well-known as a painter and psychologist, she currently teaches literature at the Universidad Centroamericana in Managua, Nicaragua.

MOYERS: When you took part in the Nicaraguan revolution, did you fight? Were you a combatant?

ZAMORA: Yes, I participated in the last part of the struggle when we were fighting throughout Nicaragua. I had to fight with a squad in the city of Managua, and I felt the bullets around me. I was the only woman in the squad. I was so afraid that I might die in the fighting that I took some provisions from my knapsack—we had to carry these knapsacks—and I put all my poems in there instead. I thought that if by chance I were killed, somebody would find them, and they were all I had to survive by.

MOYERS: You carried your poems into battle?

ZAMORA: Yes. I carried my poems all the time.

MOYERS: Writing poetry must be—

ZAMORA: It's my life. I could not live if I didn't write poetry. I have to express myself, and I cannot imagine what life would be if I were not a poet. I cannot imagine how other people live without poetry, because for me poetry is a way of living my life, a way of feeling life. It just comes naturally from the inside.

MOYERS: Is poetry that real to the people in your country?

ZAMORA: Yes. It's *very* real. It's part of our everyday life, our history, our culture. I think it's the most important cultural tradition we have. We also have a very popular sport, baseball, which is an inheritance from the United States' many invasions and interventions. So I always think that we have two national sports: baseball and poetry. *Everybody* in Nicaragua loves poetry.

*I cannot imagine how other people live without poetry,
because for me poetry is a way of living my life, a way
of feeling life.*

MOYERS: Do people turn out for poetry readings the way they have turned out here at this festival?

ZAMORA: Yes. I have been really happy here because this audience—so attentive, so sensitive, and participating so fully with questions to the poets—makes me feel as if I were still in Nicaragua. In Nicaragua poetry readings are natural occurrences, so people come and listen to you, they give you opinions on your poems, they ask questions, and they might also tell you that they wrote something similar, or that they had an idea like the one in your poem. So in Nicaragua a poetry reading is an event in which everybody participates, the audience is not just listening. After you read your poems, they immediately all start giving their different opinions about your work.

MOYERS: As a woman, you fought as a combatant in your country's revolution and yet, as a woman, you have had a hard time being a poet.

ZAMORA: That's the way life is. I mean, I was not anybody special, almost all women in Nicaragua participated in the revolution, and many women participated as combatants—some women even directed whole columns of people—but when life starts to settle down after the revolution, then you have to start ordering society, and at that point there is a tendency to go back to old cultural patterns, especially in Latin America. So it was hard for us women who had gained our space in the revolutionary process to maintain the space we had gained, and that's why my poetry also has to do with the difficulties of being a woman in everyday life, because having a revolution doesn't mean that a miracle has happened and that everything will change. The revolution is only the *beginning* of a change.

MOYERS: Your poem "Lineage" is about the difficulty of being a woman. Why did you have to look for the women of your house? Where were they?

LINEAGE

I am looking for the women of my house.

I've always known my great grandfather's story:
scientist, diplomat, liberal politician
and father of many distinguished sons.

But Isolina Reyes, married to him
from the age of fifteen until her death,
what was her story?

My maternal grandfather graduated *Cum Laude*
from the University of Philadelphia.
We still preserve his dissertation written in 1900.
He oversaw the construction of miles of track
and only a sudden death cut short his dream
of bringing the railroad to the Atlantic Coast.
Nine sons and daughters mourned him.

And his wife Rudecinda, who gave birth
to those children, who nursed and cared for them,
what do I know about her?

I am looking for the women of my house.

My other grandfather was the patriarch
beneath whose shadow the whole family lived
(including brothers-in-law, cousins, distant relatives,
friends, acquaintances, and even enemies).
He spent his life accumulating the fortune
they wasted when he died.

And my grandmother Ilse, widowed and impoverished,
what could she do but die?

I am looking for myself, for all of them:
      the women of my house.

      TRANSLATED BY MARGARET RANDALL AND ELINOR RANDALL

ZAMORA: As you see in that poem, I don't even mention the names of my grandfathers—I just say, "my maternal grandfather" and "my paternal grandfather"—but I refer to my great-grandmother and each of my grandmothers specifically by name. I mention Isolina Reyes, I mention Rudecinda, I mention Ilse; and yet, even though I give their names, I know almost nothing about them *except* their names.

MOYERS: These women were not discussed in the family? They weren't part of the family story?

ZAMORA: They were part of the family story, but all the stories you heard repeated over and over from the time when you were a small child are stories about what the men of the family did. You never heard what these women did because they were involved in minor activities which have no lasting impact. I mean, maybe they did embroidery, or maybe they cared for children, or maybe they kept all the family memories in albums, but I never learned what they *felt*. I never learned what they *thought*.

M O Y E R S :   And for sure they were not cast as heroes.

Z A M O R A :   No, these women were not considered heroes, but because the men were involved in politics and because they constructed things, the men *were* heroes. So these women are like shadows, ghosts that come in and go out, and I cannot touch them, I cannot hold on to them.

M O Y E R S :   Has your poetry helped you to connect with them? Are you better able now to experience their presence?

Z A M O R A :   Yes, of course. That's part of why I write. I want to truly know their faces. I have the photographs of some of them, and sometimes I look at them and just wonder what did these women dream? What did they feel? Nobody knows.

M O Y E R S :   One of my favorites among your poems is "Loyal Housewife." Who were you writing about here?

Loyal Housewife

Everything ended with the Honeymoon:
the orange blossoms, the love letters,
the childish weeping.

Now you crawl at your master's feet,
first in his harem,
taken or abandoned according to his will.
Mother of children who bear his name,
bemoaning your lot
            beside a clothesline heavy with diapers,
wringing your heart
            until it is purified in sheets and towels.
Accustomed to the shouts, the humiliation
of a hand held out for crumbs.
A woman cornered, a plaintive shadow
suffering migraines, varicose veins, diabetes.

A young girl kept for show
who married her first boyfriend
and grew old listening to the distant song of life
            from her place of wifely honor.

T R A N S L A T E D   B Y   M A R G A R E T   R A N D A L L   A N D   E L I N O R   R A N D A L L

ZAMORA: This poem was inspired by a real woman whom I love very deeply. She wasn't a relative of mine, she was just a lady I met when I was young who often told me the story of her marriage and how she lost all her dreams. Later, when I started listening to what was happening and looking around me, I saw that many, many women from the generation of my mother lost their lives this way. So I wrote that poem.

MOYERS: It has been as true in our culture as well as in yours: "A young girl kept for show / who married her first boyfriend / and grew old listening to the distant song of life / from her place of wifely honor."

ZAMORA: Yes, for so many women life just passes by and they sit, doing nothing. I mean, they are losing their lives.

MOYERS: Were you destined for that life, as a child? And if you were, how did you escape it?

ZAMORA: Because I was born a woman I was destined to that life, but fortunately for me there were people in my life who helped me to escape that destiny. I have a personal story which is perhaps not interesting for anybody except me, but I was born into a family of women who wanted to be different, among them my father's mother. Although she was a traditional woman in many ways, she always told me stories that made my imagination grow. She studied French and English, and she spoke both languages fluently. She read a lot, too, though she was an eclectic reader who would read anything that came into her hands and, actually, my name comes from her reading. She had read *Daisy Miller* by Henry James and she thought the name was lovely, so she named her first child Daisy. She said she was the first person to bring the name to Nicaragua.

But her daughter Daisy discovered that she had cancer when she became a young woman and, without saying anything, she decided to kill herself. She was eighteen years old when one morning she just drank poison and died. Suicide is something so striking that there is no explanation for anybody. My grandparents were deeply shocked by her death.

When her oldest son—my father—married, his first baby was a girl, and my grandmother wanted her to be named Daisy after the child she had lost, but because there was so much tragedy around the name, nobody wanted to give it to her so she got some other name. When I was born they decided it was time to give this pleasure to my grandmother, and I was named Daisy after this aunt of mine. I think my having the name caused my grandparents to pay special attention to me among all their grandchildren.

Because I knew about this tragedy, my name was a powerful influence on me as I grew up. Maybe my name also in a way determined my life because I was always reminded of how I got it. You can imagine that nobody had read *Daisy Miller* in Nicaragua, but because everybody was reading the comic strips of Donald Duck and his girlfriend, Daisy, they all said my name came from the Disney characters. So you can see why my grandmother always made a point of explaining to me how I was honored by the name.

Maybe the story of my name combined with the magical surroundings where I grew up—the atmosphere of the old house and the stories I heard and the way the city was with all the old traditional processions—all helped me to develop a different way of looking at life. In any case, I escaped the destiny of the women who had come before me and I began to look at life as a poet.

MOYERS: You wrote "Hand Mirror" for one of those women you found in your house—your grandmother Ilse.

HAND MIRROR

After so many years
my grandmother Ilse returns
with her astonished
dark and melancholy eyes,
and glances
   —slender Narcissus—
at her small silver pool,
her magic oval,
her moon of cut glass,
occupying this face
more and more hers
     and less mine.

TRANSLATED BY BARBARA PASCHKE

ZAMORA: Yes. That poem also has to do with finding your own place. It's named "Hand Mirror" because I actually have the hand mirror of my great-grandmother that my grandmother Ilse gave to me, and as I wrote I started discovering the faces of my people looking at *me*. So that was what I felt as I looked into the mirror—I saw a double image—my face and their faces.

MOYERS: You must have sensed this morning how deeply moved people were when you read "Mother's Day."

MOTHER'S DAY

—TO MY CHILDREN

I do not doubt you would have liked
one of those pretty mothers in the ads:
    complete with adoring husband and happy children.
She's always smiling, and if she cries at all
it is absent of lights and camera,
makeup washed from her face.

But since you were born of my womb, I should tell you:
ever since I was small like you
I wanted to be myself—and for a woman that's hard—
(even my Guardian Angel refused to watch over me
when she heard).

I cannot tell you that I know the road.
Often I lose my way
and my life has been a painful crossing
navigating reefs, in and out of storms,
refusing to listen to the ghostly sirens
who invite me into the past,
neither compass nor binnacle to show me the way.

But I advance,
go forward holding to the hope
of some distant port
where you, my children—I'm sure—
will pull in one day
after I've been lost at sea.

          TRANSLATED BY MARGARET RANDALL AND ELINOR RANDALL

ZAMORA: When I read that poem in Nicaragua, lots of friends and people in the street tell me that they feel a very deep identification with it. In Nicaragua, almost all newspapers have a special literary supplement that is published on weekends, and because my friends knew that I had written that poem, they asked me to publish it in the literary supplement on Mother's Day. Many people read it that day and called me to ask, "How did you know I felt that way?" But I wrote "Mother's Day" just because *I* felt that way. I thought I deserved to write a poem for myself, you know, to tell my children how *I* felt.

MOYERS: What do you mean when you say "even my Guardian Angel refused to watch over me / when she heard"?

ZAMORA: I think that Guardian Angels watch over good girls, and if you decide to be yourself then you have to be nasty sometimes. You cannot always walk the right path, you know.

MOYERS: By walking the right path you mean doing what your family wants you to do?

ZAMORA: Right.

MOYERS: You told the audience, "I wanted to be myself—and for a woman that's hard." Is that why the Guardian Angel refused to watch over you, because you wanted to be yourself?

ZAMORA: Yes. Because to be yourself you have to challenge many things that you receive as a cultural inheritance. That's the way it is in Nicaragua, and I think it's generally like that in the rest of the world, with some differences. I think it's hard in all parts of the world to be a woman because we women don't know what we are, what kind of human beings we are, what part of humanity we are considered to be. We don't know what we are to do with our lives or why we were born, or for what purpose.

This may sound very very silly to a man—because it's possible that from the time you were born you may have known what you wanted to be—but, when even as a very small child I started to think that I wanted to be a poet, I knew that meant that I wanted to be something different from what all the women in my house had been. For a man, there is nothing particularly strange about deciding to be a poet or an engineer. What seems to be simple for men is difficult for women.

MOYERS: Who are these ghostly sirens in the poem who invite you to play?

ZAMORA: They are all I received as an inheritance; that's what it is to be a woman. I keep fighting, and I imagine that until I die I will keep fighting against these ghostly sirens with their voices, that have always only come from my most inner self, making me feel guilty for trying to go my own way. I will keep fighting against them because I want to be myself.

MOYERS: Do your children understand what you are trying to tell them in this poem?

ZAMORA: Actually, I take them to my poetry readings and they comment freely afterward. They tell me that they try to understand how I feel, as both a mother and a poet, and they have made all kinds of comments about this poem. They have often said, "Well, Mom, we are trying to understand how you feel." So I think in a way they feel different because it's not only that I have to understand them, they also feel they have to understand me. They have to think that I am a person, too, and that I deserve to be a person, distinct from them.

MOYERS: This morning when you were reading about taking your mother for granted, it was so painful to one woman in the audience that she buried her hands in her hair. Was that a painful poem for you to write?

ZAMORA: Really? I didn't see that. But, yes, it was a very painful poem to write to my mother because throughout her life my mother has had a very hard time with me. When I went into the liberation movement in my country, she was even put into prison.

MOYERS: Because of you? The government locked her up because you had become a rebel?

ZAMORA: Yes. Well, she wasn't in prison very long—I think she was in prison for a month—but I was deeply hurt by it because another sister and my brothers were also involved in the struggle and my mother should not have been punished for what we were doing. It was hard for her to understand why we were all doing this after she had given so much love and after she had raised us to be happy in life. She also understandably suffered very much because she always thought that some day somebody would come and tell her I was dead. She also had to go through a divorce of mine, and that was painful for her, too, because she had to adapt her mind from traditional thinking to something different. She had to learn to love all her children—and especially her daughters—with all their different ways of looking at life and with all their different ways of building their own lives.

In my poem "Message to My Mother," I tell her that we did our best to fulfill the destiny given us by fairy tales, but we simply couldn't go on with it. The burden was too much, we had to throw all that aside, we had to become ourselves. In that poem I ask her to pardon us and to understand that we had to be ourselves.

MOYERS: Has she read your poems? Has she accepted you and the life you have made?

ZAMORA: Yes, she reads my poems, and now we have a very good relationship.

MOYERS: Do you feel you are now yourself in a world where you can make your own way? Or is it still a struggle?

ZAMORA: I think I will be at peace when I die because, as I was saying to some friends a few moments ago, I feel that we are the lost generation. We didn't want the fate of our mothers, we dreamed of being different and we are *trying* to be different. But we will never be the women we dreamed we were going to be because we all have this burden of the past—the sirens calling us to the past, every day. I also think we are the lost generation because we are the generation that is in transition to something different, but this something different will only become an actuality later on. Now we just have a glimpse of the future, so we keep growing as human beings, still struggling to achieve human wholeness and completeness.

MOYERS: How has poetry helped you live in that no-woman's-land?

ZAMORA: Yes. It *is* a no-woman's-land. In my last book, which has poems only in Spanish, I have a poem called "Nobody's Land."

MOYERS: What is it saying?

ZAMORA: It's saying what we have been talking about, that we are in no-woman's-land, filled with cross fire. But we stay here in this no-woman's-land so that there can be a next stage, beyond the cross fire and beyond the barriers against women.

MOYERS: And poetry is a record of that journey?

ZAMORA: Yes, but I also write about life—about love and separation and grief and death and everything else in life.

PRECISELY

Precisely because I do not have
the beautiful words I need
I call upon my acts
       to speak to you.
TRANSLATED BY MARGARET RANDALL AND ELINOR RANDALL

MOYERS: Your poem "Precisely" prompts me to ask if you think women in poetry are writing about love differently from the way men have written about love.

ZAMORA: Well, at least now we can say how we feel. We have always known how men felt about us, but now I feel free to write about, let's say, the body of the man I love. We have permission to say what we feel about the men we love. My poem "Vision of Your Body" is an example. That poem offers a vision I had of the man I love, lying on the bed naked at twilight. I see his body, but he doesn't know I am looking at him. He wakes, he rises from the bed, and he is different, getting his clothes and getting dressed. In the poem I just say what I feel about this experience. I say, "I shuddered / like the earth split open by lightning."

VISION OF YOUR BODY

In the dimly lit room
I had a brief glimpse of bliss:
sight of your naked body
like a god reclining.
That was all.

Quite unaware
you got up to get your clothes
just naturally
while I shuddered
like the earth split open by lightning.

TRANSLATED BY DINAH LIVINGSTON

MOYERS: You also have permission to write about your own body, or so it seems.

CELEBRATION OF THE BODY

I love this body of mine that has lived a life,
its amphora contour soft as water,
my hair gushing out of my skull,
my face a glass goblet on its delicate stem
rising with grace from shoulders and collarbone.

I love my back studded with ancient stars,
the bright mounds of my breasts,
fountains of milk, our species' first food,
my protruding ribcage, my yielding waist,
my belly's fullness and warmth.

I love the lunar curve of my hips
shaped by various gestations,
the great curling wave of my buttocks,
my legs and feet, on which the temple stands.

I love my bunch of dark petals and secret fur
keeper of heaven's mysterious gate,
to the damp hollow from which blood flows
and the water of life.

This body of mine that can hurt and get ill,
that oozes, coughs, sweats,
secretes humours, faeces, saliva,
grows tired, old and worn out.

Living body, one solid link to secure
the unending chain of bodies.
I love this body made of pure earth,
seed, root, sap, flower and fruit.

TRANSLATED BY DINAH LIVINGSTON

ZAMORA: It is important for a woman to be aware of and to recover her own body because we have been told too many times that we were born to make sure that humankind doesn't disappear; we *need* to have a consciousness of our own selves and our own bodies. I look at my body in this sacred way because I think that you have to love your own body, the body which contains your soul which, like your body, is unique. Parents, grandparents, great-grandparents, the list goes on forever of all the people who have been working through the ages to produce each one of us.

Having the consciousness that each human being is an individual and has this uniqueness has enabled me to write these poems. Maybe this perspective is nothing new for men, but for a woman, having this consciousness is important.

MOYERS: Well, I have to tell you that your poetry helps some men to find a way to live in this new world.

ZAMORA: Yes. I think that's what's so important about poetry, that you can communicate, that you can build bridges among human beings.

OCTAVIO PAZ

© William Abranowicz

Octavio Paz—poet, essayist, critic, editor, journalist, and translator—became the first Mexican to receive the Nobel Prize for Literature (1990). A man of conscience, Paz resigned as Mexico's ambassador to India in 1968 to protest his government's massacre of student demonstrators in Mexico City. He has taught at universities around the world and resides today in Mexico City.

I think the mission of poetry is to create among people the possibility of wonder, admiration, enthusiasm, mystery, the sense that life is marvelous. When you say life is marvelous, you are saying a banality. But to make life a marvel—that is the role of poetry. PAZ

I have a great belief in poetry, but not in poets. Poets are the transmitters, the conduits. They are no better than other people. Poets are vain—we have many defects. We must realize that we are human beings, and be humble. Poetry is very important, but poets are not.

Poetry, in the past, was the center of society, but with modernity it has retreated to the outskirts. It has become more and more a marginal art. The situation of poetry in the United States is terrible because poets here are genuinely outside the society. This has been a great loss, especially considering that, in the twentieth century, the United States has given the world some of its greatest poets. It's a sad irony that they are not the center of American society.

I think the exile of poetry is also the exile of the best of humankind. Our society lacks the other dimension, the dimension of light and darkness that is poetry. We live in a kind of electric light—but electric light, the light of industry, is not all the light. Both primordial light and primordial darkness are part of being human, and we have tried to hide these realities.

HERMANDAD

Homenaje a Claudio Ptolomeo

Soy hombre: duro poco
y es enorme la noche.
Pero miro hacia arriba:
las estrellas escriben.
Sin entender comprendo:
también soy escritura
y en este mismo instante
alguien me deletrea.

BROTHERHOOD

Homage to Claudius Ptolemy

I am a man: little do I last
and the night is enormous.
But I look up:
the stars write.
Unknowing I understand:
I too am written,
and at this very moment
someone spells me out.

TRANSLATED BY ELIOT WEINBERGER

RECOMMENDED FOR FURTHER READING

This introductory list includes selected titles currently in print, and unless otherwise noted, all items are poetry collections. When a subsequent title contains the contents of earlier collections, only the more recent and more comprehensive title is included. Occasionally, a title may appear which is not currently in print but which contains material not yet gathered elsewhere.

In general, this list focuses on original poetry and only incidentally includes translations, anthologies, or prose. Even a cursory search will yield many more titles in these categories.

Alegría, Claribel. *Thresholds*. Willimantic, Conn.: Curbstone Press, forthcoming in 1996.

———. *Fugues*. Bilingual Edition. Translated from the Spanish by D. J. Flakoll. Willimantic, Conn.: Curbstone Press, 1993.

———. *Woman of the River*. Bilingual Edition. Translated from the Spanish by D. J. Flakoll. Pittsburgh: University of Pittsburgh Press, 1989.

———. *Flowers from the Volcano*. Bilingual Edition. Translated from the Spanish by Carolyn Forché. Pittsburgh: University of Pittsburgh Press, 1982.

———, and Flakoll, D. J. *The Death of Somoza* (testimony). Willimantic, Conn.: Curbstone Press, forthcoming in 1996.

———, and Flakoll, D. J., editors and translators. *On the Front Line: Guerrilla Poetry of El Salvador*. Willimantic, Conn.: Curbstone, 1989.

Autry, James A. *Life and Work: A Manager's Search for Meaning*. New York: Morrow, 1994.

———. *Love and Profit: The Art of Caring Leadership*. New York: Avon, 1992.

———. *Life After Mississippi*. Oxford, Miss.: Yoknapatawpha Press, 1989.

———. *Nights Under a Tin Roof*. Oxford, Miss.: Yoknapatawpha Press, 1983.

Baca, Jimmy Santiago. *Working in the Dark: Reflections of a Poet of the Barrio* (autobiography). Santa Fe, N.Mex.: Red Crane Books, 1991.

———. *Immigrants in Our Own Land and Earlier Poems*. New York: New Directions, 1990.

————. *Black Mesa Poems*. New York: New Directions, 1989.

————. *Martin and Meditations on the South Valley*. New York: New Directions, 1987.

Barks, Coleman. *Gourd Seed*. Athens, Ga.: Maypop Books, 1993.

————, translator. *Delicious Laughter,* by Jelaluddin Rumi. Athens, Ga.: Maypop Books, 1994.

————, and Moyne, John, translators. *The Essential Rumi*. San Francisco: Harper, 1995.

————, and Moyne, John, translators. *This Longing,* by Jelaluddin Rumi. Putney, Vt.: Threshold Press, 1988.

————, and Moyne, John, translators. *Unseen Rain: Quatrains of Rumi*. Putney, Vt.: Threshold Press, 1986.

————, and Moyne, John, translators. *Open Secret,* by Jelaluddin Rumi. Putney, Vt.: Threshold Press, 1984.

Bly, Robert. *Meditations on the Insatiable Soul*. New York: HarperCollins, 1994.

————. *Iron John: A Book About Men*. New York: Vintage Books, 1992.

————. *What Have I Ever Lost by Dying?: Collected Prose Poems*. New York: HarperCollins, 1992.

————. *Selected Poems,* New York: HarperCollins, 1990.

————, editor. *News of the Universe: Poems of Twofold Consciousness*. Reissue. San Francisco: Sierra Books, 1995.

————, Hillman, James, and Meade, Michael, editors. *The Rag and Bone Shop of the Heart: Poems for Men*. New York: HarperCollins, 1992.

Chin, Marilyn. *The Phoenix Gone, The Terrace Empty*. Minneapolis: Milkweed Editions, 1994.

————. *Dwarf Bamboo*. Greenfield Center, N.Y.: Greenfield Review Press, 1987.

Clifton, Lucille. *The Terrible Stories*. Brockport, N.Y.: BOA Editions, forthcoming in 1996.

————. *Book of Light*. Port Townsend, Wash.: Copper Canyon Press, 1993.

————. *Quilting: Poems 1987–1990*. Brockport, N.Y.: BOA Editions, 1991.

————. *Good Woman: Poems and a Memoir 1969–1980*. Brockport, N.Y.: BOA Editions, 1987.

————. *Next: New Poems*. Brockport, N.Y.: BOA Editions, 1987.

Cruz, Victor Hernández. *Red Beans*. Minneapolis: Coffee House Press, 1991.

————. *Rhythm, Content and Flavor: New and Selected Poems*. Houston: Arte Público Press, 1989.

————, Suarez, Virgil, and Quintana, Leroy, editors. *Paper Dance: Fifty-Five Latino Poets*. New York: Persea Books, 1995.

Dove, Rita. *Mother Love*. New York: W. W. Norton, 1995.

————. *Through the Ivory Gate* (novel). New York: Random House, 1993.

————. *Selected Poems*. New York: Random House, 1993.

————. *Grace Notes*. New York: W. W. Norton, 1991.

————. *Fifth Sunday* (short stories). Lexington, Ky.: University of Kentucky, 1985.

Forché, Carolyn. *The Angel of History*. New York: HarperCollins, 1994.

————. *The Country Between Us*. Port Townsend, Wash.: Copper Canyon Press, 1981.

————. *Gathering the Tribes*. New Haven: Yale University Press, 1976.

————, editor. *Against Forgetting: Twentieth Century Poetry of Witness*. New York: W. W. Norton, 1993.

Hall, Donald. *The Museum of Clear Ideas: New Poems*. Boston: Houghton Mifflin, 1994.

———. *Their Ancient Glittering Eyes: Remembering Poets and More Poets.* Boston: Ticknor and Fields, 1993.

———. *Old and New Poems.* Boston: Ticknor and Fields, 1990.

———. *The One Day: A Poem in Three Parts.* Boston: Ticknor and Fields, 1988.

Harjo, Joy. *A Love Supreme* (nonfiction prose). New York: W. W. Norton, 1996.

———. *The Woman Who Fell from the Sky.* New York: W. W. Norton, 1994.

———. *In Mad Love and War.* Hanover, N.H.: University Press of New England, 1990.

———. *She Had Some Horses.* New York: Thunder's Mouth Press, 1983.

Harper, Michael S. *Collected Poems.* Champaign, Ill.: University of Illinois Press, 1996.

———. *Honorable Amendments.* Champaign, Ill.: University of Illinois Press, 1995.

———. *Images of Kin: New and Selected Poems.* Champaign, Ill.: University of Illinois Press, 1977.

———, and Walton, Anthony, editors. *Every Shut Eye Ain't Asleep: An Anthology of Poetry by African Americans Since 1945.* Boston: Little, Brown, 1994.

———, and Stepto, Robert B., editors. *Chant of Saints: A Gathering of Afro-American Literature, Art, and Scholarship.* Champaign, Ill.: University of Illinois Press, 1979.

Hass, Robert. *Human Wishes.* New York: Ecco Press, 1989.

———. *Praise.* New York: Ecco Press, 1979.

———. *Field Guide.* New Haven: Yale University Press, 1973.

———, translator. *Facing the River,* by Czeslaw Milosz. New York: Ecco Press, 1995.

———, editor and translator. *The Essential Haiku: Versions of Bashō, Buson and Issa.* New York: Ecco Press, 1994.

———, and Mitchell, Stephen, editors. *Into the Garden: A Wedding Anthology: Poetry and Prose on Love and Marriage.* New York: HarperCollins, 1993.

Hongo, Garrett Kaoru. *Under Western Eyes.* New York: Doubleday, 1995.

———. *Volcanoes* (memoirs). New York: Knopf, 1995.

———. *The River of Heaven.* New York: Knopf, 1988.

———. *Yellow Light.* New Hanover, N.H.: University Press of New England, 1982.

———, editor. *The Open Boat: Poems from Asian America.* New York: Doubleday, 1993.

Kenyon, Jane. *Constance.* St. Paul: Graywolf Press, 1993.

———. *Let Evening Come.* St. Paul: Graywolf Press, 1990.

———. *The Boat of Quiet Hours.* St. Paul: Graywolf Press, 1986.

———. *From Room to Room.* Cambridge, Mass.: Alice James Books, 1978.

Kinnell, Galway. *Imperfect Thirst.* Boston: Houghton Mifflin, 1994.

———. *Three Books: Body Rags; Mortal Acts, Mortal Words; The Past.* Boston: Houghton Mifflin, 1993.

———. *When One Has Lived a Long Time Alone.* New York: Knopf, 1990.

———. *Selected Poems.* Boston: Houghton Mifflin, 1982.

Kunitz, Stanley. *Passing Through: The Later Poems, New & Selected 1971–1995.* New York: W. W. Norton, 1995.

———. *Next-to-Last Things.* New York: Atlantic Monthly Press, 1985.

———. *The Wellfleet Whale and Companion Poems.* Bronx, N.Y.: Sheep Meadow Press, 1983.

———. *The Poems of Stanley Kunitz 1928–1978.* Boston: Little, Brown, 1979.

Lee, Li-Young. *The Winged Seed, A Remembrance.* New York: Simon & Schuster, 1995.

————. *The City in Which I Love You.* Brockport, N.Y.: BOA Editions, 1990.

————. *Rose.* Brockport, N.Y.: BOA Editions, 1986.

McCarriston, Linda. *Eva-Mary.* Evanston, Ill.: TriQuarterly Books, 1991.

————. *Talking Soft Dutch.* Lubbock, Tex.: Texas Tech University Press, 1984.

McPherson, Sandra. *The Spaces Between Birds.* Middletown, Conn.: Wesleyan University Press, 1996.

————. *Edge Effect.* Middletown, Conn.: Wesleyan University Press, 1996.

————. *The God of Indeterminacy.* Champaign, Ill.: University of Illinois Press, 1993.

————. *Streamers.* New York: Ecco Press, 1988.

————. *Patron Happiness.* New York: Ecco Press, 1983.

————. *Elegies for the Hot Season.* New Edition. New York: Ecco Press, 1982.

————. *The Year of Our Birth.* New York: Ecco Press, 1978.

Merwin, W. S. *The Vixen.* New York: Knopf, 1996.

————. *The Complete Prose Works of W. S. Merwin.* New York: Owl Books/Henry Holt, 1994.

————. *Travels: Poems.* New York: Knopf, 1992.

————. *The Rain in the Trees.* New York: Knopf, 1988.

————. *Selected Poems.* New York: Macmillan, 1988.

Mura, David. *The Colors of Desire: Poems.* New York: Doubleday, 1994.

————. *Turning Japanese: Memoirs of a Sansei.* Second Edition. New York: Doubleday, 1992.

————. *After We Lost Our Way.* New York: E. P. Dutton, 1989.

————. *A Male Grief: Notes on Pornography and Addiction.* Minneapolis: Milkweed Editions, 1987.

Nye, Naomi Shihab. *Words Under the Words: Selected Poems.* Portland, Oreg.: Eighth Mountain Press/ Far Corner Books, 1995.

————. *Red Suitcase.* Brockport, N.Y.: BOA Editions, 1994.

————. *Mint.* New York: State Street Press, 1992.

————, editor. *This Same Sky, A Collection of Poems from Around the World* (for ages ten through adult). New York: Four Winds Press/Macmillan, 1992.

Olds, Sharon. *The Wellspring.* New York: Knopf, 1996.

————. *Father.* New York: Knopf, 1992.

————. *The Gold Cell.* New York: Knopf, 1987.

————. *The Dead and the Living.* New York: Knopf, 1984.

————. *Satan Says.* Pittsburgh: University of Pittsburgh Press, 1980.

Paz, Octavio. *The Double Flame: Essays on Love and Eroticism.* Translated from the Spanish by Helen Lane. New York: Harcourt Brace, 1995.

————. *The Other Voice: Essays on Modern Poetry.* Translated from the Spanish by Helen Lane. New York: Harcourt Brace, 1992.

————. *The Collected Poems of Octavio Paz, 1957–1987.* Bilingual Edition. Edited and translated from the Spanish by Eliot Weinberger. New York: New Directions, 1988.

————. *Selected Poems of Octavio Paz.* Edited by Eliot Weinberger, translated from the Spanish by G. Aroul et al. New York: New Directions, 1984.

———. *Early Poems 1935–1955.* Revised Edition. Translated from the Spanish and preface by Muriel Rukeyser. Original title: *Selected Poems.* New York: New Directions, 1973.

———, editor. *Anthology of Mexican Poetry.* Bilingual Edition. Translated from the Spanish by Samuel Beckett. New York: Riverrun Press, Inc., 1991.

Rich, Adrienne. *Dark Fields of the Republic.* New York: W. W. Norton, 1995.

———. *Blood, Bread, and Poetry: Selected Prose, 1979–1985.* Reissue. New York: W. W. Norton, 1994.

———. *The Fact of a Doorframe: Poems Selected and New, 1950–1984.* Reissue. New York: W. W. Norton, 1994.

———. *Collected Early Poems, 1950–1970.* New York: W. W. Norton, 1993.

———. *What Is Found There: Notebooks on Poetry and Politics.* New York: W. W. Norton, 1993.

———. *Your Native Land, Your Life.* Reissue. New York: W. W. Norton, 1993.

———. *An Atlas of the Difficult World: Poems, 1988–1991.* New York: W. W. Norton, 1991.

Snyder, Gary. *A Place in Space* (essays). Washington, D.C.: Counterpoint Press, 1995.

———. *No Nature: New and Selected Poems.* New York: Pantheon Books, 1992.

———. *The Practice of the Wild* (essays). New York: Farrar, Straus & Giroux, 1990.

———. *Passage Through India* (autobiography). Bolinas, Calif.: Grey Fox Press, 1983.

———. *The Real Work: Interviews & Talks, 1964–1979.* Edited with an introduction by Scott McLean. New York: New Directions, 1980.

Stafford, William. *The Darkness Around Us Is Deep: Selected Poems of William Stafford.* Edited by Robert Bly. New York: HarperCollins, 1994.

———. *Learning to Live in the World: Earth Poems.* Edited by Jerry Watson and Laura Apol. New York: Harcourt Brace, 1994.

———. *My Name Is William Tell.* Lewiston, Idaho: Confluence Press, 1992.

———. *Passwords: Poems.* New York: HarperCollins, 1991.

———. *An Oregon Message.* New York: HarperCollins, 1987.

———. *Down In My Heart* (autobiography). Second Edition. Swarthmore, Pa.: Bench Press, 1985.

Stern, Gerald. *Odd Mercy.* New York: W. W. Norton, 1995.

———. *Bread Without Sugar: Poems.* Second Edition. New York: W. W. Norton, 1993.

———. *Leaving Another Kingdom: Selected Poems.* New York: HarperCollins, 1990.

———. *Two Long Poems.* Pittsburgh: Carnegie Mellon University Press, 1990.

———. *Selected Essays.* New York: Harper, 1988.

———. *Lucky Life.* Boston: Houghton Mifflin, 1977.

Sundiata, Sekou. *Philosophy of the Cool* (CD). New York: NuYo Records, 1995.

———, contributor. *Aloud: Voices from the Nuyourican Poets Cafe.* Edited by Miguel Algarin and Bob Holman. New York: Henry Holt, 1994.

TallMountain, Mary. *Listen to the Night, Poems for the Animal Spirits of Mother Earth.* San Francisco: Freedom Voices Publications, 1995.

———. *A Quick Brush of Wings.* San Francisco: Freedom Voices Publications, 1991.

———. *The Light on the Tent Wall: A Bridging.* Los Angeles: American Indian Studies Center, UCLA, 1990.

Troupe, Quincy. *Avalanche.* Minneapolis: Coffee House Press, 1996.

———. *Root Doctor* (CD). Los Angeles: New Alliance Records, 1995.

———. *Weather Reports: New and Selected Poems.* New York: Harlem River Press, 1991.

———, editor. *Giant Talk: An Anthology of Third World Writing.* New York: Random House, 1975.

———, with Davis, Miles. *Miles: The Autobiography.* New York: Simon & Schuster, 1989.

Zamora, Daisy. *A Cada Queen La Vida (1989–1993).* Bilingual Edition. Translated from the Spanish by Carolyn Forché. Willimantic, Conn.: Curbstone Press, 1995.

———. *Clean Slate: New and Selected Poems.* Bilingual Edition. Translated from the Spanish by Margaret and Elinor Randall. Willimantic, Conn.: Curbstone Press, 1993.

———. *Riverbed of Memory.* San Francisco: City Lights, 1993.